Ethics and Danger

The Cheese & the Worms 1970's
Carlo Ginzburg.
Montaillou   LaRoy-Ladurie
{ microhistory invented by the
                        Italians

Selected Studies in
Phenomenology and Existential Philosophy 17

Ethics and Danger

Essays on Heidegger and Continental Thought

Edited by
Arleen B. Dallery and Charles E. Scott
with
P. Holley Roberts

STATE UNIVERSITY OF NEW YORK PRESS

Published by
State University of New York Press, Albany

© 1992 State University of New York

Printed in the United States of America

For information, address the State University of New York Press,
State University Plaza, Albany, NY 12246

Production by Ruth Fisher
Marketing by Bernadette LaManna

Library of Congress Cataloging-in-Publication Data

Ethics and danger: essays on Heidegger and Continental thought /
edited by Arleen B. Dallery and Charles E. Scott with P. Holley
Roberts.
    p.   cm. — (Selected studies in phenomenology and existential
philosophy ; 17)
    Includes index.
    ISBN 0-7914-0983-X (alk. paper). — ISBN 0-7914-0984-8 (pbk. :
alk. paper)
    1. Heidegger, Martin, 1889-1976. I. Dallery, Arleen B.
II. Scott, Charles E.   III. Roberts, P. Holley.   IV. Series.
B3279.H49E87   1992
193—dc20   91-18875
                                                            CIP

10 9 8 7 6 5 4 3 2 1

Contents

v

Introduction

Can we read Heidegger as a philosopher whose thought moves us without our belonging, in the reading, to an incipient fascism? Or is Heidegger's responsibility terrifying in its demands, as David Krell suggests, terrifying because of the dangerous risks that it takes in the dangers that it reveals in our ethics and dominant ways of life? What is our responsibility as we think with Heidegger? "For me," Samuel IJsseling says, "the only appropriate motivation for a philosopher to judge Heidegger and National Socialism is the desire to become aware of National Socialist tendencies in our own thinking." Do the judgments made about Heidegger's thought come from careful—very careful—reading or with haste and in an almost automatic recoil from his personal alignment with National Socialism? Do we advance or retard incipient fascism by the spirit of our judgments? Such questions run through the chapters of the first part of this book as the authors attempt to understand both the question of politics in Heidegger's thought and the thought that gives rise to that question. The issues of Heidegger's party affiliation, his nondemocratic convictions, and his silence regarding National Socialism have been with us for many years. Now, in a period when political issues have dominated our questions, and when fascism has come to symbolize a way of living and thinking that is both evil and at a considerable distance from our judgments concerning it, the spirit of our thought in response to Heidegger comes to the fore. We pause to wonder whether something facile and self-congratulatory moves us as we gaze at events in Hitler's Germany. Some of the authors in this volume wonder whether our garrulous condemnations overlook something that Heidegger's silence preserves, whether something is missed by our lack of questions as we rush to judgment, whether something dangerous takes place in our intelligent, ethical separation from Heidegger's perverse errors.

What is clear to the authors in this book is that Heidegger's thought is not well enough understood to afford us the opportunity to summarize it and generalize it, nor do we understand well enough our own thought to speak with final confidence even in our condemnations and excited avowals of what is right and true. These encounters with Heidegger struggle to find how to think with Heidegger's work. As they read him, these authors find problems and insights; their own manners of thought are pushed to disturbing limits; their convictions are checked and placed in doubt. When, for example, his silence is engaged, the reader often finds not that Heidegger has escaped judgment or cowardice, but that 'something' more extreme than moral condemnation brings together the reader and Heidegger's thought, a gathering that does not leave moral condemnation behind, but exceeds it in claim and import. There is danger when we speak of an excess of morality. There is another danger: a world circumscribed by morality. And there is the possibility that in this silence we belong to something not avowable, not available for publicity, something that allows democracy and National Socialism to reveal their dangers in the responsibilities that they procreate.

The issue of technology frequently arises in this book. It is the issue of people's establishing the destiny of things by reference to clear goals for human life that demand efficient values and methods for achieving these goals at the expense of something fundamental for human beings. Above all it is the issue of a way of life that is inevitable at this time and that diminishes life in the pursuit of life. As one experiences dissatisfaction with Heidegger's way of addressing the issue, the issue itself looms larger. It becomes one in which the dissatisfied reader finds him or herself entangled, and one whose importance is intensified by Heidegger's inability to translate his thought into a viable politics. One wonders whether politics can bear the weight of hope that is given to it, whether that hope is too quick and too filled with the expectation of remedy in the midst of histories that are not fully understood and which might indicate that our hope is part of the problem.

The chapters' topics spread out to include many other figures: Parmenides, Aristotle, Hegel, Husserl, Benjamin, Levinas, Foucault.

And, above all, Derrida. Heidegger's engagement with his tradition and the engagements of Heidegger by those who come in his wake occupy the chapters in parts 2 and 3. These chapters are contributions to the continuing work of finding ways to speak and think in the element that Heidegger has made available to us. Must we give up entirely the language of subjectivity if we are to meet the questions posed by Heidegger? Is ethics at the end of metaphysical endeavor? Does the element of Heidegger's thought include flight from the practical world or a creative reinheritance of it? Does Heidegger miss the thought of one or another of his predecessors to such a degree that his own work must be called into question for its omission of something vital? Does his thought trip on misinterpretations? Or can his thinking tolerate serious misinterpretations while it brings us to questions and possibilities that rightfully call us away from established patterns of knowledge and certainty? Do we find in Derrida's love-hate relation to Heidegger a way of writing that brings Heidegger to bear on himself in his failures and overpowering draw?

Throughout this book there is a struggle with words. Which words are we to speak? How are words and phrases to turn in their employment away from their heritage that gave their authority and power? How are we to speak of Heidegger's thought without reinvoking the very ideas whose radical rethinking has turned us to Heidegger? How does our thought regarding Heidegger's work allow its newness, meet it, and yet hold it in question? There is in this book a notable absence of flat commentary. Rather, there are persistent attempts to think with Heidegger, to join him in thought, to rethink thinking and speaking in the process of meeting him. And throughout there is a mood of concern and worry, the mood of encountering something of moment whose implications reach to what is cherished by us and in us, something that cannot be conquered by attack, and something that is not only not fully understood but also resists the priority of understanding the thought. It is not a question of whether Heidegger is relevant. It is one of engaging a way of thought that refigures the claims which allow us to think, a way of thought that gives us to suspect that our words have lost the address that silently moves us.

In addition to worry, these essays at times both reveal and speak of outrage. The outrage of National Socialism, the outrage of being's withdrawal, the outrage of error, the outrage of spirit. Several authors say that outrage is given with being's truth—its revealing/concealing—that we find ourselves in the outrage, that our sameness is found, as William Richardson says, in the horror of darkness and not in the clarity of unshadowed light. How then are we to be? And why is that not an ethical question? Why is danger present when we find what we ought to do, when we find what we ought to say in response to Heidegger? Presumably it is because we have become subjects who are dangerous to ourselves and do not know how to think this danger. Presumably it is also because we who think, by thinking, are in the danger to which Heidegger found himself exposed. And this danger, presumably, has moved these authors to think with varying degrees of confidence that they have met, not the enemy, but the friend who found that the danger is not only in silence but also in the way we speak of it.

Note

The abbreviation "GA," followed by volume number, year of publication, and page numbers (if any), refers to the collected works of Martin Heidegger, *Gesamtausgabe*, published by Vittorio Klostermann in Frankfurt am Main.

Part 1

Heidegger and Politics

1

Heidegger and Politics

Samuel IJsseling

The facts about Heidegger's involvement in National Socialism are known. Most of these, especially what is essential, were already known in the late 1940s and early 1950s, at least by Heidegger scholars. Perhaps a few facts have been discovered in the intervening years, thanks to the research of Hugo Ott. Though the facts are known, it is something quite different to interpret and to judge these facts. The violent and heated discussions of the last two years have not had so much to do with the facts as such as with the interpretation and judgment of them. In this regard it is important to make a few distinctions, namely, a distinction between the knowledge of facts and the interpretation and judgment of them; then the distinction between interpreting facts and passing judgment on facts; and finally the question or problem of whether there are any facts without interpretation. But it is not possible to discuss all these problems in half an hour. One needs half a year because first there must be a discussion of what constitutes a justifiable judgment, what constitutes a just judgment, as well as the relation between them. By way of an introduction to my topic I would like to do three things:

First, I would like to set up a framework in which the facts can be judged; that means, to formulate the conditions of possibility and the limits of a judgment. This amounts to carrying out a kind of *Kritik der Urteilskraft*, a critique of judgment. Since what we have in view here is a question of interpretation, this necessarily involves calling

3

to mind some general principles of hermeneutics. Second, I would like to try to formulate some thoughts about the relation between a radical philosophy and a radical politics. And third, I would like to offer some thoughts about Heidegger's attitude toward democracy.

FACTS AND JUDGMENT

In the twentieth century a great deal has been published about hermeneutics, the interpretation of texts, facts, institutions, etc., as well as about the bearing this has on the philosophy of science, including the human sciences, which for their part include a science called history. Among the problems discussed in the science of history are the problems of the status of facts, of the relation between fact and interpretation, the relation between facts and their context, and, on the other hand, the problems of narrativity in the historical sciences, the scientific status of biographical matters, fictionality, etc. These and similar problems, as well as the burgeoning literature concerning these problems, seem to have been forgotten or even repressed when it comes to the interpretation and judgment of Heidegger's involvement in National Socialism. Derrida has said that if there is something that should be deconstructed, it is the *discourse* about Heidegger's political past—deconstructed so as to gain some insight into the metaphysical, theological, ideological, and, above all, ethical presuppositions and implications that are at work in that discourse.

In any case, when it comes to the facts of Heidegger's political involvements, three things have to be avoided at all costs and at every turn: simplification, haste (hasty judgments), and extrapolation (displacements) from one thing to another. Simplification, haste, and extrapolation were essential characteristics of Nazi propaganda as explicitly formulated by Goebbels. Concerning the first two, Goebbels said: "Never say something that cannot be understood immediately and by everyone. . . .We have no time to lose. National Socialism must be realized now and immediately; otherwise it is too late." There are many examples of extrapolation in the rhetoric of Goebbels: using anti-Semitism as a propaganda device is only possible on the basis of an extrapolation, one that necessarily begins by making the Jews the scapegoats for all German woes.

I must say that many of the publications in newspapers and even in the scientific journals on Heidegger's political attitudes are characterized by this rhetoric, a rhetoric of simplification, haste, and extrapolation, and that the tone of these publications is more similar to the discourse of Goebbels than to the discourse of Heidegger.

There is merit in keeping three oppositions in mind: simplification versus nuancing; haste versus trying to keep one's judgments in abeyance; and extrapolation from one level to another, etc., versus proceeding with great caution. I will try to clarify these three points. But first I must respond to a difficulty: when one tries to postpone and nuance one's judgments, as well as to avoid extrapolations, this always *seems* to be a way of making a defense and an excuse through obfuscation. More generally and principally, when one tries to understand a human deed or attitude, which implies making subtle distinctions and seeing the facts within the broader context, it always *seems* as if one is making excuses. It is in no way my intention to defend National Socialism, or Heidegger. But it is also not my intention to attack National Socialism or Heidegger. This is too facile. I will not deny that National Socialism perhaps has a dimension that is absolutely unfathomable, that withdraws from all rational structures, withdraws from every possibility of being integrated into an historical perspective, and withdraws from every sort of being rendered into words or given a justification. There are no words for it. Auschwitz is perhaps a name for this unfathomable dimension, a name that must be pronounced with the same reticence with which the Jews pronounce the name of Yahweh. But often when one speaks about Heidegger's National Socialism, there seems to be little appreciation of this absolutely unfathomable dimension. Here you see the sort of extrapolation that is at work in many of the articles on Heidegger's past. To take a concrete example: it is hardly obvious that Heidegger's having glorified Adolf Hitler in 1933–34 is tantamount to approving of what happened in the name of National Socialism after 1939.

If one is going to try to formulate a judgment about National Socialism and Heidegger, several things are necessary. First of all, one must have a sound knowledge of the historical situation, and, more specifically, one must ask what, exactly, is National Socialism. Included in a sufficiently sound knowledge is a knowledge of twentieth-century European history, German history, the social, economic, and religious elements of this history, as well as the genealogy of National Socialism. Most people lack this knowledge. And many even seem to think anti-Semitism, nationalism, and the glorification of war were inventions of National Socialism. But one should remember, for instance, that many of Germany's Jews in the early 1920s had the same attitudes. Of course, it is precarious to start to tell a lot of anecdotes. But at least I can say that apart from the Jews, almost all intellectuals, artists, and classical philologists were sympathetic with some kind of National Socialism.

Second, if one is going to formulate a judgment about National Socialism and Heidegger, one must have a sound knowledge of what National Socialism was and Heidegger's place in it. We should point out here that, at least in the beginning, National Socialism was not a monolithic figure; there were many currents and cross-currents within it that were all seeking to define National Socialism. It had and has no immutable, transhistorical essence. Perhaps some of its more salient traits were propaganda, racism, biologism, the glorification of youth, and enthusiasm, but these are precisely characteristics that never could be seen as applying to Heidegger's thinking. It is customary to call National Socialist Germany the "Evil Empire." However, this is not a critical attitude, but betrays a lack of criticism. Not everything in Russia is or was evil, and the same holds for National Socialism. We must at least make the distinction between a dangerous position and a criminal position. For instance, Heidegger's glorification of the German language together with the Greek language as *the* language of philosophy is a dangerous claim. But it is not a criminal claim. Similarly, Heidegger's claim about the mission of philosophy in the reform of the world as a whole is dangerous, but it is not criminal, and one can say the same thing about Heidegger's antidemocratic attitude: that it is dangerous and not criminal.

In order to be able to pass judgment on National Socialism and Heidegger's place in it, we must ask, What is the standpoint from which we judge? We can judge as an historian, a sociologist (these are not very good standpoints from which to *judge* about things), we can judge as a lawyer or a magistrate, a politician, a political scientist, etc. Or one can judge from an ethical or philosophical point of view. But we must always ask by what rights we judge, and what is our motivation.

Motivation: When it comes to judging, many motivations are suspect. Judgments can be born from frustration, resentment, or ignorant self-righteousness. We can say that much of the current French discussion about Heidegger's attitude toward National Socialism is motivated by an aversion to contemporary French currents in philosophy, such as Derrida, Levinas, postmodernism, and so on. A very suspect motivation is the desire to purge philosophy of all evil, a desire that all too easily satisfies itself by making

Heidegger a scapegoat. For me, the only appropriate motivation for a philosopher to judge Heidegger and National Socialism is the desire to become aware of National Socialist tendencies in our own thinking. When we say that National Socialist elements are present in Heidegger's thinking—something that certainly is not so obvious—then we can be motivated to read Heidegger very carefully, not in order to catch Heidegger "red-handed" so as to confirm our preconceptions about his National Socialism and to denounce him, but rather to discover if and to what extent our own thinking contains National Socialist elements. More specifically, because Heidegger's thinking has left its mark on all continental thinking, we must beware that our thinking, continental thinking, does not fall prey to whatever National Socialist tendencies we may want to find in Heidegger.

RADICALISM IN PHILOSOPHY AND POLITICS

Heidegger is perhaps the most radical thinker in the history of philosophy. This is what is radical in Heidegger: his early project of the destruction of previous ontologies and his *Überwindung der Metaphysik*; and later, his talk of *der andere Anfang*, and, indeed, his question of being are the most fundamental and radical issues. Radicality in philosophy pertains to the greatness of philosophy. To be radical in politics, on the contrary, does not imply a great political system or idea, but it almost always implies political terrorism. Heidegger is certainly no terrorist, but one can ask whether his siding with National Socialism was not a kind of transposition of his radical philosophy into radical politics. In other words, if one looks at the beginning and history of political thinking, one sees there are two basic options in politics: politics can be understood as *poiēsis* or *praxis*. When one understands politics as *poiēsis*, one understands it from a Platonic standpoint. According to this view the state or *polis* is seen as a work that must be made, instituted, or founded. Eventually it is seen as a work of art, or the total work of art (*Gesamtkunstwerk*). In a politics understood as praxis—that is, as negotiating, as debate, as deliberation—one is always compromising, and one must always take part in the play of the power game. In this view of politics as praxis, which is the more Aristotelian position, the state or *polis* is seen as an already existing place where one must deliberate. Radical politics is always a poetical politics, one in which the ideal society has to be built from the ground up, preferably as fast as possible and with all means available. Politics as praxis is always a politics of the feasible; it has to realize the good in this concrete situation, at this given place, at this given moment, and therefore it is involved in making compromises. For radical politics, this sort of politics is a kind of drudgery. But real democratic politics can never be anything but something based on the recognition of the difference between various meanings, opinions, and the legitimacy of conflict, and therefore a democratic politics must engage in compromise. Heidegger tends to conceive of politics as a *poiēsis*, that is, as the state-founding act. Perhaps he even tends to aestheticize politics in a way that assigns to philosophers and to the German *Volk* a specific and exalted mission. Heidegger is not the only one to have this attitude; many philosophers think that they have a preeminent political responsibility, and to see Germany as the center of Europe was certainly no invention of Heidegger. To see politics as a *poiēsis* and, still more strongly, to aestheticize politics are some of the most fundamental characteristics of National Socialism. That is the reason why it is dangerous to see politics as a *poiēsis*; it can and did lead to terrorism as one of the basic structures of National Socialism. But to repeat, a dangerous position is not a criminal position.

HEIDEGGER AND DEMOCRACY

This third point is connected with the second point. Heidegger is rather negative towards democracy. In his *Der Spiegel* interview, and in several other places, he puts quotation marks around *democracy*. It is true that for Heidegger *das Volk* plays an important role in politics, but, on the other hand, power has to be in the hands of a certain elite.

It is the case that almost all philosophers have their difficulties with democracy. And for two reasons: First, in the sciences one cannot be democratic. It is impossible to decide in a democratic way whether the sum of the three angles of a triangle equal 180 degrees, or whether there are more white or red cells in one's blood. These are things that only scientists can decide, and there is only one truth. When a philosopher thinks that a good and just society must be structured in this or that way, and he sees the necessity of its being structured in this particular way, then there is no longer a democratic discussion about the legitimacy of that insight. The second reason philosophers have difficulty with democracy is that plurality and pluriformity are usually anathema to philosophers. And democracy is essentially characterized by plurality and pluriformity. Democracy is the recognition that there exist different positions, different opinions, all of which are reasonable, justifiable, or foundable. Claude Lefort states that democracy is that system that the other in and of itself can accept. This democracy is perhaps realizable, but is not thinkable, and what cannot be thought, philosophers hate.

What is the position of Heidegger? Heidegger is an antidemocrat, but for other reasons. First, a pre-given truth about society written in Heaven, in Nature, or in Reality does not exist for Heidegger. Society must be built from the ground up; it is a project of mankind. And, second, Heidegger emphasized the idea of the unity of the thinkable, although there is always the problem of difference. The other reason why Heidegger is antidemocratic is probably the following: the problem facing contemporary politics is technology and all its concomitant problems, such as the exploitation of the earth, genetic manipulation, the progressive destruction of the environment, the impoverishment of the third world, the arms race, and possible destruction by nuclear conflict. Technology confronts man and politics with these kinds of extreme possibilities. According to Heidegger, an answer to this problem cannot be found in Americanism, liberalism, Russian communism, Christianity, or in ethical prescriptions. At least for a certain period, Heidegger saw National Socialism as a solution to this problem.

As you know, for Heidegger there is a distinction between technology and *das Wesen der Technik*; the essence of technology is not itself something technological. Problems that arise from technology cannot be resolved by technological means. Americanism and communism and even ethics are a technical solution to the problems that technology poses to us. For Heidegger democracy also is simply a technical solution to technical problems. In other words, democracy is connected with the philosophy of subjectivity, *Bewusstseinsphilosophie*, metaphysical thinking, and the heritage of Christianity. But at one time Heidegger thought that National Socialism's ideology was a nontechnical answer to the problems of technology. Now we know that National Socialism was certainly not an answer, and even Heidegger discovered this very early on. He saw the actual concrete form that National Socialism took as an accomplishment of metaphysical thinking.

For myself, I think that in our world we can only be democrats. But, for every democrat the question remains open as to whether democracy can be a solution for the problems of our time. Or let me formulate this another way: the political answer to technology is not Russian communism (who knows what that is today!) nor American liberalism, nor Christian belief, and still less, ethics in the sense of business ethics, bioethics, and medical ethics. Perhaps one can even ask oneself whether the political and the ethical as such have not lost their sense in our society. Philippe Lacoue-Labarthe speaks of *le retrait du politique*, and in the work of Levinas, which many people characterize as an ethics, we cannot find any ethics in the traditional sense of the word, much less a politics. By reading Heidegger, we at least have the possibility of discovering this problem, namely, of the withdrawal of politics and ethics. One need only think of the retreat of being.

2

Heidegger's Truth and Politics

William J. Richardson

"Mistah Kurtz—he dead." T. S. Eliot uses these words by Joseph Conrad as the epigraph for his poem, "The Hollow Men," and I propose a similar employment. Let that say that the literary context of my remarks will be Joseph Conrad's *Heart of Darkness*; the immediate inspiration for them, however, comes from John Sallis. In a remarkable paper delivered at a Heidegger symposium in September 1989, entitled "Deformatives: Essentially Other than Truth," Sallis began by asking: "What if truth were monstrous?... What if there were within the very essence of truth something essentially other than truth, a divergence from nature within nature, true monstrosity?"[1]

The paper offered a fresh analysis of Heidegger's essay, "On the Essence of Truth," delivered as a lecture in 1930 and then continually refined over thirteen years until published in 1943.[2] The reanalysis was filtered through a comparative study of the early and late versions of Heidegger's text and of the recently published *Beiträge zur Philosophie (Vom Ereignis)*, which belongs to the same period (1936–38).[3] Sallis traces in Heidegger's essay, familiar to all, the emergence of the problem of untruth at the point where Heidegger sees untruth to be more than simply the opposite of truth and, therefore, extrinsic to it (a purely metaphysical conception), but belonging to the very essence of truth itself and to be a deforming of truth, oppositionally, as it were, from the inside.

11

In the final (1943) version of Heidegger's essay, the nonessence of truth is said to be older than truth proper. We recall Heidegger's formula from section 6 of the essay: "The concealment of beings as a whole, untruth proper, is older than every openedness of this or that being. It is older than letting-be itself which in disclosing already holds concealed and comports itself toward concealing" (ET 132). What is at stake here, of course, is the *lēthē* intrinsic to *alētheia*, and we recall how Heidegger discerns two modes of it: mystery (concealment) on the one hand and errancy (concealment of concealment plus distortion) on the other. Sallis's thrust is to insist that this nontruth is "other than truth" and prior to it. He concludes by suggesting that we ponder this other: "an other that would engender, not *polemos* but outrage. An other so essentially other than truth that it would be absolved from truth, as absolutely as madness can be" (DF 18). Outrage? Madness? This theme of madness, introduced at the very end, is startling, even though Sallis had emphasized earlier, in the light of a passage from the *Beiträge*, that the effect of human involvement with truth is a "transformation of the Being of man in the sense of a de-rangement (*Ver-rückung*) of his position among beings" (DF 4). At any rate, the paper concludes: "Let us, then, ponder whether what the question of truth is all about is, in the end, akin to madness" (DF 18).

What Sallis's own intentions were in introducing themes of outrage and madness at the end of so sober and well-crafted a paper only he can say. I find those themes enormously provocative, however, especially when, in response to a question (if I understood correctly), he admitted that the other of truth might be pondered also under the guise of evil. It is this strange conjunction of outrage, madness, and evil that brings to my mind Conrad's *Heart of Darkness*, and I take it as an external frame (even paradigm) for what I think ought to be said about the relationship between Heidegger's experience of *alētheia* and his political involvement. Such a frame is not superfluous. Philippe Lacoue-Labarthe has made the point that the twentieth-century phenomenon of Nazism is not an affair of Hitler's Germany alone but has roots that go back to the beginnings of Western thought.[4]

Mr. Kurtz is part of that story, but it is told by Charlie Marlow, a low-key Everyman, who is honorable enough in his way: "You know, I hate, detest, and can't bear a lie. . . . There is a taint of death . . . in lies . . . what I want to forget."[5] His tale parallels Conrad's own experience of piloting a boat up the tortuous Congo River as it twists its way deeper and deeper into the ominous gloom of the jungle. We catch the mood in a passage such as this:

"We penetrated deeper and deeper into the heart of darkness. It was very quiet there. At night sometimes the roll of drums behind the curtain of trees would run up the river and remain sustained faintly, as if hovering in the air high over our heads, till the first break of day. . . .

"We were wanderers on a prehistoric earth, on an earth that wore the aspect of an unknown planet. . . . We could not understand [our surroundings] because we were too far and could not remember, because we were travelling in the night of first ages, of those ages that are gone, leaving hardly a sign—and no memories." (HD 50)

And Mistah Kurtz? He made his home in that foreboding darkness. He, too, was an Everyman but of a more flamboyant sort than Marlow. People spoke of him as a prodigy—as a musician, artist, painter, and especially as a man of a golden tongue—in fact, the full flower of European culture; yet plunderer, and profiteer and murderer, too, presiding sometimes at midnight dances that ended in unspeakable rites with him as their object. " 'Everything belonged to him—but that was a trifle. The thing was to know what he belonged to, how many powers of darkness claimed him for their own' " (HD 64).

But what has all this to do with Heidegger? My claim is that the other of truth that Sallis brings into focus is a *lēthē* that reaches into the heart of darkness, and this is what accounts not simply for *polemos* but for the outrage. My own view is that unless we consider Heidegger's political debacle in these terms, we do not understand it at all. The fundamental text to support this claim is precisely the one that Sallis analyzed, "On the Essence of Truth" (1943). I shall speak first of Heidegger's experience of truth, then of the relevance of this conception for his political involvement, and finally of the pertinence of both to ourselves.

HEIDEGGER'S EXPERIENCE OF TRUTH

That there are two modalities of untruth we know well enough. The first of them is the "concealing of what is concealed as a whole" and is called *mystery*. This is not terribly problematic. But the second modality of nontruth, whereby concealment not only conceals itself but beguiles Dasein into inadvertence to it, is more troublesome: this is *errancy* (*die Irre*).

> Errancy is the essential counter-essence to the primordial
> essence of truth. Errancy opens itself up as the open region for
> every opposite to essential truth. . . . Error is not just an isolated
> mistake but rather the realm (the domain) of the history of those
> entanglements in which all kinds of erring get interwoven.
> . . . every mode of comportment has its mode of erring.
> Error extends from the most ordinary wasting of time, making
> a mistake, and miscalculating, to going astray and venturing
> too far in one's essential attitudes and decisions. . . . The errancy
> in which any given segment of historical humanity must proceed
> for its course to be errant is essentially connected with the
> openness of Dasein. By leading him astray, errancy dominates
> man through and through. (ET 136)

We have only to recall how, in *Being and Time*, Dasein, though "in
the truth," is likewise "in the untruth" because "essentially falling"[6]
and to compare the language that describes this fallenness (e.g.,
verschliessen, verbergen, verdecken, verstellen) with the description
of errancy in "On the Essence of Truth" (e.g., *sich-vertun, sich-
versehen, sich-verrechnen, sich-verlaufen, sich-versteigen*) to see that
the untruth that victimizes Dasein in its presencing in *Being and
Time* is grounded in the negativity of truth-as-errancy that dominates
Dasein from the beginning.

In 1935 came the *Introduction to Metaphysics*,[7] and we are
sufficiently aware of its many ambiguities. I would recall only that
whether the theme is *physis* "that loves to hide itself" (IM 114) or
polemos, that "original struggle. . . sustained by the creators, poets,
thinkers, statesmen, against [which]. . . they set up the barrier of their
work, and. . . capture the world thus opened up" (IM 62): or *dikē*, as
the overpowering *deinon*, against which Dasein, the *deinotaton*, the
"strangest of the strange," brings power to bear but is destined to
be shattered in the end (IM 162–63): or the triple path of Parmenides,
according to which the great "de-cisions" (*Ent-scheidungen*) of history
arise from the differentiation between being, non-being and seeming-
to-be (IM 87), the fundamental issue remains the same: the struggle
between *lēthē* and *alētheia*, where *lēthē* is the other of truth—not
simply as mystery but as errancy, perverting the revelation of
alētheia. "The Origin of the Work of Art" makes this painfully
explicit: "Truth occurs precisely as itself in that the concealing denial
[*verbergende Verweigern*], as refusal [*Versagen*], provides the steady
provenance of all clearing [*Lichtung*] and yet, as dissembling
[*Verstellen*], metes out to all clearing the unremitting severity

[*Schärfe*] with which it leads Dasein astray [*Beirrung*]."⁸ *Lēthē* as errancy dominates Dasein and leads it astray; it seduces it into error and remains a corruptive force within it.

In the "Letter on Humanism" (1947), the darkness of *alētheia* takes on a more ominous, even apocalyptic, tone. The benign aspect of the process, following Hölderlin, emerges as "wholesome" (*Heilen*) but its negativity as "evil" (*das Böse*), "malice" (*das Unheile*), or "rage" (*der Grimm*). Thus:

> With the wholesome, evil appears all the more in the lighting of Being. The essence of evil does not consist in the mere baseness of human action but rather in the malice of rage. Both of these, however, the wholesome and the raging, can essentially occur only in Being, insofar as Being itself is what is contested [*das Strittige*]. . . .
> To the wholesome, Being first grants ascent into grace [*Huld*]; to raging its compulsion to malignancy [*Unheil*].⁹

At stake here, of course, is Heidegger's reading of Heraclitus's *polemos*.

All of the forementioned texts have been around for years and are common coin in the Heideggerian realm. Taken together, they say that for Heidegger *alētheia* emerges from the other of truth and remains at best a flickering struggle against the dark. Let me mention two other texts that have only recently appeared and are less familiar, since neither has yet been translated.

The first of these is *Beiträge zur Philosophie (Vom Ereignis)* (1989). Whereas *Being and Time* approached the Being-question through the fundamental-ontological analysis of Dasein, *Beiträge* is the first attempt to address the same question in terms of Being-as-history (*Seynsgeschichte*)¹⁰ insofar as this proceeds out of *Ereignis*, where it is *Ereignis* that effects the shift; and it is in this shift that the famous *Kehre* consists. Essentially, the new beginning to which Heidegger aspires here consists in thinking the "truth of *Beon* [*Seyn*] itself as the 'clearing of' or the 'clearing for' " (BP 268) the event of self-concealing. In effect, the whole work concerns the problem of truth, but in part 5 Heidegger devotes 166 pages to the essencing of truth and its negativity. He does not thematize extensively the two modalities of untruth, but the themes are there, as we may infer from his use once again of such words as *Versagung*, *Verstellung*, and *Zögerung*. He speaks of the "proper [*eigentliche*] nonessence of truth in the lecture on truth designated as errancy" (BP 347). And again, after meditating on concealment, he adds: "Now for the first time the notion of *errancy* becomes clearer and [with it] the power and possibility of the abandonment of Being [*Seinsverlassenheit*], concealment and dis-sembling" (BP 351). The significance of errancy in the negativity of truth is reaffirmed, then, in the *Beiträge* text.

And there is one more text, relatively unknown, that underlines the role of darkness in Heidegger's experience of truth. It comes from the *Zollikoner Seminare* (1987). Here Medard Boss, the Swiss psychiatrist, in publishing the protocols of the seminars conducted by Heidegger at Boss's invitation for the psychiatrists of Switzerland, includes notes from his personal conversations with Heidegger. Here Boss reports Heidegger's comments on the problem of projection in psychotherapy—that phenomenon by which one person attributes to another feelings (usually negative, e.g., anger, hate) that one has oneself:

> Psychologically, we say, someone projects an evil side of himself onto an enemy, consequently hates him as the evil one and thus avoids seeing the evil in himself. . . . But that does not have to be, by any means, a projection—indeed cannot be a projection. For in ascribing evil to another, one is merely warding off the recognition that *I too belong to evil* [*zum Böse gehöre*], like all men. . . . To each Dasein, also, always already belongs the power-to-be-evil [*Böse-sein-können*] in relation to what [it] encounters, whether this power be genuinely brought to fulfillment or not. . . .
>
> Evil is not first of all there as an abstract possibility that then somehow or other is "actualized," but the power-to-be-evil belongs to my power-to-be, that is, already in quite original fashion. It is [always] already coming-to-presence.[11]

Clearly, then, for Heidegger Dasein, in its fundamental power-to-be, is always already power-to-be-evil—this belongs (presumably) to the very structure of its fallenness. Fallenness, in turn, belongs to the very structure of Dasein, which, as the clearing of self-concealment that has *Ereignis* as its source, is permeated by a double mode of untruth: mystery and errancy. This double modality of *lēthē* is older than truth, other than truth—reaching down into the very heart of darkness.

TRUTH AND POLITICS

Let that suffice for Heidegger's experience of truth as a philosophical insight. How did he experience it on a personal level, that is, insofar as truth with its untruth had its way with him? The earliest indication we have of his reaction to self-concealing revealment is reported in Heidegger's "A Dialogue on Language between a Japanese and an Inquirer." There he reports an experience of 1921: "[I was trying] to follow a way which was leading I knew not where. Only the immediate prospect was known to me, for this was continually opening up, even if the field of vision often shifted and grew dark."[12] The experience of light and darkness was certainly there from early on, but in 1921 surely it was innocent enough.

A more serious matter is Heidegger's ambivalence—or, perhaps, his polyvalence; Hugo Ott speaks of one, Otto Pöggeler of the other. In his *Martin Heidegger: Unterwegs zu seiner Biographie* (1988), Ott traces this in detail. For example, he writes of Karl Löwith's fateful encounter with Heidegger in Rome in 1936 as follows:

> Löwith recognized with all clarity the bi-fold [*Zwiespaltige*], the twi-light [*Zwielichtige*] [character] of Heidegger that still today is unresolved: how should man and work go together; can Martin Heidegger the thinker be separated from Heidegger the political activist—[if so], in what way and to what extent? The sheer inconceivable [*unvorstellbare*] ambivalence in the structure of Heidegger's personality.[13]

But is this not unduly harsh? Both Martin Heidegger the thinker and Martin Heidegger the political activist were together the first victims of the errancy that seduced them both. *Wer gross denkt, muss gross irren* ("Who thinks great thoughts must greatly wander in errancy").[14] With regard to the ambivalence of Heidegger's personality structure, it is a structure that was itself "dominated through and through" by the errancy he described. Surely the ambivalence is there: certain texts can be read, indeed must be read, both politically and apolitically. But if Heidegger's ambivalence is really a question of structure, like some kind of astigmatism from birth, then, given his conception of *alētheia*, is it not improper to reproach him for it as if it were *as such* a moral fault? One is no doubt morally responsible for how one deals with one's personality structure, and no attempt is made here to exonerate Heidegger from such responsibility, but structure as such, like the effects of errancy, is simply an ugly fact of life. Max Müller, who knew Heidegger better than most and certainly suffered from his ambivalence, acknowledged the ambivalence as a fact that affected many aspects of Heidegger's life, including his attitude toward religion.[15] Müller simply accepted it as a fact that had to be lived with and, however unpleasant, part of the price one must pay for Heidegger's genius (MH 212).

Pöggeler's criticism is somewhat different. He remarks upon what I would call Heidegger's polyvalence rather than his ambivalence. He focuses upon the philosophical development of Heidegger's thought and comments upon the same transient enthusiasms that Ott observes—first for religion, later for political involvement:

> [We understand Heidegger's development] if we pay attention to how motives of a religious and political dimension work into Heidegger's thought. Heidegger's thought is worked over in a breathtaking, breath-crushing way by what he experienced as historical transition (*geschichtlichen Übergang*) and by what was presented to him in its concreteness every five years in a completely different way.[16]

But how could it have been otherwise? Given the fact that thought for Heidegger is a profoundly historical enterprise that engages its task in all the concreteness of a historical situation, what was there in the thought itself, that is, in *alētheia* as permeated by a double negativity, that offered any measure, or guide, for action? Given that the essence of truth includes both mystery and errancy, the scandal is not that Heidegger skidded into Nazism; the scandal is that there was nothing in his thought or experience of *alētheia* to prevent it. He himself, I suggest, fell victim to the heart of darkness.

This does not absolve Heidegger from responsibility for his behavior. It simply situates this behavior as the profoundly confounded response of a finite Dasein to Being-as-*alētheia*, revealing itself to, and simultaneously concealing itself from, this Dasein in an ineluctably dissembling way.

Marlow eventually reached Kurtz—at least he spotted the station where Kurtz lived, a long decaying building half-buried in high grass, with remains of fenceposts, their upper ends ornamented with round curved balls (HD 67–68).

> "I directed my glass to the house. . . . These round knobs were not ornamental but symbolic; they were expressive and puzzling,

striking and disturbing—food for thought and also for vultures if there had been any looking down from the sky. . . . They would have been even more impressive, those heads on the stakes, if their faces had not been turned to the house. Only one. . . was facing my way. . . . There it was, black, dried, sunken, with closed eyelids—a head that seemed to sleep at the top of the pole, and, with the shrunken dry lips showing a narrow white line of the teeth, was smiling too, smiling continuously at some endless and jocose dream of that eternal slumber." (HD 72–73)

One is reminded of the lampshades made of human skin by the "Bitch of Buchenwald." Outrage!

After a dramatic confrontation the ailing Kurtz was brought aboard ship to die:

"The brown current ran swiftly out of the heart of darkness, bearing us down towards the sea. . .; and Kurtz's life was running swiftly, too. . ., into the sea of inexorable time. . . .

"His was an impenetrable darkness. . . .

"One evening coming in with a candle I was startled to hear him say a little tremulously, 'I am lying here in the dark waiting for death.'. . .

". . .I saw on that ivory face the expression of sombre pride, of ruthless power, of craven terror—of an intense and hopeless despair. . . .He cried in a whisper at some image, at some vision—he cried out twice, a cry that was no more than a breath:

" 'The horror! The horror!' " (HD 84–85)

It was the following day that the black head of the manager's boy announced with scathing contempt: "Mistah Kurtz—he dead."

Later, back in Bruxelles, Marlow brought a few souvenirs of Kurtz to the woman who loved Kurtz and waited for him. She wanted to know Kurtz's last words.

"I was on the point of crying at her, 'Don't you hear them?' The dusk was repeating them in a persistent whisper all around us, in a whisper that seemed to swell menacingly like the first whisper of a rising wind. 'The horror! The horror!'

" 'His last word—to live with,' she insisted. 'Don't you understand? I loved him—I loved him. . .'

"I pulled myself together and spoke slowly.

" 'The last word he pronounced was—your name.' "

Marlow ceased and sat apart, indistinct and silent. . . . The offing was barred by a black bank of clouds, and the tranquil waterway leading to the uttermost ends of the earth flowed sombre under an overcast sky—seemed to lead into the heart of an immense darkness. (HD 93–94)

ETHICS AND "OUGHT"

What am I trying to get at? Two things: one concerning Heidegger, one ourselves.

If we take seriously the hypothesis that Heidegger's political debacle (his outrage) may be understood in terms of victimization by the errancy inherent in *lēthē* that stretches off into the heart of universal darkness, then there is a way to contextualize, at least, two items in the record that remain most troublesome. I am thinking, for example, of the statement attributed to the manuscript version of "The Question concerning Technology": "Agriculture is now a motorized food industry—in essence, the same as the manufacturing of corpses in gas chambers and extermination camps, the same as the blockading and starving of nations, the same as the manufacture of hydrogen bombs."[17] On the one hand, the statement can be given a reading coherent with Heidegger's thought and, in that sense, is perfectly justifiable. On the other hand, who will deny its tastelessness and gross insensitivity? But here I find a specimen of a kind of madness, at least, that may be the sort of thing John Sallis was referring to when alluding to the text of *Beiträge*, to the effect that human involvement with truth brings a "transformation of the Being of man in the sense of a de-rangement (*Ver-rürkung*) of his position among beings." At any rate, is this not a case where we can say that Heidegger's analysis is indeed a little bit *verrückt*?

I am thinking, too, about Heidegger's silence. There are, no doubt, many ways to think about it but in this context, where I propose to see him as one who faces up to his responsibility as someone who is himself a victim of errancy, what escape is there from errancy but to recognize it for what it is and to acknowledge its inescapability in the very use of the language by which we deal with it? I am thinking of the text of *What Is Called Thinking?*:

Language [*die Sprache*] plays in such a way with our process of language that it gladly lets our language wander astray in the more obvious meanings of words. It is as if man had difficulty in dwelling authentically in language. It is as if the danger to which [man] most easily succumbs is that of everydayness.[18]

Given the enormity of what had happened, it is not unthinkable that the most appropriate response to it was silence. In any case, we understand his alleged response to Elisabeth Hirsch when she argued that he ought to say something. He replied, "Aber wie?"[19]

My final observation addresses ourselves directly and concerns the ethics of Heidegger's political involvement. We are inclined to talk quite easily about the ethics of what he did (e.g., his Nazi activism) or did not do (e.g., his obdurate silence afterwards). But if we remain faithful to his thought, by what ethical standard is he to be judged? How can we justify that standard? A standard, a norm for ethical conduct, would inevitably be, it seems to me, a value of some sort—something ontic, hence a metaphysical entity, the very thing that Heidegger's entire enterprise would sabotage. Given the fact of errancy and the nature of "re-solve," there is simply no way that Heidegger's own authenticity can be judged, whether by another or even, perhaps, by himself. If we remain faithful to his thought, then, what right do we have to be scandalized by his behavior?

But the difficulty comes closer to home, for it touches the work of several among us who explore the possibility of ethics in the light, ultimately, of what Heidegger's thought has disclosed. I have in mind the work of two such thoughtful colleagues as Charles Scott and John Caputo. Scott, if I understand him, is concerned with the *question* of ethics as question, which he poses as radically and rigorously as Heidegger poses the question of ontology in *Being and Time* and of technology later on.[20] Caputo's project is quite different. He has shown how the problematics of Kierkegaard and Husserl coalesce in Heidegger's hermeneutic project of *Being and Time*, and how this, in turn, has been radicalized by Derrida's deconstructive turn. The result he calls "radical hermeneutics," a hermeneutics of the ontological difference, filtered through the template of *différance*. He then draws the ethical implications of all this in what he calls an ethics of "dissemination" or of *Gelassenheit*. Reduced to its elemental simplicity, this means an ethics of coping with the flux of *différance*, which is at once the flux of *alétheia*. "Heidegger's first, last, and constant thought, in my view, is that thinking is in the end directed at that lethic dimension, that the de-limitation of conceptual thinking issues in a *Gelassenheit* toward the *lēthē*. . . ."[21]

But *lēthē* for Caputo, as I read him, is always the *lēthē* of mystery, never the *lēthē* of errancy. This means that so far he does not really take account of the other of truth. Moreover, to sum up his ethics with Augustine's specifically Christian injunction to "love and do what you will" is not to take very seriously either the radical a-theism of *Differenz/différance* or the heart of darkness. Yet unless he does, or rather unless *we* do, we have not really come to grips with the lesson of Heidegger's debacle.

For more is at stake here than Heidegger's own sorry personal history; "In the apocalypse of Auschwitz," writes Lacoue-Labarthe, "it is neither more nor less than the very essence of the Occident that was revealed" (NI 80–81). If that is so, then ethics must do more than "cope with the flux" and "let the play be." It is simply not enough for Caputo to tell us: "There is nothing to do but face the worst, the play of the epochs, [the play] of the temporary constellations within which we live out our historical lives, to wade into the flux and try not to drown" (RH 258). Ethics, I submit, must deal with "ought." Even Heidegger, when he left Todtnauberg and moved into the world of political action, could not dispense with "ought." Listen to him in the rectorial address: "Self-governance means: to set our own task, to determine ourselves the way and manner in which it is to be realized, so that thus we shall be what we ought to be (*um darin selbst zu sein was wir sein sollen*)."[22] Ethics must deal with "ought"—some minimal "ought"—at least with the kind of "ought" that brings us together to discuss these issues. This means some kind of "value" that, however ontic in character, can at least disclose why human being as such has an importance that permits us to say that the savagery of Kurtz, the *technē* of Madame Buchenwald, the stinking ovens of Auschwitz ought not—I do not say will not—but at least *ought not* happen again.

Notes

1. John Sallis, "Deformatives: Essentially Other than Truth," forthcoming in John Sallis, ed., *Commemorations: Reading Heidegger*, from Indiana University Press; abbreviated "DF," followed by page numbers from the unpublished manuscript. Cited with permission.

2. Martin Heidegger, "On the Essence of Truth," trans. John Sallis, in Heidegger, *Basic Writings*, ed. David F. Krell (New York: Harper & Row, 1977), 117–41; abbreviated "ET."

3. Martin Heidegger, *Beiträge zur Philosophie (Vom Ereignis)*, GA 65 (1989); abbreviated "BP."

4. Philippe Lacoue-Labarthe, "Ni un accident, ni une erreur," in *Le Nouvel Observateur*, January 22–28, 1988, pp. 80–81; abbreviated "NI." Compare "Neither an Accident nor a Mistake," trans. Paula Wissing, *Critical Inquiry* 15 (1988–89): 481–84.

5. Joseph Conrad, *Heart of Darkness: A Case Study in Contemporary Criticism*, ed. Ross C. Murfin (New York: St. Martin's Press, 1989), p. 41; abbreviated "HD."

6. Martin Heidegger, *Being and Time*, trans. J. Macquarrie and E. Robinson (New York: Harper & Row, 1962), p. 264.

7. Martin Heidegger, *An Introduction to Metaphysics*, trans. Ralph Manheim (New Haven: Yale Univ. Press, 1959); abbreviated "IM."

8. Martin Heidegger, "Der Ursprung des Kunstwerkes," in Heidegger, *Holzwege*, 4. Aufl. (Frankfurt am Main: Vittorio Klostermann, 1963), 7–68, p. 43. Compare "The Origin of the Work of Art" in *Basic Writings*, 149–87, p. 177.

9. Martin Heidegger, "Brief über den Humanismus," in Heidegger, *Wegmarken* (Frankfurt am Main: Vittorio Klostermann, 1967), 145–94, pp. 189–91. Compare "Letter on Humanism," in *Basic Writings*, 193–242, pp. 237–38.

10. *Seyn* is an antiquated spelling of *Sein*. In a note added to the second edition of *On the Essence of Truth* in 1949, Heidegger tells us that it is meant to underscore Being in its *difference* from beings. I translate it by an equally antiquated spelling of *Being*, namely, *Beon*.

11. Martin Heidegger, *Zollikoner Seminare*, herausgegeben von Medard Boss (Frankfurt am Main: Vittorio Klostermann, 1987), 208–9, emphasis added. Compare "M. Heidegger's Zollikon Seminars," trans. B. Kenny, *Review of Existential Psychology and Psychiatry* 16 (1978–79): 7–21.

12. Martin Heidegger, "Aus einem Gespräch von der Sprache: Zwischen einem Japaner und einem Fragenden," *Unterwegs zur Sprache* (Pfullingen: Neske, 1970), 83–155, p. 91; compare "A Dialogue on Language between a Japanese and an Inquirer," in Heidegger, *On the Way to Language*, trans. P. D. Hertz (New York: Harper & Row, 1971), 1–54, p. 6.

13. Hugo Ott, *Martin Heidegger: Unterwegs zu seiner Biographie* (Frankfurt am Main: Campus, 1988), 131.

14. Martin Heidegger, *Aus der Erfahrung des Denkens* (Pfullingen: Neske, 1954), 17; compare "The Thinker as Poet," trans. A. Hofstadter, in

Heidegger, *Poetry, Language, Thought* (New York: Harper & Row, 1971), 1–14, p. 9.

15. Max Müller, "Martin Heidegger: Ein Philosoph und die Politik— Ein Gespräch," in *Antwort: Martin Heidegger im Gespräch*, herausgegeben vom Günther Neske und Emil Kettering (Pfullingen: Neske, 1988), 213–14; abbreviated "MH."

16. Otto Pöggeler, *Der Denkweg Martin Heideggers*, 2. Aufl. (Pfullingen: Neske, 1983), p. 345. Compare *Martin Heidegger's Path of Thinking*, trans. Daniel Magurshak and Sigmund Barber (Atlantic Highlands, N.J.: Humanities Press, 1987), 280.

17. Martin Heidegger, page 25 of manuscript version of "Die Frage nach der Technik," cited by Wolfgang Schirmacher, *Technik und Gelassenheit* (Freiburg: Alber, 1983); translation by Thomas Sheehan, "Heidegger and the Nazis," in *The New York Review of Books*, June 16, 1988, 39–47, pp. 41–42.

18. Martin Heidegger, *What Is Called Thinking?*, trans. F. D. Wieck and J. G. Gray (New York: Harper & Row, 1968), 118–19.

19. Elisabeth Hirsch, letter to the editor of *The New York Times*, March 2, 1988, p. A22.

20. See Charles E. Scott, *The Question of Ethics: Nietzsche, Foucault, Heidegger* (Bloomington: Indiana Univ. Press, 1990).

21. John D. Caputo, *Radical Hermeneutics: Repetition, Deconstruction, and the Hermeneutic Project* (Bloomington: Indiana Univ. Press, 1987), 271; abbreviated "RH."

22. Martin Heidegger, "The Self-Assertion of the German University: Address, Delivered on the Solemn Assumption of the Rectorate of the University Freiburg," trans. Karsten Harries, *Review of Metaphysics* 38 (1985): 407–80, p. 470.

3

Three Questions to Jacques Derrida

Françoise Dastur

In a round table discussion on Heidegger and politics that took place in June 1988 in Paris, Eliane Escoubas and I asked Jacques Derrida some questions about *De l'esprit*.[1] He gave his answers to our questions in a long improvised explanation of almost two hours. I asked Derrida three questions which I would like to repeat on this occasion, along with some of Derrida's remarks. The first question is about epochality and modernity and refers to chapter 3 of *De l'esprit*. The second question, concerning animality and humanity, is a commentary on note 1 (OS 120–22) in chapter 7, about Husserl's Vienna lecture. The third question is related to the problem of the radicality or banality of evil and refers to chapter 10.

"EPOCH" AND MODERNITY

My first question concerns the thought of epochality and the determination of the "epoch" in the Heideggerian history of Being and Derrida's hesitation and disquiet in this regard; the words *hesitation* and *disquiet* were used by Derrida himself in his remarks at the 1987 Essex Colloquium to which he refers at the beginning of *De l'esprit*.[2] At the end of *De l'esprit*, Derrida evokes "these trees which in Europe people an immense black forest" (OS 109; DE 179) in the shadow of which Nazism had grown. These trees, which "bear the names of religions, philosophies, political regimes, economic structures, religious or academic institutions" (OS 110; DE 179), constitute the European culture or world of spirit, which is not only the result of the Cartesian spirit of modernity but also of the Platonic and Christian spirituality which defines in itself the Western way of thinking. In France, in the debate following the 1987 publication of Victor Farías's book, *Heidegger et le nazism*,[3] the question was asked: Is Heideggerian thinking anti-modern and reactionary? In *Heidegger et les Modernes*, published in 1988 by two well-known anti-Heideggerians (and anti-Derrideans), Luc Ferry and Alain Renaut, Heidegger is presented as a neoconservative who wants to go back to tradition by criticizing technology and to impose on modernity the return to traditional values.[4]

But Heidegger, as early as 1927, formed the project of a phenomenological *"Destruktion"* or "deconstruction" of tradition, which does not concern only the modern metaphysics of subjectivity and therefore does not (as Luc Ferry and Alain Renaut declare) consider Descartes to be "the *principal* instigator of the oblivion of the [ontological] difference."[5] Derrida, on the contrary, recalls in *De l'esprit* that for Heidegger the Cartesian ontology is not a new beginning: "Descartes, then, did not displace medieval theology. In stopping at the distinction between *ens creatum* and *ens infinitum* or *increatum*, medieval theology failed to interrogate the Being of this *ens*. What passes for the rebirth or modern period of philosophical thinking is only the 'rootedness of a deathly prejudice' which held back an ontological and thematic analytics of *Gemüt*" (OS 21; DE 41). Derrida quotes here section 6 of *Being and Time* (the section dedicated to defining the task implied by the project of a "Destruktion" of the history of ontology) where Heidegger explicitly says that "the apparent new beginning of philosophy [with Descartes] shows itself as the rootedness of a fatal prejudice"[6]—a prejudice that consisted in applying to the modern "subject" the categories of medieval and Greek ontology and which therefore held back the analysis of *Gemüt*. This word *Gemüt*, as Derrida acknowledges, is difficult to translate into French, but I myself would not hesitate to translate it by *coeur* (heart), because it is a good equivalent of the German *Mut*, which means both "feeling" (mood) and "courage."[7] *Gemüt*, the traditional adequate name of the being of humanity, is therefore *not* to be understood as *anima*, that is, not as the source of life that is shared in common by all living beings, but as the *specific* manner of being human, that is, of being in some way the beings themselves, as

Aristotle said of the human soul: *hē psychē ta onta pos estin* (see SZ 14; BT 34).

This specific manner of being human can by no means be compatible with the modern determination of human being as a subject essentially defined by its egoïc closedness, as opposed to the openness proper to *Gemüt*. But does that mean that we can already find an analytics of *Gemüt* in Greek thinking and that it would be sufficient to go back to it? In fact, we cannot find it in Greek thinking, not even in the *Peri psychēs* (*De Anima*) of Aristotle, because the Greek explanation of the being of beings is also oriented towards "nature" and understands the being of humanity as something which is *vorhanden*, present-at-hand, and not *explicitly* as disclosedness. And this is a feature not only of the classical Greek thinking but also of the so-called pre-Socratic thinking: already at the very beginning of the ontological tradition, being is implicitly understood as presence (*Anwesenheit*), and long before Descartes, Parmenides jumps over (*überspringt*) the phenomenon of world, as Heidegger remarks in *Sein und Zeit* (SZ 100; BT 133); that is, jumps over the difference between presence-at-hand (*Vorhandenheit*) and readiness-to-hand (*Zuhandenheit*) by reducing world to mere "nature." If what Heidegger, much later, calls *das Gestell* is really the accomplishment of metaphysics— that is, the consecration of ontological in-difference happening as the unfolding of the being of technology—he should therefore have said not only that the atomic bomb had already exploded in the Cartesian cogito (as he did explicitly in the 1951 Zürich seminar),[8] but that it had in fact already exploded in the Parmenidean poem.[9] Because the modern meaning of being as objectivity can appear with Descartes only on the basis of its Greek meaning as presence, we must not emphasize the difference between modernity and antiquity or medieval times, but on the contrary relocate the different "epochs" of the history of Being within the great epoch of metaphysics, which could be called the epoch of re-presentation. But re-presentation here means "to render present in general" and not a rendering present of everything for the benefit of the subject, which is the peculiar feature of modernity. That is more or less what Derrida suggested in a lecture entitled "Envoi" from July 1980.[10] And in the same lecture he emphasized the fact that Heidegger does not consider the reign of representation to be at all a calamity precisely because in the accomplished metaphysics, in *Gestell* (which is the other face of *Ereignis* and as such the announcement of what is no longer "epoch-making"),[11] the "modern world begins to free itself from the space of representation and calculability."[12]

   All this should lead us to consider Heidegger not as an anti-modern but, on the contrary, as "absolutely modern" (in the sense Rimbaud meant at the end of "Une saison en enfer": "Il faut être absolument moderne") or even as postmodern. This is, for example, already the thesis of Reiner Schürmann,[13] who sees in the destinal temporality of the second Heidegger an an-archic economy of presence linked to an "anti-humanism" that understands humanity no longer as the origin of presence but as the recipient of dispatches to multiple destinations. Heidegger attributes indeed to the ultimate figure of modernity—when the object as counterpart of the subject begins to disappear and when the pure *Be-stand* replaces the *Gegen-stand*[14]—a superiority over all the other epochs so far as the thought of the ontological difference is concerned: it is the time of the reversal of peril into salvation.[15]

   But if this is really the Heideggerian thought of epochality in general, if Heidegger understands, as Derrida stresses it, *the* metaphysics as *the epochē*, or the suspensive withdrawal of Being in the epochality of all the epochs,[16] what, then, is problematic for Derrida in the Heideggerian history of Being? Derrida himself speaks in *The Post Card* of the "great epoch" of *Geschick*, of destination, which goes from Socrates to Freud and Heidegger.[17] What is in fact problematic is the *Ge-* of *Ge-schick* and its gathering *value*, by which in destination Being still destines *itself* as if it were the unified "subject" of destination (EN 137). That is why Derrida speaks in *De l'esprit*, "for provisional convenience," of "the *axiomatics* of *Destruktion* and of the epochal scheme in general" (OS 8; DE 23). Derrida stressed in his reply to my question that the word "axiomatics" is here taken in its Greek sense of "valorization" to point out the hidden teleology still to be found in the epochal scheme. In *The Post Card*, Derrida had already expressed his suspicion of what in this scheme he called the "lure" of destination in general: "To ordain the different epochs, stops, determinations, in short the whole history of Being, to a destination of Being, this is perhaps the most extraordinary postal lure" (CP 73–74; PC 44). Derrida wants to think the multiplicity of the dispensations, of the sendings, *la multiplicité des envois*, as coming from the other and not from Being it*self*, that is, as sendings back, as returns, as *renvois*, so that there is no gathering of destination but an originary dissemination or division of destiny: "This pre-ontological sending (*envoi*) does not in some way gather together with itself: it gathers together only by dividing itself, by differing from itself. . . . It does not make one with itself and does not commence with itself, in spite of the fact that it is preceded by nothing present; it emits only in already sending back, it emits only from the other, *from the other in itself without itself.* Everything commences by sending back, that is, does not commence" (EN 141).

My question on this point would be the following: Is it necessary, in order to let appear the multiplicity of the dispensations, to break off with the idea of a commencement? Rather, is it not sufficient to emphasize the an-archy of the *An-fang*? *Anfang* is a word that I try to translate by *commencement* so that it will not be identified with a mere beginning (Heidegger stresses the difference between *Beginning* and *Anfang*), because it has in German a somewhat passive sense and means something like "becoming caught into something." Heidegger tries to think what he calls, in *The Self-Assertion of the German University*, "the greatness of commencement" (*die Grösse des Anfangs*), which does not allow us to think of it as remaining behind us, in the past, but rather, "having fallen" into the future, calls to us as a task that we have to fulfill,[18] so that we must "repeat" it in a "new commencement"; is that not a thinking of destination that already "overcomes" the "axiomatics" of a predonated unity of destination? And the Heideggerian *Wieder-holung* or "repetition" of what has not yet taken place: is this not a repetition, looking forward and not backward, of a still-to-come and not already past commencement? If this were the case, then Heideggerian thinking—not only after the rectorship but during it—is not properly understood as a neoconservatism, that is, as the philosophical expression of the "conservative revolution," which is the characteristic of Nazism and fascism in general.

HUMANITY AND ANIMALITY

My second question is again related to Europe—to what Husserl in his 1935 Vienna lecture, "Philosophy and the Crisis of European Humanity," called its "spiritual figure" (*die geistige Gestalt Europas*)—and concerns the long note in chapter 7 of *De l'esprit* in which Derrida quotes the passage from Husserl's lecture where Husserl excludes from European humanity "Eskimos, Indians from travelling zoos, and Gypsies permanently wandering all over Europe."[19] This note created some indignation in France because it seemed to place on the same level "Husserl the humanist and Heidegger the Nazi." I use this formulation to summarize many commentaries without, however, thereby indicating, by any means, agreement with them. On the contrary, I think (with Derrida) that this passage of the Vienna lecture is important because it mentions the Gypsies, about whom we now easily forget that they shared the same fate as the European Jews during the Second World War. In this connection, Philippe Lacoue-Labarthe in *La fiction du politique* wants to differentiate the "spiritual logic" that commended the extermination of the Jews from another logic (political, economic, social, etc.) that commends all other kinds of slaughters, including the massacre of the Gypsies, which, he claims, has not "the same metaphysical signification" and does not follow from the "same symbolic logic" as the extermination of the Jews. Lacoue-Labarthe seems to forget, however, that evil and murder are *always geistlich*, that is, "spiritual" in a non-Christian and nonmetaphysical sense; they are *not*, as he seems to believe, sometimes *geistig*, that is, "spiritual," in the metaphysical and Christian way, as opposed to the "material," and at other times (this is for him the case with the extermination of the Gypsies) only economic or political.[20] In *Eichmann in Jerusalem*, Hannah Arendt reminds us that even Eichmann's conscience "rebelled not at the idea of murder but at the idea of German Jews being murdered" and that "this way of thinking that distinguishes between the murder of 'primitive' and the murder of 'cultured' people [is not] a monopoly of the German people," so that for many "civilized" Europeans the murder of German Jews still seems to be more monstrous than the murder of the *Ostjuden*, and the murder of the *Ostjuden* more monstrous than the murder of Gypsies.[21]

But it is also necessary to recall this passage of the Vienna lecture and quote it today, as Derrida stresses, because it is part of a discourse on spirit and on the freedom of spirit that is at the same time a discourse on exclusion. In the Vienna lecture, Husserl's main concern is to bring a remedy to naturalism or objectivism, taken to be the "deviation" of rationalism that has led to the subordination of spirit to nature—a deviation that is for him an absurdity because nature is nothing other than a formation of spirit, dependent on its "absolute historicity."[22] And this discourse on spirit ends with the Oriental and Hegelian image of the phoenix, of the immortal bird that rises again from the ashes of the great naturalist lassitude.[23] I would like to ask whether it is not the thesis of the immortality and infinity of spirit that commends the Husserlian "philosophy of history" and that allows Husserl to distinguish the types of empirical mankinds—the Chinese, the Indian, the Papuan, the Gypsy, etc., which have only a finite historicity because spirit has not yet in them become self-conscious—from the type of European mankind and its infinite teleology. And to this accomplished European type of mankind Husserl attributes also a normative value for the estimation of what he calls the abnormal varieties of mankind—the sick, the child, the old, the primitive, and even the animal, in which it is possible to discover something like a latent spirituality or rationality.[24]

It seems to me that Heidegger would consider this "continuitism" (in a very Leibnizian style) to be the last example of the thinking of the *animalitas* (as opposed to the *humanitas* as such), which is for him the metaphysical way of thinking, as he stresses in the *Letter on Humanism*.[25] Metaphysics thinks always and only the *homo animalis*, even when it understands *anima* as *animus* or *mens* and later understands *mens* as subject, person, or spirit.[26] The Husserlian affirmation of the eternity or omnitemporality of spirit in its absolute historicity does not allow us to get out of "the philosophy of life," out of the *Lebensphilosophie*, which perpetuates the nondistinction between *anima* and *animus*, between the living being and the thinking being. That is the reason why Heidegger declares that an "abyss" (*Abgrund*) separates the living being from Dasein (BH 157; LH 206). It is therefore quite ridiculous to accuse Heidegger of being an anti-humanist; he, on the contrary, accuses the metaphysical tradition of not having thought *humanitas* as such because it has always tried to understand the human being in relation to something else that it is not, the *res* or the animal. Only an analytics of *Gemüt* would be able to think the *homo humanus* and not only, as metaphysics has done since the beginning, the *homo animalis*. The metaphysical logic is a logic of addition, of *Ergänzung*: it is because human being has been reduced to mere animal organism that it seems necessary to attribute to it an immortal soul, personality, and rationality. To the metaphysical logic of addition Heidegger prefers a logic of opposition, and Derrida remarks that this oppositional logic has at least "the interest of breaking with the difference of degree" and that "it respects a difference of structure while avoiding anthropocentrism" (OS 49; DE 78). However, this oppositional logic can also function as the reconduction of the traditional gesture by which the animal is excluded from the world of spirit. And this traditional gesture not only establishes a hierarchy of humanity over animality, but it has also a homogenizing effect because *the* radical difference of structure would efface the multiple differences which do not constitute in their plurality *one* humanity opposed to *one* animality. Thus the logic of addition and the logic of opposition both seem to depend on an unavoidable anthropocentrism. Derrida sees clearly the difficulty of escaping the "program" of humanist teleology (OS 56; DE 87–88), but, on the other hand, he tries to promote the thought of contamination, which should be not a blurring of the differences but, on the contrary, their multiplication (RH 183). I can understand what is at stake, but I wonder how a thinking of contamination could escape the confusion of the Same and be the thinking of the Other. Derrida claims, "In the difference between the difference of degree and the difference of kind another difference is blurred. That is what I call *différance*, with an *a*, which is not a distinction, not a difference, either in essence or in degree" (RH 181–82). Is a new logic required here? If this new logic does not presuppose an *already present* difference of essence or degree but rather the *happening* of differences, is it not possible to find the prefiguration of such a logic in Heidegger himself, not in the lecture course from 1929–30, but later in the thought of *Ereignis?*

EVIL AND METAPHYSICS

My third question is related to the problem of evil and brings me back again to the same passage from *De l'esprit* from which I quoted at the beginning of my remarks: "Nazism was not born in the desert. We all know this, but it has to be constantly recalled. And even if, far from any desert, it had grown like a mushroom in the silence of a European forest, it would have done so in the shadow of big trees, in the shelter of their silence or their indifference but in the same soil" (OS 109; DE 179). In an interview given to the weekly magazine *Le Nouvel Observateur* in November 1987, just after the publication of Farías's book, Derrida repeats: "Nazism has not grown in Germany or in Europe like a mushroom." What is refused with the metaphor of the mushroom is the suggestion that Nazism could have suddenly exploded and rapidly propagated in *any* kind of soil. Derrida refuses this sense of the banality of evil, and thus would appear to give advantage to the idea of the radicality of evil. Hannah Arendt, however, employs the same metaphor of the mushroom against the notion of the radicality of evil in her answer to Gershom Scholem during the controversy following (and even in fact preceding) the publication in 1963 of her *Eichmann in Jerusalem*. I quote here a passage from Hannah Arendt's letter to Gershom Scholem of 14 July 1963: "It is indeed my opinion now that evil is never 'radical,' that it is only extreme, and that it possesses neither depth nor any demonic dimension. It can overgrow and lay waste the whole world precisely because it spreads like a fungus on the surface. It is 'thought-defying,' as I said, because thought tries to reach some depth, to go to the roots, and the moment it concerns itself with evil, it is frustrated because there is nothing. That is its 'banality.' Only the good has depth and can be radical."[27]

Heidegger himself, as Derrida shows in *De l'esprit*, is on the side of the radicality of evil, on the side of Kant and Schelling. He is even more radical than they were because for him evil is not external to spirit and has its center not in the material or in the sensible, but, on the contrary, *in* spirit itself. Already in *Being and Time*, section 82, when opposing his conception of time to the Hegelian one, Heidegger takes up the word *spirit* as his own, but with quotation marks. There spirit is not opposed to the temporal—as it is for Hegel, who speaks of the "fall" of spirit into time—but understood as orginary temporalization, as time itself, as Derrida remarks:

> We already perceive, behind or between the quotation marks, this spirit which is not other than time. It returns, in short, to time, to the movement of temporalization, it lets itself be affected in itself, and not accidentally, as from outside, by something like falling or *Verfallen*. We will have to remind ourselves of this much later when Heidegger insists on the spiritual essence of evil. (OS 29; DE 51)

From the very beginning, Heidegger identifies spirit and time and thinks the self-affection of spirit as an *internal* falling of one time into another, so that time is affected by an internal duplicity which renders it both proper and nonproper—*eigentlich* and *uneigentlich*.

Much later, in the essay on Trakl, Heidegger insists on the radicality of evil with formulas (as Derrida remarks) sometimes literally Schellingian. Derrida comments: "Evil and wickedness are spiritual (*geistlich*) and not simply sensible or material, by simple metaphysical opposition to that which is *geistig*" (OS 102; DE 167–68). The metaphysics of evil, which Heidegger seems then to support, is for Derrida the same metaphysics of *humanitas* and *animalitas* already expressed in the *Introduction to Metaphysics* in 1935. According to this metaphysics, evil is reserved to mankind alone because only man as a free being can disjoin his ontological fit, whereas the animal cannot get out of its natural unity. In the lecture course on Schelling from 1936 quoted by Derrida in *De l'esprit* (OS 103; DE 170–71), Heidegger tried to withdraw the Schellingian thinking of evil not only from a purely Christian space but also from the ethical horizon into which evil is always diminished. This led Heidegger to inscribe evil in the profundity of the history of spirit as its internal duality or dissension (*Zwietracht*). Dissension constantly menaces spirit insofar as spirit *is* time, that is, is always outside itself (*ausser sich*), deported from itself (*entsetzt*), thrown out of itself (*aufgebracht*).[28] Spirit is the *Flamme* which, by autoaffective spontaneity, passes ecstatically outside itself (OS 97; DE 159), while remaining, however, one in its most internal discord (OS 106; DE 175).

If we now try to see Nazism in the light of such a metaphysics of evil, we would be led to attribute to it a properly demonic dimension. But at the same time, it will become impossible for us to identify and judge those who were guilty, and we will be irresistibly inclined to take refuge in that "spiritual" construction named "the collective guilt of the German people" or even in "the guilt of the whole Platonic and Christian Occident." What will be lost is the idea that crime is always singular and individual, so that the metaphysics of *Geistlichkeit*—of a spirit that unfolds its essence in the dual possibilities of gentleness and destructiveness and has in itself the internal possibility of evil—will inevitably fall back into a mere metaphysics of *Geistigkeit*, that is, into a metaphysical construction that cannot acount for the *always* individual deeds and that appeal to metaphysical entities in order to explain what *factually* happened.[29] The identification of metaphysical and moral guilt is the risk involved with such a metaphysical construction, which proves that to withdraw the metaphysics of evil from the ethical horizon is not at all easy, just as it is not easy to get out of the purely Christian space within which evil and good have been defined. For, as Karl Jaspers wrote in *Die Schuldfrage* (translated as *The Question of German Guilt*)—a book published in 1946 that we should reread carefully today— metaphysical guilt "makes each co-responsible for every wrong and every injustice in the world, especially for crimes committed in his presence or with his knowledge,"[30] whereas, he says, moral guilt is always an individual guilt, so that it is nonsense to accuse a people, taken as a whole, of having committed a crime, and it is even more insane to accuse the Occident in general, even if, as Jaspers says, at the same time it is right to consider politically guilty the citizens of a state who have supported injustice.[31]

My question on this point would therefore be the following: Is it possible to *think* Nazism without reinforcing these "spiritual" and metaphysical constructions ("spiritual" here in the sense of *"geistig"*) by the same gesture with which we try to denounce them as undue constructions or essentializations? Hannah Arendt wrote that "evil is thought-defying" and felt therefore obliged to change her mind and to deny the radicality of evil because she was not ready to renounce judging individual criminals. The result was her affirmation of the banality of evil. Is there, as Derrida hinted in his answer to my question, a new logic that could allow us to think evil while avoiding the necessity of thinking it either as radical or as merely banal? On the one hand, to detect in Nazism a demonic dimension or a madness is still in fact a manner of reassuring oneself against the terrifying possibility of a contamination of all European discourses by the same schemes of thought and against the possibility of a "spiritual" complicity between Nazism and anti-Nazism. But, on the other hand, to affirm the banality of evil is at the same time to renounce the effort to *understand* what happened and to take refuge in the limits of the ethical point of view. In both cases, Nazism is not questioned as such, as if we already had a knowledge of what it is. It seems to me that Derrida, in *De l'esprit*, begins to destroy—to deconstruct—such a certitude and reopens the *question* of Nazism,[32] a dangerous question that deals not only with past facts but also with future eventualities.

Notes

1. Jacques Derrida, *De l'esprit: Heidegger et la question* (Paris: Galilée, 1987), abbreviated "DE"; *Of Spirit: Heidegger and the Question*, trans G. Bennington and R. Bowlby (Chicago: Univ. of Chicago Press, 1989); "OS." Where a quotation in text is followed by two page citations, the first is the source of the quotation, the second is for comparison. *De l'esprit* was originally a lecture given 14 March 1987 at the end of a conference entitled "Heidegger: Open Questions," organized by the Collège International de Paris.

2. DE 23; OS 8. See Jacques Derrida, "On Reading Heidegger: An Outline of Remarks to the Essex Colloquium," *Research in Phenomenology* 17 (1987): 171–85, abbreviated "RH."

3. See Victor Farías, *Heidegger and Nazism*, ed. J. Margolis and T. Rockmore, trans. P. Burrell and G. R. Ricci (Philadelphia: Temple Univ. Press, 1989).

4. Luc Ferry and Alain Renaut, *Heidegger et les Modernes* (Paris: Grasset, 1988), 159. See *Heidegger and Modernity*, trans. F. Philip (Chicago: Univ. of Chicago Press, 1990), 73.

5. Ferry and Renaut, *Heidegger et les Modernes*, p. 37, emphasis added. Compare *Heidegger and Modernity*, p. 14.

6. Martin Heidegger, *Sein und Zeit* (Tübingen: Niemeyer, 1963), 25; abbreviated "SZ." Compare Heidegger, *Being and Time*, trans. J. Macquarrie and E. Robinson (New York: Harper & Row, 1962), 46; "BT."

7. Derrida recalls (DE 41–42; OS 21–22) that the first translators of *Sein und Zeit* into French took up the Latin word *mens* to "translate" *Gemüt* and so escaped the worst confusion, which would have been the translation by *esprit*, given that *Geist* and *Gemüt* are usually translated into French by the same word *esprit*. Heidegger writes also the word *Gemüt* with quotation marks to indicate that it is a traditional—Kantian—expression and not his own (the Heideggerian word is *Dasein*), but he does not ask to avoid it, as in the case of *Geist*, which can only with difficulty be dissociated from the Hegelian discourse into which it is defined in connection with (absolute) knowlege. It should be emphasized that *Gemüt* is a *collective* name and means in the Kantian discourse the gathering of two different "faculties" or "sources," sensibility and understanding, opposed as receptivity and spontaneity, which are not without similarity to the two fundamental existentials of *Befindlichkeit* (disposition) and *Verstehen* (comprehension). So Kant's understanding of the being of humanity as *Gemüt*, even if its (temporal) unity remains unknown to him, is the nearest in the tradition to the Heideggerian Dasein, mainly because the dimension of receptivity or openness is not only present but, as Heidegger stresses in his Kant interpretation, dominant in it.

8. Martin Heidegger, "Séminaire de Zürich," (6 November 1951), trans. (German to French) F. Fédier, in *Po&sie* 13 (Summer 1980): 52–62, p. 58: "La bombe atomique a déjà explosé depuis beau temps; exactement au moment—un éclair—où l'être humain est entré en insurrection par rapport à l'être, et de lui-même a posé l'être, le transformant en objet de sa représentation. Depuis Descartes. Représenter l'être comme objet, par un sujet, voilà qui est accompli en connaissance de cause depuis Descartes. Cette provocation de la nature a n'être qu'objet caractérise le comportement fondamental de la technique, et en lui repose toute science moderne. Science physique moderne, ce n'est que développement du déploiement de la technique, dont nous ne savons encore que peu de chose. Il nous est impossible de surmonter la technique avec de la morale. La technique n'est ni simplement, ni même en premier lieu seulement quelque chose d'humain. La technique est en son déploiement une espèce tout à fait précise d'ouverture de l'être, par laquelle il faut, destin de l'être, que l'homme d'aujourd'hui passe." To my knowledge, the original German text has never been published.

9. To my knowledge, Heidegger never said explicitly that the atomic bomb had already exploded in Parmenides' poem. But we can find some hints going in that direction in *What Is Called Thinking?*, trans. J. G. Gray (New York: Harper & Row, 1968), 234 (compare *Was heisst Denken?* [Tübingen: Niemeyer, 1954], 142), in a commentary on the Parmenidean being:

If the Being of beings, in the sense of the being here of what is present, did not already prevail, beings could not have appeared as objects, as what is objective in objects—and only by such objectivity do they become available to the ideas and propositions in the positing and disposing of nature by which we constantly take inventory of the energies we can wrest from nature. This disposition of nature according to its energy supply arises from the hidden essence of modern technology.

If *einai*, Being of beings, did not prevail—in the sense of the being here and thus objectivity of the inventory of objects—not only would the airplane engines fail to function, they would not exist. If the Being of beings, as the being here of what is present, were not manifest, the electric energy of the atom could never have made its appearance, could never have put man to work in its own way—work in every respect determined by technology.

But the clearest indication is to be found at the beginning of the lecture, "The Thing," in Heidegger, *Poetry, Language, Thought*, trans. A. Hofstadter (New York: Harper & Row, 1971), 165–82, p. 166, where Heidegger explicitly considers the explosion of the atomic bomb as "the mere final emission of what has long since taken place": the terrifying "merging of everything into the distanceless" that does not allow us to sojourn in the nearness of the thing itself, which only occurs when world worlds. Compare Heidegger, "Das Ding," in *Vorträge und Aufsätze* (Pfullingen: Neske, 1954), 164.

10. Jacques Derrida, "Envoi" (abbreviated "EN"), in *Psyché: Inventions de l'autre* (Paris: Galilée, 1987) ("PS"), 109–43, pp. 121–22: "Le fait qu'il y ait de la représentation ou de la *Vorstellung*, cela n'est pas, suivant Heidegger, un phénomène récent et caractéristique de l'époque moderne de la science, de la technique et de la subjectivité de type cartésiano-hegelien. Ce qui serait caractéristique de cette époque en revanche, c'est l'autorité, la généralité dominante de la représentation. C'est l'interprétation de l'essence de l'étant comme objet de représentation. Tout ce qui devient présent, tout ce qui *est*, c'est-à-dire est présent, se présente, tout ce qui arrive est appréhendé dans la forme de la représentation. L'expérience de l'étant devient essentiellement représentation."

11. Martin Heidegger, "Summary of a Seminar on the Lecture 'Time and Being'," in Heidegger, *On Time and Being*, trans. Joan Stambaugh (New York: Harper & Row, 1972), p. 53: "Between the epochal formations of Being and the transformation of Being into Appropriation [*Ereignis*] stands Framing [*Ge-stell*]. Framing is an in-between state, so to speak. It offers a double aspect, one might say, a Janus head. It can be understood as a kind of continuation of the will to will, thus as an extreme formation of Being. At the same time, however, it is a first form of Appropriation itself." Compare Heidegger, "Seminar Protokoll zu Heidegger's Vorlesung 'Zeit und Sein'," in *Zur Sache des Denkens* (Tübingen: Niemeyer, 1969), 56–57.

12. Jacques Derrida, EN 122: "Bien entendu, ce règne de la représentation, Heidegger ne l'interprète pas comme un accident, encore moins comme un malheur devant lequel il faudrait se replier frileusement. La fin de *Die Zeit des Weltbildes* est très nette à cet égard, au moment où Heidegger évoque un monde moderne qui commence à se soustraire à l'espace de la représentation et du calculable."

13. Reiner Schürmann, *Le principe d'anarchie: Heidegger et la question de l'agir* (Paris: Seuil, 1982). See *Heidegger on Being and Acting: From Principles to Anarchy*, trans. Christine-Marie Gros (Bloomington: Indiana Univ. Press, 1987).

14. Martin Heidegger, "The Question concerning Technology" (abbreviated "QC"), in Heidegger, *The Question concerning Technology and Other Essays*, trans. W. Lovitt (New York: Harper & Row, 1977), 3–35, p. 17 (collection abbreviated "QT"): "The name 'standing-reserve' [*Bestand*] assumes the rank of an inclusive rubric. It designates nothing less than the way in which everything presences that is wrought upon by the challenging revealing. Whatever stands by in the sense of standing-reserve no longer stands over against us as object [*Gegenstand*]." The interplay of *stand* and *stehen* is evident in the original; compare Heidegger, "Die Frage nach der Technik" (abbreviated "FT") in VA 13–44, p. 24: "Das Wort 'Bestand' rückt jetzt in den Rang eines Titels. Er kennzeichnet nicht Geringeres als die Weise, wie alles anwest, was vom herausfordernden Entbergen betroffen wird. Was im Sinne des Bestandes steht, steht uns nicht mehr als Gegenstand gegenüber."

15. See QC 28 (FT 36) where Heidegger quotes Hölderlin's verse from "Patmos":

But where danger is, grows
The saving power also.

See also Heidegger, "The Turning," QT 36–49, p. 42 (compare "Die Kehre," in *Die Technik und die Kehre* [Pfullingen: Neske, 1962], pp. 37–47, p. 41), where Heidegger stresses that peril as such is what brings salvation.

16. Jacques Derrida, "Le retrait de la métaphore," PS 63–93, p. 79: "Le concept dit 'métaphysique' de la métaphore appartiendrait à *la* métaphysique en tant que celle-ci correspond, dans l'époqualité des ses époques, à une *épochè*, autrement dit à un retrait suspensif de l'être."

17. Jacques Derrida, *The Post Card: From Socrates to Freud and Beyond,* trans. Alan Bass (Chicago: Univ. of Chicago Press, 1987), pp. 42, 191; abbreviated "PC." Compare *La carte postale: De Socrate à Freud et au-delà* (Paris: Aubier-Flammarion, 1980), pp. 69, 205–6; "CP."

18. Martin Heidegger, *Die Selbstbehauptung der deutschen Universität: Rede, gehalten bei der feierlichen Übernahme des Rektorats der Universität Freiburg* (Frankfurt am Main: Vittorio Klostermann, 1983), 12; compare "The Self-Assertion of the German University: Address, Delivered on the Solemn Assumption of the Rectorate of the University Freiburg," trans. Karsten Harries, *Review of Metaphysics* 38 (1985): 470–80, p. 473.

On the necessity of repeating the commencement, see my article, "La fin de la philosophie et le nouveau commencement de la pensée," in *Heidegger: Questions ouvertes* (Paris: Osiris, 1988), p. 129: "Le commencement, à cause de sa soudaineté, ne peut être maintenu que s'il est répété, recommencé. Et recommencer, c'est toujours commencer autrement: c'est ce qui garantit que la répétition, pas plus qu'elle ne consistait en 1927 à redevenir aristotélicien, ne signifie dix ans plus tard 'ne philosopher qu'en présocratique et dénoncer tout le reste comme malentendu et décadence'."

19. DE 94–95; OS 120–22. This passage was curiously absent from the first published version of the lecture (the Strasser version translated into French by Paul Ricoeur in 1949).

20. Philippe Lacoue-Labarthe, *La fiction du politique: Heidegger, l'art, et la politique* (Paris: Christian Bourgois, 1987), 76. See *Heidegger, Art, and Politics: The Fiction of the Political*, trans. Chris Turner (New York: Basil Blackwell, 1990), 49.

21. Hannah Arendt, *Eichmann in Jerusalem: A Report on the Banality of Evil* (New York: Penguin Books, 1964), 96.

22. Edmund Husserl, "Philosophy and the Crisis of European Humanity," in *The Crisis of European Sciences and Transcendental Phenomenology: An Introduction to Phenomenological Philosophy*, trans. David Carr (Evanston, Ill.: Northwestern Univ. Press, 1970), appendix 1, "The Vienna Lecture," pp. 269–99: "Here the spirit is not in or alongside nature; rather, nature is itself drawn into the spiritual sphere. . . . The universality of the absolute spirit surrounds everything that exists with an absolute historicity, to which nature is subordinated as a spiritual structure" (p. 298). Compare *Die Krisis der europäischen Wissenschaften und die transzendentale Phänomenologie* (The Hague: Martinus Nijhoff, 1962), 346, 347.

23. Husserl, "Philosophy and the Crisis," p. 299: "If we struggle against this greatest of all dangers as 'good Europeans' with the sort of courage that does not fear even an infinite struggle, then out of the destructive blaze of lack of faith, the smoldering fire of despair over the West's mission for humanity, the ashes of great weariness, will rise up the phoenix of a new life-inwardness and spiritualization as the pledge of a great and distant future for man: for the spirit alone is immortal." Compare *Krisis*, 348. On Hegel's image of the phoenix, see Jacques Derrida, *Glas* (Paris: Denoël/Gonthier, 1981), 164–65; compare *Glas*, trans. J. P. Leavey, Jr., and R. Rand (Lincoln: Univ. of Nebraska Press, 1986) 116–17.

24. There is a thematic discourse in Husserl about normality and abnormality (see, for example, the fifth Cartesian Meditation, sec. 55) that deals with differences in age, health, culture, animality, and humanity, a discourse that prompts the following questions: What constitutes the norm in itself, if not a reference to a "we," meaning "we who are discoursing about normality and abnormality," that is, "we who are fully spiritual or rational beings"? Why do we find in Husserl a discourse of normativity, that is to say, a discourse on *Geist*, and not a discourse on *Gemüt*, or heart, if not because he is still privileging, like the entire Western tradition, the intellectual dimension of mankind against the "affective" one?

25. Martin Heidegger, *Brief über den 'Humanismus'*, in *Wegmarken* (Frankfurt am Main: Klostermann, 1967), 145–94, p. 155 (abbreviated "BH"): "Die Metaphysik denkt den Menschen von der animalitas her und denkt nicht zu seiner humanitas hin." Compare "Letter on Humanism" ("LH"), BW 193–242, p. 204.

26. BH 155: "Man denkt in Prinzip stets den homo animalis, selbst wenn anima als animus sive mens und diese später als Subjekt, als Person, als Geist gesetzt werden." Compare LH 203.

27. Hannah Arendt, *The Jew as Pariah: Jewish Identity and Politics in the Modern Age*, ed. Ron H. Feldman (New York: Grove Press, 1978), 250–51.

28. Compare Heidegger, "Sprache im Gedicht: Eine Erörterung von Georg Trakls Gedicht," *Unterwegs zur Sprache* (Pfullingen: Neske, 1959), 35–82, p. 60; "Language in the Poem: A Discussion on Georg Trakl's Poetic Work," *On the Way to Language*, trans. P. D. Hertz (New York: Harper & Row, 1971), 159–98, p. 179. Spirit is time, but it can also be evil. We should remember that the word *Böse* (evil) in German has also the sense of anger and originally means "swollen" or "distended," and that the "distension" of the soul (which is time itself for Augustine) is the condition for this other distension of the soul which is anger and evil.

29. This is what happens in *La fiction du politique* when Lacoue-Labarthe sees in the extermination of the Jews the accomplishment of the essence of the Occident; see pp. 62–63 (*Heidegger, Art, and Politics*, p. 37). It is also what happens when Jean-François Lyotard in *Heidegger et "les Juifs"*, in spite of all his caution, is led to invoke an essence of "the Jews" (with quotation marks as opposed to the real Jews)—which is nothing else than sublimity itself understood as nonrepresentability—in order to "understand" their extermination. Such a contempt for facts and such a "willing" to submit history to the mere power of ideas and essences is not far from the Hegelian "logicization" of history and leads in fact to a mere inversion in value of the Hegelian figure of the Jew. See *Heidegger et "les Juifs"* (Paris: Editions Galilée, 1988), *Heidegger and "the Jews"*, trans. A. Michel and M. S. Roberts (Minneapolis: Univ. of Minnesota Press, 1990).

30. See Karl Jaspers, *Die Schuldfrage: Ein Beitrag zur deutschen Frage* (Heidelberg: Schneider, 1946), p. 31; *The Question of German Guilt*, trans. E. B. Ashton (New York: Capricorn Books, 1961), 32.

31. Jaspers, *Die Schuldfrage*, p. 39; *Question of German Guilt*, 39–40.

32. The fact that Derrida in a long note to *De l'esprit* (DE 147–54; OS 129–36) marks (*with* and not *against* Heidegger) the limits of the questioning attitude, does not mean that he should abstain from questioning and withdraw "from the infinite legitimacy of questioning" but only that it is necessary to situate—as Heidegger does—the question itself in the more originary dimension of hearing, which should be understood in this case as listening to the events themselves without any "presupposed" ideas and ready-made explanations.

4

Spirit and Danger

John D. Caputo

I shall speak here of spirit and danger, and likewise of what Jacques Derrida, in *De l'esprit*,[1] calls the law of the quotation marks.

Two by two, Derrida says, these little marks stand guard over the word *Geist* in Heidegger's *Being and Time* and prevent its entry. Or again, like little hooks, Derrida says, they hold up a curtain that is half-opened so that the word is still visible under the marks, only partly erased. Then, at a certain point, just six years later, this curtain is suddenly lifted. Onto the stage strides the impressive figure of *Geist*, well clad in full military uniform, in blazing, flaming color, and (if we are to believe Hugo Ott) with no little display of academic pomp and circumstance.[2] We can hardly believe our eyes. This is not the same figure we thought we saw through the partly opened curtain. Maybe it is just a ghost. But it is a "terrifying" moment, Derrida says, not a little intimidating to the spectators (OS 31).

I shall speak here of two things. First, of the fearsome figure which is cut by *Geist* when it enters the stage in Heidegger's rectorial address and in *An Introduction to Metaphysics*. I will take my lead from a remark of Derrida's, in which he speaks of the "proportion" between "spirit" and "danger" (OS 45), and then extend and reinforce his analysis, proceeding, let us say, as much in the spirit of *De l'esprit* as in its letter. Second, I wish to say something about the law of the quotation marks, about the operation of the stage machinery, about the lifting itself, and hence about what was set aside in order to

43

allow the striking figure of *Geist* to make its appearance. I shall show
that the law of the quotation marks makes use of what I call the law
of the "economies" (to use Derrida's term) that govern the deployment
of individual words like *Geist*.

THE SPIRIT OF DANGER

As soon as Heidegger lifts the ban that was in place on *spirit*
in *Being and Time*, as soon as he suspends the law of quotation marks
which caused the feet of *spirit* to dangle in the air (of mention) above
the ground (of use), as soon as *Geist* gets its feet on the ground,
something very dangerous breaks loose. As soon as spirit is let in the
door and let on stage, something inflammatory flares up, a fiery
spectacle occurs on stage (the stage that is also the scene or place of
Being's comings and goings) (OS 32). This is not an innocuous and
merely immaterial blaze which does not really burn. This fiery figure,
this very German *Geist*, is dangerous; indeed, it can be defined by
its dangerousness, or by its love of danger, its willingness to endure
fiery pain.[3]
  In the 1930s, danger is the flame of the spirit.
  In *De l'esprit*, at the end of chapter 5, which is devoted to
Heidegger's rectorial address and *An Introduction to Metaphysics*,
Derrida remarks that "the experience of spirit appears proportional
to 'danger'," that for the Heidegger of the 1930s "the most spiritual
people" is the "most endangered" (OS 45). Although the thematics
of danger is not a dominant one in Derrida's own discussion, I want
to show just how right Derrida is. The entire problematics of the
Entmachtung—the enfeeblement—of the spirit, which Derrida
discusses in chapter 7, is a function of the question of danger, for the
power of the spirit is measured by its love of danger.
  Derrida is referring to the famous pincers passage in *An
Introduction to Metaphysics*, in which Heidegger speaks of the menace
of having too many neighbors; it is, Heidegger says, very dangerous.
Heidegger wants to keep his neighbors at a distance. As fond as he
is of nearness and of what is nearby, he likes his neighbor to be at
least a good walk down the road, as far away as it takes to smoke
a pipe (*Being and Time*, sec. 23). He does not like crowded neighbor-
hoods—or crowded continents. The nearby neighbor ought to be kept
at a safe distance; otherwise it is dangerous.
  In *An Introduction to Metaphysics*, the Germans are called—
this is their vocation as the most endangered people—to be the most

spiritual people. They have been situated by the "geopolitics" (OS 44) of Being in the middle. This is a destiny (*Schicksal*) that has been sent the Germans' way, not by Being's history but by Being's geography. It is this people's unique vocation (*Bestimmung*), their destiny, to struggle in and from out of that middle. We are certain of this, Heidegger says; there is no doubt of it (*derer wir gewiss sind*).[4]

That is very interesting. In a book devoted to making everything questionable, one that wants to expose everything to the question of Being, that makes everything tremble with the possibility of its non-being, which exposes it to the abyss of asking why-it-is-rather-than-not, Heidegger seems to think there is no need for questioning why *this* should be so rather than not. It does not fall within the domain of the question of Being to wonder whether Germans have this destiny rather than not, whether they are the center of the map, whether there are not other maps on which they are not the center, whether even the center is the privileged place rather than not, or whether any place at all should be privileged (which is what one might have thought if all there really is, is the *es gibt* which gives without why). It does not occur to Heidegger to wonder whether this is not all a massive "tautology," as Derrida says, rather the way that you can only think *Sein* and have *Geist* in the German language (OS 71–72).

Be that as it may, Heidegger is saying that the certain destiny of the Germans is to rise up out of that middle, to let all of the great spiritual power of what is German unfold and spill over from that middle, and this in virtue of Germany's endowment as the metaphysical people par excellence. In that way, this middle, metaphysical, spiritual people will be able to push itself—and thereby Europe—out of this cramped middle and back into the originary sphere where the powers of Being prevail (EM 41–42; IM 38–39). For Europe is Germany's responsibility, and this people seems to be certain of this, too, and eager to assume this responsibility.[5]

We see now all the terms of what Derrida calls the "proportion" between danger and spirit. Our people (*unser Volk*) is the most overladen with neighbors (*das nachbarreichste Volk*), which makes it the most endangered people (*das gefährdetste Volk*), and this most endangered people is the most metaphysical people (*das metaphysische Volk*). The measure of this *Volk* is taken ultimately by its metaphysicality, which is itself what uniquely endows it with the ability to deal with danger, and danger is just what has been assigned to it by Being's geography or "geopolitics." It is in virtue of being the most metaphysical people that this spiritual people can rise to the danger of the neighbor. This most spiritual of all peoples has been granted the destiny of being the most metaphysical people in one and the same granting in which it has been granted the destiny of being endangered by its neighbors.

Now let there be no misunderstanding. Heidegger is not complaining. This is not a piece of bad luck. He is not lamenting the fact that Russia or the United States, who have fewer neighbors, have it easy and therefore are better off. On the contrary, in matters of the spirit, danger is a gift of destiny, and the lack of danger is dangerous, the highest and deepest and most perilous danger of all. Those who have been given danger have been given a great gift— which is the gift of spirit itself. It is not a question of bad luck but of destiny, for in matters of destiny resoluteness drives out everything accidental (*Being and Time*, sec. 74). This people has been granted a destiny; they have been given greatness, singled out by destiny in order to fulfill an historical role. That is why Heidegger's rhetoric in the early 1930s turns on a call for danger, a call to danger, a warning about the danger of dangerlessness, of being unendangered (*ungefährdet*) (EM 160; IM 151). Complete safety would no doubt distress Heidegger very much.

We see this for the first time in 1929–30, in *Die Grundbegriffe der Metaphysik*, where the Germans are warned—for this is dangerous—about the distress (*Not*) of lacking distress (*Notlosigkeit*). Speaking in 1929, in Weimar Germany, Heidegger says that there is a deep and pervasive boredom besetting "us." (Who is this "us"? And how does Heidegger know this about "us"? Is this a matter of sociological fact or a kind of essential intuition he has?) This boredom cuts more deeply than any or all of the multiple problems which are all around us today: "contemporary social misery, political confusion, the impotence of science, the hollowness of art, the groundlessness of philosophy, the debility of religion."[6]

But, one might ask Heidegger, what about all the parties, groups, and associations that are organized to meet these needs and have programs aimed at offsetting these ills? Heidegger's rejection of such undertakings could not be more complete. Such ventures, he thinks, are worse than nothing, for they serve only to cover over the real need, need as a whole, to consign to oblivion a more profound void.

What truly besets and oppresses us, Heidegger thinks, is the fact that we are cognizant only of particular needs and that we do not feel more deeply beset and oppressed. The real need is found in the "absence of an essential oppression of our Dasein as a whole" (GM 244). There are many bureaucrats administering one program or another but no "administrator of the inner greatness of Dasein and its necessities." We have nothing to make us great, because the only way to be great is to face up to an "inner terror" (*innerer Schrecken*). This absence of distress is the most distressing of all and lies at the basis of the void of boredom. These bureaucrats are trying to induce in us "a generally complacent comfort in dangerlessness" (GM 245). Heidegger continues:

> This comfort in the very ground of our existence, despite all the multiple needs, leads us to believe that we have no more need to be strong [*stark*] in the ground of our existence. We trouble ourselves about teaching skills. The present is full of pedagogical problems and questions. But by heaping up skills we will never replace power and might [*Kraft und Macht*]; if this sort of thing does anything at all, it will only choke them off. (GM 245)

The liberal institutions of the Weimar state, of bourgeois democracy, lack inner greatness and power because they are concerned with making life comfortable, with meeting our needs, with curing our ills. They are making us soft. Presumably, then, we need something to make us hard.

We have forgotten, Heidegger warns, that it is only by putting one's shoulder to the "ownmost burden" of existence (GM 248), by bearing the unbearable heaviness of Being, that we can restore weight to things and to our human being (cf. EM 9; IM 11). Dasein, Heidegger says, is not like a car one can take for a relaxing cruise: "But because we are of the opinion that it is no longer necessary to be strong and to have to resist danger, we have all of us together snuck out of the dangerzone [*Gefahrzone*] of Dasein, and so relieve ourselves of the need to take over Dasein" (GM 246–47).

What, then, to do? What does it mean to shoulder one's existence? Just this, to procure genuine knowledge (*Wissen*), which will enable us to be ourselves. But how is that possible? Only by letting ourselves be overtaken by this void, by letting it transfix our existence, and by *not taking action against it*. (What would that actually mean? Would we abandon every program to help society's most helpless?) In Heidegger's view, the trouble is that we multiply our efforts to fill up this void with one quick fix after another and with hastily conceived programs instead of pushing Dasein into its extreme condition. We have buried deep boredom under an avalanche of depth psychology and psychoanalysis. Heidegger does not seek piecemeal reforms, to undertake local action here or there, but rather to make everything turn on a radical, inner—let us say spiritual—

transformation. Only a revolution can save us. This will be possible only if we let things drift into their most extreme destitution and thereby test the mettle of our Dasein against inner terror, putting it to the test of the greatest difficulty and danger. Hard and dangerous is the great.

Spirit needs distress. Spirit needs to be needy. Neediness (*Notdürftigkeit*) is necessary (*notwendig*) for spirit. It is our fate, our necessity (*Notwendigkeit, anankē*) and we need it. We must have it. It is not safe to lack danger; we can never be saved if we are safe.

The saving and the safe are dangerous. The danger is in the safe. Where the safe and saving are, danger grows. We see here the original Jüngerian form of the later and better-known Hölderlinian formula— where the danger is, the saving grows. The latter formula is the mirror image of the Jüngerian motif and the result of a remarkable *Kehre*. In the 1930s, that is, in the economy of spirit, there is no talk of moving beyond danger to the saving. On the contrary, in this Heideggerian-Jüngerian economy, the movement is exactly the opposite, from the saving, the safe, the unendangered, to the danger. Furthermore, Jünger's formula implies an active nihilism, a voluntary pushing of humanity into extreme destitution, which Heidegger seemed to accept in the early 1930s, while the Hölderlinian version of the formula expresses acceptance of the drift towards the extreme state as a movement beyond human control.[7]

That is why in his rectorial address, delivered just a few years later in 1933, Heidegger issues a call to danger in and as the call to spirit:

> If we will the essence of science understood as the *questioning, unguarded holding of one's ground in the midst of the uncertainty of the totality of what-is, this* will to essence will create for our people its world, a world of the innermost and most extreme danger, i.e., its truly *spiritual* world.[8]

For spirit is danger; thus a spiritual world is one filled with the spirit of danger. Now to pique the spirit, to raise it to its highest peak, the German people must submit itself to its Greek beginning and return to the Promethean insight that knowing (*Wissen*)—Heidegger's translation of *technē*—is far weaker than necessity (*anankē, Notwendigkeit*). Among the Greeks there was no flight from neediness and necessity, no attempt to soften the hard necessity of life, no attempt to make things easy. The Greeks knew the one thing necessary, which is that knowing should fling itself against necessity and let itself shatter in a defiant display of creative impotence (*schöpferische Unkraft*) (SdDU 11; SGU 472). Knowing knows that it will be overwhelmed by the overwhelming power (*Übermacht*) of its destined fate, that it will fail before it. But that is precisely what makes it strong and gives it its truth.

Knowing, for the Greeks, is no cultural ornament but the willingness to persevere against impossible odds, against the insuperable, unalterable concealment of Being. Knowing is a willingness to pit oneself against, to do battle with, an unfathomable abyss. Science is no safe (*gefahrlos*) occupation, without danger. On the contrary, it is unguarded exposure (*ungesetzten Ausgesetzsein*) before the uncertainty of Being's own abyssal questionability (SdDU 13; SGU 474). For "us," knowing is no academic game, not a matter for school teachers or conferences, no occasion for careerism. "But for us this knowledge is not the settled taking note of essences and values in themselves; it is the most severe endangerment [*Gefahrdung*] of human being [*Dasein*] in the midst of the overwhelming power of what is" (SdDU 16; SGU 477). Knowing is self-endangering; it throws away all the security and safety of life and casts itself into an abyssal danger, the danger of the "questionability of Being."

That is why, Heidegger insists, we must rouse these professors out of their academic sleep and push them out ahead of the student body which is already awake, already on the march. The students started marching before the professors. They are already ahead of the faculty, which is no way to conduct an academic procession or a military march. The professors must not think they have a safe profession, behind the front, for theirs is a call to battle (*Kampf*), even presumably without helmets (uncovered), a battle over, with, about Being (*Kampf um das Sein*: EM 114; IM 107). We must challenge the teaching body to assume these most dangerous posts (*äusserste Posten der Gefahr*: SdDU 14; SGU 475), for we have learned from Plato that greatness is always attended by the storm. The greatness of the spirit is its readiness for the storm, its readiness for danger.

In *An Introduction to Metaphysics* Being itself is the storm. For Being is determined, following Heraclitus (fragment 53), as *polemos*, which Heidegger translates sometimes as *Auseinandersetzung* (strife, confrontation) and sometimes as *Kampf* (battle). This is, of course, no human war but the aboriginal conflict among the elements which gives all things their unity (*logos*) and order of rank. Still, this aboriginal *Kampf*, if it is not outright war, nonetheless communicates with concrete human Dasein. It is the origin of the human creators—the poets, thinkers, and statesmen—who continue the *Kampf* and carry it on (*tragen*). These human creators are as it were a barrier, a block, a bastion—but ultimately a futile and impotent one—against the overwheming power (*überwaltigendes Walten*) with which they must contend. When the creators are gone from the nation, when their authentic *Kampf* ceases, when the hand they lend to the aboriginal *Kampf* grows still, then we are left only with decline, decay, the loss of the world (EM 66–67; IM 62–63). What does not battle and grow stronger can only weaken; when things are soft and safe, the real danger sets in.

In *Antigone* the aboriginal *Kampf* of Being is determined as *deinon*. *Deinon* means, on the one hand, the terrible itself (*das Furchtbare*) in the sense of the overwhelming power that compels terror and anxiety; on the other hand, *deinon* means the one who wields or uses power (*Gewalt-tätig*), who contends violently (*gewaltig*) with the overwhelming. Thus *deinon* names alternately the terrible power of Being itself and the terrible one, human being, who deploys his power against Being. Such a man the poet calls *to deinotaton*, which Heidegger translates as "the most uncanny one" (*das Unheimlichste*), not in order to hide his violence but in order to accentuate it. "We understand the *Un-heimlich*," Heidegger says, "as that which casts out of the 'home-ish,' i.e., the homely, the customary, the familiar, the unendangered [*Ungefahrdeten*]" (EM 160; IM 150–51). The violent, uncanny one, the one who leaves the warmth of the hearth, the comforts of the familiar, is one who renounces safety, who wades into the danger, who does not shrink from impossible odds, who embraces the danger of the *Kampf* with appearance, the battle to wrest Being from appearance. The great Greek poet, whose formula in *Antigone* gives us "the authentic Greek definition of man" (EM 160; IM 151), that is, the authentic definition *simpliciter*, wants to give us back our danger, wants to see to it that man does not suffer from the neediness of lacking need. He sees to it that man will be exposed to the danger that constitutes Being-there: uncovered exposure to the abyss of the terrible power of Being.

On Heidegger's reading, the violent one ventures, sets out, breaks out upon (*Aufbruch*) the stormy sea in order to subdue it; he disturbs the tranquility of the earth by breaking into it (*Einbruch*) with mighty plows; he violently snares the peaceful animal with his net (EM 163; IM 154). With his wind-swift understanding he has learned to rule over cities and to subdue even the elements of unpropitious weather.

So this *technē* that pits itself against the overwhelming has all the marks of the *Gestell* but with this one difference—that such *technē* serves the flame of the spirit, *this* spirit, which is marked by its love of violence (*Gewaltsamkeit*) and struggle. No tender tending of the earth, no letting be and letting in (*einlassen*), but rather breaking in and breaking up. (This too reflects the earlier, Jüngerian economy.)

But however far the uncanny, violent one ventures, he is always thrown back on the paths he himself lays out: "All violence shatters against *one* thing. That is death. . . . Here there is no breaking-out or breaking into, no capture or subjugation" (EM 167; IM 158). With the power of his *techne* the uncanny one wrestles with (*erkämpft*) the overwhelming, trying to subdue and stabilize it in his works, his art:

> Yet he can never master the overwhelming. . . . Every violent curbing of the powerful is either victory or defeat. Both, each in its different way, fling him out of home, and thus, each in its different way, unfold the dangerousness [*Gefährlichkeit*] of achieved or lost being. Both, in different ways, are menaced by disaster. The *violent one*, the creative man, who sets forth into the un-said, . . . stands at all times in risk and venture [*Wagnis*] (*tolma*). (EM 170; IM 161).

Such a shattering against death is not a lesson in *Gelassenheit* but a test of courage. Without home or hearth, risking death and disaster, the creative one wrestles with the overwhelming power, only finally to shatter against it. He holds up the barrier of his work—statue or state, text or temple—which for a passing moment gives the appearance of stability, only to go under in the mighty rolling wave of the overwhelming power. The uncanny one dares all, risks all, and finally loses all.

Now that is spirit—that's the spirit—and we should get it (OS 125–27, n. 8). That's hard, tough spirit; no tender spirit this. The violent one flings himself against the terrifying and shatters against it. He is tough, "bad," a lover of dangerous seas and wild game, a violent knower/doer (*techne*), a being of danger, risk, hazard, who in the end is torn to shreds, dispersed by the overwhelming, a victim of the insuperable odds of fate. But that is what makes him great. For if he is indeed crushed by the aboriginal *polemos*, which is no human war, he will be a fearsome opponent in the purely ontic wars with his neighbors ("but who, Lord, is our neighbor?")[9] in which he must be engaged, for this is a point of honor for the *Geist*.

We would say in English that such a fearsome figure "does not know the meaning of danger," which means of course that he really does know it, where *Wissen* is *techne*, where knowing is doing. Indeed that is the very greatness of his spirit.

THE LAW OF THE ECONOMIES

Now I return to the law of the quotation marks. I want to identify the lever that operates this curtain, that lifts it up and down, the machinery that lets the word *Geist* dangle in the air or get a footing on the ground. That law I will call, invoking a notion of which Derrida often makes use, the law of the "economies." That law governs the following proposition, the defense of which I can only sketch here: the spirit of danger is and is not Nazi talk. This is a dangerous way to talk. I admit it. But everything I like and everything I dislike about Heidegger—both at once—are contaminated by this talk of danger, flirts with the danger of this danger, is and is not dangerous, is and is not a Nazi danger.

The "spirit" of "danger" *is* Nazi talk—but it is talk from a philosopher who has set out to make the meaning of "is" tremble, to make it waver in instability.

The "spirit" of "danger" *is* Nazi talk—but it is being read by a philosopher (for Derrida is a "certain" kind of philosopher) who reads through the lens of undecidability.

The "spirit" of "danger" *is* Nazi talk, but I am commenting upon it, for I have signed my name to this piece, and I am speaking of Heidegger and Derrida, of *Geist* and *De l'esprit*, as one who does not believe in essences, as one who thinks that Derrida has shown that we cannot reduce a word or a work to a fixed, identifiable, essential-izable meaning. (This also has a profound effect on my reading of Heidegger's discourse on the *Wesen* of this or that, not only of truth, but also of pain when the spirit returns in the Trakl essay.) With Derrida, I do not think that a word has a meaning "in itself," that its sense is fixed and fitted inalterably in one direction or another, and this certainly holds for the words *danger* and *spirit*. For Derrida, words do not have meanings but, rather, they belong to changing economies, and everything depends upon the economies into which they are entered.

All of this is another way of saying that there are no words about which we can comfort ourselves that just by using them, by protesting loudly that we are on their side and that we stand with them, we can thereby show *we are in the right*. There is no assurance that we are in the right just because we say we are against danger, or against struggle, or against the strength of the spirit, or against the spirit of danger. For there is no danger "in itself," no spirit "in itself." Conversely, there is nothing about *national* or *socialism* that proves that we or anyone else are in the wrong.

The economy of spirit and power in the 1930s is very detestable. I have tried to make it as detestable as possible, that is, to let everything detestable about it stand out without mask or disguise— something I have been doing recently with regard to other texts of Heidegger, to the dismay of many old friends, and it is hard to see where it will stop![10] But I want to conclude this chapter by pointing out (and this is by no means to be construed as a full-fledged demonstration) that this discourse on danger and hardness is not without a *history* in Heidegger's texts and hence that it has been subject to a number of economic shifts. That means that it has taken other forms, has belonged to other economies, has had other senses.

On the one hand this discourse has had a prehistory that goes back to Heidegger's earliest interest in Aristotle and Kierkegaard.[11] Towards the beginning of *An Introduction to Metaphysics* Heidegger says that "philosophy by its very nature never makes things easier, only more difficult" (EM 13; IM 11). He adds that "making things difficult gives the weight [*Gewicht*] (the Being) back to things, to beings." To take things lightly, to make life easy, is to rob things of their weight, to expose them and oneself to the unbearable lightness of Being, to let everything float away in ontological weightlessness. In *An Introduction to Metaphysics* this whole notion of difficulty is immediately tied to the origin of everything "great," which is itself tied to the "destiny" of an "historical people." In short, it is entered into the economy of the spiritual danger that we have just rehearsed, which is, I say, detestable. For that is what lets *Geist* enter in full military garb through the opened curtains.

But that represents a change, a fundamental transformation of Heidegger's standpoint that could not have developed before the late 1920s and had already gotten a foot in the door of *Being and Time*, especially in section 74. For one who has been reading the work of the early 1920s this invocation of the thematics of "difficulty" is a reference to Aristotle. In fact it is practically a translation of the text in the *Nicomachean Ethics* (1106b28ff.) where Aristotle observes that there are many ways to miss the mark of virtue but only one way to hit it and that therefore the former is easy but the latter is difficult. Heidegger thought that this Aristotelian notion, to which he attached, in my view, a very Kierkegaardian significance, was just the thing he needed.[12] For Heidegger was trying to shake philosophy loose from the spell of Husserlian "neutrality" and to shift it into the mode of difficulty and struggle, for which he even used the word *Kampf* some four years before *Mein Kampf*. *Kampf*, struggle, difficulty, venture, all stand there, in that economy, in differential opposition to transcendental neutrality.

In this Aristotelian, Kierkegaardian, even Lutheran economy, Heidegger was striving with the bloodless subject of transcendental philosophy and seeking to reinstate the rights of what he called in those days "factical life." He was talking about the difficulty of factical living, of the "danger" of simply drifting along with the downward pull of daily existence, of the struggle in which we are all engaged to hit the mark. He had in mind, too, the "danger" that genuine philosophizing about factical life would be suffocated by its academic setting.

Now that is not a detestable economy. In fact, I would say it hits the mark.

But somewhere in the mid- to late 1920s this discourse underwent a momentous and ominous economic shift—very likely under the impetus of the encounter with Ernst Jünger[13]—from Aristotle and Kierkegaard to Nietzsche. These economies are complicated: for even as this had been a very Kierkegaardian Aristotle, so too this would be a very Jüngerian Nietzsche. With that shift, "difficulty" became "danger" and the lever that controls the lifting of the quotation marks was pulled, allowing this fiery German figure of *Geist* to make its entrance.

But even as the discourse on the spirit and danger had a prehistory, so too does it have a subsequent history. *An Introduction to Metaphysics* raises the question of Being with a radicality that is such as to make everything tremble, including and above all itself, a radicality that it itself compromises, that it indeed betrays. Thus this fiery figure of *Geist* turns out to be nothing less than the question of Being in military uniform—after it has been turned over by Heidegger himself (one would have thought him its most trusted admirer) to the military authorities. The question of Being withdraws the security and comfort of Being from beings, letting them waver in uncertainty and insecurity. But Heidegger tried to draft this question into the army, to deck it out in a shining, blazing uniform, to enlist it into one of the three services of the rectorial address. Nonetheless, the power of this question twists free from this domestication, nationalization, and militarization—shall we say it goes AWOL?—and ultimately troubles all of Heidegger's own discourse about *Geist, Volk, Dienst, Kraft und Macht,* and *Gefahr.*

Indeed, in the later works the *Gefahr* became the danger that we are not thinking, a very salutary, saving danger, and the whole movement between saving and danger is reversed, with the goal of moving beyond the danger to the saving. This is not to say that I am not profoundly troubled by what I have elsewhere called the later

Heidegger's "phainesthetics" or about the place of the "victim" and the meaning of "evil" in the history of Being.[14] Nor do I think that they are adequately addressed by pointing to the phenomenon of errancy (*die Irre*) in Heidegger. Errancy is not evil. These are serious issues and grave problems for me, and they have (irreversibly, I fear) affected the way I will henceforth think about Heidegger. But nothing Heidegger has said or failed to say manages to suppress the enormous power of the question of Being and the questioning of the history of metaphysics that irrupts in his later writings.

For me the most powerful pages that Heidegger has written occur at the end of the last lecture in *Der Satz vom Grund*, where Heidegger writes that Being is "without why,"[15] a formula that invokes both the rhythms and the vocabulary of the Rhineland mystical tradition. Being plays because it plays. There are—*es gibt*—only the various epochs of Being, the comings and goings of Being's multiple economies, whose only law is play without why. Here Heidegger formulates the law of the economies.

There is—*es gibt*—and that is all. It gives because it gives. And that is all.

It is our exposure to this groundless ground, to the loss of principles and of primordial assurances, of overarching stories and reassuring essences, that constitutes the originary difficulty of life.

Shall we not call that also the danger of the "postmodern" fix we are in, and can we not say, this time in English, that we need the spark, the nerve, the spirit, to come to grips with it? May the spark of that spirit return! *Viens, revenant!*

Notes

1. Jacques Derrida, *Of Spirit: Heidegger and the Question*, trans. G. Bennington and R. Bowlby (Chicago: Univ. of Chicago Press, 1989), hereafter "OS"; translation of *De l'esprit: Heidegger et la question* (Paris: Galilée, 1987).

2. Hugo Ott, *Martin Heidegger: Unterwegs zu seiner Biographie* (Frankfurt am Main: Campus, 1988), 171–72. Likewise, it is Ott's documentation of Heidegger's fondness for matters military, and not just during the rectorship, that prompts the militarizing of the figure of *Geist* in the present essay.

3. Ernst Jünger, "Über den Schmerz" (1934), in *Werke* (Stuttgart: Klett Verlag, 1960–65), 5:149–98. Incidentally, the original version of Heidegger's remark in the 1942 lectures, cited by Derrida (OS 4), in which Heidegger

says, "Tell me what you think about translation and I will tell you who you are" (Heidegger, *Hölderlins Hymne "Der Ister,"* GA 53 [1984], 74), is to be found on the first page of Jünger's essay: "Nenne mir Dein Verhältnis zum Schmerz, und Ich will Dir sagen, wer Du bist."

4. Martin Heidegger, *Einführung in die Metaphysik,* GA 40 (1983), 41; abbreviated "EM." Translations are mine, but they closely follow the English translation; compare *An Introduction to Metaphysics,* trans. Ralph Manheim (New Haven: Yale Univ. Press, 1959), 38 ("IM").

5. See Martin Heidegger, "Letter to the Rector of Freiburg University, Nov. 4, 1945," in Karl A. Moehling, "Martin Heidegger and the Nazi Party: An Examination" (Ph.D. diss., Northern Illinois University, 1972), 265.

6. Martin Heidegger, *Die Grundbegriffe der Metaphysik,* GA 29/30 (1983), 243; abbreviated "GM."

7. For more on the Jünger-Heidegger link, see Michael Zimmerman's study, *Technology, Politics, and Art: Heidegger's Confrontation with Modernity* (Bloomington: Indiana Univ. Press, 1990).

8. Martin Heidegger, "The Self-Assertion of the German University: Address, Delivered on the Solemn Assumption of the Rectorate of the University Freiburg," trans. Karsten Harries, *Review of Metaphysics* 38 (1985): 470–80, p. 474; abbreviated "SGU." Compare *Die Selbstbehauptung der deutschen Universität* (Frankfurt am Main: Vittorio Klostermann, 1983); abbreviated "SdDU."

9. That there might be a biblical alternative to the question of neighbor and friendship is suggested by Derrida in "The Politics of Friendship," trans. Gabriel Motzkin, *Journal of Philosophy* 85 (1988): 632–44, p. 644.

10. John D. Caputo, "Heidegger's *Kampf:* The Difficulty of Life," *Graduate Faculty Philosophy Journal* 14:2–15:1 (1991): 61–83; "Heidegger's Revolution: An Introduction to *An Introduction to Metaphysics,*" forthcoming in James Risser, ed., *Heidegger: The Texts of the Thirties* (State Univ. of New York Press); "Heidegger and the Ethics of Responsibility," forthcoming in Hubert Dreyfus and Michael Zimmerman, eds., *Applied Heidegger* (Indiana Univ. Press); "Thinking, Poetry, and Pain," *Southern Journal of Philosophy* 28, Supplement, *Heidegger and Praxis* (1989): 155–82.

11. See the study of John van Buren elsewhere in this volume for an excellent introduction to this issue.

12. More specifically, Aristotle held that the practice of virtue became easier with time and habit (*hexis*), but Kierkegaard always resisted that side of Aristotle, insisting on the need to reenact from moment to moment the choice of the good. Kierkegaard regarded settled practices as a lulling to sleep of the will, and in its place he put decisive choices in the existential moment.

See George Stack, *Kierkegaard's Existential Ethics* (University Park: Univ. of Alabama Press, 1977). This view depended on an Ockhamistic-Cartesian conception of time in which being must be created from moment to moment by divine freedom instead of being steadily conserved. Kierkegaard's reading of Aristotle was decisive for Heidegger in *Being and Time*, who, on this point, interestingly enough, is using a more Christian and Cartesian conception of time and not a Greek conception at all. See John D. Caputo, *Radical Hermeneutics: Repetition, Deconstruction, and the Hermeneutic Project* (Bloomington: Indiana Univ. Press, 1987), 18. It seems grossly ungrateful of Heidegger to complain about the Christian distortion of the Greek experience of Being and time when it is just this Christian conception which he is using to challenge Greek parousiology.

13. I take the appearance of Jünger's "Die Totale Mobilmachung" (*Werke*, 5:123–47), which appeared in 1930 in a collection entitled *Krieg und Krieger*, to be a significant date in this history.

14. See John D. Caputo, "Heidegger's Scandal: Thinking and the Essence of the Victim," in the volume of studies forthcoming (spring 1992) from Temple University Press, edited by Joseph Margolis and Tom Rockmore, on Victor Farías's *Heidegger and Nazism*. For an account of Heidegger in terms of errancy, see William Richardson's contribution elsewhere in this volume; see my response to Richardson in "Thinking, Poetry, and Pain," 176–80.

15. Martin Heidegger, *Der Satz vom Grund* (Pfullingen: Neske, 1957), 187–88. Compare "The Principle of Ground," trans. K. Hoeller, *Man and World* 7 (1974): 207–22.

5

Of Spirit and the Daimon:
On Derrida's De l'esprit

David Farrell Krell

Allow me to continue posing questions to Derrida's *Of Spirit*, precisely in the spirit of Jack Caputo and Françoise Dastur.[1] My questions look suspiciously like assertions, but they are more like sheer phantasms, and they seem to hover about three themes: (1) *Geist* and *Geschlecht*, in Derrida and Heidegger; (2) the daimon, which has been at the center of my own recent work; and (3) the perverse politics of responsibility, avoidance, and hesitation. I will move very quickly through matters I do not understand very well, precisely where hesitation alone would be in order.

In the first set of questions, on *Geist* and *Geschlecht*. I try to resist Derrida's suggestion that the thought of spirit in Heidegger organizes what Heidegger says about sex, race, or generation—to mention only three meanings of the word and the matter called *Geschlecht*. I suggest that in both Heidegger and Derrida the thought of *Geschlecht* is not only the more powerfully organizing thought but also the more disruptive one. It touches on the issues of a dual sexuality, divine embodiment, and what the ontotheological tradition called *evil*.

In the second set of questions, I pursue the issues of duality, sexuality, embodiment, and evil in the direction of what Heidegger in 1928 called the daimonic, τὸ δαιμόνιον, meaning by that not some sort of diabolism or demonism but what I am calling *daimon life*.[2] The daimon seems to be the organizing power for what Heidegger calls finite transcendence, temporality, freedom, the overpowering, and the holy. For all these are bound up, in some bedeviling way, with animality and sexuality. Bound up by the word *benommen*, 'dazed, bedazzled, stupefied, benumbed.' It is the highly unlikely thought of *Benommenheit* that allows us to link in a positive way what Heidegger and Derrida call variously "bestrewal" and "dissemination," which are the very marks of daimon life.

The third set of questions—on responsibility avoidance, perversion, and hesitation—tries to speak to the political character of Derrida's *Of Spirit*. In so doing, it breaks with the positive thrust and receptivity of the earlier remarks and engages in a polemic. If Heidegger is right when he says that the very posture one adopts in polemic precludes the possibility of thinking, then readers would do well to pay this third set of remarks no mind.[3] If Derrida is right when he says (DE 65–66; OS 40) that discourses of responsibility always burn our own fingers, then responsible readers would do well to ignore these final remarks of mine. Yet if spirit *is* this treacherous burning, and if *being itself* has abandoned us to whatever posture we might assume—if, in a word, spirit is evil and being is a real bastard—then we might as well engage. Albeit with hesitation.

GEIST AND GESCHLECHT

The book *Of Spirit* is a kind of bastard. It arrived on the scene unexpectedly, usurping the rightful place of the *third* generation of *Geschlecht*, which, at least according to Aristophanes' myth, ought to have been the androgynous generation. The first generation of *Geschlecht* was devoted to sexual difference and ontological difference in Heidegger's *Being and Time* and in the 1928 logic course; the second generation took up Heidegger's *hand* in *Was heisst Denken?*; the fourth tried to hear with Heidegger's *ears* the harmonious yet polemical "voice of the friend" in *Being and Time* and in later texts. One, two, four—yet where is the *third* of those who only yesterday promised to join us here?[4]

The third-generation *Geschlecht*, the androgynous one, is an unfinished typescript by Derrida on Heidegger's "placement" of Georg Trakl's poetry, "Die Sprache im Gedicht." Why does it lie unfinished? Why is the line of descent in these generations interrupted? Because Heidegger's text is so difficult, says Derrida, as though easy texts

were his line. The third-generation *Geschlecht,* unfinished, breaks off
at the point in Heidegger's text where Heidegger announces, a bit
shyly, the friend's intention to become a brother to the departed
brother who haunts Trakl's poetry, a brother to the defunct brother
who withdraws in apartness, *Abgeschiedenheit.* By becoming a
brother to the brother who haunts the rim of the forest at eventide,
says Heidegger, the friend will "thereby become a brother to the
sister," thus assuaging the discord of the sexes and achieving the
gentleness of a more confluent twofold, in that way fulfilling the
primeval promise called *man.*[5]

If *De l'esprit* interrupts the generations, upsets the genealogy
of *Geschlechter,* it does not do so alone; the bastard *Of Spirit* is
accompanied by two siblings (there are more than two, of course; I
am oversimplifying), namely, *Psyché,* the sister-soul of spirit, and
"Chôra," the mother and nurse of γένεσις.[6] Like any proper bastard,
De l'esprit nevertheless claims to be the nodal point of and for all the
generations: in the moment of gravest hesitation, spirit-as-gathering
rises to tie the four threads of Derrida's inquiry—questioning the
question, essence and contamination, animality, and epochality—into
a knot, or to weave them into a weft, if not a tapestry. Derrida promises and even "counts on" coming back to the way in which the words
Geist, geistig, and *geistlich* "organize the thought of *Geschlecht* at this
stage of Heidegger's path" (DE 22). Yet I wonder whether it is not
Geschlecht that does the organizing for spirit, and not the reverse;
whether it is not *Geschlecht* that weaves and ravels at once all the
strands in both Heidegger's and Derrida's texts. Or, rather, whether
it is not daimon life that organizes both *Geschlecht* and *Geist.* Is not
Geist but a ghostly response to the choreographies of the sister (who
dances to the rhythms of her own lunar voice in Trakl's poems) and
the arts of the mother (her aporias that bastardize all reasoning and
calculation since Plato's *Timaeus*)? What should the solar theologians
know of the dance?

Yet speaking of bastards and theologians. . . . Recall the strokes
that produce the twofold (*Zwiefalt*) of the sexes, or something like the
sexes, in Heidegger's Trakl essay, and the discord (*Zwietracht*) into
which the twofold incorrigibly falls. Heidegger implies, and Derrida
insists, that there are two strokes, and that only the second of the
two is the stroke of evil. The most subtle and supple of ontotheologists,
F. W. J. Schelling, at a decisive point in his treatise *On Human
Freedom,* says that there is only one stroke, the single stroke of "an
eternal deed" that casts and shapes the human body as such *in Einem
magischen Schlag,* "in one magic stroke."[7] However, if there is only

one stroke, then the question of bodying spirit *is* the question of evil. Of an evil so intrinsic in spirit that the very distinction between good and evil founders in "indifference."

Schelling craved to know the magic of that one fateful and fatal stroke. He knew that it would have to involve the restive, longing, langorous *body* of God, the God whose every path culminates in embodiment. And he was terrified of her, terrified of the body of God. Such a langorous God could only be a δαίμων, a bastard spirit or bitched *Mittelwesen*, a creature that binds and unravels at the same time in one magic stroke.[8]

Could it be that such a daimon organizes Heidegger's and Derrida's thoughts of spirit and *Geschlecht*? Might not all engagements with the daimon exceed the opposition of good and evil? Might not such engagements unsettle even the most self-righteous of moralizing discourses, even when the latter disguise themselves as political discourses? Might not all invocations of the daimon drive to distraction even the most self-torturing of ethical and political discourses?

THE DAIMON

I wonder whether both "spirit" and "sexuality" in Heidegger are not in fact organized by a daimon. Not merely by the demon of demonism, which Heidegger invokes in his 1935 lectures, published in 1953 as *Introduction to Metaphysics*[9] and which Derrida discusses in *De l'esprit* (DE 101–2); not only by the demonic disenfranchisement of being (*die Entmachtung des Geistes*) in a tenebrous and ever-darkening world; but also by the figure that Heidegger invokes earlier and elsewhere, in a marginal note to his 1928 lecture course on logic (MA 211 n. 1). There he designates finite transcendence as *wesentlich ontologisch differenter*, "essentially *differenter* in an ontological manner," "unfolding in an essentially ontological way as *differenter*." How to understand the daimonic word *differenter* lexically and syntactically? Is the transcendence that is implicated in temporality, that unfolds as time itself, both deferring and differentiating? Is transcendence therefore always only on the *verge* of temporalizing?[10]

However that may be, in this same note Heidegger suggests that to transcendence belongs "the understanding of being as the overpowering [*Übermächtigem*], as holiness [*Heiligkeit*]." Much earlier in the lecture course he refers to the sky (in Aristotle's vision of it) as the "encompassing" and the "overwhelming," in a word, as "the overpowering." Under the burning gaze of the sun-resplendent sky we are whelmed, bedazzled, even stupefied and benumbed, *benommen* (MA 13).

A year earlier, in *Being and Time*, Heidegger had used the word *benommen* to designate not only a Dasein that is bemused and bedazzled by its *worldly concerns* but also, astonishingly, the Dasein that is dazed in the flash of an eye (*Augenblick*) by its own *proper being*, benumbed by its *ownmost* possibility as descried in care and anxiety. In the whole of *Being and Time* there is no more consequential a confusion, no more monstrous a crossbreeding of terms. In only two years' time, with the 1929–30 lectures, published as *Die Grundbegriffe der Metaphysik: Welt—Endlichkeit—Einsamkeit* ("The Fundamental Concepts of Metaphysics: World—Finitude—Solitude"), it becomes clear what the resulting hybrid or mutant will have to be: Dasein proper proves to be an animal, an animal that it must and yet cannot be.[11] For in those 1929–30 lectures Heidegger uses the word *benommen* to designate the ontological status of animal behavior as opposed to human comportment. Meanwhile, in the 1928 logic course, between *Being and Time* and the 1929–30 lectures on biology, the overpowering that dazes us has to do with neither the world nor our proper being nor the animal but the *divine*. Hence the divine, uncannily, seems to be strangely animated, alive, embodied, well-nigh animal. In a word, daimonic.

The idea of being as an excess of power (*Übermacht*) can only be understood, Heidegger says in that marginal note to his 1928 lectures, if we relate it to what he has earlier in the lecture course called semination, *Streuung*, bestrewal. He refers us to section 10, proposition 6, of the logic course, a passage that stands at the nodal point of Derrida's first-generation *Geschlecht* and that remains as bedazzling as ever. Heidegger writes: "In general, Dasein harbors the inner possibility of factical dissemination [*Zerstreuung*] into embodiment [*Leiblichkeit*] and thereby into *Geschlechtlichkeit*"—let us say, into something like sexuality (MA 173). He emphasizes that such dissemination or dispersion is not wholly negative; it is not a mere splitting or splintering, in spite of what all the words that begin with *Zer-* suggest (e.g., *Zersplitterung, Zerspaltung,* "*Zerstörung*"); he invokes the "metaphysically neutral concept" of an original *Streuung*, a primordial semination or strewing that "only in one particular aspect" is a dissemination or dispersion, *Zerstreuung*. If the latter casts existence onto the shoals of embodiment, dual sexuality, historicity, space, and time, original semination is the originating leap, the *Ursprung*, of all these things at once, in one magic stroke, as it were. Yet it is a stroke that cannot be identified straightforwardly as evil. If spirit is the unifying and gathering One, if *Geist* is *Versammlung*, then its origin too is a seminal leap, a bestrewal that would be "older" than any gathering and "mightier" than any mere dispersal. Perhaps even older and mightier than the exclusively masculine figures of semination would suggest, perhaps as primal and as irresistible as langor. Here the allegories of both the Titan and the Goddess, both Λόγος and 'Ανάγκη, would be inverted and interlaced in order to form something more bedeviling than spirit, something more brazen than the sky, something more dazzling than the flame. Something that Hölderlin's and Nietzsche's Empedocles saw in the mouth of the crater.

In his marginal note on transcendence Heidegger relates this entire complex of semination and dissemination to the overpowering and the holy. But not the holy of holy pictures and of pious prattle, for in a parenthetical remark he adds: "(It remains for us to ponder being and δαιμόνιον; better, understanding-of-being and δαιμόνιον. Being as ground! Being and nothing—anxiety.)"

In this bizarre and bedazzling (if marginalized) scene of the overpowering, of original semination, the holy, the nothing, and anxiety, we confront—not spirit, not quite spirit, and not the animal, not quite the animal, and not God, not quite God, nor even Dasein, whether brutalized by beings or rapt to its own tremulous being, but— the δαίμων. Elsewhere, somewhat later, but also somewhat earlier, Heidegger will call and will have called that daimon *life*.

RESPONSIBILITY, AVOIDANCE, PERVERSION, AND HESITATION

In an extended footnote to *De l'esprit* (DE 152–53; OS 134), Derrida conjures up what he calls a "perverse reading" of Heidegger. Such a reading would range through Heidegger's text like a voracious mechanical animal—a gnawing rat or the turbo-mouse of a word processor—following to the letter and with a vengeance Heidegger's own commands: Avoid spirit! Cross through being! Cross out the animal's world! Do not utter propositional sentences! Do not even think them! And, whatever you do, never insist on the piety of questioning!

For the moment, another kind of perversion in Derrida's note intrigues me. At the very time Derrida calls for a rereading of the

Heideggerian corpus in terms of *responsibility*, he shows with devastating precision and disarming candor that Heidegger himself was never closer to acceptance of responsibility and adherence to duty (*Verantwortung, Verpflichtung*), never more responsive to the call of something higher, indeed, to the call of *le plus haut*, never more disposed to elevation and exaltation, never more capable of a kerygmatic response to the call to infinite responsibility, in short, never more docile and responsive (*fügsam*) with regard to ethical and political responsibilities than in 1933–34, the year of his rectorship at the University of Freiburg. Will that perverse paradox chasten us responsible ones as we drag the accused to the bar? For the tribunals are by now established, the briefs have been prepared, the advocates and judges, having mastered the arts of emancipatory discourse, communicative praxis, and endless conversation, are now prepared to set them to work; they have secured a social-critical purchase on thought, and have seen all the newsreels on the Weimar Republic; they will not be duped, and they will have historic rectification and apocalyptic retribution. We shall have a public burning. All is in readiness.

And Derrida? He refuses to light the match. He hesitates. Abashed, he admits his perversity. Abashed or not, he will be burned for that hesitation, has already been burned for it, twice over, without hesitation. Yet his question concerning spirit remains unanswered: How to avoid the flame if flame is spirit and spirit inevitably returns to haunt? Hesitation in the face of responsibility, responsibility *as* hesitation, a hesitation never to be avoided: such perversity is, as Derrida says, *of* spirit.

Yet it seems to me that the drama of spirit does not begin in 1927, as Derrida suggests it does. It does not commence as the avoidance of *spirit* in *Being and Time*, proceeding thence in 1933 to the solemn installation of the *spiritus rector*, and culminating in 1953 with spirit as the (dis)spiriting flame of Trakl's poetry. The drama begins in the earliest lecture courses by Heidegger that we have, the early Freiburg lectures of 1919–23.[12] From the outset of his career as a phenomenological researcher Heidegger sees the university as the only possible site of his and his students' factical lives. True, the very metabolism of such life is catabolism; the animatedness of factical life is ruinance, ruination, the plunge. Yet a counterthrust and a resistance are possible, insists Heidegger, the ardent researcher and teacher, and they are possible only in the university, in a fundamentally transformed and revitalized university; a university, he says, in which we can *live*. The avoidance of *spirit* in 1927 is in service to what Heidegger perceives as the genuine possibility of phenomenological research as a "how" of life, the restive, gnawing propensity toward illumination (*die Erhellungstendenz*). No doubt, such a propensity is the luminous flame of spirit that burns in this young researcher. But it is spirit condemned to *life*, spirit haunted by daimon life.

The tragic drama of ruinance—the peripety or reversal of plummeting life—never seems to come to an end in Heidegger's thought. His invocation of the rage of malignancy and the malice of evil as something quite beyond the baseness of human beings certainly seems like one more act in that play.[13] Yet is it an act that has played itself out? Do we today understand what Heidegger might have been saying in this regard? So many want to know whether Heidegger can be trusted any longer, whether he ever could be trusted. I want to know whether he can ever be understood. So many want to know why he should not be burned. For the moment, at least, I want to ask how far one must go with Heidegger; how far one must go with rage and with the malice of evil. Which—let us make no mistake about it—is the malice *of being*, no matter how perverse such an ontological malediction may seem. Being itself, malicious? How can that be? The answer is contained in two very similar-looking words:

Seinsvergessenheit, oblivion of being. We always "translate" it as *our* forgetting of being, objective genitive. Yet Heidegger insists always and everywhere that it is not *we* who do the forgetting, although we never push him on this. Being appears to be well housed, well shepherded, and ably safeguarded in the Heideggerian text; being is the sending and the sent, the well-rounded destination and providential dispensation for which we can only be thankful. No point in pushing the question. *Gelassenheit* in all things. And so we "translate" another word that looks just like *Seinsvergessenheit* in the identical fashion. . . .

Seinsverlassenheit, abandonment of being, objective genitive. Shame on us, we abandoned being, we are real bastards, we are worse than rats, worse even than turbo-mice. When did we abandon being? Did we ever do that? No, says Heidegger, frustrating our eager embrace of guilt: no, it is not we who have abandoned being, it is being that has abandoned us; being itself does the abandoning; the genitive is strictly subjective, precisely in order to resist the metaphysics of subjectivity; being is the only bastard there is.

In a text written between 1944 and 1946, "Nihilism as Determined by the History of Being," Heidegger leaves no doubt about

such abandonment: "Das Seiende ist vom Sein selbst verlassen";
"Beings are abandoned by being."[14] Being withdraws, is in default;
being absents and omits itself; even the nihilism it leaves in its wake
is disingenuous, *uneigentlich*; the essential unfolding of nihilism,
while wreaking unmitigated havoc, is nonetheless inessential; it is
nonessence (*Unwesen*) as such. Being is reticent, we acolytes say.
Being is diffident. Being is timid (poor thing!) and keeps to itself.
Being withdraws itself and expropriates us, leaving human beings
to flounder and founder in the turmoil of something that is not even
proper nihilism—although there is "nothing negative" in this,
Heidegger hastens to assure us, as always (SB 369). Nevertheless,
the rhetoric here is alarming: the mystery of being is a riddle, the
riddle is a dissonance, and cacaphonous being serves us with
insolence. *Geheimnis, Rätsel, Misston,* and *Zumutung* are words for
being. They are the final words of fugitive being. They are the
bedeviling words of bastardly being.

Does Heidegger merely glorify evil as dastardly being, bastardly
being, being in default and omission, being *as* the nothing, in order
to distract us from our responsibility or to avoid his own? Or is there
something in the clamorous call to responsibility that is invariably
haunted by ghosts? In the calamitous epoch and ἐποχή that is being
itself, being-in-suspense and in suspension (SB 383), whatever we
might call "being" pops up (*auftaucht*) only as the spook of mere
abstraction, *das Gespenstische der blossen Abstraktion* (SB 396). Is
not Heidegger's discourse on being plagued by spooks? Spooks of
abstraction? Is not the contorted discourse of fickle being sufficient
to condemn him and all his works and ways? Did not he himself admit
as much immediately after the war when he conceded the impotence
of his own (and ostensibly all) thinking?[15] And have not all the
journalists and intellectuals of contemporary Germany who have
written on Heidegger avowed that his Achilles' heel is the very
language of being that he concocted? A language so spookily abstract
that it sanctions the worst of political naiveté and violence?

If then we finally succeed in burning him, purging ourselves of
him at long last in a public burning, will we be shut of his perturbèd
spirit? Or will he and all the shades of malevolent being continue
to haunt and bedazzle us?

There can be no doubt that Heidegger's being is insolent,
perfidious, a dirty rat, a gigolo. Shall we abandon Heidegger's being?
Yes?

Yes. Let us strike a match and abandon being.

Provided, of course, that being has not already abandoned us, the bastard, and already long ago, as grandfather used to say.

We have to learn as much as we can about Heidegger's terrifying sense of responsibility; as much as we can about his situation, his actions, and his omissions. We dare not multiply or reinforce in any way his silences. Yet the very engagements in which we fulfill this responsibility threaten us with our own version of the very worst: the daimon dwindles and becomes the sanctimonious, hand-wringing, O-so-sincere deceptive demon or sprite of retribution; righteous indignation descends like a fog and almost covers our acres of ignorance; the spirit of revenge rises from the frustrations we cannot face and guides us safely back to a past for which *others* were responsible; and the professional ambition of university professors craves to make a killing on the book market, a market that cries for exposés and public burnings, even in translation.

No wonder Derrida speaks of moments of gravest hesitation. In a book that shows us something absolutely devastating about the spirit of Heidegger, Derrida hesitates to light the match, refuses to abandon what used to be called the matter of thinking. It certainly looks like an avoidance of responsibility, a shirking, a perverse complicity, an act or an omission stemming from cowardice. I suspect on the contrary that his hesitation is a moment of unheard-of courage, and that its daimon is of life.[16]

Notes

1. Perhaps also in the spirit of my earlier discussion of Derrida's *De l'esprit*, "Spiriting Heidegger," in *Research in Phenomenology* 18 (1988): 205–30. I shall refer to Jacques Derrida, *De l'esprit: Heidegger et la question* (Paris: Galilée, 1987), with the abbreviation "DE," followed by the page number. The excellent English translation, which appeared only after my text was completed but to which I refer by "OS," is by Geoffrey Bennington and Rachel Bowlby: *Of Spirit: Heidegger and the Question* (Chicago: Univ. of Chicago Press, 1989). In my opening sentence I am referring, of course, to the contributions by Françoise Dastur and John D. Caputo in this volume.

2. See the published version of the 1928 logic course in Martin Heidegger, *Metaphysische Anfangsgründe der Logik im Ausgang von Leibniz*, GA 26 (1978), 211 n. 1; abbreviated "MA." See also David Farrell Krell, *Daimon Life: Heidegger and Lebensphilosophie*, forthcoming from Indiana University Press.

3. Martin Heidegger, *Was heisst Denken?* (Tübingen: M. Niemeyer, 1954), 49. Compare "What Calls for Thinking?" *Basic Writings*, ed. David Farrell Krell (New York: Harper & Row, 1977), 345–67, p. 354; collection abbreviated "BW."

4. For the first two generations of *Geschlecht*, see "*Geschlecht*: Différence sexuelle, différence ontologique" (1983) and "La main de Heidegger (*Geschlecht II*: 1984–1985)," in Jacques Derrida, *Psyché: Inventions de l'autre* (Paris: Galilée, 1987), pp. 395–414 and 415–51, respectively. An English translation by Ruben Berezdivin of the first essay appears as "*Geschlecht*: Sexual Difference, Ontological Difference," in *Research in Phenomenology* 13 (1983): 65–83; a translation by John P. Leavey, Jr., of the second essay has been published as "*Geschlecht* II: Heidegger's Hand," in John Sallis, ed., *Deconstruction and Philosophy: The Texts of Jacques Derrida* (Chicago: Univ. of Chicago Press, 1987), 161–94. The third generation of *Geschlecht* has not yet been published. The fourth, "Heidegger's Ear: Philopolemology (*Geschlecht* IV)," will appear in John Sallis, ed., *Commemorations: Reading Heidegger*, forthcoming from Indiana University Press.

5. See Martin Heidegger, "Sprache im Gedicht: Eine Erörterung von Georg Trakls Gedicht," in Heidegger, *Unterwegs zur Sprache* (Pfullingen: Neske, 1959), 35–82, pp. 69–70; abbreviated "US." Compare "Language in the Poem: A Discussion on Georg Trakl's Poetic Work," in Heidegger, *On the Way to Language*, trans. Peter D. Hertz (New York: Harper & Row, 1971), 157–98, pp. 187–88 ("OW"). More precisely, Derrida's typescript breaks off long before that point in Heidegger's text is reached; "*Geschlect* III" begins to comment on the initial passage on the duality and discord of the sexes (US 50; OW 170) and then breaks off. For a discussion of Heidegger's Trakl article, see David Farrell Krell, *Intimations of Mortality: Time, Truth, and Finitude in Heidegger's History of Being* (University Park: Pennsylvania State Univ. Press, 1986), chap. 11.

6. For *Psyché*, see note 4 above. "Chôra" appears in Alfred Adler et al., *Poikilia: Etudes offertes à Jean-Pierre Vernant* (Paris: Ecole des Hautes Etudes en Sciences Sociales, 1987), 265–96.

7. F. W. J. Schelling, *Sämmtliche Werke* (Stuttgart and Augsburg: Cotta, 1860), 7:386–87.

8. On the daimonic in Schelling's text, see his *Werke*, 7:380. I have commented on these admittedly bizarre ontotheological issues in "The Crisis of Reason in the Nineteenth Century: Schelling's Treatise on Human Freedom (1809)," in John Sallis, Giuseppina Moneta, and Jacques Taminiaux, eds., *The Collegium Phaenomenologicum: The First Ten Years* (The Hague: Martinus Nijhoff, 1989), 13–32.

9. Martin Heidegger, *Einführung in die Metaphysik* (Tübingen: M. Niemeyer, 1953), 35. Compare *An Introduction to Metaphysics*, trans. R. Manheim (New Haven: Yale Univ. Press, 1959), 46.

10. See David Farrell Krell, *Of Memory, Reminiscence, and Writing: On the Verge* (Bloomington: Indiana Univ. Press, 1990), chap. 6.

11. Martin Heidegger, *Die Grundbegriffe der Metaphysik: Welt—Endlichkeit—Einsamkeit*, GA 29/30 (1983), part 2.

12. See Martin Heidegger, *Zur Bestimmung der Philosophie*, GA 56/57 (1987); *Phänomenologische Interpretationen zu Aristoteles: Einführung in die Phänomenologische Forschung*, GA 61 (1985); and *Ontologie (Hermeneutik der Faktizität)*, GA 63 (1988). I have discussed these in "Heidegger's Rectification of the German University," in Richard Rand, ed., *Our Academic Contract: "Mochlos" in America*, forthcoming from Univ. of Nebraska Press.

13. Martin Heidegger, "Brief über den 'Humanismus'," in *Wegmarken* (Frankfurt am Main: V. Klostermann, 1967), 145–94, pp. 189–91. Compare "Letter on Humanism," BW 193–242, pp. 237–38.

14. Martin Heidegger, "Die seinsgeschichtliche Bestimmung des Nihilismus," *Nietzsche*, 2 vols. (Pfullingen: G. Neske, 1961), 2:335–98, p. 355, abbreviated "SB"; "Nihilism as Determined by the History of Being," trans. Frank A. Capuzzi, in *Nihilism*, ed. David F. Krell, vol. 4 of *Nietzsche* (San Francisco: Harper & Row, 1982), 197–250, p. 215.

15. Heidegger, *Was heisst Denken?*, 161. Compare *What Is Called Thinking?*, trans. J. Glenn Gray (New York: Harper & Row, 1968), 159.

16. My thanks to P. Holley Roberts for her careful work on my paper.

6

Alētheia and Oblivion's Field:
On Heidegger's Parmenides Lectures

Véronique M. Fóti

Martin Heidegger insists, in his 1941–42 lecture course on Friedrich Hölderlin's "Andenken," that it is the poet who institutes (*stiftet*) history, whereas the thinker establishes its foundation (*gründet*).[1] In his Parmenides lectures of the following year,[2] Heidegger interlinks this poetico-philosophical understanding of historical origination with the problematic of *alētheia* which, by his own account, had preoccupied him intensely since the early 1930s,[3] and which he then still understood in the sense of truth, rather than in the later sense of the pure opening (*Lichtung*).[4] Although, as Jürgen Habermas points out, Heidegger "rigidly maintained the abstraction of historicity (as the condition of historical existence itself) from actual historical processes,"[5] his effort to think historicity as rooted in the aletheic "power to bring to word," which he pits against "a crude biological interpretation of history" (PL 83), carries historicopolitical import. This import and concern are not explicitly thematized; but they account for the fact that, as Manfred Frings notes, "long stretches of the lecture hardly deal with Parmenides himself" but seem to ramble over a bewildering plethora of topics.[6] Frings advocates conjoining the text with Heidegger's 1943–44 lectures on Heraclitus which continue to develop a similar problematic. The present essay, however, will focus strictly on the Parmenides lectures. It will seek

71

to show not only that this text is meaningfully organized and internally coherent, but also that it reveals certain important aspects of the historicopolitical dimension of Heidegger's thought.

ALĒTHEIA

Heidegger, characterizing essential history as ongoing change in the understanding of truth and therefore of manifestation, points to the Greek thought of truth as *alētheia* as one of the "inconspicuously rare moments" in which history "pauses" because the essential being (*Wesen*) of truth gives itself over to beings in an originary way (PL 80–81). This revelatory pause, Heidegger finds, has not only been covered over and obliterated, but access to it has become blocked by a thought-configuration that links the Roman understanding of truth as defensive posit (*veritas*; cf. PL 69–79) to the representational concept of rightness or *rectitudo*, and finally to the Nietzschean analysis of the "justice" of truth as the self-assertion of a will to power (PL 77).

This sequence, as Heidegger understands it, culminates in the stance of domination, the word of power (*Machtspruch*) as unconditional command, and the totalizing organization characteristic of the technical enframing or "posure" (*Ge-stell*). These are complemented, in turn, by the technicized and telically oriented model of historiography which Heidegger seeks to discredit, understanding his own (the "thinker's") role as a salvific mission in a destinal transition involving a retrieval of the Greek thought of *alētheia*. Such a retrieval must renounce the model of mimetic reproduction, or even of dialectical reappropriation, as being incompatible with the very nature of what is to be retrieved. The place of this model is taken by the Hölderlinian gesture of a "greeting" which allows what is greeted to safeguard its essential enigma (cf. HA 42–56). This gesture characterizes Heidegger's own retrieval of the Parmenidean meditation on *alētheia*.

It is striking that Heidegger, throughout these lectures, presents Aletheia as a divinity, the goddess of Parmenides' poem. He is careful not to ascribe this identification explicitly to Parmenides (who refers to the goddess only once, at Bl, 22, leaving her unnamed)[7] but indicates that it is "given only by the whole of the 'didactic poem' " (PL 6). Nevertheless, in that his interpretive method involves elucidating individual texts in terms of the "guiding thought" which, in turn, must show itself in these elucidations, and in that he does not examine the fragments sequentially or in their entirety but prepares his own selection, he obliquely insinuates that the selection is Parmenidean. His textual selectivity allows him to evade the difficult question as to how the goddess, if indeed she is Aletheia, can announce (B8, 50–53) that she will now cease her "trustworthy discourse and thought about truth" (*piston logon ēde noēma amphis alētheiēs*) so as to articulate (at great length) a "deceitful formation of words" (*kosmon . . . epeōn apatēlon*).

In keeping with Heidegger's observation that the originary does not show itself without our contribution (PL 28), one is led to ask why the presentation of Aletheia as a divine figure is so important to Heidegger that he contributes it to the poem. First, this contribution helps to sever the Greek understanding of *alētheia* from any modern association with human subjectivity, knowledge, or judgment. In Greek thought, Heidegger remarks, "concealed" and "unconcealed" are characteristics of being as such, not of observation or mental grasping (PL 35). He emphatically dissociates *alēthes* from some of its ordinary meanings, such as "sincere" or "without reserve," albeit Parmenides does use the adjective in contexts stressing persuasion and trust.[8] Heidegger also points to the ambiguity or "twofold unity" of *alēthes*, which can mean both "unconcealed" and "unconcealing," as bespeaking the differing of beings and their being (PL 49). The divine figure of Aletheia thus marks the differing as it addresses itself to mortal hearing and saying.

Second, Aletheia, as a goddess who offers "indications" (*Weisungen*) for crossing over into "an altered domain of truth," resists the insidious annexation of Greek thought by what Heidegger, with reference to ancient Rome, calls an "imperial" framework of understanding. Such change by assimilation (*Anverwandlung*), he remarks, is, by its very subtlety, "the most dangerous but also the most enduring form of domination" (PL 67). In entrusting the word as *mythos, epos,* or *logos* to the mortal seeker, the goddess, by contrast, safeguards the lethic aspect of its manifesting power. She inspires and embodies the reticent and respectful awe which Heidegger calls *aidōs*, taking this term to be the "essential word" of Pindar's poetry (PL 110). Divinities are figures of *aidōs*, which refuses to violate the lethic or chthonic aspects of manifestation. Once the gods have fled, *aidōs* is unheeded, and sheer obliteration (*die Vergessung*) holds sway. Heidegger understands such oblivion and deprivation to be an uproar of self-affirming will that takes the form of ideological fanaticism:

> The distinguishing trait of modern disclosure [*Ent-schlossenheit*] is "the fanatical." By contrast, the Greek experience of dis-closure [*Ent-schlossenheit*] as a self-concealing opening-up [*Aufschliessung*] to being has another essential origin, namely, out of being which is otherwise experienced, out of *aidōs*. . . . But against *aidōs*, *latha* holds sway, the concealment which we call oblivion [*Vergessung*]. (PL 112)

An age from which the figures of the divine have withdrawn is thus an age caught up in *Vergessung* or sheer oblivion, which obliterates precisely the lethic aspect of *alētheia*; and it is therefore given over to fanaticism.

Finally, the Parmenidean goddess whom Heidegger calls Aletheia not only speaks to the mortal traveler but, in welcoming him, clasps his hand with her own. Through the figure of the goddess, Heidegger draws attention to the aletheic function of the hand which "like the word, safeguards the laying claim [*Bezug*] of being to man, and only thereby the relation [*Verhältnis*] of man to beings," in the "pragmatic" mode (PL 125). The "essential interconnection" between word and hand is, for Heidegger, consummated through *grammē*, the writ, which signs the disclosive word into the very midst of beings. Through the writ, the beings that are things are first brought into the aletheic draw of unconcealment. Heidegger deplores here the technicization and mechanization of writing as, in Pindarian language, a "signless cloud" that obscures the way man is from the outset drawn into the differing; for "being, word, *legein* [*die Lese*], writ name an essential interconnection, to which the writing hand belongs" (PL 125). The withdrawal of the gods then marks not only the loss of *aidōs* but also the signless severance of writing from the human hand (which Heidegger discusses with respect to print and typewriter, but which certainly has become more decisive today).

It is not feasible, within the limits of the present study, to explore the relationship of Heidegger's writ to Derridean grammatology or to Derrida's own thematization of the Heideggerian hand, nor yet to Celan's understanding of the poem—the poetic word—as handclasp.[9] What needs to be pointed out here, however, is that Heidegger's discussion of the hand, which initiates action (*Handlung*) from out of the prevailing modalities of unconcealment, forms the connecting link, in the organization of the lectures, between the problematic of *alētheia* and an analysis of the historicopolitical domain.

POLIS AND PRAXIS

Heidegger understands *ta pragmata*, the aletheic domain of action (*Handlung*), to be the realm of entities revealed in the modalities of being present-at-hand (*vorhanden*) or ready-to-hand (*zuhanden*). Given that (according to the third of the "indications" Heidegger gleans from the very word *alētheia*) the aletheic domain is conflictual, *lēthē* or self-withdrawing concealment enshrouds *ta pragmata*. In Greek thought, Heidegger finds, the inseparability of *lēthē* and *alētheia* in the happening of manifestation bespeaks itself only as *mythos*. The myth that Heidegger considers crucial here is the "political" myth of Er in Plato's *Republic* (614b–621b), given that, for the Greek epochal type of man (*Menschentum*),[10] the *polis* constituted the revelatory center of human existence.

Precisely because the essence of the *polis* has to be understood from out of the conflictual nature of *alētheia*, it cannot be grasped in terms of modern conceptions of the political. The *polis*, according to Heidegger, is a gathering pole (*polos, Pol*) of the happening of manifestation, thought as *pelein* or 'arising into un-concealment'. What reveals itself in its deployment around such a pole is the whole of beings, so that the *polis* becomes the gathering locus (*Ort*) and the articulated locality or "placescape" (*Ortschaft*) of an historical configuration of unconcealment. In that it is revelatory, in a certain way, of the whole of beings, the *polis* stands in a primary if oblique relation to the being of beings (see PL 132–33).

The obliqueness is due to the aletheic tensions which the *polis* polarizes in such a way as to introduce distortions, obscurations, and oblivion (*Verstellung, Vergessung*) into the historicopolitical context. In the *polis* as the "essential site" (*Wesensstätte*) of a form of historical human existence, the extreme "counteressence" of beings in their being comes into its own as disaster and terror. Heidegger recalls here Jacob Burckhardt's emphasis on the "tragic" dimension of the *polis*, linking it to the thematization of "the ascent and precipitous fall of man in his historical site" in Greek tragedy.[11] A fuller discussion of Greek tragedy and of the *polis* in the context of essential historicity requires, for Heidegger, an engagement with Hölderlin's reading of Sophocles, particularly of the *Antigone*. Heidegger thus embeds such a discussion in his 1942 lecture course on Hölderlin's hymn "Der Ister."[12]

The locality of the *polis* is not mapped out as one of establishment but rather of man's "death-gravid" (*todesträchtiger, thanatophoros)* passage. In their passage through the political locality, human beings do not complete the circle-path or revolution (*periodos*) of their existence; and Heidegger therefore repeats the Platonic question as to what awaits them in death. This question also underlies Heraclitus's statement, in fragment B27, that "for mortals in their dying there abide those things which they do not expect nor form any conception of."[13]

The point of giving the question its Greek formulation is to bypass any Christian-theological concern with the afterlife (and the above reference to Heraclitus might have served Heidegger better in this regard than does the Platonic text). It is a question, then, not of the afterlife but of the very life of mortals as drawn into the draw of the differing.

During their participation in the *polis*, the life of mortals remains exposed to the radiance of being which, as the "uncanny," "shines into all that is canny, that is, into beings, [and] which often, in its shining, merely grazes beings like the shadow of a cloud soundlessly passing" (PL 150). Being, in the self-donation of its *phainesthai*, is to be thought of as *to daion* or self-giving gift. Heidegger links this term to the notion of the daimon who, as an intermediary between the divine and mortal realms, mediates this self-donation in such a way as to keep mortals mindful of the gift. With oblique reference to the preeminence that Plato grants to Eros as a great daimon, Heidegger remarks that the daimones are attuners (*die Stimmenden*) who determine all essential feeling-tones (*bestimmen jede wesentliche Gestimmtheit*) through which the "soundless voice" (*Stimme*) of the "word" attunes mortals to the claim of being (PL 157). Whereas the mediating daimones (or the Hölderlinian demigods) are associated with the attuning voice, the divine self-giving, in the manner of *phainesthai*, occurs through the luminous glance. Heidegger here points out the close similarity between the Greek words *théa* (glance, view) and *theà* (goddess). He understands the glance not only nonrepresentationally but in a proto-Levinasian way as a bestowal of alterity:

> If man, however, does not experience his own glancing, which here means the glance of man, through "reflection" on himself as one who represents himself glancing, but if man, allowing for an encounter without reflection, experiences the glance as the looking-at-him of the human being who comes towards him, then it becomes evident that the glance of the human being encountered shows itself as that wherein the human being itself waits towards the other, that is, appears and is. (PL 152–53)

Being, or, in Greek parlance, divinity (*to theion*), offers itself, through the glance that bestows alterity, in the aspect of what is manifest or familiar, while at the same time uncannily subverting the tendency of beings to absolutize themselves, entrenching themselves in their supposed self-sufficiency. The "glance of presencing," which is the glance of the goddess, brings unconcealment in the modalities of *physis* and *idea* as well as of *historia*, which Heidegger construes etymologically as "bringing into view" (PL 165).

From being claimed, in their death-gravid course through the *polis*, by the uncanniness of the divine glance, mortals must at last pass on to the lightless realm (Hades, the Unseen) where they come to the outermost place, the place of *krisis*, in the topology of the uncanny. From this place they must reenter the *polis*, beginning another death-gravid course. Heidegger, following Plato, interprets this place as *to tēs Lēthēs pedion*, Oblivion's Field, which, in its counter-position to *alētheia*, refuses all coming-to-appearance and "withdraws everything." Oblivion's Field is suffused with the uncanniness of the divine glance that "fills" its emptiness without abolishing it. In that it mediates the sheer donation of emptiness as the self-withdrawing core of manifestation, Oblivion's Field is a "demonic place" (*topos daimonios*).

This *topos daimonios*, nevertheless, is also demonic in the sense of being sinister and menacing, since all care of being is here in danger of being forgotten. The lethic lure of emptiness is more potent than that of the aletheic domain. Heidegger, indeed, describes the desolate terrain of Oblivion's Field, with its seared, scarred, and smoldering ground and its air "which brings everything to suffocation" (PL 174), in images which, notwithstanding their Platonic provenance, disturbingly call to mind the burning and desolation of the death camps in the historicopolitical context of his writing.

Rather than developing or making explicit any contemporary allusions, however, Heidegger points out that those who pass through Oblivion's Field must each drink a measure of the "uncontainable waters" of Lethe which inundate the terrain; and through these waters the very nature of the place, oblivion, enters into and overcomes the drinkers. Some, however, according to the Platonic myth, drink in excess of measure, so that they reenter the *polis* bereft of responsiveness to the divine glance. Instead of receiving, in Oblivion's Field, the donation of emptiness which is the root of any ethical relationship, they have become afflicted with utter unmindfulness (*Vergessung*) and return to the *polis* as bringers of desolation.

THE QUESTION OF HISTORY

In accordance with the very law of origination, Heidegger insists, ancient Greek thought failed to consummate its own insight into the differing, the insight that bespeaks itself in the discourse of *alētheia*. He notes that although any first beginning is decisive, it is not fully originary in the sense of illumining itself and the essential domain that it opens up. Origination in this radical sense (*das Anfängnis des eigentlichen Anfangs*) happens, paradoxically, last of all (PL 202).

Western history, as Heidegger understands it, is instituted and comes into its own, in the manner of *Ereignis*, through the thought of *alētheia*. The Occident (*Abendland*) is now an "as yet undetermined and undelimited landscape of the earth" situated in this historical continuum and lying in the shadow of the evening (*Abend*) of an historical and essential closure. Since this evening, however, has developed out of the originary arising, it shelters within itself a new morning waiting to irradiate a terrain without national or geographic boundaries (PL 219). This quasi-eschatological vision articulates what Derrida aptly refers to as "Heideggerian hope."[14]

Despite his earlier strong emphasis (sustained in texts ranging from the rectorial address of 1933 to the lecture course on "Andenken" on the destinal and spiritual mission of the German people as an Occidental people of poets and thinkers, to retrieve and carry to fruition the Greek beginning of Western thought,[15] Heidegger now castigates nationalism and *Volkheit* or ideologies of national identity as the inheritors of the metaphysics of subjectivity and of its representational thought-structures. He notes that such ideologies become "capable of history" only in consequence of the metaphysical effort to ground truth—the truth of beings as a whole—upon (transcendental) subjectivity, and that, without this effort, the founding of "the peoplehood of peoples" remains unthinkable (PL 204). Thus—although Heidegger, as late as the *Spiegel* interview of 1966,[16] insists on an "inner kinship" between the German and the Greek languages and therefore on a certain destinal mission of Germany—to charge him, as does Habermas, with a "crude nationalism" as an "invariant feature of his thought" (WW 445) is to oversimplify. Heidegger's strong nationalistic tendencies become tempered by the realization that the retrieval of *alētheia* undercuts ideologies of national identity. The Parmenides lectures are important partly for the reason that this realization first announces itself there; and it is re-marked, in the *Spiegel* interview, by the transposition of the (supposed) Greek and German affinity into the essential realm of language.

Heidegger insists that what is at stake in the present "unique moment of history" is more than "the being or non-being of our historical people or even of European culture," but is rather "Being and non-being themselves. . . in their essential nature" (PL 241, 236). What needs to be retrieved in this time of *krisis* is the twofold nature of disclosure or *Ent-bergung* which, on the one hand, overcomes lethic obliteration as well as dissembling and distortion (*pseudos*) and which, on the other, brings about a sheltering (*bergen*) into unconcealment (PL 198). Dis-closure as *Ent-bergung* thus both removes and safeguards concealment. The safeguarding honors the lethic dimension of *alētheia*, that is, the differing, into which "political" man remains initiated by his mythical provenance out of Oblivion's Field, while yet, in the balance of the safeguarding, the temptation to yield utterly to the intoxication of *lēthē* as unmindful obliteration is held in check. Human existence remains thus sheltered in the freedom of the Open which Heidegger (at pains to distinguish it from Rilke's cognate but supposedly still metaphysical notion)[17] understands as the claim and draw of being to which human being responds through envisagement (*theōria*) and word (*logos*). This consignment to the Open forms the fourth "indication" that Heidegger gleans from Aletheia (in accordance with the double sense of *Weisung*). *Legein* and *theōrein* thus constitute the mindful, originary thinking and poetizing protected by Mnemosyne, the mother of the Muses, among whose daughters is Clio, the Muse of history.

The fundamental conviction that bespeaks itself in these complex analyses and speculations is that a salutary historicopolitical turning cannot be instigated by theories based on empirical analysis but can only spring unforeseeably (as pure advent) from a profound intellectual as well as spiritual alteration in human self-understanding. Heidegger characterizes this envisaged but still horizonal change as the retrieval and consummation of the essential unthought of Greek thought, which was discerned by Hölderlin but remains to be fully articulated by contemporary poets and thinkers. This conviction accounts for Heidegger's often criticized refusal to speak to historical and political actuality, his tendency to avoid concrete issues and to resort to what Habermas calls "abstraction by essentialization" (WW 453). Notwithstanding the importance of this critique, which charges the philosopher, ultimately, with abdication of moral responsibility and disregard for social justice, it is too facile to dismiss his fundamental position as escapist. Its central claim is a powerful one that needs to be heeded and evaluated precisely for what it is.

The Parmenides lectures do not, of course, offer a sufficient basis for the evaluation of Heidegger's claim. They show, however, how his grappling with this focal issue leads him to repudiate nationalism and to articulate a critique of totalitarian thinking. Given that Heidegger, at the time of these lectures, is willing to resituate National Socialism—as a result of his prolonged and agonized "confrontation" with it—from the side of salvific promise to the side of the gathering nihilistic danger,[18] the question still remains whether this move leaves him committed to a structural validation of the totalitarian ideology. Since Heidegger's historical schema focuses on the nadir of danger as the turning point for a possible inversion which, in the Idealist sense, commutes negativity into something positive, and since he characterizes technological rationality, along with racist and biologist modes of interpretation, as consummate metaphysical and totalizing thought-structures, these are ultimately validated as a destinal extreme. On Heidegger's understanding of historicity— which, as he admits, is what propelled him into political engage- ment[19]—the extremity of danger alone can provide the momentum for a restitutive turning to aletheic mindfulness, and the latter alone can ultimately resist totalization. The validation to which he remains committed is therefore not only structural but economic, hearkening back to the "closed economy" (in the language of Derrida and Bataille) of metaphysics. With respect to the essentially unnameable event referred to as the Holocaust, however, economic discourses unmis- takably betray moral failure.

Notes

1. Martin Heidegger, *Hölderlin's Hymne "Andenken,"* ed. C. Ochwadt, GA 52 (1982), 3–4 (abbreviated "HA"). Translations from the German, unless otherwise noted, are mine.

2. Martin Heidegger, *Parmenides*, ed. M. S. Frings, GA 54 (1982); abbreviated "PL."

3. Martin Heidegger, "The Rectorate 1933/34: Facts and Thoughts," trans. Karsten Harries, *Review of Metaphysics* 38 (1985): 481–502, p. 482.

4. For Heidegger's own discussion of these changes in interpretation, see "The End of Philosophy and the Task of Thinking," trans. Joan

Stambaugh, in Heidegger, *Basic Writings*, ed. David Farrell Krell (New York: Harper & Row, 1977), 373–92, p. 389. See also the Zähringen seminar in Heidegger, *Vier Seminare* (Frankfurt am Main: Vittorio Klostermann, 1977), 110–38, pp. 134–37.

5. Jürgen Habermas, "Work and Weltanschauung: The Heidegger Controversy from a German Perspective" (abbreviated "WW"), trans. John McCumber, in Arnold I. Davidson, ed., "Symposium on Heidegger and Nazism" ("SH"), *Critical Inquiry* 15 (1988–89): 431–56, p. 437.

6. Manfred S. Frings, "Parmenides: Heidegger's 1942–43 Lecture Held at Freiburg University," *Journal of the British Society for Phenomenology* 19 (1989): 15–33.

7. Citations from the Parmenidean fragments are based on David Gallop, ed. and trans., *Parmenides of Elea: Fragments* (Toronto: Univ. of Toronto Press, 1984). They conform to the Diels-Kranz numbering.

8. See the following Parmenidean fragments: B1, 29; B2, 4; B8, 39, 50.

9. On the hand, see Paul Celan, "Brief an Hans Bender," *Gesammelte Werke*, ed. Beda Allemann and Stefan Reichert, 5 vols. (Frankfurt am Main: Suhrkamp, 1983), 3:177; and Jacques Derrida, "*Geschlecht* II: Heidegger's Hand," in John Sallis, ed., *Deconstruction and Philosophy: The Texts of Jacques Derrida* (Chicago: Univ. of Chicago Press, 1987), 161–94.

10. See Reiner Schürmann's discussion of *Menschentum* in *Heidegger on Being and Acting: From Principles to Anarchy*, trans. Christine-Marie Gros (Bloomington: Indiana Univ. Press, 1987), 72–77.

11. See Jacob Burckhardt, *Force and Freedom: Reflections on History*, trans. J. H. Nichols (New York: Pantheon, [1943], 1964).

12. Martin Heidegger, *Hölderlins Hymne "Der Ister,"* ed. Walter Biemel, GA 53 (1984), 63–152.

13. The translation is mine and follows the text established by Jean Bollack and Heinz Wismann in *Héraclite ou la séparation* (Paris: Editions de Minuit, 1972), 124.

14. Jacques Derrida, "Differance," *Margins of Philosophy*, trans. Alan Bass (Chicago: Univ. of Chicago Press, 1982), 3–27, p. 27.

15. Martin Heidegger, "The Self-Assertion of the German University: Address, Delivered on the Solemn Assumption of the Rectorate of the University Freiburg," trans. Karsten Harries, *Review of Metaphysics* 38 (1985): 470–80.

16. Martin Heidegger, " 'Only a God Can Save Us': The *Spiegel* Interview (1966)," trans. William J. Richardson, in Thomas Sheehan, ed., *Heidegger: The Man and the Thinker* (Chicago: Precedent, 1981), 45–67.

17. See PL 224–50; and Martin Heidegger, "Wozu Dichter?," *Holzwege*, 4. Aufl. (Frankfurt am Main: Vittorio Klostermann, 1963), 248–95. Compare English translation by Albert Hofstadter: "What Are Poets For?" in Heidegger, *Poetry, Language, Thought*, ed. Albert Hofstadter (New York: Harper & Row, 1971), 91–142.

18. This relocation is also remarked upon by Arnold I. Davidson, "Questions concerning Heidegger: Opening the Debate," SH 407–62. Although Heidegger thematizes the notion of saving in the Parmenides lectures (see PL 178), the full-fledged schema of danger and saving appears in other contexts, notably in "Die Frage nach der Technik," *Vorträge und Aufsätze*, I (Pfullingen: Neske, 1967), 5–36; compare "The Question concerning Technology," trans. William Lovitt, in Heidegger, *Basic Writings*, 287–317.

19. See Karl Löwith, *Mein Leben in Deutschland vor und nach 1933* (Stuttgart: Metzler, 1986), 57, as cited by Thomas Sheehan, "Heidegger and the Nazis," *New York Review of Books*, June 16, 1988, 38–47, p. 38 n. 4.

7

Questioning Heidegger's Silence: A Postmodern Topology

Babette E. Babich

INTRODUCTION

Martin Heidegger's silence regarding his Nazi past is not simply a failure to condemn the fascist trajectory of thirteen years of Nazi rule. As the silence of a philosopher who was repeatedly questioned on the matter of Auschwitz, the same matter that crushed but did not silence Adorno, Heidegger's silence speaks as a deliberate failure to name the name of the Jews, the victims of the Holocaust. What can be said about this failure, about this silence, philosophically and otherwise?

For his part, Heidegger's reflections on language as saying (and silence as a mode of discourse) enjoin silence: "Saying will not let itself be captured in any statement. It demands of us that we achieve by silence the appropriating, initiating movement within the being of language—and do so without talking about silence."[1] Thus, Heidegger's "A Dialogue on Language" investigates language as a saying correspondence from within language rather than as discourse about language. The Japanese partner observes, "The course of such a dialogue would have to have a character all its own, with more silence than talk." Heidegger's own interlocutor reinforces this description: "Above all, silence about silence. . . ." In turn, the being "silent of silence" is named "authentic saying."[2]

How can one speak about silence without language, without words on silence? In what follows, I cannot be silent about silence—as, indeed, Heidegger himself was not and could not be. I seek to address not language but silence. It is my intention thereby to come to some understanding of Heidegger's own de-etherealized, convicted silence on his past. In this endeavor it may be recalled that what we know about the guilt and volubility of silence is not just a legacy of Freudian psychoanalysis or Nietzschean genealogies but is also the effort of hermeneutic phenomenology, which is the gift of Heidegger's reflection on thought.

I seek to pose the question of Heidegger's silence as a question in the Heideggerian sense. Beyond questions of reception and the issue of political, ideological condemnation, the question of Heidegger's silence entails a special consideration of Heidegger's understanding of the significance of silence. The question of what may be called Heidegger's *silences* then comprises the questions concerning his political, factual silence as well as his philosophical questioning of the nature of language and silence. Below, I hope to articulate the resulting play of silences as a productive ambivalence coordinately enhancing an understanding not only of the philosopher's silence but silence itself.

What was Heidegger's understanding of silence? What was the significance of his silence, particularly his silence on his own words, his publicly proclaimed and published statements: the troublesome *Rektoratsrede*; the passages proclaiming the "inner truth and greatness"[3] of Nazism which were never silenced even if—and this too is debated—abridged. We cannot begin to answer these questions without a double consideration of Heidegger's own philosophic understanding of silence and the convicted, unremitting silence that damns him in our eyes.

Essentially ambiguous, the question of the proposed conjunction of Heidegger's silence as philosophically articulated and Heidegger's silence on his involvement and philosophic complicity with the political principles of Nazism requires such a duplication of terms. But such a doubling of silences is not proposed for the sake of equivocation. Both silences are to be interrogated, the reflective as well as the public silence, in order finally to resolve the positive tension of ambiguity or else to abandon this dyad within the blinking duplicity of scandal. Whatever the outcome, it is clear that without a hermeneutic of the question of Heidegger's silence, the inquiry must fail as an inquiry. This is also to say, and it is important to say it, that lacking the very Heideggerian question of the question, the question of Heidegger's silence has not yet been and cannot be posed as a question.

For an authentic questioning, it is imperative that we heed Heidegger's recollection of the nature of questioning. In his investigation into the nature of language, Heidegger noted that all questions require "the prior grant of whatever it is they approach and pursue with their queries."[4] This gift or grant is the antithesis of calculating challenge. Hence, what is wanted in questioning "is not a putting of questions—rather, it is a listening to the grant, the promise of what is to be put in question" (NL 71). We shall find that such an attending to "what is to be put in question" is hard to achieve and even more difficult to sustain. Just as questioning is always guided in advance by what it seeks, listening, in its necessary correlevance, shares the anticipatory structure of questioning as a listing inclination. Seen from within its own hermeneutic and phenomenological prospect, listening is always a listening *for*. As seekers, as listeners, our "listening is a listening for the countering word." The countering word is the word of recognition, the answering word. But in wary attunement, in the sensitivity of thoughtful response, the countering word also awaits challenge. Thus, like questioning, listening is a *possibility* of attentive comportment. We are always ahead of ourselves as listeners, but without listing balance if we listen without regard for this dispositional response. Then listening becomes a demand that "develops into our asking for the answer" (NL 75), and fails to listen for the answering word of attunement.

On the early Heidegger's understanding of questioning, "every seeking gets guided beforehand by what is sought."[5] This projective understanding remains central to Heidegger's thought; in the 1957 essay, "The Nature of Language," we find, "Every question . . . is already borne up by the grant of what is to come into question" (NL 75). For the present hermeneutic purpose of questioning questioning, I will need to distinguish two styles of questioning.

The first, ordinary question—and indeed, the immediate question concerning Heidegger's silence, questioning the significance of that silence in terms of what his silence confesses concerning his guilt—is a *problematical* kind of questioning. This kind of questioning listens for nothing like a countering attunement. Instead, problematical questioning demands a plain account—an answer guided by the facts it has in advance. In the Kantian spirit, the satisfaction of this questioning demand corresponds to the concurrence of the witness, whether that witness be nature, or a text under investigation, or a criminal suspect, or, indeed, a philosopher. But the answer-directed, satisfaction-compelling question of a given problematic—in the case at hand, the advance conviction of the question of Heidegger's guilt and the matter of Heidegger's shame—is not the only way of questioning.

Where problematical questioning starts out at its goal, the alternative style of questioning takes its point of departure from "that which is to be found out by the asking" (NL 75). This way of questioning is authentic just because it has the character of a seeking.[6] For Heidegger, the challenging force of problematical questioning does not correspond to the essence of the questioning he called the *piety of thought*. For Heidegger, "the true stance of thinking cannot be to put questions, but must be to listen to that which our questioning vouchsafes" (NL 72). If the question of this present chapter is to be posed in an authentic or essential fashion, what is to be found out is the questionableness of Heidegger's silence as such.[7]

But if there are two ways of posing the question of Heidegger's silence, there are also two ways to understand the notion of silence itself in this same context. Heidegger's silence can be heard privatively, as a Nazi, effectively anti-Semitic silence betraying personal failure and granting shameful consent—complicity—without the least admission of guilt. This is the now-standard interpretation of Heidegger's silence, and it accuses and condemns Heidegger's vain involvement with Nazism and his cowardliness and pettiness in whitewashing and denying his intimate and ongoing concord with the Nazi ethos in public statements made in the years after 1945. But beyond this standard statement of Heidegger's guilt, Heidegger's silence can be understood to be an authentic disclosure in the light of Heidegger's philosophic reflections on language and thought.[8] As such a disclosure, it can be said that the project of the later Heidegger *is* silence. In "The Way to Language" he writes, "Silence corresponds to the soundless tolling of the stillness of appropriating-showing Saying" (WL 131). By this correspondence, in speaking of the ringing of silence as *geläuter Stille*, Heidegger understands "the soundless gathering call, by which Saying moves the world-relation on its way" (NL 108). This soundless invocation is "the ringing of stillness. It is: the language of Being." So understood as the soundless, gathering calling that calls without a caller, the Saying that Says without a Sayer, silence is the poetic touchstone: "the breaking up of the word." This breaking up means that "the sounding word returns into soundlessness. . .into the ringing of stillness." This gathering echo is "the true step back on the way of thinking."

In the postmodern schema, aligning the intellectual culture of suspicion and indifference, the topological register of silence is always a pregnant one, always multifarious, and always betraying and betrayed.[9] This is not least because of the echoing of silence, its implicit address to another. In the distal echoing of its significance, the silence of refusal—the voice that fails to speak in silence—is heard to confess its own guilt. This distant and foreign silence speaks from the side of defiance, pride, and shame. Such silence does not conceal its contempt for the human demand for community and understanding. Yet silence can also be understood proximally—from the side of forbearance or reverent intimacy and solicitous regard. Thus conceived from within, silence is the mask or surface of a receptive species of *reticence*, relinquishing judgment, acknowledging failure, and deflecting and recoiling from disappointment, in the quiet that tentatively awaits the possibility of the redemption of ambiguity. What is glimpsed in this redemption is the flash of the impossibility of comprehension.[10] This realm of silence is the shadowed side of the thinker's recognition of his own finitude as it admits the thinker into a community of finitude and the pain of realizing that all vectors of human redemption—whether offering a salvation granted by the "spirit" of a people or represented by one man or one political movement or ideology, even one philosophy—are sometimes, more than ordinarily but dismally, horrifyingly flawed.[11] This same recognition is also the silent joy, as Nietzsche names it, ringing in the character of Oedipus at Colonus. Defeated and wounded, finally freed of his excess of vision and in the quiet wisdom of the mystic's *Gelassenheit*, Oedipus affirms his Sophoclean darkness, with a benediction and the same equanimity with which Odysseus faced Nausicaä, blessing life. If Heidegger's silence may be similarly conceived, although distanced from the heroic image of tragedy, we can regard silence as the nontactical, nontaciturn but still open reticence of a thinking that attends but does not calculate understanding.[12] As the reticent expression of the thinking that has learned how to listen, the tentative word of silence waits.

THE QUESTION OF HEIDEGGER'S SILENCE

I have claimed that it is essential to trace the question of Heidegger's silence by noting the terms that are at stake in the debate regarding Heidegger's Nazism. I hold that one must ask why

Heidegger kept and maintained silence on a topic that all the world has talked about and which continues to terrorize the human heart. It is this same silence which his followers have more or less sought to preserve, while nevertheless capitulating to the public pressure for a final word, so that the premature (if one considers Heidegger's own schedule and plan) publication of the *Beiträge* is a concession to public pressure for free access to texts representing Heidegger's thought in the Nazi era, as the important years in controversy. To those of us, apologists as well as detractors, who find Heidegger's silence lacking, who hear it as a mark of Heidegger's shameful and factual complicity with the Nazi ethos, what is in question is whether this silence should be spoken of as a crime.

I have conceded that the crime of everyday silence is denial. What is oppressed by this silence is the past, and it is this past that is ever newly manifest in the guilty return of the obliterated, the conviction of the repressed. This guilty caesura marking the moment of ordinary, criminal silence thus repeats in the obliteration of traces, in the imposition of a supplement, in the addition of parentheses, in the suppression of a manuscript page. Hence, the ordinary, problematical questioning concerning Heidegger's silence questions the significance of that very silence in terms of what his silence confesses about his past and lifelong guilt, or, abysmally, the horror to which his silence has given consent.

Why not speak the name of the Jews in the name of the mass crime that was done against them, in the name of the Holocaust, the Shoah? Why not speak out in the name of the Jews, cry out for the sake of the Jews, pronounce the nature of the crime in the name of its victims? In earnest and, above all, exasperation, why not confess one's own shame and guilt, one's own responsibility as a participant on so many levels in this sad century of unspeakable horror, its impossible wars, its tactical logics, and its continuing techniques of terror as they are dispersed and regathered in the simulacra of the Western world?[13] This is the very fulcrum and these are the sore points of the question of Heidegger's "terrible silence," in Derrida's words, or, following Levinas's damning judgment, his near consent "to horror."[14] For, make no mistake, the question is not the question of an assault on modernity, the issue is not merely that of believing in the "inner truth and greatness" of a political movement—apart from anti-Semitism, biologism, and the final solution—but these very things at their impossible extreme. It is to this issue, the issue of anti-Semitism, as the issue of Nazism and the Holocaust, that we pose and cannot but pose the questions: Why not speak? Why not apologize? Why not confess redemptive remorse? Why not denounce one's past, the shame of one's people?

But there are, as suggested above, at least two ways to pursue such needful questions. On the one hand, the question of Heidegger's silence can be posed as it has been up till now, poised to condemn and thus answered in advance. As we have seen, this is the problematical questioning that accuses. But, on the other hand, along the path of questioning I have sought to undertake in this essay, the question may be posed hermeneutically. Here, deliberately following Heidegger in order to track Heidegger in this question, one seeks to know where one does not claim to know in advance, one seeks to understand where a judgment has not already been uttered.

It may be possible, of course, to hold and to prove that Heidegger's political insights or allegiances have no more to do with the substance of his thought than the fondness he may have had for rustic footwear, Swabian soups, or whole-grain breads. Or else it may be that his political acts, different from personal preferences regarding dress or food, involve his philosophy with important implications for the practical or principial philosophical question, "What must I do?"[15] If the latter is true (as, along with many others, I believe), we are not released from the responsibility of the hermeneutic interrogation already begun. There is no ready negative judgment by association.[16] To continue this question of the question, we must be prepared once again to follow the Heideggerian project for thinking. This time we must attend not to Heidegger's way but to the way of Heidegger's way of thought, asking questions (after Heidegger's fashion) in thoughtful reappropriation. The task is not easy, and it is likely to be unfulfilling and, at least for a time, possibly unfulfilled. As William J. Richardson cautions in another context: "Foundational thought . . . is always an indigent thing. . . . it can never be anything more than tentative."[17] In the present context, the issue is the relevance of the tentative character of all beginnings, all attempts. When one eschews problematical calculation in favor of the questioning of thought, it is essential to forbear, to do without an automatic or advance answer, if only for the sake of listening.

THE REPRESSION OF SILENCE

To begin again (we may have to be prepared to begin again and yet again from now on, such is the task of uniting philosophy and politics), what is to be questioned is the silence of a philosopher and, by extension, a philosophy conceived with reference to the *issues* of Nazism. The philosopher's silence regarding the Holocaust betrays or fails to address the issue of horror. To recognize, to name, the ashes, cinders, dust of the Holocaust is an act of commemoration; for these cinders are not the tokens of Christian sinfulness but the very bodily ashes of the dead, filtering the dull penumbra of the Holocaust which drifts and cannot settle.

The declaration of the survivors of the death camps—which includes everyone—and the Passover invocation of Jews today, supplementing the promise of Jerusalem's redeeming gold, is the imperative: "Never forget!" This is not a promise of commemoration but an injunction issued to mortal beings, to human animals—in the classic humanistic ideal: *zoon logon*. The memories of rational animals work across the bar of ratio, installed in the disproportionate tension between the timeless circuit of the unforgetting, uncomprehending currents of the unconscious and the limits of conscious attention and recollective rationalization. Hence the vow, "Never forget!" is a solemn vow of silence, a vow to break silence, even in silence, perpetually.

The vow is necessary as a command just because the animal body forgets. Yet it is only because of animal, bodily forgetfulness that silence *can* articulate the unconscious brought to speech in the body, carried by the misspoken word, the accidental, the unwithheld.[18] In the same way, I submit that it is because of human forgetfulness (of the question of Being) that silence can be an *Erschweigen*, a *telling silence*, the foundation for what Heidegger calls another thinking.

And yet as important a commentator on just these affairs as Jürgen Habermas maintains that Heidegger's silence does not tell of anything but Heidegger's own guilt, nor does it admit of any ringing or resonant response. Heidegger's silence, once demystified in accord with the sensitively humanistic historical perspective of critical theory, *betrays* his insensitive, even petty detachment "from all relation to surface historical reality."[19] Inherently duplicitous, this blind detachment is undermined by the self-exoneration typical of the bourgeois "post-war mentality" of Heidegger's time, "the milieu of the Adenauer era of repression and silence" (WW 459). Thus Habermas fits Heidegger's silence within the ranks of the everyday, repressed or guilty kind.

I have suggested that opposed to the refusing, morally paralyzing silence of commission, featuring the insensitivity that denies community, is a finite, faltering, or *reticent* kind of silence. For Heidegger, reticent, stammering, ringing silence as such—and not the absence of speech or indeed the taciturn refusal of speech—is the very condition of the possibility of speech: "Everything spoken stems in a variety of ways from the unspoken, whether this be something not yet spoken, or whether it be what must remain unspoken in the sense that it is beyond the reach of speaking" (WL 120). The poverty of reticent silence is what can await the advent of mystery or the unknown: "that which must remain wholly unspoken is held back in the unsaid, [and] abides in concealment as unshowable" (WL 122).

In his "Letter on Humanism," written (let us to take care to iterate the historical cascade of crises we can barely remember, let alone understand) in the postwar followed by the war and its unwinnable inversion in genocide, followed again by the postwar world, Heidegger had wondered, "Perhaps, then, language requires much less precipitous expression than proper silence" (LH 223). Such a "proper" silence, the needful silence that belongs to language, corresponding "to the soundless tolling of the silence of appropriating-showing Saying" (WL 131), is, it can be said, what Heidegger would call *Gelassenheit*. The path of silence is then the succession of a thinking that rings the circuit from the early Heidegger (I) to the later Heidegger (II) as *another thinking*. Because this thinking is another beginning (*Anfang*) and because this is the description of the *Beiträge*, the difference between Heidegger I and II is not the difference of reversal but only the inclination of a turning, and indeed a turning within and not away.

This other thinking is the thinking that is otherwise than modern. It is here that Heidegger's own path of thinking traces the topography of the postmodern. I examine the significance of the controversial "postmodern" later. Here it is only important to note that if a thinker is postmodern, it is not to be thought that the thinker is premodern or even anti-modern. Rather, the postmodern is the condition, willy-nilly and despite all protests against the tastelessness of composite terms, of our own contemporary condition after the apices of modern achievement in the atomic age (bomb), the information age (computer), the age of imaginary transportation (the space shuttle), and so on. Beyond the innocence of an ideal of modernity that is no longer possible in such innocence, precisely because of the still unspeakable horror of the Holocaust, is the final, irrevocably consummate death of God and end of man. After this failure, what calls for thinking must abandon the centrality of the subject. This thinking is ex-centric to—Other than—ordinary, modern thinking. This otherness is foreign not just to ourselves but also, if we take him at his word, to Heidegger himself. To overcome this distance would require a finesse beyond even Nietzsche's wildest dreams for a thinker, a philosopher with exceeding fine fingers, possessing "that filigree art of grasping and comprehending."[20] Citing Nietzsche's physiological exigence ("Our thinking should have a vigorous fragrance, like a wheatfield on a summer night"), Heidegger shares Nietzsche's melancholy wish when he asks in Nietzsche's name and almost in Nietzsche's voice, "How many of us today still have the senses for that fragrance?" (NL 70). In this same spirit of tenuous hope, Heidegger could repeat, "Who of us today would want to imagine that his attempts to think are at home on the path of silence?" (LH 223).

Perhaps it is in this sense—speaking of the fragile, mortal significance of silence—that we may speak of the flawed, insecure path of silence. It may be that this path also reflects the difference between the early and the later Heidegger, between "Heidegger I" and "Heidegger II." But then (and I have already indicated my dissatisfaction with this extension), the movement of the turning, the *Kehre*, could be understood as the transformation of "Heidegger I" following upon the failure of the popular-political movement of National Socialism. Yet Heidegger himself thus articulates the topology of his thought: "The thought of [Heidegger] I becomes possible only if it is contained in [Heidegger] II."[21] In the same way and along the same continuum, we can understand why Philippe Lacoue-Labarthe—expressing the conviction of the later Heidegger who never chose to alter the damning passage in *Introduction to Metaphysics* underlining the "inner greatness" of Nazism—refuses to speak of accidents or mistakes: "Nazism, whatever its 'reality' might have been, . . . had the possibility Heidegger saw in it. . . at least in some of its traits, with respect to the destiny of Germany and that of the West."[22] After Auschwitz, after Dachau, as after Hiroshima and Nagasaki, this fictitious "possibility" is the failed essence of the West: the real meaning of the "death of God," a disappointment and a devastation haltingly observed by Paul Celan and commemorated by Maurice Blanchot. In Lacoue-Labarthe's expression of this essential decomposition, in a sentiment Emmanuel Levinas, too (among many, many others), does have personal cause to confirm: "In the apocalypse at Auschwitz, it is no more or less than the essence of the West that is revealed—and that has not ceased since that time to reveal itself" (NA 484). This revelation is denied an echo or a preface in Heidegger's work, early or late. According to Lacoue-Labarthe, "It was the thought guiding this event that Heidegger failed to recognize" (NA 484). Indeed, the Heidegger of 1949 testifies to the magnitude of this failure, when he is quoted as saying: "Agriculture [*Ackerbau*] is now a mechanized food industry. As for its essence, it is the same thing as the manufacture of corpses in the gas chambers and the death camps and the reduction of countries to famine, the same thing as the manufacture of hydrogen bombs."[23] Levinas, drawing out the incredibly leveling effect of this comparison, says of this passage that it is "beyond commentary" (AI 487).

It is by way of the trope of an express failing, the word that suddenly falters, by way of what scholars call *aposiopesis*—that is, the silence that breaks off speaking with pregnant exultancy, silence itself tumbling forth the obvious or else failing with a shuddering that plainly names what need not be spoken—that Levinas succeeds in rendering provocative and even eloquent commentary precisely where Heidegger's silence as well as Heidegger's words must fail to offer any account of themselves before the accusation of complicit guilt and repressed shame. And yet, if Heidegger's silence is not (or not only) the closed, taciturn silence of guilt but also, as I would suggest, the open silence of tentative finitude or reticent mortality, if silence can be heard under two species, that of guilt and that of listing, listening reticence, then Heidegger's words yet falter—*nonetheless and in the same fashion*.

The unspeakable mechanization of agriculture and death reflects the diabolical malignancy of the *Unheil* in the danger that is the calculative or productive essence of technology. This essence is difficult to conceive because the essence of technology in its current expression reveals the destiny of the "truth of Being, a truth that lies in oblivion" (LH 220). To think along with what Heidegger says here, and thereby to go beyond commentary, is to recover the trajectory of Heidegger's question of the truth of Being. For this approach to the essence of technology, it is essential to challenge the encroaching rule (*Ge-Stell*) of its achievements. Before one can think the essence of something that is in essence as neutral or ordinary as factory farming, as effectively innocent of political and economic forces as agriculture, one must relinquish both the convicted innocence of technology together with the vision of human stewardship, that is, humanistic omnipotence. In Heidegger's words: "Man is not the lord of beings" (LH 221).

For Heidegger, the ruling sway of technology obviates its societal aura of neutrality. In the banal technicization of agriculture, in accord with the all-too-routine encroachment of technology, factory farming is obviously no longer farming in the traditional sense. Today's mechanical, factory model agribusiness is not the same as the aboriginal cultivation of the earth. Technologized, devitalized, and mechanized, agriculture is yet one more postindustrial expression of the cultural domination of what Fredric Jameson, for one, calls *late-capitalism*.[24] Its effects match those of technology in any other field.

For a limited example that, if controversial, may offer some commentary on the force of Heidegger's impossibly banal comparison of agriculture with "the manufacture of corpses in the gas chambers," recall the modern functioning of agra-culture in contemporary practice: the food industry, including the production of grains, vegetable and fruit production, and indeed meat production. To take only the last element in the industrial extension of agriculture, just because the point in the former instances is necessarily subtler, it is worth attending to the economic function and definition of farm *animals*. In today's food industry, what is called *livestock* (read: live animal inventory or production units) is both figuratively as well as literally the material stock in trade of the meat industry. In commercial fact, then, livestock represents, in brutal but exact expression, no more than a self-renewing resource that is, in the end, "Bestandstücke eines Bestandes der Fabrikation von Leichen."

Rendered in this context, I am well aware that this example may be intellectually offensive and marginal, affectively postmodern and, of course, emotionally disturbing. We are not comfortable with the routine proximity of the image presented or its blatant parallel with the death camps of the latter comparison,[25] and, finally, we cannot be comfortable with the style of discourse. Yet owing to our discomfiture at its offensiveness, it may well unfold Heidegger's meaning where he writes in a text roughly contemporaneous with the *"Ackerbau"* quotation: "To healing Being first grants ascent [*Aufgang*] into grace; to raging [*dem Grimm*] its compulsion [*Andrang*] to malignancy" (LH 238).[26] How are these two texts to be conjoined?

The meaning of the conflict between healing grace and raging malignancy is what might be called, following Schürmann's usage, the "bifrontality" of technology. In Heidegger's essay "The Turning," first presented in 1949, the danger that reigns in the enframing essence of technology also succors what saves; yet this "saving power is not secondary to the danger. The selfsame danger is, when it is *as* the danger, the saving Power."[27] If it is the free essence of humanity that is endangered, this free essence is challenged only in terms of its responsibility. The heightening of technology is the danger posed against the free essence of humanity claimed to be necessary for "the safekeeping of the coming to presence of truth."[28] Before one can think the essence of technology—related as it is to truth—as a destiny within the truth of Being, one must conceive the complicit responsibility of humanity as "the shepherd of Being" (LH 221). When one relinquishes claim to lordship, a claim secured by the forgetful flight from Being, one can begin to approach "the essential poverty of the shepherd, whose dignity consists in being called by Being itself into the preservation of Being's truth" (LH 221).

What has truth, much less poverty and sheep herding, to do with technology? What have such romantic—transcendent *and* bucolic—images to do with the brutal conversion of human beings into corpses, the theft of human mortality that is extermination, the world-historical reality that was and continues to emerge in each new avatar as the Holocaust? What—if anything at all—has truth to do with agribusiness? We can ask this question by once again underlining as above the oddness or inappropriateness of the metaphoric invocation of the shepherd's affairs. Thus, in the *Republic* (343b), Thrasymachus ridiculed Socrates who sought to use a similar trope to illustrate the aim of practical art; the shepherd's interest, Thrasymachus claimed, is not the good of his flock but his own advantage, which last profit is ultimately secured at the slaughterhouse. Of course, the shepherd of whom Heidegger speaks and the aspect of the shepherd intended by Socrates is the poetic ideal of the shepherd dwelling alongside and for the sake of his flock. Against Thrasymachus—and even against Nietzsche, who spoke against the lamb even if he never spoke on behalf of the shepherd—the possibility of a shepherd's care is real beyond the idealism of Socrates, Heidegger, or, indeed, because this is a Western metaphor, Christ. And, if we can think it apart from the passage of time, the metaphor works. The ideal of the shepherd's care entails a genuine involvement with the flock, thus, at least temporarily, superceding the idols of the marketplace. This ideal possibility is the attentive tenderness that grows in every farmer's child, an openness to the animal as an essential being that grows and claims responsibility, until the subject's heart hardens into the sure conviction of right and the settling of societal debts—the accession to the position of the father—must finally close it off.

According to Heidegger, there is more to technology and its overwhelming success than can be fathomed by humanistic achievement: "It is the constellation of Being that is uttering itself to us" (TU 48). The postsubjectivist perspective of the postmodern is the perspective that could begin to attend to this utterance. This perspective is otherwise than Being, post-American-centrist, and thus—but not with any guarantee and not without the risk of confusion—potentially nonhierarchically pluralistic. Even where he himself may not track this perspective, Heidegger emphasizes the imperative need for such a new commencement because "we do not yet hear, we whose hearing and seeing are perishing through radio and film under the rule of technology" (TU 48).

If we can attend to the constellation that utters itself to us in the bifrontal essence of technology, we can begin to address the question of Heidegger's silence. Heidegger's "failure," to use Lacoue-Labarthe's expression, or Heidegger's consent to the "diabolical," in Levinas's unflinching words, is the failure of Heidegger's understanding vis-à-vis the Nazi movement. It is the meaning of Auschwitz that Heidegger cannot seem to comprehend, as Habermas implies: "Heidegger dealt with the theme of humanism at a time when the images of the horror that the arriving Allies encountered in Auschwitz and elsewhere had made their way into the smallest German village" (WW 449). But we would be as remiss as most readers of the infamous "*Ackerbau*" passage if in reading and discussing this passage we yet failed to observe that it offers, in spite of its obvious insufficiency and its startling dissonance, a veritable tour of the geographic promiscuity and escalation of the pinnacle of evil. For in that passage, among whatever other references there may be, Heidegger refers to the horror of Auschwitz *and* the final solution, as well as to the plight of Berlin during the blockade, to the Ukraine "reduced to famine" by Stalin, and finally to the hydrogen bomb that devastated the Japanese cities of Hiroshima and Nagasaki.

To say that these multifarious expressions of the aggressive essence of technique are "the same" is in no voice to excuse or absolve them, as some have claimed. "The essence of evil does not consist in the mere baseness of human action but rather in the malice of rage" (LH 237). The horror of thinking this accession to evil is the fearsome side of piety: "The coming to presence of technology gives man entry into That which, of himself, he can neither invent nor in any way make. For there is no such thing as a man who, solely of himself, is only man."[29]

I have observed that we do not wish to hear this fearsome expression of piety as the admission and reception of the worlding of the world, as "the nearest of all nearing that nears," or as any kind of openness to thinking apart from metaphysics. We do not hear Heidegger's words as the anguished speaking that breaks off (as reticent silence), but only, in Levinas's pronouncement, "as if consenting to horror." Thus, it is as if we would rather hear from Heidegger a bourgeois expression of shock, no matter if feigned or confused or exaggerated; it is as if we would prefer the sob of Christian repudiation, or moralizing self-denunciation, even the *mea culpa* of an honest confession, or, in Habermas's words, a "sober account of the facts" (WW 450).

These expectations are as question-worthy as the issue of Heidegger's rectitude. To question them, we can consider what Heidegger says concerning the destitution of our era and its senselessness. Towards the end of the text "Nihilism as Determined by the History of Being," composed during the years 1944–46 and included in Heidegger's volumes on Nietzsche, Heidegger writes:

> As the veiled and extreme need of Being, however, needlessness [*Notlosigkeit*] reigns precisely in the age of the darkening of beings, our age of confusion, of violence and despair in human culture, of disruption and impotence of willing. Both openly and tacitly, a boundless suffering and a measureless sorrow proclaim the condition of our world a needy one.[30]

Hearing this, let us first interrogate the persuasive ideology that compels us to take Heidegger to be speaking of anything but the need to think the terrifying destructiveness of "the planetary domination of the unthought essence of technicity" (OG 60) in its worst and, at that time—as Heidegger writes in the Nietzsche passage, in the "age of the darkening of beings"—in its impossibly palpable expression, "both overt and tacit," of "a boundless suffering and a measureless sorrow." It requires little hermeneutic skill to render this text in its lived context and to hear in it a reference to the overwhelming crimes of the recent world war(s). That we do not find this simple reading interesting or satisfying reveals as much about our demands as it does about Heidegger's silence. Heidegger goes even further when he writes, "The default of the unconcealment of Being as such releases the evanescence of all that is hale in beings. The evanescence of the hale takes the openness of the holy within it and closes it off" (NI 248, altered). Levinas is entitled to write, "Say what you will, the diabolical gives food for thought" (AI 488), but the value of that recognition should not be permitted to negate the similarity to be heard in Heidegger's earlier warning, "The closure of the holy eclipses every illumination of the divine. The deepening dark . . . conceals the lack of God" (NI 248).

THE TOPOLOGY OF POSTMODERNISM

Luc Ferry and Alain Renaut conclude the last chapter of their book, *Heidegger and Modernity*, by decrying the inauthenticity of Heidegger's anti-humanism, the tradition of a code—"(if only that of the history of Being)"—as making possible "the return of the nationalistic myth and the fanatical hatred of modernity."[31] Thus Ferry and Renaut epitomize the debate on Heidegger in its "deepest significance" as "hinging on the criticism of modernity," which they take to exemplify the values of subjectivity and humanism (HM 53). To say that Heidegger is anti-modern or postmodern is also to say that he is an anti-humanist. This anti-humanism is, then, the ultimate significance of his critique of subjectivity. For Ferry and Renaut, it was indeed only because of Heidegger's recidivist humanism, and in opposition to the principles of his philosophy, that he could, as a "fact" they acknowledge again and again, "criticize the biologizing reifications of Nazi anti-Semitism" (HM 107).

The project of this paper does not permit me to address the question of humanism, with its special polarization in favor of the realm of the spirit and its corresponding negation of the animal—or its denial of life, to use Nietzsche's language. The question of humanism is a labyrinth of hidden barbs, chasms, and well-appointed blind corridors. Here, in the context of the present effort, and by way of preparing a conclusion, I must address Heidegger's anti-modernism, which is also to say, the question of his postmodern standing.[32] But to discuss Heidegger's postmodernity, yet another consideration of the eminently debatable meaning of the postmodern is necessary.

According to the canonic author of philosophical postmodernity, Jean-François Lyotard, the postmodern is the condition of representational knowledge in an age of information. Heidegger characterized this epistemological condition as the triumph of ratiocination, calculative, productive thought. In the technological domain, knowledge is the still-surviving, dominant expression of the reign of metaphysical hope. Referring to Wall Street and NASA, Lyotard dubs this the economic mystique and exigence of calculation.[33]

The postmodern is not a moment (neither, contra Habermas, future utopian nor retro-nostalgic) beyond the modern.[34] Instead, what is represented by the postmodern is the unmasterable, disappointed condition of the Enlightenment ideal of modernity "after Auschwitz." That is, the postmodern is the modern in the wake of the impossible conflagration—disintegration—of the ideal of progress. The rational image of the modern, of the ideal of progress, is the representational essence of the scientific project of the West. This logical essence has suffered an irrefragable eclipse, and the postmodern simply names the persistence of its occlusion. Knowing this, we know that the insistence of the eclipse is what calls for the necessity of silence. To speak of the occlusion as accomplished blinds us to its continuing advent.

Both Heidegger and Nietzsche named the crisis of Western metaphysical values *nihilism*. The same occlusion of values is renamed by the condition of the postmodern because in the face of the modernist ideal of human-ascendant and liberating progress, what nihilism named persists. The nihilizing occlusion of values is not a description of a fixed condition; it is rather a procession of representations, what Baudrillard names *simulacra*, the decomposition or withering of values. These (de)valuations persist in their decomposition, and the postmodern is the condition of the ineluctability of inadequacy.

Although "after Auschwitz" we have resolved never to forget, a resolution cannot eliminate the knottings of repression, as Lacan explains its ergonomic Freudian topology. If we remember six million Jews, if we remember the violent issue of anti-Semitism, if we remember the silent mass crimes of fascism, is it necessarily or somehow obliquely required that we thereby simultaneously purchase as we do the oblivion of the six or seven million others who *are said* also to have died in the death camps—that is, that we overlook the components of the "racially unfit," a catchall expletive including (along with Jews) cripples, the mentally handicapped, Gypsies, homosexuals, Jesuits, Slavs, and so on? We may yet find it necessary to prepare a historical or social hermeneutic in order to question the rhetorical hesitation that effects an eclipse of this order, so that these millions *cannot* (or should not) be counted. It is clear that it is a bitterly reprehensible crime to pretend that the Nazis did not systematically and monstrously kill Jews. It is a further crime to claim that this systematicity, this monstrous genocide, this unmasterable Holocaust was not, in many crucial and still unthought senses, unique. But it remains as much a crime to forget that the death camps had jaws wider than the anti-Semitism which gorged them. If we cancel the memory of six or seven million for the sake of the commemoration of six million, we achieve the continuation of another kind of anti-Semitism. By the anti-Semitic expedient of despising, excluding, and monologizing, we thus invent other Jews.[35]

But even an orgy of naming victims, even a frenzy of metonymic place-designations, adding Polish and Russian names to the name of Auschwitz, cannot resolve the question of the Holocaust because we are not yet able to ask it. As we bring the still recalcitrant issue of silence to mind, we are confronted with the inarticulate expression of a horror that cannot be touched by the resolve, "Do not forget." The polished boots of the SS at Auschwitz and the metallic black of futuristic appliances repeat the same. The silence continues in silencing silence.

Thus the question that has ever to be opened up is the automatic refusal of the question, as if it were only a Nazi issue, only an issue of anti-Semitism, only a silence that is only a bourgeois silence, a shamed silence. If we can remember the protean structure of the different expressions of the will to power, we can begin to understand the impotent self-assertion Heidegger has named *needlessness*—the expression of the homeless, uprooted, essence of humanity, its failure as Da-Sein. In the many guises of European world history it may be that only the *infrastructure*, only the tools, only the globalization of the impotent structures for preserving and increasing power differ. But who actually speaks when the impotence of power cries out? And what of truth, what of illusion? Is there any thinker, any thinking that can ask here, *whose* truths? What is wanting is a way of thought that could jostle us in our confidence. What fails is a way of disturbing the quietude of our disquiet that could engage us with such finesse that we would be able to rest in being so rustled: this is a drumming on our souls that would beat with the rhythm of the heart, teasing us, shaming us out of any imaginary phantasm of justice, by asking, ever so lightly, *whose* illusions? What thinker remains who can see any of this, even after Marx, Freud, and Nietzsche?

CONCLUSION

Heidegger was silent on the question of the Holocaust, except in ways that are too faltering for words. In the question posed to and not simply raised in accusation against Heidegger's silence, inquiry must also seek the meaning of silence conceived "as a mode of discoursing," whereby "reticence Articulates the intelligibility of Dasein in so primordial a manner that it gives rise to a potentiality-for-hearing which is genuine, and to a Being-with-one-another which is transparent" (BT 208).

Attentive reticence, or silence here understood as the possibility of authentic listening, is at the very least an essential condition for a more than merely (post)traditional community. By its nature, the necessarily confessional, public, or expressly declarative expression of a traditional community is exclusive, separating a select people from its enemies (others), installing the monolithic sense of an admitted and pledged *we* in opposition to a despised and designated *them*. In contrast to the ancient oppositional polarities now at least superficially eschewed by a postmodern, culturally pluralistic world, a reticent, that is, *listening and attending*, community is the indispensable condition for the possibility of a genuine pluralistic engagement between human beings in terms of and across all differences.

Seen in this engaged light, Heidegger's period of Nazi involvement failed at nothing so much as silence. Lending his voice to the confessional community of the Nazi party, Heidegger forsook the insight the early Heidegger had understood and that the later Heidegger had so much cause to recall: silence does not hold thoughtful understanding at bay, but keeps itself in readiness for understanding. We should not be surprised to find that this perspective endures as expressed for posthumous publication in the *Spiegel* interview, where Heidegger describes the "tentative, unassuming character of thought that strives to ponder [the] unthought" (OG 60).

In addition to the problematical reading of silence, which confesses Heidegger's human weakness, and far from the sullen refusal of historical community but conceived in its philosophical aspect, Heidegger's silence is a redemptive, glancing address that sponsors authentic listening as "a potentiality-for-hearing which is genuine" and "a Being-with-one-another which is transparent." This attentive, waiting address reflects Being, which "in its giving of light, simultaneously keeps safe the concealed darkness of its origin as the unlighted" (TU 45). As Walter Benjamin has described the task of commemoration, "To articulate the past historically does not mean to recognize it 'the way it really was' (Ranke). It means to seize hold of a memory as it flashes up at a moment of danger."[36] Benjamin's metaphor is the metaphor of redemptive acquisition. But Nietzsche focuses on the inventive technique, against the photographic ideal of objectivity: "Man spins his web over the past and subdues it, thus he gives expression to his artistic drive—but not to his drive toward truth or justice. Objectivity and justice have nothing to do with one another."[37] As Heidegger captured and spun his own memory of his own past, it is possible that he saw in it the wake of the perpetuity of the modern, the passing of the subject and his own efforts as striving "along narrow paths that do not stretch too far" (OG 65). Even this limited past can claim what Benjamin would call a *weak* redemption, woven from Heidegger's words. It is this redemption that waits in the flash of the stilling grace and malignancy that would sustain and bind a genuine community and an authentic gratitude of a thought exceeding humanism.

Notes

1. Martin Heidegger, "The Way to Language" (abbreviated "WL"), *On the Way to Language*, trans. Peter D. Hertz (New York: Harper & Row, 1971), 111–36.

2. Martin Heidegger, "A Dialogue on Language," *On the Way to Language*, 1–54, pp. 52–53.

3. Martin Heidegger, *An Introduction to Metaphysics*, trans. R. Manheim (New Haven: Yale Univ. Press, 1959), 199. This passage expresses Heidegger's distance from National Socialism, but it also confirms his convicted interest in its projects, its "inner truth," as he saw it. On this point, see Graeme Nicholson's excellent article, "The Politics of Heidegger's Rectoral Address," *Man and World* 20 (1987): 171–87. For Nicholson, "it is not malice, rancour, power-lust, or vengence that marks the moral and political character of [Heidegger's] intervention. . . . Heidegger was betrayed by *hybris* that his mere words could transform National Socialism" (p. 185). I have not to date seen any argument that controverts this analysis. See too George Kovacs, "On Heidegger's Silence," *Heidegger Studies* 5 (1989): 135–51; and for an interesting historical reading of both the circumstances of the *Rektoratsrede* and Heidegger's trajectory of Nazi involvement, developed in opposition to Hugo Ott's interpretation in *Martin Heidegger: Unterwegs zu seiner Biographie* (Frankfurt am Main: Campus, 1988), see the lecture by Ott's University of Freiburg colleague, the philosopher H. Tietjen, "Martin Heideggers Auseinandersetzung mit der Nationalsozialistischen Hochschulpolitik und Wissenschaftsidee," delivered in Budapest and, in a shortened English version, at Yale University in fall 1989. The lecture is part of a work in progress.

4. Martin Heidegger, "The Nature of Language" (abbreviated "NL"), *On the Way to Language*, 57–108, p. 71.

5. Martin Heidegger, *Being and Time*, trans. J. Macquarrie and E. Robinson (New York: Harper & Row, 1962), 24; abbreviated "BT."

6. For Heidegger, such inquiry has as its guide that which "is asked about...that which is interrogated...and that which is to be found out by the asking." NL 75.

7. Inquiry reaches its term when the question of Heidegger's silence has been posed and thought as a question. Authentic questioning seeks for what is to be found out by the asking. The problematic or inauthentic question has this information implicitly or analytically in advance and asks for a legitimation or demands a justification. Because what is to be found out by the asking is already given, the question is itself questionable.

8. See Heidegger's discussion of the possibility of discourse as "*keeping silent*," BT 204–8. Heidegger holds that "speaking at length" (*Viel-sprechen*) is the best way of covering something up, bringing "what is understood to a sham clarity" (p. 208). On the other hand, he submits that "in talking with another, the person who keeps silent can 'make one understand' (that is, he can develop an understanding), and he can do so more authentically than the person who is never short of words" (p. 208). Thus "*keeping silent* is [an] essential possibility of discourse." Heidegger's later reflections on language continue the spirit of this distinction.

9. Thus, so far from being an utter silence, Heidegger's silence has quite literally said volumes to us, without of course revealing itself, and producing in response a stream of books, articles, parentheses, and disquisitional footnotes. Heidegger recognized this phenomenon as the origin of language not as a "phonetic-acoustic-physiological" event but as the "ringing stillness" (WL 121, 122). Thus: "A man may speak, speak endlessly, and all the time say nothing. Another man may remain silent, not speak at all and yet, without speaking, say a great deal" (WL 122). My purpose in this paper is to draw out the communicative difference of this latter reticence because it characterizes the spirit of Heidegger's thought on language from the start. See BT 204–8.

10. Thus, when Victor Farías's *Heidegger et le Nazisme* (1987) first began to cause a stir in literary publications in the English-speaking world, another student of Heidegger's, Professor Elisabeth Hirsch, was moved to write a clarifying letter to the *New York Times* (March 2, 1988). Hirsch reported a continuing context of deep concern on Heidegger's part, not the unrepentant Nazism attributed to him, and recalled that she had asked him to give an account of his Nazi past. Heidegger, she said, agreed that something needed to be said, "—Aber wie?" *But how?* From the privileged report of a student and a friend, Heidegger's silence can be approached, if not ever resolved, as testifying to the reticent provisionality of the impossibility of language.

11. See Martin Heidegger, " 'Only a God Can Save Us': The *Spiegel* Interview (1966)," trans. William J. Richardson, in Thomas Sheehan, ed., *Heidegger: The Man and the Thinker* (Chicago: Precedent, 1981), 45–67 (abbreviated "OG"), p. 62: "No single man, no group of men, no commission of prominent statesmen, scientists, and technicians, no conference of leaders

of commerce and industry can brake or direct the progress of history." Compare this with Martin Heidegger, *Discourse on Thinking*, trans. J. Anderson and E. H. Freund (New York: Harper & Row, 1966), 52, 55; originally published as *Gelassenheit* (Pfullingen: Neske, 1959), 20, 23. See also Martin Heidegger, "On the Essence of Truth," trans. J. Sallis, *Basic Writings* (abbreviated "BW"), ed. David Farrell Krell (New York: Harper & Row, 1977), 117–41, esp. pp. 131–32; and so on.

12. In the poverty of this reticence, "thinking is what it is according to its essential origin." Martin Heidegger, "Letter on Humanism" (abbreviated "LH"), BW 193–242, p. 196.

13. By such "simulacra of the Western world" I refer to the third world, as well as the "fourth," "fifth," and however many other subaltern and secondary worlds.

14. For the first quote see Jacques Derrida, "Heidegger's Silence: Excerpts from a Talk Given on 5 February 1988," in G. Neske and E. Kettering, eds., *Martin Heidegger and National Socialism: Questions and Answers,* trans. L. Harries and J. Neugroschel (New York: Paragon House, 1990), 145–48, p. 148. The original text was part of a colloquium on Heidegger's thought held in Heidelberg, with Hans-Georg Gadamer and Philippe Lacoue-Labarthe, February 5, 1988. The second quote is from the title of Emmanuel Levinas, "As If Consenting to Horror," trans. Paula Wissing, *Critical Inquiry* 15 (1988–89): 485–88, p. 485; abbreviated "AI."

15. See Reiner Schürmann's distinction between principial (archic) and an-archical thought: *Heidegger on Being and Acting: From Principles to Anarchy*, trans. Christine-Marie Gros (Bloomington: Indiana Univ. Press, 1987), 13; abbreviated "HB."

16. If we do not wish to follow the path of Heidegger's questioning, we must at least be able to limn its direction so that we know what we foreclose in our own way. As Reiner Schürmann shows, the question of the relevance of Heidegger's thought for action, that is, practical and political world-historical engagement, requires a reappropriation of Heidegger's thought, because anything short of this does not address the question of practical responsibility in a time of faltering principles; see HB, esp. parts 1 and 4.

17. William J. Richardson, *Heidegger: Through Phenomenology to Thought* (The Hague: Martinus Nijhoff, 1963), 551; abbreviated "HTP."

18. Note then that the silence of the body, like the silences of animal beings, is not to be thought as a wordless silence. Although animals lack a language, Heidegger does note that "they are not thereby suspended wordlessly in their environment": LH 206.

19. Jürgen Habermas, "Work and Weltanschauung: The Heidegger Controversy from a German Perspective," *Critical Inquiry* 15 (1988–89): 431–56, p. 449.

20. Friedrich Nietzsche, "Why I Am So Wise," *Ecce Homo*, trans. W. Kaufmann (New York: Randon House, 1969), 223. See too Nietzsche, *Twilight of the Idols*, trans. R. J. Hollingdale (Harmondsworth: Penguin, 1968), 30.

21. Martin Heidegger, "Vorwort": "Aber I wird nur möglich wenn es im II erhalten ist." In HTP xxii–xxiii.

22. Philippe Lacoue-Labarthe, "Neither an Accident nor a Mistake," trans. Paula Wissing, *Critical Inquiry* 15 (1988–89): 481–84, p. 482; abbreviated "NA."

23. Martin Heidegger, quoted in Wolfgang Schirmacher, *Technik und Gelassenheit* (Freiburg: Alber, 1983), 25. Schirmacher refers to page 4 of a then-unpublished text of Heidegger's "Das Ge-stell." Schirmacher's context does not approximate Levinas's nor indeed that of Lacoue-Labarthe. For Schirmacher, the problem at hand is the danger of technology, that is, understood in its essence: "Zur Beherrschung jedoch waren wir niemals in der Lage und keine Technologie wird uns dies in Zukunft ermöglichen" (p. 24). For the further context of this quote, Schirmacher precedes its introduction with another citation from another unpublished text, "Gefahr," where Heidegger characterizes the victims of the Holocaust as so many "Bestandstücke eines Bestands der Fabrikation von Leichen" (p. 25). A more comprehensive reading of these texts is offered by Otto Pöggeler, *Martin Heidegger's Path of Thinking*, trans. Daniel Magurshak and Sigmund Barber (Atlantic Highlands, N.J.: Humanities Press, 1987); originally *Der Denkweg Martin Heideggers* (Pfullingen: Neske, 1983). The *"Ackerbau"* passage is quoted in AI 487 and in Arnold Davidson (citing Lacoue-Labarthe but giving this same source), "Questions concerning Heidegger: Opening the Debate," *Critical Inquiry* 15 (1988–89): 407–26, p. 423.

24. Fredric Jameson, "Postmodernism, Or The Cultural Logic of Late Capitalism," *New Left Review* 146 (1984): 53–92.

25. It is however significant, following the suggestion of Isaac Bashevis Singer in just this connection, that from the perspective of animals "we are all Nazis." See "The Slaughterer," *The Animals' Voice Magazine* 2 (1989): 38–41.

26. I have included the German words because if we hear this in the German, its significance is compelling (although it may yet remain, in another sense, "beyond commentary"). The original text is as follows: "Sein erst gewährt dem Heilen Aufgang in Huld und Andrang zu Unheil dem Grimm." Martin Heidegger, "Brief über dem Humanismus," *Wegmarken* GA 9 (1978), 313–64, p. 357.

27. Martin Heidegger, "The Turning" (abbreviated "TU") in *The Question concerning Technology and Other Essays*, trans. W. Lovitt (New York: Harper & Row, 1977), 36–49, p. 42; collection abbreviated "QC."

28. Martin Heidegger, "The Question concerning Technology," QC 3–35, p. 33.

29. Heidegger, "Question concerning Technology," 31. See also Martin Heidegger, *Discourse on Thinking*, 53.

30. Martin Heidegger, "Nihilism as Determined by the History of Being," *Nietzsche*, trans. Frank A. Capuzzi, ed. David Farrell Krell, vol. 4 (San Francisco: Harper & Row, 1982), 197–250, p. 245, translation slightly altered; abbreviated "NI." Compare Heidegger, "Die Seinsgeschichtliche Bestimmung des Nihilismus," *Nietzsche*, 2t. Bd. (Pfullingen: Neske, 1961), 335–98, p. 392.

31. Luc Ferry and Alain Renaut, *Heidegger and Modernity,* trans. F. Philip (Chicago: Univ. of Chicago Press, 1990), 108; abbreviated "HM." Originally published as *Heidegger et les Modernes* (Paris: Grasset, 1988).

32. Russell Berman and Paul Piccone, "Hidden Agendas: The Young Heidegger and the Post-Modern Debate," *Telos* 17 (1988): 117–25, claim that the continuing impetus for the "Heidegger debate" turns on the spurious "*necessary* connection between Heidegger's Nazi politics, his philosophy and, *ipso facto*, post-modernism and deconstruction" (p. 119).

33. "Not only is it necessary to represent, but one must also calculate, 'estimate' in advance the represented quanta and the quanta of the representatives. This is the very definition of economic knowledge." Jean-François Lyotard, *Heidegger and "the Jews"* trans. A. Michel and M. S. Roberts (Minneapolis: Univ. of Minnesota Press, 1990), 40–41.

34. If only for this reason alone, the postmodern is not merely the elliptical fancy of a new rage. It will not do to convert the "post" of the postmodern into an anti- or amodernity. The implication of transit, of a passage through modernity is essential, for this the contemporary condition is characterized by nothing so much as a history, with all its effects, of being modern.

35. When Adorno and Horkheimer observe, "There are no more anti-Semites," they are asserting that anti-Semitic "psychology has been replaced by mere acceptance of the whole Fascist ticket, the slogans of aggressive big business." *Dialectic of Enlightenment*, trans. J. Cumming (New York: Herder & Herder, 1972), 200–201.

36. Walter Benjamin, "Theses on the Philosophy of History," *Illuminations*, trans. Harry Zohn (New York: Schocken Books, 1969), 253–64, p. 255.

37. Friedrich Nietzsche, "On the Uses and Disadvantages of History for Life," *Untimely Meditations*, trans. R. J. Hollingdale (Cambridge: Cambridge Univ. Press, 1983), 91.

Part 2

Heidegger's Thought

8

Ever Respectfully Mine:
Heidegger on Agency and Responsibility

Peg Birmingham

No aspect of Heidegger's thinking evokes more discussion and criticism than the question of whether his work allows for the possibility of practical philosophy. The debate centers on Heidegger's location of authentic selfhood in the moment of Dasein's anticipatory resoluteness in Being-toward-death.[1] In its Being-toward-death the authentic self appears to be so radically individuated as to allow for no possibility of authentic *Mitsein*. Lacking this possibility, the prospects for an ethical or political philosophy seem nonexistent.

My contention in this essay is that Heidegger's analysis of the Kantian understanding of *respect* in the 1927 lecture course published as *The Basic Problems of Phenomenology*, together with his earlier analysis of *anxiety* in the 1925 lecture course published as *History of the Concept of Time*, provides important illumination of the moment of authentic selfhood in *Being and Time*. Thinking together the two discussions of respect and anxiety (a thinking-together that, I submit, Heidegger's own analysis suggests) reveals that *Mitsein* is radically implicated in Dasein's Being-toward-death.[2] This implication, in turn, suggests that Heidegger is questioning whether the authentic self can be located in anything like an autonomous sphere, and, moreover, whether the *activity* of the self can be understood in terms of autonomous agency. Finally, the radical implication of *Mitsein* in Dasein's Being-toward-death suggests that Heidegger is challenging two tenets of modern liberal political theory: the inviolability of the subject and the right to self-preservation.

RESPECT AND THE DEMAND OF THE OTHER

In *The Basic Problems of Phenomenology* Heidegger, discussing the Kantian understanding of the self, states, "Kant's interpretation of the phenomenon of respect is probably the most brilliant phenomenological analysis of the phenomenon of morality that we have from him."[3] Although he will argue that Kant does not go far enough in his analysis of respect, nonetheless, Heidegger's analysis of Kant's understanding of the feeling of respect remains *positive*. Like any disposition, this feeling, Heidegger argues, "directly uncovers and makes accessible that which is felt, and it does not, to be sure, in the manner of intuition but in the sense of a direct having-of-oneself" (BP 133; GP 188). At the same time the *direct having-of-oneself* discloses the self. Thus, all dispositions are twofold:

> In having a feeling *for* something there is always present at the same time a *self*-feeling, and in this *self*-feeling a mode of becoming revealed to oneself. The manner in which I become manifest to myself in feeling is determined in part by that for which I have a feeling in this feeling. Thus it appears that feeling is not a simple reflection upon oneself but rather a feeling of *self* in having a feeling *for* something. (BP 132; GP 187)

The feeling for something determines who the self is.

Specifically, the feeling of respect gives Dasein's authentic self: "This feeling of respect is the true mode in which man's existence becomes manifest, not in the sense of pure ascertainment or taking cognizance of, but in the sense that in respect I myself *am—*am *acting*" (BP 137; GP 194). It is important to note in this analysis of respect that Heidegger is thinking the problem of the authentic self and, further, that he locates authenticity in the sphere of action. More precisely, Heidegger locates the authentic self in the sphere of *responsible* action:

> Although Kant does not press directly in this direction, nevertheless the possibility is present in reality. . . . Respect reveals the dignity before which and for which the self knows

itself to be responsible [*verantwortlichkeit*]. Only in responsibility does the self first reveal itself—the self not in a general sense as knowledge of an ego in general but as in each case mine.. . .(BP 137; GP 194)

"Mineness" (*Jemeinigkeit*) only occurs in the feeling of respect. Only in the feeling of respect *for something* does Dasein's authentic self reveal itself as a responsible, acting being.

Heidegger then argues that the feeling of respect is the *ontical* manifestation of the individual's responsibility to determine itself in its potentiality-for-being. In this sense Heidegger agrees with Kant's understanding of the person as self-determining end. Dasein's peculiar ability to be lies in its "choosing itself" and determining its existence from that choice. Heidegger locates this ability to choose in the phenomenon of "purposiveness":

To this being belongs purposiveness, more precisely, self-purposiveness. Its way of being is to *be* the end or purpose of its own self. This determination, to be the end of its own self, belongs indisputably to the ontological constitution of the human Dasein. (BP 141; GP 199)

Yet, Heidegger argues that Kant does not go far enough in asking about the very possibility of Dasein's purposiveness, that is, its capacity to choose:

The Dasein exists: that is to say, it is for the sake of its own capacity-to-be-in-the-world. Here there comes to view the structural moment that motivated Kant to define the person ontologically as an end, without inquiring into the specific structure of purposiveness and the question of its ontological possibility. (BP 170; GP 242)

In other words, to understand Dasein's purposiveness is to understand Dasein as a self-determining end. To do this is to grasp the ontological basis of responsible action, which, as we saw above, defines the authentic self.

In order to grasp Dasein's purposiveness, it is necessary first to reflect upon Kant's understanding of the person as a self-determining end. Of course, this is the question of agency. To be a self-determining end is to have the capacity to choose one's own ends. The capacity to choose marks the Kantian self. The self, understood as this capacity, must be prior to the ends it chooses. In other words, the self is an end-in-itself:

> Rational nature is distinguished from others in that it proposes an end to itself. . . . Now this end can never be other than the subject of all possible ends themselves, because this is at the same time the subject of a possible will which is absolutely good; for the latter cannot be made secondary to any other object without contradiction.[4]

The priority of the subject over its ends marks the radical autonomy of the Kantian subject. As Michael Sandel points out in *Liberalism and the Limits of Justice,* Kant formulates a notion of the self as "antecedently individuated."[5] The self is individuated in advance and is given prior to its ends. This position of autonomy is the original position of the Kantian self.[6]

Although Heidegger agrees with Kant that the self must be grasped as an acting being having a capacity to choose, he argues, however, that Dasein's purposiveness is *not* due to any original position (to use Rawls's phrase) of autonomy. On the contrary, this capacity must be grasped from out of an original *transposition*:

> Yet it is only on the basis of an *antecedent* "transposition" that we can, after all, come back to ourselves from the direction of things. The question is only how to understand this "transposition" and how the ontological constitution of Dasein makes it possible. (BP 161; GP 229)

There is, according to Heidegger, no antecedently individuated self. The original position, as it were, is a transposition. Heidegger, therefore, thinks the authentic self and its activity from out of a position of radical heteronomy.

Going further, Heidegger argues that this transposition must be grasped as Dasein's transcendence, and in the lecture course of 1929 published as *The Metaphysical Foundations of Logic* he clarifies the relation between Dasein's purposiveness (its capacity to choose) and its transcendence:

> But a for-the-sake-of-which, a purposiveness [*Umwillen*], is only possible where there is a willing [*Willen*]. Now insofar as transcendence, being-in-the-world, constitutes the basic constitution of Dasein, Being-in-the-world must also be primordially bound

up with or derived from the basic feature of Dasein's existence, namely, freedom. Only where there is freedom is there a purposive for-the-sake-of, and only here is there world.[7]

Before turning to the "for-the-sake-of" which marks Dasein's capacity to choose, it is important to note again that Heidegger does not locate Dasein's selfhood in anything like an autonomous sphere of egoism. Transcendence is a peculiar trans-position:

> Dasein is itself the passage across. And this implies that transcendence is not just one possible comportment (among others) of Dasein toward other beings, but it is the basic constitution of its Being, on the basis of which Dasein can at all relate to beings in the first place. (MF 165; MA 211)

Dasein's selfhood, authentic or inauthentic, cannot be taken to reside in a sphere of immanence. Moreover, insofar as Dasein's transcendence is identical with its freedom, freedom is not an attribute of an autonomous will but is the basis of Dasein's capacity to choose in its Being-in-the-world.

As noted above, Heidegger understands Dasein's purposiveness, its capacity to choose, as "for-the-sake-of":

> To be for its own sake is an essential determination of the being of that being which we call Dasein. This constitution, which we will now, for the sake of brevity, call the for-the-sake-of, provides the intrinsic possibility for this being to be itself, i.e., for selfhood to belong to its being. (MF 189; MA 243)

We need to recall that Dasein's purposiveness is the ontological basis for the ontical feeling of respect. Again, the feeling of respect is twofold: In having a feeling-for, Dasein's authentic self is revealed as a responsible, acting being. At the ontological level of purposiveness, Heidegger also argues that only in Dasein's being "for-the-sake-of" is its self determined. Insofar as these two levels are distinguishable, yet inseparable, Heidegger is suggesting that the feeling of respect accompanies authentic purposiveness.

At this point the question of the "for" must be clarified. Recalling that Dasein's purposiveness is its capacity to choose, Heidegger suggests that the authentic self is given *only* in its being "for-the-sake-of" of its *Being-with* (*Mitsein*):

> Many times, even ad nauseam, we pointed out that this being qua Dasein is always already with others and always already with beings not of Dasein's nature. . . . In choosing itself Dasein really chooses precisely its being-with others and precisely its being among beings of a different character. (MF 190; MA 245)

In *Being and Time*, Heidegger argues the same point:

> According to the analysis which we have now completed, Being with Others belongs to the Being of Dasein, which is an issue for Dasein in its very Being. Thus as Being-with, *Dasein 'is' essentially for the sake of Others*. . . . In Being-with, as the existential "for-the-sake-of" of Others, these have already been disclosed in their Dasein.[8]

In contrast to Kant, Heidegger's understanding of purposiveness articulates a radically different relation between the self and its ends. The self does not exist prior to its end; instead, the self is given only in choosing for the sake of an end other than itself. Specifically, only in choosing for the sake of the other as end is there revealed Dasein's own self.

To be sure, Being-with (*Mitsein*) is not a *mediating* moment through which Dasein's self is given. Here again, Heidegger rethinks Kant. Kant's proof for the Law of Humanity begins with the assumption that every rational being exists as an end in itself. At the same time, the proof argues, every other rational being thinks of its existence in this way as well. The same rational grounds that hold for me as a rational being also hold for every other rational being. Therefore, one ought to treat all others as ends in themselves, deserving of the respect one accords to oneself. The proof is based on the direct experience of the self as an end possessing dignity and the analogizing transfer of this experience to the other.[9]

Heidegger, on the other hand, argues that the analogizing transfer is unnecessary. It is not the case that Dasein has some original experience of the self, and, then, there occurs a type of transference to the other in a second moment. Nor does the self proceed from the other. Being-with (*Mitsein*) belongs to the ontological constitution of Dasein. *I am only in the activity of Being-with.* Heidegger clearly articulates this in his analysis of feeling, which, he says, directly uncovers and makes accessible that which is felt, and it does this not, to be sure, in the manner of intuition but in the sense of a direct having-of-oneself. Both moments of the structure of feeling must be kept in mind: feeling as feeling-for and simultaneously the self-feeling in this having-feeling-for. (BP 133; GP 187)

In the event of the feeling of respect, the other is given immediately with the feeling of self. This immediacy must be grasped as *equiprimordiality*. In this sense the other "breaks in on" or "befalls" Dasein. Therefore, Dasein never chooses simply for itself. Nor does it choose for the other as if he or she were the same as the self. (This marks the difference between empathy and respect. Here Heidegger's critique of empathy in section 26 of *Being and Time* needs to be recalled.) As Being-with, Dasein is ontologically obligated to solicit the other in his or her potentiality-for-being.

In both *The Basic Problems of Phenomenology* and *The Metaphysical Foundations of Logic,* Heidegger's discussion of Dasein's purposiveness, its capacity to choose in its Being-with, clarifies the moment of emanicipatory solicitude in *Being and Time.* Purposiveness is possible only because Dasein is always beyond itself. This transcendence marks the realm of freedom: "Only where there is freedom is there a purposive for-the-sake-of, and only here is there world. To put it briefly, Dasein's transcendence and freedom are identical" (MF 185; MA 238). Again, Heidegger does not locate freedom in an autonomous, sovereign will; instead, freedom is understood to be a space wherein Dasein has the capacity to act with others: "The *realm-of-ends* is the *being-with-one-another,* the *commercium of persons* as such, and therefore the realm of freedom" (BP 139; GP 197).

Thinking together transcendence, freedom, and Being-with (*Mitsein*), Heidegger suggests that Dasein's purposiveness must be understood as the capacity to choose for the sake of the other's freedom. Dasein's purposiveness, its capacity to choose, is only possible in the realm of freedom, which, Heidegger argues, is the realm of Being-with (*Mitsein*). Dasein's purposiveness is for-the-sake-of this realm. This is the moment of emanicipatory solicitude wherein authentic Dasein lets the other be in the sense of allowing its potentiality-for-being to become transparent. Rather than marking the self as an autonomous end-in-itself, Dasein's purposiveness marks its heteronomy, its responsibility to the other as end. In other words, Dasein's capacity to choose, its "I am able," marks the moment of obligation.

This obligation is given in the feeling of respect, a feeling that "has 'something analogous at once' to inclination [*dioxis*] and fear [*phuge*]" (BP 136; GP 193). The feeling of respect includes a self-subjection or yielding (*phuge*) to the other who has the force of absolute exteriority and who makes the demand of emancipatory solicitude. Indeed, the inadequacy of the self to meet this demand instills respect for the other who makes this demand; it reveals the dignity of the other "before which and for which the self knows itself to be responsible." Thus, the feeling of respect is sublime. In one's yielding to the other as to a demand, the other, who has the force of exteriority, is never fully present such that there could be an adequate fulfilling of one's obligation. The other always remains in part undisclosed, nontransparent. At the same time, the feeling of respect has a moment of inclination (*dioxis*) wherein the self who attempts to meet this demand of responsibility is first revealed to itself—"the self not in a general sense as knowledge of an ego in general but as in each case mine" (BP 137; GP 194).

BEING-TOWARD-DEATH: ANXIETY AND RESPECT

The objection might be made that although Heidegger's analysis of respect is important for illuminating Dasein's authentic selfhood, the fundamental disposition that determines Dasein's authentic self is the disposition of anxiety. I suggest, however, that Heidegger's discussion of respect in *The Basic Problems of Phenomenology* is a thinking further and clarification of his earlier analysis of anxiety. That this is the case can be seen by turning to the 1925 lecture course published as *History of the Concept of Time*.

In *History of the Concept of Time* Heidegger argues that authenticity must be grasped in the literal sense of "having itself for its own in intimacy with itself."[10] At the same time, he points out that such self-possession is only a modification of Dasein's immersion (*Verfallen*) in the world. Authenticity always carries immersion along with it. Insofar as *Verfallen* is a "flight of Dasein from itself," authenticity as the moment of individuation carries with it this flight. Clearly, from his earliest writings forward, Heidegger is rethinking the very notions of "self-possession" and "ownness."

Going further in this analysis, Heidegger argues that this flight can be understood as either a "fleeing" or a "falling back before something." Fleeing, he argues, is grounded in fear and is characterized by the flight from a definite object. Falling back before something characterizes Dasein's flight from itself and is given in the phenomenon of anxiety. Indeed, all fleeing has its ground in the more primordial flight in the sense of "falling back."

Like the feeling of respect, the disposition of anxiety is twofold: it contains the two moments of the "of-which" and the "about-which." Again, the moments are equiprimordial: one does not mediate the other. Heidegger argues that the moment of the "of-which" is the moment of Dasein's Being toward its uttermost and unsurpassable end, that is, its death. This is a "flight" in the sense of a "falling back before." Dasein falls back before its uttermost and ownmost end. And only in this falling back, this yielding, as it were, is Dasein concerned about its being.

This flight (*phuge*) underscores again the nonrelatedness of Dasein to its ownmost and uttermost end. Let us pause briefly to consider this discussion of Being-toward-death in *Being and Time*. Heidegger argues here that death is not something that one can actualize, nor is it a possibility that can be dwelled upon: "Death, as possibility, gives Dasein nothing to be 'actualized', nothing which Dasein, as actual, could itself *be*" (BT 307; SZ 348). If death is the possibility of the impossibility of existence, and, further, if Dasein cannot project upon its own death as a possibility of its being, then it must be the case that the individual Dasein cannot be in a relation with its own death. Death is the nonrelational, uttermost and absolute limit; it is absolute exteriority and it is nonintegrable.

Heidegger argues, therefore, that Dasein can only anticipate this uttermost possibility: "Anticipation turns out to be the possibility of understanding one's *ownmost* and uttermost potentiality-for-Being—that is to say, the possibility of *authentic existence*" (BT 307; SZ 349). Now in *History of the Concept of Time*, Heidegger argues that anticipation marks the flight of anxiety before death: it marks Dasein's falling back before this uttermost end, a falling back which opens up Dasein's authentic possibilities for Being-in-the-world. Thus, while death is Dasein's uttermost and *ownmost* possibility, the aspect of "ownmost" is called into radical question. That which is most my own is never my own; I am always falling back, falling away from that which is properly mine.

This is precisely why Heidegger insists that *Verfallen* (immersion, decay, falling apart) is an existential, and, furthermore, why there is no contradiction between Heidegger's earlier argument in *Being and Time* that *Befindlichkeit, Verstehen,* and *Rede* are inseparable structures of Dasein's authentic disclosure and his later argument that *Befindlichkeit, Verstehen,* and *Verfallen* are inseparable structures of Dasein's authentic disclosure. Rather than follow Pöggeler in drawing the conclusion that these statements are contradictory and, further, that there is no possibility of authentic discourse, we can read in them Heidegger's demand that we think *Rede* and *Verfallen* together. Indeed, the demand is to do more. Insofar as *Rede, Befindlichkeit,* and *Verstehen* are inseparable, it is not the case that there can be an authentic state of mind and understanding on the one hand, and on the other an inauthentic discourse, as if it were the case that Dasein would be authentic in staring mutely at its situation. If *Rede* must be thought with *Verfallen,* then *Befindlichkeit* and *Verstehen* also must be thought with *Verfallen.* This calls into question anything like the possibility of "pure" authenticity; or, at the very least, it calls into question any understanding of authenticity that is free from the shared realm of discourse. This is precisely the reason why Heidegger argues that authenticity is only a modification of *"das Man"* and, moreover, why Dasein, wrenched from the anonymity of *"das Man,"* remains essentially Being-with:

> As the non-relational possibility, death individualizes—but only in such a manner that, as the possibility which is not to be outstripped, *it makes Dasein, as Being-with,* have some understanding of the potentiality-for-Being of Others. (BT 309; SZ 350–51; emphasis added)

Anticipating death in the flight (*phuge*) of anxiety, Dasein determines itself in a codetermination of Being-with (*Mitsein*) wherein the indifferent and deficient mode of solicitude becomes emancipatory: the other is freed to be who he or she is in his or her potentiality- for-being.

Now we must recall that in *The Basic Problems of Phenomenology* Heidegger characterizes the moment in the feeling of respect wherein the self yields to the other as the moment of self-subjection or *phuge*:

> Respect has "something analogous at once" to inclination and fear. To understand this remark we may briefly recall that ancient philosophy already characterized practical behavior in the broader sense, orexis, by dioxis and phuge. Dioxis signifies following in the manner of pursuit, a striving toward something. Phuge signifies a yielding, fleeing, retreat from, striving away from. (BP 136; GP 193)

Significantly, in *History of the Concept of Time*, Heidegger uses the word *phuge* to characterize Dasein's falling back before its own end. The similarity in language with the later discussion of respect is striking:

> All fleeing is grounded in fearing. But not every falling back before something is necessarily also already a fleeing and so a being afraid.
>
> These two meanings are generally intermingled in the ancient concept of *phugē* and in the medieval concept of *fuga*, both of which we simply translate as "flight." (HC 283; PG 392)

Thinking together these two discussions of *phuge* is to think together the feeling of respect with Dasein's anxiety before its own death. To think these two discussions is to think Dasein's self-subjection (*phuge*) before the other with Dasein's falling back before (*phuge*) its uttermost end. In still other words, to think together these two discussions is to think Dasein's anxiety before death *as* Dasein's respect before the other. To stand resolutely in anticipation of one's ownmost and uttermost end is to act responsibly for-the-sake-of the other's potentiality-for-being. This is why Heidegger calls anxiety "uncanniness" (*Unheimlichkeit*). To be anxious before one's uttermost end is to be not at home, which means, to be responding to the other. And only in this position of uncanniness is Dasein's own being at issue.

HOBBES AND HEIDEGGER: THE ANTICIPATION OF DEATH

Of course, the anxious anticipation of death lies at the origin of modern political theory, namely, in the thinking of Hobbes. Pausing briefly to examine this "anticipation" in Hobbes is to grasp how radically Heidegger is challenging modern liberal political theory with its foundation in the inviolability of the subject and the right to self-preservation.

Briefly, Hobbes's understanding of the anticipation of death has its basis in his understanding of method, language, and motion. Insofar as his methodology looks to Galilean science, Hobbes argues that all of nature, including human nature, can be resolved into clear and simple elements. Language as well can be resolved into clear and simple elements, specifically, definitions: "So that in the right definition of names lies the first use of speech."[11] It is precisely Hobbes's nominalistic understanding of language that Heidegger calls into question in *The Basic Problems of Phenomenology*, a discussion that follows immediately upon Heidegger's discussion of the Kantian notions of respect and purposiveness. In this discussion, Heidegger critiques Hobbes's understanding of assertion and points out that Hobbes's theory of language breaks down insofar as it cannot account for the significative aspect of assertion—that for the sake of which the assertion is made.

As is well known, in Hobbes's thinking humans are atomic entities with a capacity for motion and a desire to keep moving. All movement, then, is self-interested. Because the individual is only interested in his or her own ability to keep moving and, moreover, because all other individuals have an equal ability coincident with an equality of hope to attain this end of continued self-movement, Hobbes argues that individuals are natural enemies. Therefore, each individual must *anticipate* destruction at the hands of the other, "seeking mastery of the persons of all men so long till he see no other power great enough to endanger him" (LE 99). Fearing violent death at the hands of another, the Hobbesian individual must anticipate means of self-preservation. Anticipation, then, includes both the fear of the other and the reckoning of how to avoid this threat. And, it is this twofold anticipation that founds the fundamental right of self-preservation:

> The right of nature, which writers commonly call *jus naturale*, is the liberty each man hath, to use his own power, as he will himself, for the preservation of his own nature; that is to say, of his own life; and consequently, of doing anything, which in his own judgment and reason, he shall conceive to be the aptest means thereunto. (LE 103)

This right to self-preservation, itself rooted in the anticipation of the violence of the other, is prior to and founds political obligation.

Contrary to this, Heidegger argues that Dasein is fundamentally Being-with (*Mitsein*). Dasein's anticipation of its ownmost and uttermost end is an anticipation of the ownmost and uttermost end of the other. As shown above, this anticipation is not marked by fear but by respect: Dasein's self-subjection is its yielding to the other, to a demand to act responsibly for the sake of the other's potentiality-for-being.

Here something like the Kantian moral law emerges. Death is the possibility of the impossible. To stand in anticipation before this uttermost possibility, which is to stand before the uttermost end of the other, is to let this possibility stand as a possibility:

> I have already indicated that the relationship of being to a possibility must be such that it lets the possibility stand as a possibility, and not such that the possibility becomes reality, perhaps by causing my own death in suicide. By suicide I surrender the possibility precisely as possibility; it is radically reversed, for it becomes a reality. The possibility is however just what it is only when it is left standing, that is, when it is left standing before us as impending. (HC 317; PG 439)

In other words, the relation between Dasein's being and the uttermost possibility of death calls for the inviolability of the possible. In a later essay, "Overcoming Metaphysics," Heidegger calls this "the inconspicuous law of the possible."[12] This law is "different from the will to will which forced the impossible upon the possible." This inconspicuous law of the possible demands that one act so that the impossible does not force itself, in the sense of a goal to be actualized, upon what must stand impending as the uttermost possibility. This is the law given both in the feeling of anxiety and the feeling of respect, which, I have argued, Heidegger thinks as the same. The inconspicuous law of the possible demands that one act so that the possibility of the impossible not be made actual. This law gives the "ground" of emancipatory solicitude: to let the death of the other be as its uttermost possibility so that the other is free to be in his or her authentic potentiality-for-being.

In conclusion: rather than understanding the authentic self from out of the sphere of an autonomous, willing subject—which, in turn, would be to understand "mineness" or "ownness" in terms of self-preservation (the inviolability of the subject)—Heidegger thinks authentic selfhood from out of Dasein's immersion (*Verfallen*) wherein Dasein always carries with it a flight from itself. This flight allows Heidegger to think the capacity to choose (which marks the authentic self) as purposiveness, for-the-sake-of. Dasein's purposiveness, its capacity to choose, is for the sake of the other in its Being-with (*Mitsein*). The authentic self is given only in responsible action wherein there is an authentic response to the other. To stand responsibly before the other is to stand before the inconspicuous law of the possible: the inviolability of the other.

Notes

1. For a discussion of this debate, see, among others: Jean-François Lyotard, *Heidegger and "the Jews"*, trans. Andreas Michel and Mark S. Roberts (Minneapolis: Univ. of Minnesota Press, 1990); Jean-Luc Nancy, *La Communauté désoeuvrée* (Paris: Christian Bourgois, 1986); Otto Pöggeler, *Martin Heidegger's Path of Thinking*, trans. Daniel Magurshak and Sigmund Barber (Atlantic Highlands, N.J.: Humanities Press, 1987); Jacques Taminiaux, "Poiesis and Praxis in Fundamental Ontology," *Research in Phenomenology* 17 (1987): 137–69.

2. I am indebted to Paul Davies, who first raised with me the question of Dasein's Being toward the other in its Being-toward-death. I am also indebted to Robert Madden who gave an extensive commentary on an earlier draft of this chapter.

3. Martin Heidegger, *The Basic Problems of Phenomenology*, trans. Albert Hofstadter (Bloomington, Ind.: Indiana Univ. Press, 1982), 133; abbreviated "BP." See original, *Die Grundprobleme der Phänomenologie*, GA 24 (1975), 189; abbreviated "GP."

4. Immanuel Kant, *Foundations of the Metaphysics of Morals*, trans. L. W. Beck (Indianapolis: Bobbs-Merrill, 1959), 56.

5. Michael Sandel, *Liberalism and the Limits of Justice* (Cambridge: Cambridge Univ. Press, 1982), 55.

6. Of course, as Sandel's argument points out, this is Rawls's starting point for his "original position," which, in turn, provides the foundation for Rawls's theory of justice. Insofar as Heidegger, in his attempt to think the basis of responsible action, rejects this "original position of autonomy," it would be most fruitful to consider something like a Heideggerian theory of justice and how this might challenge Rawls's theory.

7. Martin Heidegger, *The Metaphysical Foundations of Logic*, trans. Michael Heim (Bloomington, Ind.: Indiana Univ. Press, 1984), 185; abbreviated "MF." See original, *Metaphysische Anfangsgründe der Logik im Ausgang von Leibniz*, GA 26 (1978), 238; abbreviated "MA."

8. Martin Heidegger, *Being and Time*, trans. J. Macquarrie and E. Robinson (New York: Harper & Row, 1962), 160, emphasis added; abbreviated "BT." See original, *Sein und Zeit*, GA 2 (1977), 164; abbreviated "SZ."

9. Kant, *Foundations of the Metaphysics of Morals*, 47.

10. Martin Heidegger, *History of the Concept of Time: Prolegomena*, trans. Theodore Kisiel (Bloomington, Ind.: Indiana Univ. Press, 1985), 282; abbreviated "HC." See original, *Prolegomena zur Geschichte des Zeitbegriffs*, GA 20 (1979), 390; abbreviated "PG."

11. Thomas Hobbes, *Leviathan*, ed. Michael Oakeschott (London: Collier, 1962), 37; abbreviated "LE."

12. Martin Heidegger, "Overcoming Metaphysics," in *Nietzsche, Vol. II: The End of Philosophy*, trans. Joan Stambaugh (New York: Harper & Row, 1973), 110.

9

Metaphysical Presence:
Heidegger on Time and Eternity

Tina Chanter

INTRODUCTION

Heidegger's claim that the idea of presence dominates metaphysical thinking has been much discussed of late. Many contemporary critics are wary of embracing the idea of metaphysical presence. Their suspicion extends to several other traditional philosophical concepts to which that of metaphysical presence bears some relation. The concept of subjectivity, which construes the subject as masterful, controlling, and fully present to itself; the articulation of identity as fixed and determined by the self; the ideal of absolute truth—all these "metaphysical" ideas are, we are told, to be avoided, although there is little clarity about precisely what is wrong with them. This is true for those who have read and rejected the work of Jacques Derrida and his contemporaries, and moved on to something new. While rejecting deconstruction as passé, they nevertheless retain some of its terminology, often on the basis of a partial understanding of what they claim to have surpassed. This chapter is an attempt to elaborate the complex Heideggerian background of metaphysical presence, one of the ideas informing Derrida's relationship to the philosophical tradition.[1]

What exactly does it mean to say that the tradition of Western philosophy has been characterized by a metaphysics of presence? I address this question here by examining a text that has been rather neglected, although it has been published since 1954 and available in English translation since 1968. I consider the final sections of part 1 of *What Is Called Thinking?* where Heidegger deals with Nietzsche.[2] But I am not so much concerned with his interpretation of Nietzsche as with the light this discussion sheds on Heidegger's earlier, more systematic and protracted treatment of temporality in the Marburg period.[3] Not only *Being and Time* but also major portions of the lectures in that period were devoted to the relation of Being and time.[4]

There has been some debate about how the lectures—more or less contemporaneous with *Being and Time*—contribute to our understanding of temporality, but I am not aware of any studies specifically focused upon the problem of time in the brief but illuminating sections of the later lectures published as *What Is Called Thinking?*[5] It is often assumed that after the period of *Being and Time* the question of time was no longer a pressing question for Heidegger—except in his 1962 essay, "Time and Being." Therefore, if we can reconstruct Heidegger's discussion of Nietzsche so as to make clear his view of time, not only will we have made some headway in answering the question, What happens to time in the later Heidegger?; we will also have shown that the concerns of "Time and Being" are neither so elliptical nor so surprising as they have sometimes been represented.

Having situated the problem I want to address, the remainder of the chapter falls into four sections. In the first part I make some brief observations about Heidegger's account of temporality in the Marburg period. Next I discuss Heidegger's reading of Nietzsche's conception of revenge and the "it was" in *What Is Called Thinking?* The third part focuses on eternity, and the last on the problem of presence.

TIME: THE EARLY VERSION

The early Heidegger is generally considered to have challenged the common account of time by calling into question the predominant role traditionally given to the present. Instead of emphasizing the present, Heidegger's analysis of death in *Being and Time* offers an interpretation of time that treats the future as primordial. The significance Heidegger attaches to finitude, to the mortality of Dasein, to the fact that I must die, is at the same time a way of emphasizing the future. Heidegger's point is that the present is always lived within an understanding of the future; I am determined by my finitude in such a way that the present only makes sense in terms of an anticipated future.

However, it would be a mistake to take Heidegger's insistence upon the importance of death as simply a claim that the future, instead of the present (as the tradition thought), is primary. The primacy that the future holds for Heidegger is more complex than this. It is not simply a matter of changing the order of importance of the three ecstases of time: past, present, and future. Despite the primacy Heidegger accords to the future, he understands the future to be a "coming-toward-oneself from one's ownmost peculiar possibility" (BP 265; GP 375). Not only is the priority of the future based upon taking over oneself as possibility, but equally primordial are the other two ecstases of time. Coming-toward-oneself occurs within the unity of present, past, and future. Heidegger says: "Since the Dasein always comes-toward-itself from out of a possibility of itself, it therewith also always *comes-back-to* what it has been. Having-been-ness, the past in the existential sense, belongs with equal originality to the future in the original (existential) sense. In one with the future and the present, [the past as] having-been-ness first makes existence possible" (BP 266; GP 376; brackets in translation).

Heidegger, then, is not merely claiming for the future the priority traditionally accorded to the present. He is also disrupting the very idea that there can be only one ecstasis that is primary. The priority he accords to the future is, at the same time, a priority of the whole, of the totality of life. It is the unity of the three ecstases—past, present, and future—that is primordial for Heidegger. His point is that in understanding the present we have already, although implicitly, grasped the whole of time; we have understood the present as coming out of the past, as having a particular history, and as going toward a specific future. The present has built into it, as it were, a no-longer and a not-yet. It is the interconnectedness of life that is essential for Heidegger. To be sure, the special quality that the future bears is its relation to death. But death has a bearing on life as a whole, not just on the end of life. Indeed, the meaning of death is specifically not to be found at the end of life. For death is peculiar in that I can never experience it as such; I cannot know what death is directly, for to die is precisely to cease being there. The meaning of death is no less important, however, despite the unknowability of death as such. Death is that which individualizes Dasein; it is that which no other Dasein can take on for me. Although I can give my life for another, no one can ultimately take my death away from me. No one can stand in for me when it comes to dying. Finitude determines the character of my life from the start, whether or not I become explicitly aware of it, and whether or not I understand anxiety—the experience of which, according to Heidegger, brings me closest to death. It would seem, then, that the future has no inherent priority for Heidegger, except insofar as it recoils into a priority of the whole, the unity of past, present, and future.

REVENGE AND NIETZSCHE'S "IT WAS"

In *What Is Called Thinking?*—a series of lectures delivered by Heidegger between 1951 and 1952 at the University of Freiburg—there is an instructive discussion of temporality. Instructive, because it sheds retrospective light upon Heidegger's earlier explorations into the problem at hand, the problem of whether the future or present is considered by Heidegger to be the primordial ecstasis of time—or indeed whether it makes sense to privilege one temporal ecstasis over another. If the whole of time is precomprehended in understanding each particular mode of time—past, present, and future—what kind of priority could the future, or the present, or even the past, have?

The last two lectures in part 1 of *What Is Called Thinking?* include what is, in effect, a condensed account of the complexities that Heidegger discusses in great detail between the years 1925 and 1928, in *History of the Concept of Time, Being and Time, The Basic Problems of Phenomenology,* and *The Metaphysical Foundations of Logic.* The 1951–52 discussion of time in *What Is Called Thinking?* can be read in terms of what Heidegger later came to see to be the salient points in his earlier understanding of ecstatico-horizonal temporality.[6]

In part 1, lecture 9, of *What Is Called Thinking?* Heidegger discusses Nietzsche's description of revenge in *Thus Spoke Zarathustra,* as "the will's revulsion against time and its 'It was'" (WI 93; WH 37). Supplementing the idea of time as active and projective, the "it was" of time reveals the capacity time has for weighing us down, when, for example 'history catches up with us', as we say.[7] The weighing of time takes its toll. "Willing endures the contrary within itself as a heavy burden, it suffers from it—that is, the will suffers from itself" (WI 92; WH 37). For Heidegger, this way of thinking time is characteristic of the kind of thinking for which "that which is present has been regarded as what is" (WI 92; WH 36); in other words, the thinking that is naively oriented toward the present. This is precisely the kind of inadequate thinking that Heidegger wants us, in *What Is Called Thinking?* to "unlearn" (WI 8; WH 5) if we are to begin to learn thinking proper; it is "representational" thinking, the thinking that issues in "correct" but not "truthful" ideas. The distinction Heidegger is making is between *Wahrheit* and *Richtigkeit* (WI 38; WH 14). The "representational" way of forming correct (*richtig*) ideas is the way of revengeful thinking, the thinking that characterizes Nietzsche's last man (WI 72; WH 69), the thinking which the Overman has to overcome. This way of thinking hides the growing of the "wasteland" (WI 64; WH 63), issuing from the idea of humanity that unthinkingly takes for granted the conception of human being as "*animal rationale.*" This thinking still thinks in terms of objects and subjective states.

According to Heidegger, the "it was"—the passing of time— characterizes not only the past but the present and the future, too. All time passes. The passing of time is essential to our ordinary experience of time. It is a fundamental feature of time as thought by representational thinking. Revenge, perhaps in the form of nostalgia for the past, resents the passing of time and wants to hold on to time. According to the commonsense view of the world, the only reality that is accepted as correct, is what is, the actual, the extant. The "it was" is not just about the past; equally it concerns the present and the future. For time, all time, is essentially transitory; its nature is precisely such that it passes away.

It appears then that we will have to revise any impression that Heidegger's discussion of the "it was" of time is concerned primarily with the past and not with the future. We will have to revise it for two reasons: First, because we are now in a position to see that Heidegger understands Nietzsche's "it was" not to be solely concerned with the past but rather to permeate present and future, too. Second, because this idea of time characterized by passing is a representational idea of time. Heidegger will complicate the idea. He will introduce a question about the *possibility* of this representational way of thinking time.

Because we ordinarily tend to view time as that which passes, and yet we only accept as reality what is present, we resent the passage of time. Not wanting to let go of the past, we attempt (in nostalgia, for example) to preserve it. We are revengeful against the passing of time, which we are nevertheless powerless to prevent. "The revulsion of revenge remains chained to this 'It was'," says Heidegger. In the same way, "there lies concealed in all hatred the abysmal dependence upon that from which hatred at bottom always desires to make itself independent—but never can, and can all the less the more it hates" (WI 103-4; WH 42-43). To resent the passage of time is to remain determined by precisely that against which one objects most vehemently, and precisely to the extent of the violence of one's objection. Heidegger pushes further the tension contained in the representational idea of time: the idea of time both (1) as transitory or as that which passes away, ceases to be, and (2) as what must be present. He claims that metaphysics has failed to see the consequences of this tension: "Metaphysics leaves something essential unthought: its own ground and foundation" (WI 100; WH 40). In asking the question, What is being? metaphysics has already understood Being as present (*anwesend*): "Beings are more in being the more present they are...the more abidingly they abide, the more lasting the abiding is" (WI 101; WH 41). So time has been conceived in terms of Being, but in terms of "a totally specific interpretation of 'Being'— Being as being present [*Anwesenheit*]" (WI 102; WH 41). Furthermore, Heidegger goes on to say, "this interpretation of Being has been current so long that we regard it as self-evident." Heidegger will suggest why it can no longer be regarded as self-evident.

ETERNITY

The question for thinking, as Heidegger puts it in *What Is Called Thinking?* is the question, What *is*?— a question about the present as presence, or rather the "presence of what is present" (*Anwesen des Anwesenheit*) (WI 244; WH 149). The idea of time at the bottom of representational thinking is that "it is, in that it constantly is not" (WI 99; WH 78). Here, in the account Heidegger gives of the inadequacy of the metaphysical proclivity for understanding time on the basis of the now, he refers specifically to Aristotle's *Physics* (IV, 10-14) as the source of his interpretation. Aristotle's essay on time was a cornerstone of Heidegger's discussion of time in the lectures published as *The Basic Problems of Phenomenology*. Yet it is remarkable that Heidegger's critique of the Aristotelian tradition in *What Is Called Thinking?* barely mentions the future, that aspect which is so crucial for his earlier account. Even when he does mention the future in *What Is Called Thinking?* it receives no special treatment but is classed along with the other aspects or ecstases of time, past and present. This is because the determining feature of time, as it is usually represented, is not its futurity but its passing, the fact that it continually passes away. Time, as we say, waits for no one.

Not only is the future hardly mentioned in *What Is Called Thinking?*; only the briefest of references are to be found to death. Heidegger says, for example, that we are reminded of the "temporal" (*Zeitliche*) "when we are told that someone's 'time was up' " (WI 99; WH 78). Because time is not "a bundle in which past, future, and present are wrapped up together" (WI 96; WH 39), the future is taken simply to be another way in which time passes. "Time goes," says Heidegger. He continues:

> And it goes in that it passes away. The passing of time is, of course, a coming, but a coming which goes, in passing away. What comes in time never comes to stay, but to go. What comes in time always bears beforehand the mark of going past and passing away. This is why everything temporal is regarded simply as what is transitory. (WI 96; WH 39)

By interpreting the future, as well as the past and present, in terms of Nietzsche's "it was," Heidegger understands the future, Dasein's finitude, in terms of the fact that time passes away. The future seems to take on significance only as a further example of the passing of time. Heidegger says:

> This passing away is conceived more precisely as the successive flowing away of the "now" out of the "not yet now" into the "no longer now." Time causes the passing away of what must pass away, and does so by passing away itself; yet it itself can pass away only if it persists throughout all the passing away. Time persists, consists in passing. It is, in that it constantly is not. (WI 99; WH 78).

With this last thought we return to Aristotle's famous aporia, the classic paradox of time: time is what it is not.

Heidegger's argument rests upon the failure of metaphysics to acknowledge that while on the one hand it rules out the possibility of eternity—since it thinks of time as that which constantly passes away—on the other hand it tacitly appeals to eternity. For it is eternity that is implicitly the model for the now as constant presence, as abiding reality, which underlies the concept of time as that which passes away. Heidegger explains:

Since in all metaphysics from the beginning of Western thought, Being means being present [*Anwesenheit*], Being, if it is to be thought in the highest instance, must be thought as pure presence [*reine Anwesen*], that is, as the presence that persists [*die anwesende Anwesenheit*], the abiding present [*die bleibende Gegenwart*], the steadily standing "now" [*das ständige stehende "jetzt"*]. Medieval thought speaks of *nunc stans*. But that is the interpretation of the nature of eternity. (WI 102; WH 41–42)

The metaphysical idea of time thinks of Being as eternal, that is, as independent of time. But Being itself is assumed by the tradition to be present! Hence Heidegger asks the crucial question:

Is not this [the metaphysical] definition of Being ruled by the view of presence [*Anwesenheit*], the present [*Gegenwart*]—ruled, that is, by the view of time, and of a time of such a nature as we could never surmise, let alone think with the help of the traditional time concept? What about Being and Time? . . . Does this not show, then, that something was left unthought at the very core of metaphysics—something essential in the essential nature of Being? The question "Being and Time" points to what is unthought in all metaphysics. (WI 103; WH 42)

The guiding thought here is that the definition of Being is ruled by a view of time that "we could never surmise, let alone think, with the help of the traditional time concept." The very idea of presence that dominates the tradition, according to Heidegger, is informed by eternity. That is, it is informed by a static phenomenon, the idea of the now as *nunc stans*, an abiding now, which runs contrary to the essence of time as that which by its nature, being necessarily transitory, passes away. When Schelling thinks Being as "independent of time," as primal willing, he thinks it as outside of time, and thus as eternal. But, Heidegger asks, how can we conceive of eternity without being ruled by our understanding of time? What is eternity, except a present that never goes away? The difficulty is that since time is essentially what passes away, the traditional concept of time does not have available to it the means for thinking such an eternal presence. *The ground for metaphysics must remain unthought.* Being, as independent of time—that is, eternity—is ruled by a view of the present that is unthinkable. It is ruled by the contradictory notion of the present as unthinkable. It is ruled by the notion of eternal presence. Such a notion is unavailable to metaphysical thinking, which thinks time as passing away, and reality as what stays here, unchanging.

PRESENCE

What is left unthought *cannot* be thought by metaphysics. Although everything about the passing of time suggests motion, philosophers, in order to think this essential transitoriness, have in fact depended upon the static idea of the eternal: time is still understood, as in Plato, to be a moving image of eternity.

The basic question for metaphysics, Heidegger says, is, What is being? (*was ist das Seiende?*) (WI 100; WH 40). Because metaphysics asks about Being in this way—that is—with reference to beings—when it examines the nature of time, the question it asks about the truth of time is, What in time is truly in being? Now, whatever sense "in being" has, already interprets time, insofar as whatever is in being is taken to be *present*. The question as to the truth of time, or what time is present or is in being, receives the answer: the "now"; it is the now which proves to be in being, or to be present. The now is the truth of time. "But," says Heidegger, "each 'now' is in its present being by virtue of its passing" (WI 101–2; WH 41); for the very essence of time is its passing. Precisely what is present in time, as the truth of time, is only present insofar as it is also passing. So time both is— and it is not.

Heidegger observes, as we saw earlier, "The essential nature of time is here conceived in the light of Being and, let us note it well, of a totally specific interpretation of 'Being'—Being as present [*Anwesenheit*]" (WI 102; WH 41). Heidegger brings under scrutiny precisely how this interpretation holds, whereas metaphysical thinking not only regards this interpretation of Being, as Heidegger says, as "self-evident." Metaphysics, according to Heidegger, cannot even articulate this self-evidence because it does not pose the question of Being in a radical way. Heidegger claims that the "view of time" that rules the definition of Being as eternal, or as independent of time, as being-present, as a present now—this view of time cannot possibly be thought in terms of "the traditional time concept" (WI 103; WH 42); for that view presupposes the passing of time, or the notion that time does not stand still.

As we have seen, Heidegger points out that the concept of eternity underlies the idea of enduring presence. The eternal, or unchanging, cannot be thought within a time that passes. The problem for metaphysics is that it is caught within a circle: time is thought with the help of Being, but Being can only be thought with the help of time. The problem is the fact that metaphysics cannot acknowledge that asking about the nature of time always rules out in advance an unproblematical answer. This is because it asks its question on the assumption that time is a being, and because it has already understood Being in terms of "being present" (*Anwesenheit*). So when metaphysics asks about the nature of time, it asks about the Being of time; but in the very asking of the question it has already interpreted Being in terms of time and, moreover, in terms of a specific character or aspect of time: time as present.

Heidegger is at pains to point out that the tradition has neglected to give enough thought to the nature of presence as Being, and thus has not adequately thought through the difference between the presencing of the present and the presencing of absence.[8] Aristotle's indefinite postponement of the question as to whether or not time exists, and his consequent pursuit of the question as to the nature of time (which presupposes that time must exist in some sense) serves to confirm Heidegger's suggestion. To investigate the nature of time without having first decided whether time exists, not only takes for granted *that* it exists, but also assumes a particular type of existence, namely, the present-at-hand existence of a being.

At this point, before concluding, let me note that in order to develop the significance of the points made in this chapter, one would need to show the positive effects of Heidegger's claim that we cannot properly understand time by starting with an implicit appeal to eternity. There is only time to gesture, however inadequately, toward the consequences of Heidegger's rethinking of time in terms of the restlessness of the technological age.

In order to direct his readers toward a clearer understanding of the essence of technology, in his essay "The Question concerning Technology" Heidegger finds it necessary to elaborate precisely the problem we have addressed.[9] He suggests that the traditional understanding of essence, or that which is most real, has been thought as an enduring permanence. But the tradition has not acknowledged that such an interpretation of essence draws upon an unexamined and contradictory notion of time, namely, a kind of eternal presence. Heidegger suggests that the Platonic notion of Idea, for example, understands enduring only as "permanent enduring" (QT 30; FT 39). His own view is that "*only what is granted endures*" (QT 31; FT 39). He goes on to say, "That which endures primally out of the earliest beginning is what grants." What Heidegger means by "earliest beginning" is elaborated in terms of *Ereignis* in the essays "The Way to Language" (especially section 3) and "Time and Being," an examination of which must be left for another time.[10] What can be seen from these brief remarks, however, is that at the heart of the confusion that Heidegger claims to see in the traditional conception of essence conceived as endurance, is the problematic of time. Far from being left in abeyance, as is sometimes assumed, the relation between Being and time remains pivotal in the texts that follow *Being and Time* and precede "Time and Being."

CONCLUSION

We began by pointing out the problematical priority of futural Being-toward-death in Heidegger's early account of time. We have seen how the early emphasis upon Dasein's finitude leads Heidegger to a reconsideration of the relation between time and eternity.[11] Let us conclude by recalling Heidegger's suggestion that metaphysics leaves unthought the ground of its thinking. According to Heidegger, since metaphysics has consistently failed to raise the question of Being, it has also neglected to articulate properly the way it (metaphysical thinking) gains access to an understanding of time. Philosophers have understood the truth of time in terms of that which is most real. But what is assumed to be most real, most in Being, already interprets time. Reality, for the tradition, implies a sense of duration. The tradition therefore understands by time that which passes, but tacitly appeals to the constant presence of reality. By construing reality as some kind of enduring presence, the tradition implicitly assumes that time is modelled upon an image of eternity. Such an assumption, however, is inconsistent with its idea of time as transitory. Heidegger claims to have departed from the tradition insofar as he explicitly confronts the question of Being in relation to time. By demonstrating this confrontation, I hope to have clarified a number of points: first, why Heidegger finds the traditional way of understanding time inadequate; second, precisely how Heidegger himself understands time in the 1950s. The third point I have tried to clarify is the relation between time and Being in Heidegger's thinking, and how this problematical relation underlies his criticism of the Platonic conception of essence. Most importantly, I hope to have clarified the Heideggerian claim, to which appeal is often made but which is rarely elaborated, that Western philosophical thinking is dominated by an unexamined metaphysics of presence.

Notes

1. Although I deal with Heidegger's discussion of Nietzsche, it is not my purpose in this chapter to take up the question of whether Heidegger does justice to Nietzsche's conception of time. I restrict myself to clarifying the details of Heidegger's critique of the Western tradition of time in order to highlight the confusion he claims to find in the priority philosophers have tended to accord to the present.

2. Martin Heidegger, *Was heisst Denken?* (Tübingen: Max Niemeyer, 1954), hereafter abbreviated "WH"; *What Is Called Thinking?* trans. J. Glenn Gray (New York and London: Harper & Row, 1968), abbreviated "WI."

3. In his 1953 essay "Who Is Nietzsche's Zarathustra?" Heidegger makes clear how his reading of Nietzsche's conception of time as the "it was" relates to Nietzsche's "eternal recurrence of the same." "Nietzsche," he says, "thinks the three phases of time in terms of eternity as the constant now. Yet for him the constancy consists not in stasis but in a recurrence of the same"; in *The Eternal Recurrence of the Same*, trans. David F. Krell, vol. 2 of Heidegger, *Nietzsche*, 4 vols. (San Francisco: Harper & Row, 1974–1987), 211–33, p. 218; essay abbreviated "WZ." The essay is also translated by B. Magnus in *The New Nietzsche*, ed. D. Allison (New York: Dell, 1979), 64–79. Compare original, "Wer ist Nietzsches Zarathustra?" in Heidegger, *Vorträge und Aufsätze* (Pfullingen: Neske, 1954), 109; (abbreviated "WN"). The three phases of time to which Heidegger refers are specified by Nietzsche in *Also Sprach Zarathustra (Thus Spoke Zarathustra)* as "the today" (present), "one day" (future), and "formerly" (past). Heidegger regards Nietzsche as the "last metaphysician"; accordingly, he assumes that Nietzsche thinks revenge "metaphysically" (WN 114; WZ 223). Elsewhere Heidegger says, "Despite all his overturnings and revaluings of metaphysics, Nietzsche remains in the unbroken line of the metaphysical tradition when he calls that which is established and made fast in the will to power for its own preservation purely and simply Being, or what is in being, or truth." "The Word of Nietzsche: 'God Is Dead'," in Heidegger, *The Question concerning Technology and Other Essays*, trans. W. Lovitt (New York: Harper & Row, 1977), 53–112, p. 84; compare "Nietzsches Wort 'Gott ist tot'," *Holzwege* (Frankfurt am Main: Klostermann, 1972), 221.

4. Martin Heidegger, *Prolegomena zur Geschichte des Zeitbegriffs*, GA 20 (1979); *History of the Concept of Time*, trans. T. Kisiel (Bloomington: Indiana Univ. Press, 1985). Heidegger, *Sein und Zeit* (Tübingen: Max

Niemeyer, 1984); *Being and Time*, trans. J. Macquarrie and E. Robinson (Oxford: Basil Blackwell, 1980). Heidegger, *Die Grundprobleme der Phänomenologie*, GA 24 (1975), abbreviated "GP"; *Basic Problems of Phenomenology*, trans. A. Hofstadter (Bloomington: Indiana Univ. Press, 1982), ("BP"). Heidegger, *Metaphysische Anfangsgrunde der Logik im Ausgang von Leibniz*, GA 26 (1978); *The Metaphysical Foundations of Logic*, trans. M. Heim (Bloomington: Indiana Univ. Press, 1984).

5. Robert Mugerauer provides a detailed interpretation of *What Is Called Thinking?* in his book, *Heidegger's Language and Thinking* (Atlantic Highlands, N.J.: Humanities Press, 1988). Although he touches upon the theme of time (see pp. 71 and 74 especially), he does not develop it, and neither does he make any attempt to show the relationship between his reading of *What Is Called Thinking?* and Heidegger's earlier, more systematic treatment of it.

6. Whether or not it was Heidegger's explicit aim to rework the discussion of temporality in his earlier lectures, the parallels—and differences—between Heidegger's consideration of time in *What Is Called Thinking?* and the earlier work of the Marburg period are instructive, perhaps all the more so if Heidegger was not self-consciously either developing or deviating from his earlier views.

7. Alphonso Lingis, "A Time to Exist on One's Own," in vol. 6 of *Analecta Husserliana*, ed. A.-T. Tymeniecka (Dordrecht: D. Reidel Publishing Co., 1977), 31–40, maintains that Heidegger's interpretation of time is entirely active and projective. I am offering an interpretation of Heidegger that shows him to be more receptive to the weight of time, to time as a burden, in *What Is Called Thinking?* than Lingis suggests he is in *Being and Time*.

8. Martin Heidegger, "Zeit und Sein," in *Zur Sache des Denkens* (Tübingen: Max Niemeyer, 1969), 1–25, abbreviated "ZS"; "Time and Being," in *On Time and Being*, trans. J. Stambaugh (New York: Harper & Row, 1969), 1–24 ("TB"); see especially ZS 7; TB 7.

9. Martin Heidegger, "The Question concerning Technology," in *The Question concerning Technology and Other Essays*, 3–35; essay abbreviated "QT." "Die Frage nach der Technik," in *Vorträge und Aufsätze*, 13–45, abbreviated "FT."

10. Martin Heidegger, "The Way to Language," trans. Peter D. Hertz, in *On the Way to Langauge* (New York: Harper & Row, 1982), 111–32; "Der Weg der Sprache," in *Unterwegs zur Sprache* (Pfullingen: Neske, 1971), 241–67.

11. To suggest that Heidegger no longer appeals to Dasein's finitude in his later work would be an oversimplification. He does, of course, refer to death, particularly in thinking the relation that humans have as "mortals"

to the other members of the fourfold: earth, sky, and divinities. See, for example, "Das Ding," in *Vorträge und Aufsätze*, 163–81, esp. pp. 176–81; "The Thing," in *Poetry, Language, Thought*, trans. A. Hofstadter (New York: Harper & Row, 1971), 163–82. See also "Bauen Wohnen Denken," in *Vorträge und Aufsätze*, 145–62, esp. 150 and 159; "Building Dwelling Thinking,"in *Poetry, Language, Thought*, 143–61. My point is that death is no longer at the center of Heidegger's philosophy—at least not in the same way in which it directed Heidegger's earlier thinking. To develop this point, one would have to show how Heidegger's analysis of death must change for the same reasons that his analysis of temporality changes; for Dasein's finitude is the key to temporality in the early work. In *Being and Time* the question of time is raised in the context of Heidegger's questioning of Dasein as an entity with ontico-ontological priority. Far from being pushed aside, the problem of time, and with it the problem of death, proves that Heidegger's early framework of fundamental ontology is inadequate to it. Even if Heidegger would ultimately want to construe the problem of death in *Being and Time* as "letting death be," he has set up his enquiry into Being in terms that are in danger of collapsing the problem of death into a problem of Dasein's self-understanding. By taking as his starting point the ontico-ontological status unique to Dasein, Heidegger's questioning of Dasein's finitude in *Being and Time* is still dictated by the requirements of a strategy that would make explicit what is already implicit in the characterization of Dasein as a being whose Being is an issue for it.

10

Framing Redemption: Aura, Origin, Technology in Benjamin and Heidegger

Rebecca Comay

My remarks will be somewhat programmatic, leading in the direction of a possible "encounter" between Martin Heidegger and Walter Benjamin. I take as my starting point the historical encounter that failed to take place in the 1930s, a non-encounter whose failure was determined by the usual factors—Heidegger's indifference, Benjamin's rather allergic contempt—and which today calls for rethinking.

I have two reasons for suggesting that such a posthumous encounter is both necessary and urgent today. First, because Benjamin articulates in an exemplary fashion two strands of the ontotheological (or rather, onto-theo-technological) tradition that remain at once both most susceptible and yet most recalcitrant to Heidegger's diagnosis of "metaphysics" (also most recalcitrant to each other). I mean Marxism and Judaism. Two currents kept alive by Benjamin in their greatest possible tension—neither reconciled nor split apart—during the 1930s, which is to say at the historical juncture where both come to crisis (the one, perhaps, having been co-opted, the other on the verge of being, quite literally, annihilated) through the very political forces to which both Heidegger and Benjamin—in equally palpable, if no doubt opposite ways—were most subject. For this last reason alone, Marxism and Judaism represent two strands

139

in urgent need of redemption, *before we forget*—by assigning too quickly to metaphysics, thereby only continuing the unilateral work of metaphysics—just what they could offer.

Second, because precisely in mobilizing, in his own idiosyncratic fashion, the conceptual and ethical resources of these two subtraditions within "metaphysics," Benjamin promises to provide a kind of historical concretion or focus to Heidegger's thinking—both a date and a place—a focus which, I believe, might bring out some of the practical resources still latent (despite everything) in the Heideggerian system, resources still potent for politics today.

FACE-OFFS

To orient this discussion I would like to begin by bringing together two texts published the same year (1936): Benjamin's "The Work of Art in the Era of Its Technical Reproducibility" and Heidegger's "The Origin of the Work of Art."[1] Neither text is a response to the other, but in a sense surely both are a response to the same thing. It is no mere coincidence that, a year after Leni Riefenstahl had raised to an exquisite degree (had both raised and foreclosed) the question of art's political possibilities in the era of its technological reproduction, we find both Heidegger and Benjamin (by this time on opposite sides of the Rhine) offering parallel reflections on the political reality of the work of art today.

These are texts which in themselves and in context point to the extreme difficulty of simply splitting the differences between Heidegger and Benjamin as thinkers of technology and history. They are texts that beg to be read with and against one another, and yet which resist the more obvious terms of opposition.

For if it is tempting to pit Heidegger against Benjamin as spokespersons, respectively, of aesthetic autonomy and popular culture, or of disinterestedness and engagement—the "self-sufficiency" of the artwork pitted against the disseminating flux of the media, the disinterested (Kantian style) refusal of purpose pitted against the utilitarian insistence on practical ends, the apparent exclusion of scientific reason ("Science is not an original happening of truth") pitted against the apparent celebrations of "polytechnic" skill—this is not the debate I would like to stage today. I do not want to use these texts to rehearse the familiar enough debates between "high culture" and "popular culture"—a debate that even in its most sophisticated (which is to say, Adornian) version, is unproductive in that it leaves unproblematized much of what is at stake. In this instance such a debate would be severely distracted by the numerous red herrings that litter both texts (e.g., Heidegger's privileging of "great art," Benjamin's Brechtian enthusiasms; Heidegger's somewhat loaded appeals to autochthony, Benjamin's celebrations of the utopic displacement and mobility of the traveling image; Heidegger's example of the Greek temple, Benjamin's example of the movie theatre; Heidegger's mandarin tastes, Benjamin's somewhat studied anti-elitism, and so on). Nor do I want the discussion, at least not at the outset, to be determined by the rather loaded oppositional matrix which no doubt indeed also governs this nonexchange, in its biographico-geopolitical (and that means also, always, metaphysical) dimension: country versus city, Freiburg versus Paris, home versus abroad, German versus Jew, "inner emigration" versus exile, and so on.

It is not always easy to resist such a set of oppositions. For (on the one hand) does not Heidegger's very identification of art as an origin (indeed as *the* essential event of origination, "prior" to all production and all technological becoming)—unique, unrepeatable, unassimilable to all exchange—seem to privilege the very terms of reference Benjamin would have demolished under the name of *aura*? If aura, according to Benjamin's somewhat cryptic formulation, is defined by "the unique appearance of a distance, however close it may be," and if this uniqueness is further determined as a "presence in time and space, [a] unique existence, at the place where it happens to be" (KW 479, 475; WA 223, 220), Benjamin will have declared such a distance and such uniqueness to be authoritarian and coercive—fetishizing of transcendence, obfuscating of power, legitimating of tradition—and, finally, in any case, already rendered obsolete by the media. For what would seem to have been displaced or deposed by the advent of reproductive technologies, by Benjamin's account, would be just that singularity which marks "origin" as origin—erasing the ontological distinction between original and double, collapsing the temporal distinction between early and late, eliding the spatial distinction between here and there, thereby (suggests Benjamin) overcoming the social distinction between author and recipient, between "producer" and consumer, as between consumer and consumer (all this is what happens, or might happen, when photography is invented)—an effacement of hierarchy that would dethrone every privilege, shattering the tyranny of tradition, introducing a generalized proximity or "closeness," establishing for humankind a "sense" (I quote Benjamin silently quoting part 1 of *Capital* with exquisitely understated irony) "of the equality of [all] things."[2]

Leaving open room (on the other hand) for the potentially Heideggerian rejoinder that such a displacement of origin and effacement of hierarchy would, in their undialectical hastiness, only flatten the space of difference—replacing authority with mere indifference, thus diminishing the very scope of possible intervention. Leading one to wonder, in Heidegger's language, whether Benjamin's very celebration of such a displacement would not simply bespeak his final immersion in the realm of *Technik*—the celebration of the replacement of *Kultwert* with *Ausstellungswert* (cult value with exhibition value) only attesting to Benjamin's own dependence on the idiom of the *stellen* series. (And it would not be too hard to trace the ways in which the *stellen* morpheme in fact determines the whole of Benjamin's corpus.) And so—thus the accusing question would seem to follow—does not the cinematic victory of *Ausstellung* (as pure exhibitionality) not instantiate precisely, in Heidegger's terms, the very supremacy of the *Gestell*? Would not the reduction of the world to the indifferent object of pure vision (present, available, exchangeable, identical) involve precisely the culmination of the modern reduction of world to *Weltbild*? (That is to say—to recapitulate very briefly the Heideggerian symptomatology—the reduction to an object represented to and by a controlling subject (*Vorstellung*), "pursued" and "trapped" by the calculations of science (*Nachstellung*), "set up" by physics to "exhibit" itself as observable matter (*Aufstellung, Ausstellung*), "ordered" by humanity to render itself disposable on demand (*Bestellung*), "distorted" in its very visibility so as to "block" or "dissimulate" the possibility of authentic appearance (*Verstellung*), and so on?)[3]

And does not the contraction of social space resulting from the reproducibility of the image (Benjamin speaks of bringing things and people "closer") not invoke precisely that "frantic abolition of all distances" cited by Heidegger at the beginning of his essay, "The Thing"—where indeed the media will be cited as the proximate cause of the current exhaustion?[4] Or, to pose the question in somewhat different, but no doubt related, terms, does not the creation of a "distracted" public—Benjamin's rather Kracauerian description of the movie-going crowd finally released from the mesmerizing tyranny of the art fetish—does not this "distraction" come perilously close to that homogeneous dispersal described in *Sein und Zeit* (section 27) under the same rubric of *Zerstreuung*, that is to say, under the more general rubric of *das Man*?

And so on. But this is not where I want now to push these texts. For if it would be more or less mechanical to draw up a kind of ledger of the differences—targetting Heidegger, through Benjamin's eyes, as "pro-aura" (hence, reactionary), or, conversely, targetting Benjamin, through Heidegger's eyes, as "pro-*Gestell*" (hence, oblivious) (for the examples on either side could easily multiply)— this may not be the most productive way to proceed. The entanglement may indeed be more complex.

REGARDING AURA

For one thing, Benjamin's so-called ambivalence must at least be noted. It is not without irony, no less aching for being understated, that the post-auratic, post-cultic product is described by Benjamin in the very language of the commodity (this is surely at least one of the forces of the allusion to the "universal equality of things"). And it is not without irony that the distracted public, freed from the mesmerizing grip of an oppressive aura, is described in essentially consumerist terms: never too late to tune in, never too early to tune out, free, as Brecht insisted, to come and go, to switch the radio on and off,[5] ingesting, or, as Benjamin says, "absorbing" the product rather than being "absorbed" by it (note the options: eat or be eaten), distractedly rummaging about through the debris of modern culture to gather the scraps and leftovers of an exhausted epoch. It did not require Adorno's nagging (Adorno's word)[6] to remind Benjamin just what the effects of such distraction might be. Or, more precisely, what the cost. The epilogue alone—where Benjamin speaks most pointedly of fascism as being the aestheticization of politics which results when the destruction of aesthetic autonomy goes unaccompanied by changes in property relations—should itself warn against taking this essay to be in any sense an unmodulated celebration of the media.

It was perhaps as a result of Adorno's intervention that Benjamin, in his revised Baudelaire essay of 1939, was to register a certain dismay as he describes modern experience precisely in terms of a clammy sensation of proximity—the collapse of spatial distance through the frenetic jostlings of the crowded city, the collapse of social distance through the uniformities of wage labor, the collapse of temporal distance through the jerky accumulation of empty moments—in short, the catastrophic occlusion of auratic distance through the amorphous homogeneity of the given.[7] But it is neither opportunism nor duress that motivates this expression of dismay. In other texts, and without the editorial pressures of Adorno—texts written not only before and after but even indeed concurrently with the "Work of Art" essay—Benjamin had voiced a repeated elegy for the deteriorated aura. For if aura, in its institutionalized or "cultic" form, would seem to be guilty of just that authoritarianism which makes all culture, as Benjamin puts it finally, a place of barbarism,[8] it had also promised the utopia of a reconciliation beyond every domination and all control.

This is no doubt the point of Benjamin's alternative definition of aura as the perception of the object's ability to "return the gaze"—a definition that hints not only of the historical reconciliation with external nature (what Marx perhaps meant by the "humanization of nature," and what both Novalis's sense of auto-reflexion and Baudelaire's notion of *correspondances* elicit for Benjamin), but also of the social reciprocity between human beings, manifested perhaps especially in the space of erotic intimacy, with its peculiar blend of distanced nearness and the special reciprocity which marks its structure as that of care. Benjamin's oft-quoted formulation—a formula which Brecht, for one, found "pretty ghastly" and privately snubbed as "mysticism"[9]—could perhaps still do with some rereading.

> There is the expectation, when we look at someone, that the recipient of the gaze [literally, the one to whom it is given, *sich schenkt*] will return [*erwidert*] our look. When this expectation is met (which, in the case of thinking, can be attached equally to the mental gaze of attention or to the literal act of seeing), there is the experience of aura in its fullness. . . . The experience of aura rests on the transfer [*Übertragung*] of a response common in human society to the relationship between inanimate or [living] nature and man. The person who is seen, or who believes himself to be seen, returns the gaze [*Der Angesehene oder angesehen sich Glaubende schlägt den Blick auf*]. To experience the aura of a phenomenon means to invest it [*belehnen*] with the ability to look at us in turn [*den Blick aufzuschlagen*]. The findings/funds [*Funde*] of the *mémoire involontaire* correspond to this experience. (UM 646f; SM 188)

What is the sense of this economy? If looking is a "gift," what kind of gift would it be that would carry with it the expectation of a reciprocation or countergift? What kind of "transfer" would convey from humanity to nature the essential properties of social intercourse?

And whose projection, exactly, is this? Does the expectation of reciprocity begin with the looker or the looked-at object? How does the one who only "believes himself to be seen" manage to open his eyes to return a gaze which might not, in the first place, exist? From where would the "funds" of memory be replenished? If looking is always an "investment" (*Belehnung*) which assumes a returning dividend and even perhaps a supplementary surcharge (*Aufschlag*) on its contribution, how exactly would such an economy function? Or, to pose the question very simply: Is the auratic moment already inscribed within the restricted economy of restitution and exchange which marks the egological order of the Same? Is the reciprocity of the gaze subsumed within the totalizing order of appropriation and return-to-self—the narcissistic movement of Lacan's Imaginary, or what Levinas calls "*l'avidité du regard*"?[10] Or is a more "generous" (Levinas)—that is, more "general" (Bataille)—economy at play?

It is true that lurking behind the Baudelaire essay is the specular epistemology of German Idealism. In his *Kunstkritik* dissertation, Benjamin had already invoked the Romantic *topos* of nature's self-reflexive *Wiederspiegelung* in order to describe the mimetic doubling of every gaze. If, as Schlegel puts it, "everything that is thinkable, thinks itself," it follows, explains Benjamin, that every object is itself a subject, and thus that all cognition is already self-recognition. Or, as Novalis, echoing Empedocles slightly, puts it: "The eye sees nothing but an eye, the organ of thought nothing but an organ of thought." Or, more precisely, again Novalis: "In all the attributes with which we see the fossil, it sees us."[11]

But if we are tempted, according to our habitual assumptions, to read the Romantic epistemology outlined here as simply another expression of the metaphysics of the subject—the ego consolidating itself through a movement of reflexive totalization or mediated return-to-self through the Other—Benjamin would have it otherwise. By Benjamin's slightly idiosyncratic reading, the specularity and redoubling at work in nature's self-apperception would seem to exceed the closure of subjective (and indeed intersubjective) space. Eyeing the other's eye—eyeing the other *as* eye, or facing the other's face as a face—would in his reading (as Levinas might also remark) break the appropriative circle of identification of every ego and thus dislodge the very economy of the Same.[12]

In "On the Mimetic Faculty," Benjamin speaks of the decayed phylogenetic capacity of perceiving and "producing" affinities.[13] The auratic "transference" or expectation of a countergaze would appear to be cognate with the mimetic faculty of seeing external nature as one's own counterpart or "semblable." This is not—or not quite—the empathic fusion Benjamin will later denounce as the conformist minglings of historicism, and which he will relate to the homogenizing movement of the commodity.[14] Nor is it the "pathological suggestibility" that masks the "idle curiosity" (*Neugier*) of the empiricist.[15] There is in fact no time for such appropriative blurrings to take place. Nor is there the opportunity. For the "similarities" appear in a "flash," like a "flame," "flitting past" with the speed—and this is crucial—of writing or reading.[16] A "textual" moment would apparently have already invaded the immediacy of the living present. In their very incandescence, the "similarities" would seem to exceed all possible identification by rupturing the narcissistic interiority of the standing present and thereby, too, of the self-present self.

The specular economy would thus seem to be disrupted. The "funds" or "data" of the involuntary memory are "unique," remarks Benjamin, insofar as they are "lost to the memory which tries to incorporate them" (UM 647; SM 188). In "The Image of Proust" Benjamin remarks that Proust's "impassioned cult of similarity" leads him away from the prosaic day world of identity to the dream world of resemblances—a world "in which everything that happens comes up not in identical but in similar guise, opaquely similar to one another"[17]—a world in which a rolled-up stocking in the laundry hamper can be, for a child, both a "bag" and a "present." The child knows better, remarks Benjamin, than to try to hold on to the present, to make the gift, in fact, into something "present"—in this respect the Bataillean gift economy is in full swing—for the stocking is only waiting to be "instantaneously" unravelled or unrolled, just as (and indeed for the same reason) the "dummy" of the ego is waiting to be divested of its tangible selfhood "in order to keep bringing in that third thing, the image" (BP 314; IP 205).

The auratic image is, therefore, "a fragile reality" (BP 314; IP 205). Far from reinforcing the egological order of the visible through the self-confirming exchange of looks, such an image rather opens up a space of reciprocity that, paradoxically, undermines the very symmetry it renders possible. For the flash in its transience reveals the countergaze of the other to be in fact irreducible to the projective identifications of my own gaze. Like the "face" [*visage*] in Levinas which "looks back" at us (*qui nous vise*)[18] precisely in refusing to be thematized or captured in any eidetic optic and which therefore disturbs the superficial symmetry of the ethical "face-to-face," the auratic image similarly disrupts the specular scene of recognition and introduces perhaps a similar "curvature of intersubjective space" (cf. TI 291). In "A Small History of Photography," Benjamin remarks that the auratic countergaze of the Other is precisely not the coy "they're looking at you" of commercially photographed animals and babies which "so distastefully implicates the buyer."[19] Nor would it be the seductive mirroring he sees in the blank eyes of Baudelaire's prostitutes—eyes that "charm" precisely because, in reflecting everything, they simultaneously crowd and vacate the space of intimacy, substituting for the distanced nearness of erotic love the claustrophobic remoteness that Benjamin calls *sex* (UM 647; SM 189). Or, as Benjamin puts it, with telling precision—and with an almost Heideggerian pathos: "In eyes that mirror, the absence of the looker remains complete. It is precisely for this reason that such eyes know nothing of distance" (UM 648; SM 190).

Thus the *Projektion*[20] or *Übertragung* (UM 646) from man to nature is not the imperialistic transfer it might appear to be. Nor would the "metaphor" (if that is indeed the word for it) achieve the totalizing adequation of the transposed terms. Indeed, it is ultimately uncertain from which direction the alleged transfer comes. For if the auratic perception of nature's gaze involves a humanization, or perhaps, still better, a socialization of the natural, Benjamin carefully resists the obvious inference. That is, that a massive anthropocentric subsumption is at work. Despite the humanistic overtones of Benjamin's description, closer scrutiny suggests that we should not take for granted just what either *man* or *nature* have come to mean.

In a letter of 1940,[21] Benjamin rejects Adorno's suggestion that the auratic experience of a "humanized" nature involves simply the recognition of the "forgotten human residue in things"[22]—that is, the reified traces of human labor that have been obscured by commodity fetishism. Or rather, he suggests not that this Marxist interpretation is incorrect but simply that it is insufficiently radical. If "all reification is a forgetting" (to quote Adorno's familiar formula), what Adorno himself seems to forget, according to Benjamin, is that there is a forgetting even prior to the reification of labor through the occultation of its social form. Subtending and thus, perhaps, subverting—at the very least extending—the Marxist narrative of the Fall as the alienation of labor (objective genitive) is, on Benjamin's reading, the biblical narrative of the Fall as the alienation *by* labor, that is, the alienation *of* labor (subjective genitive)—in other words, alienation *as* labor.

The experience of the aura would thus appear to be anterior even to the Marxist utopia of unalienated labor and thus both to condition and to exceed its visionary hope. Just as the tree and the bush are not the product of human "making," writes Benjamin to Adorno, "there must be something human about things which is not the result of labour"—an affinity which is based, no doubt, on the "common origin" or shared physical createdness of both human and nonhuman nature, and which thus both precedes and exceeds the productive order of work as such.[23] The "mutual attraction of all created things" would take place in a "sphere deeper" than that of labor.[24] According to Benjamin's reading of Genesis, this latter productive order, even in its nonalienated state, would already be the result of a decline or Fall—the Fall from the Adamic naming of the animals to the "prattle" of signs, the Fall from noncoercive cohabitation to "the arbitrary rule over things"—and in this sense the reification of labor in commodity fetishism would be already a second-order decline, the Fall of a Fall, the reification of reification, or, perhaps—to speak Heideggerian— the forgetfulness of a forgetfulness.[25]

For if labor as such is a product of forgetfulness or of "original sin"—a loss of the primal affinity between the speechless "language of things" and the Adamic language of naming[26]—the reification of labor in commodity fetishism would be simply a doubling or compounding of that sin. For in occluding the very process of labor, it would constitute a forgetfulness of that original forgetfulness which instituted the regime of work as such. In "Franz Kafka," Benjamin speaks of forgetting as a "distortion" (*Entstellung*) of both space and time, a twisting of the "care" (*Sorge*) of the family man into the hunchbacked deformities of wage labor, a redoubling of primal guilt (*Schuld*) into the criminality of the everyday. He quotes Willy Haas commenting on the nexus of guilt and accusation that informs the structure of the *Trial*: "The object of this trial, indeed, the proper hero of this incredible book is forgetting, whose main feature . . . is that it forgets itself."[27]

The layered reminiscence at work in the (re)experience of the aura thus exceeds the egocentric grasp of a humanistic self-consciousness and indeed points to a humanity beyond human self-production and control. If, indeed, *humanity* is still the word for it. In his essay on Karl Kraus, Benjamin speaks of the "theological" quality of *tact*. "Tact," explains Benjamin, would be the "ability to treat social relations, while not departing from them, as if they were natural, indeed as paradisiacal relations"[28] (note how this formula would apparently reverse the direction of auratic "projection" as defined by the Baudelaire essay), culminating in the "more real humanism" which Benjamin sees announced by Kraus. This new humanism heralds not a "new man" (*neuer Mensch*) but rather a "nonhuman," a "monster" (*Unmensch*). Such an "inhuman" humanism would displace the "cosmopolitan rectitude" projected by bourgeois idealism, with its inherent spiritualization of the natural and its essentialization of *homo sapiens* (KK 363; KR 271). "Humanity" would receive its materialist determination.

But such an anti-humanist determination of *das Menschliches* would not involve a naturalism along biologistic or organicist lines. For "nature" too is being refunctioned. If the naturalizing movement of tact would "win back" nature in making it the "answer" to human criminality (KK 340; RE 245)—hence Kraus's fondness for dogs and other animals—Benjamin resists the temptation to turn "nature" into a new foundation. In his Fuchs essay, he severely reproaches the vulgar Marxist tendency to derive historical development from natural laws—a tendency he relates to the organicist aesthetics of "living form" and sees as culminating in the ideological productions of Social Democracy, with its familiar appeals to spontaneity and inevitability, and its Darwinist representations of social change.[29] In "Zentralpark," he speaks of the curious "contradiction" in Baudelaire between the "theory of natural correspondences and the renunciation of nature" (ZP 658). "How is this to be resolved?" asks Benjamin.

Answer: it cannot. For if Baudelaire's theory of *correspondances* involves establishing "similarities" between the human and the natural, Benjamin insists that this would not involve an idealization of the organic. Unlike traditional efforts to spiritualize humanity by seeking a "warranty" or "security" in external nature (ZP 680), Baudelaire himself—urbanized, dandified, artificer par excellence—seeks rather to problematize any essentialism of either humanity or nature by means of an allegorical "destruction of the organic" (ZP 669). He thus undermines the economic "community" with nature which the notion of *correspondances* would at the same time render possible. "His dream . . . declines community with earthly nature and gives itself over to the clouds" (ZP 680).

But then the *Übertragung* or transfer from the human to the natural would be less a simple carrying over or vertical transmission than a vertiginous transition in which neither pole remains intact. In his essay "The Task of the Translator," Benjamin insists on the radical circumscription of the human within the sphere of the "unforgettable."

> Certain relational concepts retain their good, indeed even their best meaning when they are not immediately and exclusively referred to humanity. Thus one could speak of an unforgettable

life or moment even if all men had forgotten them. If the essence of such events demanded that they not be forgotten, that predicate would not be false, but rather would be a demand not fulfilled by men, and no doubt also a reference to a sphere in which it would be fulfilled: the remembrance of God.[30]

"HOW THINGS WITHSTAND THE GAZE!"

No *theoria* could therefore cast or catch the auratic glance at or of the Other. Vision would indeed here reach its limit. For this reason, no doubt, Benjamin speaks equally of the aura as something "breathed,"[31] smelled (BP 323; IP 214), and even heard, read, and spoken, as with the "nonsensuous similarities" in every language (MV 212; MF 335). He remarks that Kafka himself was no "seer": "Kafka listened to tradition, and he who listens hard, does not see."[32] The phenomenal order as such would appear to be subverted. Or rather—since it is indeed for Benjamin explicitly a question of a quasi-Platonic "saving of the phenomena" (or, as he also puts it, a question of capturing the phenomenal in and as the noumenal)[33]—it is perhaps more exact to speak of a kind of phenomenality beyond the phenomenological. Beyond the self-evidence of eidetic vision (*Schau*), it is a movement to an opaque translucency that both conceals and reveals the Other precisely by responding to its prior claim. If "knowledge," as Benjamin insists, is "possession," then "truth," in contrast, would resist the appropriative order of intentionality and exceed the interiority of every ego. Truth "evades every projection [*Projektion*] into the realm of knowledge" (DT 209; GT 29). Beyond the projective phantasms of the specular subject, the auratic "projection" (*Übertragung*) would outstrip every visualization and hence all possession and control.

> The being of ideas absolutely cannot be thought of as the object of an intuition [*Anschauung*], even of intellectual intuition. For even in its most paradoxical transcription [*Umschreibung*], as *intellectus archetypus,* intuition does not participate in the mode of givenness peculiar to truth, a givenness that remains withdrawn from every kind of intention.... Truth is the death of intention. (DT 216; GT 35–36)

Or, to evoke again only one of the many quasi-Heideggerian formulations that could be mobilized here: "Truth is not an unveiling that destroys the mystery, but rather a revelation that does it justice" (DT 211; GT 31). Such an aletheic movement would involve the restorative but radically finite revelation which constitutes the proper "rhythm" of original disclosure. "That which is original," remarks Benjamin, "is never revealed in the naked and manifest existence of the factual" (DT 226; GT 45). Such a movement beyond facticity would exemplify the radically nonempiricist materialism or the antiphenomenological phenomenology of Benjamin's auratic vision. Or perhaps, to use a term of Goethe's that Benjamin liked well enough, we might speak of a "tender empiricism" (BK 60).

But it is not only the evidence or "givenness" of phenomenological intuition that would have been subverted by the fragile image of the auratic "gift." Equally subverted would be the greedy libidinal gaze of Lacan's Imaginary—the narcissistic search for confirmation through the (m)other's mirroring gaze—with its familiar appropriative structures and its specular attachment to the Same. Such translucency would have been (always, already) interrupted by an absence even prior to the institution of the symbolic order and to the establishment of the paternal law.

"How things withstand the gaze!" comments Benjamin, in "surprise," in 1932, while taking notes on a hashish trip. The drug trance had induced a feeling of familiarity so overpowering as to suggest that "all men are brothers." "I saw only nuances, yet these were the same." Gazing at a newspaper clipping, he had read that one "should scoop sameness [*das Gleiche*] from reality with a spoon." The cobblestones of Marseille had become like "bread" to his hungry eyes (HM 414–15; H 142–44). Even in the face-to-face of the hallucinatory encounter, the gaze would be interrupted at the point of being returned. In "A Small History of Photography," Benjamin describes the initial shyness of the early subjects, how they "drew back" at the moment of being photographed, how their very withdrawal constituted their essential "look" (KG 380; SH 251).

It is an absence defined by time as such. For the distance of aura is defined precisely in terms of "a strange weave of space and time" (KG 378; SH 250)—a weave that would introduce precisely the delay of memory and thus the irreducible alterity of an (again, to speak Levinasian) absolute past. In his reading of Baudelaire's sonnet "Correspondances" ("L'homme y passe à travers des forêts de symboles/ Qui l'observent avec les regards familiers"), Benjamin insists that the "*regards familiers*" returned in the temple of nature are "burdened with distance" (UM 649; SM 190). The face-to-face reduces to the "'*tête-à-tête sombre et limpide*' of the subject with itself"

(ZP 659), both familiar and radically defamiliarized—no doubt the Freudian *unheimlich* would be the word for it: the unfamiliar familiarity or "opaque similarity" that marks the temporal order as the order of repetition itself. Such unfamiliar familiarity would disrupt the familial order of proximity—Baudelaire's satanic snobbery, remarks Benjamin, was to disrupt the "coziness" (*Gemütlichkeit*) of every dwelling (ZP 675)—opening experience to the "temporal abyss" (ZP 679) that structures every time.

In Baudelaire, writes Benjamin, "there are no simultaneous correspondences, such as were later cultivated by the symbolists" (UM 640; SM 182). The "murmur of the past" would have already invaded the interiority of every present, making every life a "*vie antérieure*" to itself, rendering problematic any notion of a final return-to-self and thereby disrupting the restricted economy of the home. For this reason, strictly speaking, there can be no "nostalgia" for the aura, for it had never in the first place offered itself in the immediacy of a "lived experience." Its presence would have been indeed just the absence that marks the order of time itself. Its loss or *Verfall* would have thus been quite inevitable. For in a sense aura is nothing other than the structure of every loss. Its loss would be therefore the loss of loss—a dissimulation of dissimulation or a decline of decline. Its decline or fall would be interior to it or "original," rather than accidental and external. For its finitude (to use Heidegger's language) would have already determined its destiny as the self-effacing destiny of the trace.

"Refinding" it, therefore, would involve the "elegiac happiness" which defines *le temps retrouvé*. Rather than exulting in the repossession of a mislaid property or past immediacy, such happiness would involve the abyssal and transcriptive movement of time itself. Proustian experience, writes Benjamin, reveals only the truth that there never was an "experience":

> [Proust] is pierced by the truth that none of us has time to live the true dramas of the existence that are destined for us. This ages us. Nothing else. The wrinkles and lines on our faces are the entries of the grand passions, vices, perceptions that called on us—but we, the masters [*wir, die Herrschaft*], were not at home." (BP 320; IP 211)

Such is the uncanny "too late" that marks the structure of lived time as such. It is a lateness that disrupts the inevitability of every destiny, dislodges every claim to "mastery," disappropriates every comfort

of being "at home." Memory, then, assumes the involuntariness—
ungewolltes Eingedenken, Proust's *mémoire involontaire*—of a seizure
without closure. Reminiscence becomes the recapitulation of what
never did, in the first place, take place. For Benjamin, such a loss
had the power to counter every form of nostalgia and fuelled the
impatience for revolutionary change.[34]

For the very asymmetry of the auratic experience—its non-
reciprocal reciprocity—opens up desire to a vertiginous intensity that
threatens the stable economy of every regime. Such desire, fuelled
by the uneasy presence of what cannot be possessed as such, exceeds
the scope of all consumption and therefore challenges the (Imaginary,
or equally capitalist, or for that matter "metaphysical") order of
property and control. Benjamin remarks that the auratic distance of
the artwork—like the flower, and unlike the commercial photo-
graph[35]—fulfills a desire which it simultaneously thereby further
stimulates.

> The painting we look at reflects back at us [*an einem Augenblick
> wiedergeben*] that of which our eyes will never be sated. That
> which fulfills the [original] desire. . . would be the very thing
> on which this desire incessantly feeds. What distinguishes
> painting from photography is therefore clear. . .: to the gaze
> which can never be sated with a painting, photography is rather
> like food for the hungry or drink for the thirsty. (UM 645; SM
> 187)

Such desire—both revolutionary and erotic—has the desperate
impatience which refuses every partial nourishment and thus can
never be bought off by the consolations of available goods. This is
not the greedy craving of the consumer. As a desire whose very
satisfaction is to refuse all finite satisfaction—corresponding thus
roughly to what Bloch called "the other, transcendental hunger"—it
would break through the comfortable horizon of the culinary, that
is, the restricted circuit of self-preservation that defines Marx's "realm
of necessity." It would be a hunger so aching it would stretch towards
the infinite. (Levinas speaks of a "lack inconvertible into needs, and
which, being beyond plenitude and void, cannot be gratified" [TI 155].
Bataille speaks of the "avidity not to be satisfied.")[36] Unlike the Social
Democrats who gathered both past and future into the "granaries
of the present" (EF 475; F 358)—reducing the eschatological order
of time to the stable present of a standing reserve—and unlike their
historicist counterpart, Nietzsche's "spoiled idler" gorging in the

garden of knowledge (BG 700; PH 260), Benjamin's revolutionary has the simultaneously ascetic and voracious desire which grows only stronger in being satisfied and hence resists accommodation to any regime.

This is not an otherworldly denial of the body and its appetites. If Benjamin speaks of a simultaneous "promise and renunciation" (UM 649; SM 190), the point is not abnegation for its own sake but precisely the radical sacrifice that promises to free the body for pleasures unconceivable within the restricted economy of self-reproduction, with its modest hedonism and its pregiven needs.

A "Marxist" defence of aura is thus both plausible and suggested. In the *Passagen-Werk*, Benjamin remarks on the link between libidinal and political potency (PW 457). Marx had already commented in 1844 that sexual relations would always be an index of the political possibilities of the day. Benjamin speculates that the human upright posture made face-to-face—that is, auratic—orgasms for the first time possible, enabling at once both (and for the same reason) erotic fantasy and the utopian yearning for social change (EF 497; F 378). He goes on to suggest that the decline of erotic/auratic eye contact would imply the dissipation of the revolutionary urge as such. "The distance which, in the eyes of the beloved, draws the lover on, is the dream of a better nature. The decline of aura and the withering of the fantasies of a better nature—owing to the defensive position of the class struggle—are one and the same. The decline of aura and the decline of sexual potency are in the end the same" (PW 457). Poetic aura creates just this urgency. Its very distance or withdrawal would provide the utopian space in which longing for a better future arises precisely in the experience of lost time: "a long past moment in which the future nests so eloquently that we can rediscover it in looking back" (KG 371; SH 243).

Marxist? Perhaps, equally, Heideggerian? The special quality of this eros still needs to be examined. In his Kraus essay, Benjamin speaks of the peculiar "withdrawal" (*ziehen*) underlying erotic "seeing" (*sehen*)—"how the beloved grows distant and lustrous, how her minuteness and her glow withdraw" (KK 362; KR 268)—a withdrawal that turns love itself into the infinite "gratitude" (*Dank*) that renounces all satisfaction and finds its promise in the pure "name." In *Was heisst Denken?* Heidegger writes of the special tug exerted by the receding ebb of being—a "draw" (*Zug*) which attracts or draws thinking on (*anziehen*) in its very withdrawal (*Entzug*)—creating the ecstatic structure of temporality by carving out a future in memory's wake.

What withdraws from us draws us along by its very withdrawal, whether or not we notice it immediately or at all. Once we are drawn into the withdrawal [*in den Zug des Entziehens gelangen*], we are—but altogether unlike migrating birds [*Zugvögel*]— drawing toward what draws us by its withdrawal [*was uns anzieht, indem es sich entzieht*]. When we, being so drawn, draw towards what draws us, our essence is already stamped as "drawing towards..." [*auf dem Zuge zu...*].[37]

Benjamin writes similarly of being drawn into the wake left by the awakening of the auratic gaze. "Wherever a human being, an animal, or an inanimate thing thus invested [*belehnt*] by the poet lifts up its gaze, it draws [*zieht*] him into the distance. The gaze of nature thus awakened dreams and pulls the poet after its dream" (UM 647n; SM 200n).

CONSTELLATIONS

But what of aura in the age of technical reproduction? How would one face the radical effacement of the face-to-face?

Heidegger announces the "turning" at the heart of *Technik* as the intensifying "flash" (*Blitz*) of repetition. It is worth recalling that enigmatic passage in "Die Kehre" where Hölderlin's apocalyptic phrase in *Patmos*—"Wo aber Gefahr ist, wächst das Rettende auch"— is parsed out and elaborated as pointing to the catastrophic moment of memory as such, in both its interiorizing and reversing tendencies.[38] Here forgetfulness, redoubled as the forgetfulness of an original forgetfulness or the concealment of Being's concealment, "turns inward" (*kehrt ein*) in its intensity and thus awakens the spark of a future memory.

Here the *Gestell* reaches its climax and thereby pushes towards its own displacement. In the homogeneities of the modern epoch, the metaphysical drive to presence comes full circle and thus has the potential to invert itself. The technological ordering of the world to full availability (*Beständigkeit*) simultaneously perfects and subverts the very law of objectivity, such that, as Heidegger puts it, "what stands by in the sense of standing-reserve [*Bestand*] no longer stands over against us as object [*Gegenstand*]" (FT 16; CT 17). In the flattened space of the *Gestell*, where even the "subject" has become reduced to a standing reserve of "human resources" (the "challenger" is in turn "challenged"), the subject-object relation defining modern metaphysics reaches its limit and in turn, suggests Heidegger, comes to erase itself.

For Heidegger, the full experience of our homelessness involves the defamiliarization or uncanniness that (from *Being and Time* on) marks repetition as the site of difference. To recognize this homelessness would be precisely to experience the withdrawal of Being as the essential condition of our historicity. This is essentially what Heidegger means when he speaks of stepping back from *Technik* to the essence of *Technik*. To experience the *Gestell* as a "destining of revealing" (FT 25; CT 25) would be to "hear the claim" that speaks in the modern framework.[39] To experience the mutual challenging of man and Being under the imperative of calculative ordering would be to recognize that the confrontation (*sich stellen*) in fact derives from a prior imbrication or "mutual belonging" (ID 33/97): the specific mutuality of "man" and Being which defines the *Konstellation* of the modern age.

From *Ge-stell* to *Kon-stellation*: on such a minute displacement the apocalyptic force of history would seem to turn. For both Heidegger and Benjamin, such a constellation, like every constellation, would find its peculiar destiny in the encounter between the "most recent history" and what is primordially past. For both thinkers, such an encounter would contract the historical continuum into the radical intensivity of the "moment"—a political moment, according to Benjamin—cutting through the apparent homogeneity of "tradition" with the apocalyptic closure of first and last things. To recognize even the *Gestell*, in Heidegger's terms, as a "destining of revealing," would be to grasp the hidden unity determining the history of Being as such. A "straight line of admirable simplicity," remarks Heidegger at one point;[40] elsewhere he speaks of a tangle of many loose threads.[41] To hear the "claim of Being" in the modern "framework" would be precisely to hear what is primordially "early" in the radically new.

For Benjamin, such historical contraction defines the peculiar temporality of the "dialectical image." He writes of the peculiar layered quality of Kafka's metamorphic memory: "everything forgotten mingles with what has been forgotten of the prehistoric world" (FK 430; KA 131). In the *Passagen-Werk*, such mingling reveals the "secret affinity" (PW 1045) between the phantasmagorias of modernity and the archaic prehistory of myth—an affinity which, supervening between two oblivions, opens memory to a radical future. To experience the *Gestell* as a "destining of revealing" (to return to

Heidegger's idiom) would be precisely to glimpse the hidden affinity between modern *Technik* and its precursors in the history of Being. Such an affinity would refer this latest forgetfulness to the primal forgetfulness that inaugurated the regime of metaphysics as such. In the space between these two forgetfulnesses, thinking would indeed achieve a kind of memory. Such a memory would be free of all nostalgia: freed, as Heidegger puts it, from a "thinking back" to a "thinking forward which is no longer a planning" (ID 41/106). Freed, in Benjamin's terms, from historicist retrospection to a future more radical than all utopian blueprints and all progressive formulas of social change.[42]

In such a "constellation" the *Gestell* both perfects and has the means to surpass itself. The imbrication of Being and thought is indeed a form of identity in which "man's" complicity—but thereby his greatest hope—can be brought to light. In the *Ereignis* or "appropriation" of "man" by Being—but equally of Being by "man"— what had been passively suffered in unconscious complicity becomes explicitly grasped just *as* complicity. If what is most dangerous about the danger is, as Heidegger puts it, that "it is not experienced *as* the danger"—such is the ultimate meaning of the "forgetfulness of forgetfulness"—*Ereignis* is the danger that comes to mark itself reflexively "as danger" (TK 37–40; QT 37–41). Much like Benjamin's dream about dreaming which strangely prefigures its own awakening (PW 492), *Ereignis* involves an "awakening from [*aus*] the oblivion of Being to [*zu*] the oblivion of Being" (SD 32; TB 30). An "active forgetfulness," in Nietzsche's sense.

Such a turn from a prereflective submission to technology to the "quasi-transcendental"[43] grasp of its "essence" involves, for Heidegger, an epistemological turn as well. It is a turn from a contemplative or eidetic "looking" to a radically insecure "glancing": from the representational grasp of the world as *Weltbild* to the glimpse of a prior "lighting." This fragile illumination occurs in a region prior to the theoretical apperception of every object, and simultaneously determines and undermines the latter's possibility. "Everything depends," writes Heidegger, "on catching sight of [*erblicken*] what comes to presence in *Technik* instead of simply staring [*starren*] at the technological" (FT 32; CT 32).

But in such a turn—corresponding roughly, in Benjamin, to the movement from the acquisitive gaping of the "historicist" to the momentary grasp of the "historical materialist"—the very direction of vision becomes strictly undecidable. In the sudden "flash" of

Ereignis, the glance in fact *glances back* (strictly speaking, the real meaning of "glance" contains just this tropic quality, as in the beam of light glancing off or back from a reflective surface), a redoubling that exceeds the specularity of intersubjective space. Thus Heidegger etymologizes *Ereignis* as *Eräugnis*—"owning" as a kind of "eyeing"— a seeing that precedes all eidetic vision and in which seen and being seen become, in fact, quite intertwined.[44]

"Insight [*Einblick*] into that which is," writes Heidegger in "Die Kehre," is not that transitive or unilinear "inspection" that habitually determines our relation to the ontic—not an *Einsicht* into *das Seiende*—but is rather the intransitive "in-flashing" (*Einblitz*) in which man, seeing, is equally seen (K 44f; T 46f). In such an epiphanic moment, man is caught sight of (*erblickt*) by that which he catches sight of (*blickt*)—beamed down or "struck" by the very flash with which Being reveals itself and thus makes its greatest claim. In *Der Satz vom Grund,* Heidegger distinguishes the ontic seeing (*Sehen*) which passes transitively from subject to object from a prior ontological glancing (*Blicken, Erblicken*). The intensive prefix *er-* no doubt says it all. To glance at something (*erblicken*), he remarks, is "to glance at that which in the thing seen turns its glance to us [*anblickt*]." "We see too much," he adds, and "glimpse [or glance at] little."[45]

Despite the specular appearances of such reversal (which Heidegger will indeed characterize as a *Spiegelspiel* or mirror-play [K 43; T 45]), this glance in fact exceeds the closure of every chiasmatic whole. In "The Way to Language," such an excess is related to the specific finitude that defines the hermeneutic circle as such. Insofar as "we are always inside language," Heidegger remarks, we can never step outside it so as to "see it in the round [*umblicken*]. We are able to catch sight of [*erblicken*] the nature of language only insofar as language has already appropriated us, holds us in view [*angeblickt*]" (US 266; WL 134). Benjamin speaks in somewhat similar terms of the distanced eros or "Platonic love" between man and language: "the more closely you look at a word, the more distantly it looks back" (KK 362; KR 267). Such "love" carves out a circularity beyond the circulation of commodities, a "transfer" (*Übertragung*) beyond adequation and all recompense.

Benjamin—starting always (or nearly always) with what Brecht called the "bad new things" (UB 121)—sees in this "flash" the specific rhythm of technology. The "flashing image [*aufblitzende Bild*] flickering in the moment of danger"—quoting here from the Fifth

Thesis on history—both repeats and transfigures, transfigures by repeating, the jolty rhythms of modernity (all those jerks described in the Baudelaire study, from the jostles of the Parisian crowd, to the switch of the assembly line, to the flick of the matchstick, to the snap of the gambler's hand, to the click of the telephone receiver, to, finally, the flash of the camera, perfect instrument of the *Zeit des Weltbildes*). In the flickering light of film—and by the mid-1930s Germany saw all those images, saw itself in those images, was becoming just those images, and had given these images a revealing name: "Triumph of the Will" (a film dominated in the extreme by both its director and its direction or destiny)—one sees the sharpest image of the danger. Both the sharpest and, of course, the most distorted. For Benjamin, as for Heidegger, the task of history is to convert danger into saving—that is, in Benjamin's terms, redemption. This is the task and the exclusive privilege of politics.

Art has its place here. It is a place rendered most visible in the displacements of the media, an origin carved out precisely in the duplications of the image. It is not by turning away from these images that Benjamin sought to redeem art for politics: in this sense his term "dialectical image" (*Bild*) is precise and could not be more provocative. For the moment of redemption, in Benjamin, both simulates and displaces the dangers of technology. It is the task of allegory to realize this. In the "frozen unrest" of its images (PW 410)—transfixed, as though by Medusa, by the very reifications it would reflect—allegory in its abstraction and fragmentation both repeats and apotropaically resists the devaluating movement of the commodity. Here, writes Benjamin, the commodity "seeks to look itself in the face." In being captured allegorically, the phantasmagoria of capitalism would both achieve and resist their final "distortion" (*Entstellen*) in the flattened space-time of pure exchange (ZP 671). Repetition would introduce the face-to-face of an aura beyond aura: beyond the cultic transcendence of the earlier auratic art-object to the expanded or "profane illumination" of a revolutionary age.[46] Baudelaire, "secret agent" in the enemy camp of the marketplace, finding originality in the very replications of the cliché and "stereotype" (ZP 664), exposes "for the first time" the uncanny force of the *Immerwiedergleiches* (ZP 680), and thereby opens repetition to the force of difference. He is for Benjamin in this respect exemplary.

For it is by meeting image with image—a flight from images into image (*Bilderflucht*, PW 410)—that the (bad) mimesis of imitation (to speak Platonic) turns into the (good) mimetic perception of similarities; that the bad infinite of reproduction (to speak Hegelian) turns into the speculative focus of repetition; that the quantitative flatness of the commodity (to speak Marxian) turns into the qualitative breadth of real collectivity; that the servile and depressive "sameness" of the eternal recurrence (to speak Nietzschean, that is, to quote a certain dwarf in *Zarathustra*) turns into the ecstatic "yet once again" of the real return; that the numbing tedium of *spleen* (to speak Baudelairean) turns into the allegorical richness of *l'idéal*; and that the sterile obsessions of the repetition compulsion (to speak Freudian) turns into the healing "work" of true remembrance. Or— to speak Heideggerian—that the reductive and homogeneous identity (*Gleiche*) of *Gestell* turns into the supple "sameness" (*Selbe*) of *Ereignis*. Benjamin, who of course spoke all these idioms quite fluently except for one, could not quite come to think this last point.

For this is no doubt Benjamin's own version of Heidegger's "turning." Such an articulation is not exhausted, though it is certainly determined, by the two major foci of his thinking: the Marxist dialectical determination of capitalism (i.e., the "universal expropriation" that defines civil society) as being both the antithesis and the precondition of communism, and the Jewish apocalyptic determination of redemption as a catastrophic reversal of profane history.

And if the era of art's mechanical reproduction gives the *Gestell* its historical determination as the triumph of *Ausstellungswert*—the final supremacy of value exhibiting itself as the value of sheer exhibition—the "turning" in this case would involve precisely that minute (but utterly uncompromising) shift from spectacle to performance. Or, as Benjamin puts it, in a formula too easily dismissed (and of course far too easily recited)—and it is unnecessary to insist on the Heideggerian syntax of this formulation—the turn from the "aestheticization of politics" to the "politicization of art." A turn from *Triumph of the Will* to—something else. (I hesitate to give examples.) A turn, we might paraphrase, from the *Gestell* as the perfection (but also the exhaustion) of the *Weltbild* to *Ereignis* as the flicker of remembrance; from the spectacular reduction to the image to the performance of historical action. Only action, for Benjamin, could give to memory its authentic movement—this is what the politicization of art is all about—rupturing the static *Weltbild* of the contemplative order of vision with the (in every sense of the word) "ecstatic" concentration of the Messianic. If Being's "oblivion" here reaches its limit (as Heidegger insisted), this is because its recognition (as Benjamin insisted) involves also the *ontic* identification of those who were, in fact, most forgotten: the victims of history whose fragile image appears fleetingly in the most reified recapitulations of the present. Such an ontic memory would not be inconsistent with the remembrance of the ontico-ontological difference: indeed the very finitude of that difference should have, strictly speaking, required precisely such attention to the specific differences that are the stuff of history. Such attentiveness would have easily redeemed Heidegger's notion of "historicity" from the sneering charge of "abstractness" which both Adorno and Benjamin—not without some justice, but without real cause—were to insist on levelling.[47]

If for Heidegger the *Gestell* appears as a kind of "photographic negative" of *Ereignis*,[48] Benjamin insists that this negative imprint must be developed. "Dialectical materialism" would be for Benjamin both the medium and the method of such development. "The dialectical materialist," he writes, "focuses" (*feststellt*) the image, "presses the shutter, removes the photographic plate," and lets concepts "develop" it (CB 1165). On his fortieth birthday, he writes that our "most important images" are the ones in which "we ourselves are seen." He adds that such images must be developed within "the darkroom of the lived moment."[49] A dark room indeed, by the time of Benjamin's last reflections.

Unlike Heidegger, Benjamin gives the *Gestell* a name— fascism—and a specific material place—capitalism. For more than one reason, he had to. Only thus could the final spectre of aestheticism be contested.

Notes

Key to abbreviations (complete bibliography is to be found in the note whose number follows the abbreviation):

BG (8): Benjamin, "Über den Begriff der Geschichte"
BK (11): Benjamin, "Der Begriff der Kunstkritik in der deutschen Romantik"
BP (17): Benjamin, "Zum Bilde Proust"
BR (6): Benjamin, *Briefe*
CB (14): Benjamin, *Charles Baudelaire: Ein Lyriker in Zeitalter des Hochkapitalismus*
CT (3): Heidegger, "The Question concerning Technology"
DT (15): Benjamin, *Ursprung des deutschen Trauerspiels*
EF (29): Benjamin, "Eduard Fuchs, der Sammler und der Historiker"
F (29): Benjamin, "Eduard Fuchs, Collecter and Historian"

FK (27):   Benjamin, "Franz Kafka: Zur zehnten Wiederkehr seines Todestages"
FT (3):   Heidegger, "Die Frage nach des Technik"
GS (1):   Benjamin, *Gesammelte Schriften*
GT (15):   Benjamin, *The Origin of German Tragic Drama*
H (2):   Benjamin, "Hashish in Marseille"
HM (2):   Benjamin, "Haschisch in Marseille"
HW (1):   Heidegger, *Holzwege*
ID (39):   Heidegger, *Identity and Difference*
IL (1):   Benjamin, *Illuminations*
IP (17):   Benjamin, "The Image of Proust"
K (38):   Heidegger, "Die Kehre"
KA (27):   Benjamin, "Franz Kafka: On the Tenth Anniversary of His Death"
KG (19):   Benjamin, "Kleine Geschichte der Photographie"
KK (28):   Benjamin, "Karl Kraus"
KR (28):   Benjamin, "Karl Kraus"
KW (1):   Benjamin, "Das Kunstwerk im Zeitalter seiner technischen Reproduzierbarkeit"
MF (13):   Benjamin, "On the Mimetic Faculty"
MV (13):   Benjamin, "Über das mimetischen Vermögen"
OW (1):   Heidegger, "The Origin of the Work of Art"
OWS (19):   Benjamin, *One Way Street*
PH (8):   Benjamin, "Theses on the Philosophy of History"
PL (1):   Heidegger, *Poetry, Language, Thought*
PW (24):   Benjamin, *Das Passagen-Werk*
QT (3):   Heidegger, *The Question concerning Technology and Other Essays*
RE (2):   Benjamin, *Reflections*
SD (40):   Heidegger, *Zur Sache des Denkens*
SG (41):   Heidegger, *Der Satz vom Grund*
SH (19):   Benjamin, "A Small History of Photography"
SM (7):   Benjamin, "On Some Motifs in Baudelaire"
T (38):   Heidegger, "The Turning"
TB (40):   Heidegger, *On Time and Being*
TI (10):   Levinas, *Totalité et Infini*
TK (3):   Heidegger, *Die Technik und die Kehre*
UB (5):   Benjamin, *Understanding Brecht*
UK (1):   Heidegger, "Der Ursprung des Kunstwerkes"
UM (7):   Benjamin, "Über einige Motive bei Baudelaire"
US (44):   Heidegger, *Unterwegs zur Sprache*
VA (4):   Heidegger, *Vorträge und Aufsätze*
WA (1):   Benjamin, "The Work of Art in the Age of Mechanical Reproduction"
WL (44):   Heidegger, *On the Way to Language*
ZP (20):   Benjamin, "Zentralpark"

A short version of this chapter was presented at the 1989 SPEP meeting in Pittsburgh. This expanded version was presented in April, 1990, at the conference on Walter Benjamin at State University of New York—Buffalo.

1. Walter Benjamin, "Das Kunstwerk im Zeitalter seiner technischen Reproduzierbarkeit," second version (abbreviated "KW"), in *Gesammelte Schriften*, 7 vols. (Frankfurt: Suhrkamp, 1980–89), I.2:471–508 ("GS"); trans. Harry Zohn, "The Work of Art in the Age of Mechanical Reproduction" ("WA"), in *Illuminations* (New York: Schocken, 1969), 217–251 ("IL"). Martin Heidegger, "Der Ursprung des Kunstwerkes" ("UK") in *Holzwege*, 6. Aufl. (Frankfurt: Klostermann, 1980), 1–72 ("HW"); trans. Albert Hofstadter, "The Origin of the Work of Art" ("OW") in *Poetry, Language, Thought* (New York: Harper & Row, 1971), 15–87 ("PL"). Translations are generally my own (for reasons of consistency), but the standard English translations will also be indicated throughout this essay.

2. KW 480; WA 223. The quote, which appears as early as 1932 in "Haschisch in Marseille" ("HM") (in GS IV.1:414; trans Edmund Jephcott, "Hashish in Marseille" ["H"], in *Reflections* [New York: Harcourt, Brace, Jovanovich, 1978], p. 142 ["RE"]) is actually taken from Johannes Jensen, *Exotische Novellen* (Berlin: S. Fischer, 1917), pp. 41f. The source is also acknowledged in the first (1935) version of the "Work of Art" essay, in GS I.2:440. But note the crucial changes from 1932 to 1935. In the 1932 text, the appreciation of "alles Gleichartige in der Welt"—which by 1935 Benjamin rewrites to "das Gleichartige in der Welt"—is invoked to capture the hallucinatory intimacy of the hashish trance: a sense of differentiated unity in which "I saw only nuances, and yet these were the same [*gleich*]" (p. 414). In this early text, such a hallucinatory sensation of "sameness" is contrasted explicitly with the experience of the "thoroughly mechanized and rationalized" order of modernity. This is how Benjamin, quoting Jensen against himself, contrasts his own "insight" with what he declares to be Jensen's own original intention ("war die neue Einsicht durchaus anders"). But clearly such an "auratic" communion would be opposed to the mundane identities of the marketplace—a qualitative similarity that outstrips the quantitative identities of the everyday.

By the first edition of the "Artwork" essay in 1935, Benjamin, requoting the quote or, in effect, translating the translation, will have apparently rewritten Jensen's sentence to correspond to what he had identified in 1932 as the author's original intention. For now the "sense of equality" is related precisely to the advent of technical rationality: it is mechanical reproduction, rather than a drug trance, that has obliterated the distinctions between things. But if the significance of the quote seems to have been converted from an "auratic" to a radically anti-"auratic" interpretation, it would also appear to have been pulled free of its original author (whose name is also, by the second edition of 1936, dropped). For by using the quoted phrase "das Gleichartige in der Welt" without attribution, Benjamin subtly invokes the

Marxist subtext. In the politicized context created by the "Artwork" essay, it is the commodity chapter of *Capital* that surely comes to mind. See *Das Kapital*, in *Marx-Engels Werke* (Berlin: Dietz, 1962), 23.1:85–98. Although the exact words do not, in fact, appear in *Capital*, the proximity to the latter's discussion of abstract "equality" (*Gleichheit*) is unmistakable, creating a quotation-effect or *déjà vu* exemplary of Benjamin's own complex theory of quotation.

3. See Martin Heidegger, "Die Frage nach dem Technik" ("FT"), in *Die Technik und die Kehre* (Pfullingen: Neske, 1962), 5–36, pp. 20f. ("TK"); trans. William Lovitt, "The Question concerning Technology" ("CT"), in *The Question concerning Technology and Other Essays* (New York: Harper and Row, 1977), 3–35, pp. 20f. ("QT").

4. KW 479; WA 223, and Martin Heidegger, "Das Ding," in *Vorträge und Aufsätze* (Pfullingen: Neske, 1954), 163 ("VA"); trans. "The Thing," PL 165.

5. See Walter Benjamin, "Was ist epische Theater?" in GS II.2:524; trans. as "What Is Epic Theatre? [First Version]," in Benjamin, *Understanding Brecht*, trans. Anna Bostock (London: New Left Books, 1973), 1–13, p. 6 ("UB").

6. Letter from Adorno of Aug. 2, 1935, in Walter Benjamin, *Briefe*, hrsg. Gershom Scholem and Theodor W. Adorno (Frankfurt: Suhrkamp, 1978), 683 ("BR"); also in GS V.2:1135.

7. Walter Benjamin, "Über einige Motive bei Baudelaire" ("UM"), in GS I.2:605–53; trans. "On Some Motifs in Baudelaire" ("SM") in IL 155–200.

8. Walter Benjamin, "Über den Begriff der Geschichte" ("BG"), in GS I.2:696; trans. "Theses on the Philosophy of History" ("PH"), in IL 256.

9. Bertolt Brecht, *Arbeitsjournal*, 2 vols., ed. W. Hecht (Frankfurt: Suhrkamp, 1973), 1:16.

10. Emmanuel Levinas, *Totalité et Infini* (The Hague: Martinus Nijhoff, 1961), 50 ("TI"); compare *Totality and Infinity: An Essay on Exteriority*, trans. A. Lingis (Pittsburgh, Pa.: Duquesne Univ. Press, 1969), 50.

11. Walter Benjamin, "Der Begriff der Kunstkritik in der deutschen Romantik" ("BK"), in GS I.1:55–56.

12. I am very grateful to Miriam Hansen for making this point clear to me. See her excellent essay, "Benjamin, Cinema, and Experience: 'The Blue Flower in the Land of Technology'," *New German Critique* 40 (1987): 179–224.

13. Walter Benjamin, "Über das mimetischen Vermögen" ("MV"), in GS II.1:210ff; trans. "On the Mimetic Faculty" ("MF") in RE 333ff.

14. BG 696; PH 256. Compare the notes for *Charles Baudelaire: Ein Lyriker in Zeitalter des Hochkapitalismus* ("CB"), in GS I.3:1179.

15. Walter Benjamin, *Ursprung des deutschen Trauerspiels* ("DT"), in GS I.1:234; trans. John Osborne, *The Origin of German Tragic Drama* (London: New Left Books, 1977), 53f. ("GT").

16. MV 213; MF 335. In the *Trauerspielbuch,* Benjamin similarly speaks of the allegorical *Augenaufschlag* or awakening of a personified nature as a "form of writing" (DT 360; GT 184f.).

17. Walter Benjamin, "Zum Bilde Proust" ("BP"), in GS II.1:314; trans. "The Image of Proust" ("IP"), in IL 204.

18. Emmanuel Levinas, "Ethique et esprit," *Difficile liberté: Essais sur le judaïsme* (Paris: Albin Michel, 1976), 15–24, p. 21; compare "Ethics and Spirit," *Difficult Freedom: Essays in Judaism,* trans. S. Hand (Baltimore: Johns Hopkins Univ. Press, 1990), 3–10, p. 8. For a good recent discussion of the face-to-face in Levinas, see Jill Robbins, "Visage, Figure: Reading Levinas' *Totality and Infinity,*" *Yale French Studies,* 79 (1991): 135–49.

19. Walter Benjamin, "Kleine Geschichte der Photographie" ("KG"), in GS II.1:380; trans. Edmund Jephcott and Kingsley Shorter, "A Small History of Photography" ("SH"), in *One Way Street* (London: New Left Books, 1979), p. 251 ("OWS").

20. "Zentralpark," in GS I.2:655–90, p. 670 ("ZP").

21. Letter of Benjamin to Adorno, May 7, 1940, in BR 849; also in GS I.3:1134.

22. Letter of Adorno to Benjamin, in GS I.3:1132.

23. DT 272; GT 93. See Hansen, "Benjamin, Cinema, and Experience," p. 212.

24. DT 272; GT 93, and Benjamin, *Das Passagen-Werk* ("PW"), in GS V.1,2:579.

25. See DT 407; GT 233. For an extremely lucid explication of the Fall motif in Benjamin's early writings, see Irving Wohlfarth, "On Some Jewish Motifs in Benjamin," in Andrew Benjamin, ed., *The Problems of Modernity: Adorno and Benjamin* (London: Routledge, 1989), 157–215. Wohlfarth has a slightly different reading of the "second" Fall or "double reification," which he relates to the ideological institutionalization of linguistic arbitrariness in the semiotic conception of language (p. 163). No doubt these two readings could be reconciled.

26. "Über Sprache überhaupt and über die Sprache des Menschen," in GS II.1:151; trans. "On Language as Such and on the Language of Man," in OWS 117.

27. "Franz Kafka: Zur zehnten Wiederkehr seines Todestages" ("FK"), in GS II.2:429; trans. "Franz Kafka: On the Tenth Anniversary of His Death" ("KA") in IL 131.

28. "Karl Kraus" ("KK"), in GS II.1:339; trans. "Karl Kraus" ("KR") in RE 244. This definition echoes Benjamin's earlier discussion of Baroque anti-humanism, with its tendency to treat ethical relations by means of naturalistic "metaphors" and thereby to "blunt all tendency to ethical reflection" (DT 168; GT 89).

29. "Eduard Fuchs, der Sammler und der Historiker" ("EF"), in GS II.2:487f; trans. "Eduard Fuchs, Collector and Historian" ("F"), in OWS 369f.

30. "Die Aufgabe des Übersetzers," in GS IV.1:10; trans. "The Task of the Translator," in IL 70.

31. KW 479; WA 223. The Latin etymology of *aura* refers, of course, to breath or wind.

32. Letter of Benjamin to Scholem, June 12, 1938, in BR 762; trans. "Some Reflections on Kafka," in IL 143.

33. DT 214; GT 33. See also the early Kant essay, "Über das Programm der kommenden Philosophie," in GS II.1:157-71.

34. See Rebecca Comay, "Redeeming Revenge: Nietzsche, Benjamin, Heidegger and the Politics of Memory," in Clayton Koelb, ed., *Nietzsche as Post-Modernist* (Albany: State Univ. of New York Press, 1990), 21-38.

35. In "A Small History of Photography," Benjamin allows, as we have seen, "auratic" moments in the early photographs.

36. Georges Bataille, *Le Coupable,* vol. 5 of *Oeuvres Complètes,* 12 vols. (Paris: Gallimard, 1970–89), 402.

37. Martin Heidegger, *Was heisst Denken?* (Tübingen: Niemeyer, 1954), 5-6; trans. J. Glenn Gray, *What Is Called Thinking?* (New York: Harper & Row, 1968), 9. Such a withdrawal would constitute a giving so radical it would refuse the propriety of the standing present—a 'gift' irreducible to every 'present'—inducing a "thinking" (*Denken*) inseparable from a "thanking" (*Danken*), that is, from the memory (*Gedächtnis*) of that which never offered itself as an immediacy to be possessed. See pp. 91–95 and 157–59; trans. 138–47.

38. Martin Heidegger, "Die Kehre," ("K") in TK 41f.; trans. "The Turning" ("T") in QT 42f.

39. Martin Heidegger, *Identity and Difference*, bilingual ed. trans. Joan Stambaugh (New York: Harper & Row, 1969), 34/98 ("ID").

40. Martin Heidegger, *Zur Sache des Denkens* (Tübingen: Niemeyer, 1969), 49 ("SD"); trans. Joan Stambaugh, *On Time and Being* (New York: Harper & Row), 46 ("TB").

41. Martin Heidegger, *Der Satz vom Grund* (Pfullingen: Neske, 1957), 154 ("SG").

42. See BG 700, 704; PH 260, 264.

43. I borrow Rodolphe Gasché's superbly efficient term. See *The Tain of the Mirror: Deconstruction and the Philosophy of Reflection* (Cambridge, Mass.: Harvard Univ. Press, 1986).

44. Martin Heidegger, "Der Weg zur Sprache," *Unterwegs zur Sprache* (Pfullingen: Neske, 1959), 260 ("US"); "The Way to Language," trans. Peter Hertz, *On the Way to Language* (New York: Harper & Row, 1971), 129 ("WL").

45. SG 85. In his *Parmenides* lectures of 1942–43, Heidegger (in the course of a curious attack on Rilke which surely deserves to be scrutinized) emphatically contrasts human "seeing" (and being seen) with the blind staring of animals. GA 54 (1982), 230–40.

46. Walter Benjamin, "Der Surrealismus," in GS II.1:297; trans. "Surrealism," in RE 179.

47. PW 577f. Compare Theodor Adorno, "Die Idee der Naturgeschichte," *Gesammelte Schriften*, 20 vols. (Frankfurt: Suhrkamp, 1973–86), 1:345–65.

48. Martin Heidegger, *Vier Seminare* (Frankfurt: Klostermann, 1977), 104.

49. Walter Benjamin, "Aus einer kleiner Rede über Proust, an meinem vierzigsten Geburtstag gehalten," in GS II.3:1064.

11

The Young Heidegger, Aristotle, Ethics

John van Buren

Over the years the unpublished manuscripts and student transcripts of Heidegger's youthful lecture courses and essays from 1919 through the early 1920s acquired the reputation of a kind of literary treasure trove of possibilities for interpreting the development and meaning of his thought. Hannah Arendt even spoke about the young Heidegger's reputation as the "rumor of the hidden king" that spread through the German philosophical circles at the time.[1] As work on the edition of his collected writings moves along at a brisk pace, we are finally getting a chance to see many of these youthful lecture courses and essays,[2] and to explore what Hans-Georg Gadamer called "the revolutionary genius of the young Heidegger."[3] These writings will give us important insights into the origins of Heidegger's thought in his critical appropriations of Aristotle, Husserl, Dilthey, and the original Christianity of Paul, Augustine, the young Luther, Pascal, and Kierkegaard.[4]

In what follows, I want to focus on the young Heidegger's reading of Aristotle and pursue the following themes: the young Heidegger's philosophical project, the role of Aristotle's practical philosophy in this project, Heidegger's indications for reorienting ethical thought along Aristotelian lines, his later distancing from Aristotle, and finally the significance of his youthful thought for coping with the difficulties of his later philosophy.

Heidegger's themes of "the end of philosophy" and "the other beginning" are familiar to us primarily from his later writings after 1930, but already in his 1921–22 lecture course *Phänomenologische Interpretationen zu Aristoteles* he states that his task is nothing less than effecting the end of philosophy and another genuine beginning. "Skepticism is a beginning," he tells his students, "and as the genuine beginning it is also the end of philosophy" (PA 35). By *philosophy*, Heidegger meant here the whole history of Western thought from its first beginning with the Greeks through its various transformations and restructurings in the Middle Ages and modernity (PA 2–3, 170). Borrowing from Luther's 1518 Heidelberg Disputation, where Luther spoke of destroying (*destruere*) the pseudo-wisdom of Greek philosophy and of Scholasticism's "theology of glory," Heidegger proposed an ontological destruction (*Destruktion*) or deconstruction (*Abbauen*) of the history of philosophy, so as to expose its unacknowledged origins in concrete historical life, in terms of which philosophy could be repeated or retrieved in a new beginning.

Heidegger expressed this beginning in the formula "Leben = Dasein, in und durch Leben '*Sein*' "; "life = there-being, '*being*' in and through life" (PA 85). This means that being has to be explored not as it is in itself, but rather as it is given to human life in the form of the sense of being or being-sense (*Seinssinn*). Human life, which Heidegger calls *there-being* (Dasein), is the there (*Da*) of being (*Sein*), in and through which being is given. His name for the question of being was at this point the questionableness of being (*Seinsfraglichkeit*) (PA 189) in the historical situatedness of factical life. He was able to adopt creatively Husserl's concept of intentionality in order to articulate his notion of being-sense into the following three intentional moments: First, there is the content sense (*Gehaltssinn*) of there-being, that is, being as the intentional object of world, which is articulated into the technical environing world (*Umwelt*), the interpersonal with-world (*Mitwelt*), and the personal self-world (*Selbstwelt*). Second, there is the relational sense (*Bezugssinn*) of there-being, that is, human being in the manner of intending the world that Heidegger calls *care*. And, finally, there is the fulfillment-sense (*Vollzugssinn*) or temporalizing-sense (*Zeitigungssinn*) of there-being, the fulfillment of the whole intentional world-care relation as historical time (PA 52–53). In 1919, Heidegger called this temporal sense of being the "it worlds" (*es weltet*) of the world and the appropriating event (*Ereignis*) of the person-world relation (IP 63–76). His threefold intentional sense of being was expressed in his 1922 definition of philosophy as "phenomenological ontology": "*Philosophy is principally knowing comportment to that which is as being (being-sense), and indeed in such a manner that, in the comportment and for it, it is also decisively a matter of the being (being-sense) of the having of the comportment at a particular time"* (PA 60).

Between 1921 and 1926, Heidegger gave a number of lecture courses and seminars on Aristotle.[5] In 1922, he planned to publish what Husserl called a "large and fundamental work on Aristotle" that was to have appeared in Husserl's *Jahrbuch* in the following year.[6] How did Heidegger envisage Aristotle's place in his own philosophical project in the early twenties? Aristotle was both a foil and an ally; he belonged to the metaphysical tradition that was to be brought to an end, but also occupied a special place in the violent repetition of this tradition in Heidegger's new beginning. He interpreted Aristotle's thought as a falling away (*Abfallen*) from the three intentional senses of being: Aristotle's categories of being were a "de-worlding" (*Entweltlichung*) or covering-over of the content-sense of the environing world; his emphasis on theory and the assertoric statement was a "de-living" (*Entleben*) of the relational sense of our practically interested, lived experience (*Erlebnis*); and his focus on substance and eternal being was a "de-historicizing" (*Entgeschichtlichung*) of the temporal fulfillment of the person-world relation.[7] Heidegger's intent was to dismantle Aristotle's metaphysical formulation of the being-question back down to the life-world from which his concepts had been derived (HF 74). This meant understanding it in the sense of a "hermeneutics of facticity" in which life had indirectly brought itself interpretively to language and was still, as it were, audible.[8] For example, in Aristotle's term *ousia* Heidegger could still detect an echo of the practical world of the household (PA 92). The word *thēoria* pointed back to the sight of the artisan (AJ 4), and the term *logos* pointed to the dimension of social discourse (PA 96, 112; LW 1–3). The models that Heidegger adopted for his destruction of Aristotle included the young Luther's attack on Aristotle and Aristotelian scholasticism (PA 6): ancient skepticism (LW 4, 19, 54); Kierkegaard's critique of objective philosophy; and Aristotle's own critique of Plato's idea of the Good, which Heidegger in effect turned against Aristotle's own metaphysical intentions.[9]

But Heidegger's destruction of the metaphysical Aristotle was inseparably bound up with his attempt to find the genuine Aristotle in his practical writings and in his *Physics*, which were retrieved within Heidegger's own project of a new beginning. This is what Heidegger meant by approaching Aristotle's thought within what he called a "hermeneutical situation," that is, critically appropriating

Aristotle's past thought in light of its futural possibilities for present philosophizing. The genuine beginning of philosophy was already implicitly present in Aristotle and had only to be explicated and radicalized. In his 1921–22 lecture course on Aristotle, Heidegger writes that modern philosophy

> has its intellectual and active historical roots in *Greek philosophy*, and indeed in such a way that, in the latter, both motives for beginning are alive (original explication of experience and categorial theoretical explication), and that one of them simply got lost in the process of levelling the original element. (Cf. *ousia*, "having," "household," "property".) (PA 92)

Heidegger indicates that the three intentional moments of his notion of being are to be understood as creative retrievals of corresponding elements in Aristotle's analyses of human praxis and *kinēsis* (movement).[10] His analysis of world (content-sense) was a retrieval of Aristotle's notions of the household (*oikos*), the social-political community (*polis*), and the individual's moral stance (*ethos*), which, as both Aristotle and Heidegger would say, are different expressions of the for-the-sake-of-which (*hou heneka*) of human praxis. The Heideggerian concept of the environing world was influenced by Aristotle's analysis of productive knowing (*technē*) which discloses things as ends and means. Aristotle's *Politics* and *Rhetoric* provided a model for Heidegger's concept of the social with-world. And the Heideggerian notion of the self-world is rooted in Aristotle's analysis of *ethos*.

As for the relational sense of being, Heidegger's concept of care found a precedent in Aristotle's notion of striving (*orexis*) that has action itself as its end. He was also influenced by Aristotle's analyses of mood (*pathos*), discourse (*logos*), the practical interpretive understanding of *phronēsis*, truth (*alētheia*), and excess (*hyperbolē*) and deficiency (*elleipsis*) in relation to what is fitting in action. Heidegger adopted the last-mentioned terms to describe inauthentic human existence that has fallen away from itself into abstract public life ("the hyperbolic") and thus falls short of what is fitting for it in its own situation ("the elliptic"). Heidegger's fulfillment-sense or temporalizing-sense of being was a retrieval of the Aristotelian theme of human praxis as a kind of coming forth (*physis*) in the sense of movement (*kinēsis*) towards ends that are fulfilled in situations (*kairos*).

Heidegger also creatively appropriated Aristotle's method in practical philosophy, which consists in laying out the factual "that" (*to hoti*) of our pregiven practical understanding in an "outline" of the analogical principles (analogy of proportion) visible here, that is, of the structural similarities of different practices (for example, the means-end relation). This outline does not give the invariable truth of "science" (*epistēmē*) but rather a rough sketch that has to be interpretively applied to changing practical situations. Heidegger himself spoke of a hermeneutics of facticity that unfolds our pre-understanding of being and formalizes it in the formal indication (*formale Anzeige*) of "*hermeneutical* concepts" that do not indicate a truth in itself, but rather can only be interpretively applied to and fulfilled with the particular content of historical situations. He was here also influenced by Kierkegaard's "indirect communication" and Husserl's investigation of "occasional expressions" (PA 21, 112, 192; AJ 32).

Gadamer has said that what took place in the young Heidegger's critical appropriation of Aristotle was the original model of his own notion of a hermeneutical "fusion of horizons."[11] It was a fusion of horizons between Aristotle's practical philosophy and Heidegger's own concern to rethink the question of being within the horizon of factical life, a concern motivated by a cluster of antimetaphysical traditions that included Dilthey's philosophy of life, Jaspers's philosophy of existence, Husserl's Sixth Investigation, Kierkegaard, and the young Luther. Heidegger used Aristotle's practical writings not only for his new beginning in ontology but also for his suggestions about rethinking ethics, a concern he took over also from Kierkegaard (PA 182). He understood his ontology to provide formal indications that could be concretized in practical disciplines such as theology and ethics.[12]

In his comments on ethics, Heidegger's approach was again that of destruction and retrieval. His destruction was directed specifically against neo-Kantian philosophy of value and against Husserl's and Scheler's phenomenology of value. In Heidegger's reading, these traditions were modern forms of Platonism. His interpretation, in its basic outline, runs as follows: The modern revival of Plato's approach to ethics begins with Hermann Lotze's struggle against positivism and his interpretation of the Platonic ideas as normative and teleological forms of validity (*Geltung*). Insofar as Lotze takes over Fichte's interpretation of Kant, which stresses "the primacy of practical reason as 'value-feeling' reason," he really effects a "founding of logic in ethics" (PW 139–39; compare LW 62–79). Lotze's idea of "the primacy of practical reason, the founding of theoretical scientific thinking in practical belief and the will to truth" (PW 143) is taken up in Wilhelm Windelband's and Heinrich Rickert's philosophy of value and made more explicit with the transformation of his notion of validity into the concept of value. Kant's three critiques (logic, ethics, aesthetics) are accordingly interpreted to demarcate different spheres of value (the true, the good, the beautiful). Eventually, Kant's investigations into religion are also taken to set the boundaries of the sphere of "the value of the sacred," so that God, too, becomes a value (LW 82–84). The task of philosophy is to develop a self-enclosed system of values and a scientific worldview that can normatively guide concrete scientific culture. Transcendental philosophy of value is, in Windelband's words, quoted by Heidegger, a "critical science of universally valid values" (PW 146).

Heidegger notes that Husserl's critique of psychologism was directed primarily at the psychologizing of logic, but also at the psychologizing of ethics. Husserl took over the Lotzean and neo-Kantian notion of the ideal validity of values in order to show that every ethics "presupposes a theoretical discipline, and that, as the foundational discipline of the normative science, this theoretical discipline cannot be psychology; rather, analogous to how logic deals with the pure content of propositions, ethics must likewise deal with the pure content of norms, i.e., with values."[13] Scheler's phenomenology of values then "took up this type of questioning and worked it out in the field of ethics, of practical philosophy, as an ethics of value."[14]

Modern philosophy of value, Heidegger maintained, pursued an "absolute ethics," an "absolute *system of morality* [*Sittlichkeit*], of ethical values and value-relations that are valid in themselves" (PA 164, 165). If we put this modern philosophy of value into Heidegger's language of the threefold intentional sense of being, we can say that it determined the content-sense of ethical experience as the objectivity and universality of values; relational sense as rational judgment for which values are necessarily binding; and temporalizing-sense as the static presence of purportedly atemporal ideality. Heidegger saw in value-philosophy a transcendental restatement of Plato's idealist ethics, whose three intentional moments are content-sense as the universal idea of the Good, relational sense as theory, and temporalizing-sense as eternal being (LW 53–88). In other words, he took value-philosophy to be a "de-worlding," "de-living," and "de-historicizing" of the "living morality" (PA 164) that Aristotle had defended against Plato's intellectualism.

In fact, Heidegger effectively turned Aristotle's critique of the Platonic idea of the Good against modern value-philosophy, which had revived Plato's equation of science (*epistēmē*) and practical wisdom (*phronēsis*), of metaphysics and ethics. Aristotle argued against Plato that there is no separate, universal idea of the Good that can be known in theory. Rather, there are many goods given in the "that" of human life, and these goods are always bound up with one's *ethos*, one's ethical being-at-home in a political community. He argued, further, that practical goods only show themselves interpretively to practical insight (*phronēsis*) in individual situations as what is fitting (*to deon*) in relation to us (*pros hemas*), that is, in relation to each individual in his or her own circumstances.

Following Aristotle, Heidegger raised the question of the relation (*methexis*) between ideal values and the historicity of concrete life. He took value-philosophy to be a falling away from the situational character of human praxis and, therefore, an instance of Aristotle's notion of excess in the sense of being out beyond (the hyperbolic) and thus falling short (deficiency, the elliptic) of the fitting measure (*das gebührende Mass*) in historical situations (PA 108–9, 103). He writes: "The ideality of values and the like, which are dressed up as atemporal and posited as eternally valid in enthroned nobility, flutter about like phantoms. ... Philosophy should think about giving up as principal knowing the swindle of aestheticizing intoxication of itself and its contemporaries" (PA 111). Taking up Kierkegaard's critique of the aestheticism of speculative philosophy, Heidegger saw in philosophy of value a form of quietism that was just a more refined expression of the inauthenticity of everyday life, which he described with the following phrases: making it easy for oneself, security, self-satisfaction, presumption, masking, blinding, and ruinance (PA 108–9, 120, 122). As a motto to his 1921-22 lecture course on Aristotle, Heidegger quotes from Kierkegaard's *Training in Christianity*:

> "The whole of modern philosophy is, both ethically and Christianly, based on easygoingness. ... Philosophy, as abstract, floats in the indefiniteness of the metaphysical. Instead of now admitting this about itself and thus directing human beings (the individual man) to the ethical, to the religious, to the existential, philosophy has aroused the illusion that human beings could, as one prosaically says, speculate themselves out of their own good skin and into pure light." (PA 182)

Heidegger attempted to dismantle the pretensions of modern value-philosophy back to "living morality" as it had been described

by Aristotle and Kierkegaard. The three intentional moments
Heidegger saw as operative in Aristotle's understanding of practical
life are content-sense as the concrete moral ends given in *ethos* in
its connection with social-political community; relational sense as
striving (*orexis*), practical understanding (*phronēsis*), and social
discourse (*logos*); and temporalizing-sense as the movement (*kinēsis*)
of interpretively applying futural moral ends, given by past tradition,
to one's situation (*kairos*). In the following passage from his 1921–22
lecture course, Heidegger forcefully expresses his indications for
rehabilitating practical philosophy along Aristotelian and
Kierkegaardian lines:

> One can project an absolute *system of morality*, of ethical values
> and value-relations that are valid in themselves and can
> meanwhile—I am not saying: be a bad person; to start here with
> this argument is out of place. But precisely with and through
> these absolute relations of validity and laws, one can be blind
> to objects and affinities that usually come forth at a particular
> time in living morality, that is, in facticity as the how of its
> possible being-sense and fulfillment-sense. One says maybe:
> some day, and intends to exaggerate; man is after all at bottom
> a sad subject—but for the same reason this does not continue
> to bother the philosopher.
>
> By measuring with absolute relations of value, one can
> discover that one seldom or never completely "realizes" them.
> In a gesture of modesty, one notes a falling short of the ideal.
> But this is at bottom inconsequential and immediately forgotten
> again. What is the point of taking into account such
> imperfections and awkward difficulties, and indeed even in
> principle such that these also speak in the very definition of the
> sense of being of factical life? The basic situation remains: one
> is an undisturbed advocate of an absolute ethics. ...
>
> Prior to all comfortable calculations about validity and
> objectivity for humanity stands the reflection on what we
> actually have and can have before us [*eigentlich vorhat und
> vorhaben kann*], on the available ways of fulfilling this; and
> further that one stays free from all wide-ranging exaggerations,
> with whose novelty one musters oneself, if need be, to an
> exceptional paragraph with the man in the street [*bei Überweg-
> Heinze*], but nothing otherwise. (PA 164–65)

The young Heidegger's position on ethics, as on authenticity in
factical life in general, is not that of decisionism,[15] the arbitrary use of

unlimited freedom that Sartre, for example, sometimes comes close to expressing. Rather, following Kierkegaard's notion of the ethical self as a synthesis of possibility and actuality, past and future, Heidegger's position is that in moral action one's "possibilities" are bound up with one's "actuality," one's destiny (*Schicksal*) or heritage, which is enacted interpretively within one's current situation.[16] In Aristotle's language, this means that the ends of action are not chosen ex nihilo but rather interpreted.

Even though Heidegger was intensely interested that his ontology provide the conceptual formal indication that could indirectly be of help in reforming Christian theology (he even wrote to Karl Löwith in 1921 that he was not a philosopher, but "a Christian theo*logian*"),[17] he nonetheless maintained a sharp distinction between ontology, which is atheistic, and theology (PA 197). Similarly, he followed Aristotle's separation of ethics and metaphysics, and thus sought to affirm (in Julius Ebbinghaus's words) "the intrinsic lawfulness of ethical-religious life that is independent of scientific theory" (PA 198). "Philosophy," Heidegger wrote in 1919, "is not art (poetry), not life-wisdom (giving of practical rules)" (IP 24). "As critical science, philosophy is *not identical* with a doctrine of worldview" (IP 10). In the spirit of Aristotle and Kierkegaard, Heidegger maintains that neither ontology nor ethical theory can legislate a universal, transhistorical concept of the good that is known by a privileged individual or group. There is no such thing as a philosopher-king, philosopher-prophet, speculative know-it-all, or world-historical Führer, who can know the good once and for all and choose for other individuals.

The following passages, again from Heidegger's 1921–22 lecture course, have to be read against the backdrop of the cultural crisis in Germany after the horrors of the First World War, a time when Spengler's *Decline of the West* was the book of the day. In these passages, Heidegger renounces prophetic universal solutions and Führers with such visions:

> [The formally indicative definition of philosophy] guards precisely against being able to preach philosophy from some elevated but basically indefinable place, as if it could put up bail for the coming cultural periods and destinies of humanity, such that one does not know who speaks for whom and for what, and what is the point of these prophecies and schools of wisdom, and who has assigned them such a cultural mission. (PA 66)

> Where they speak of the university, [these investigations] stand in principle beyond discussions about the goal and means, the necessity or superfluousness of the so-called *university reform*. These discussions about reform...are all uncritical; they overlook the question of competence and forget the question about the suitable time. For us here it is a matter of philosophically seeing the actual situation without prophecy and Führer-illusions. (One writes today about the Führer-problem!) (PA 69–70)

> And if we "go into decline," then there again stands before us only
> *either*: ...radical existentiell concern...
> *or*: degenerating into the padding of mythical and theosophical metaphysics and mysticism, and into the dream-state of a preoccupation with piety, what one calls religion. (PA 70)[18]

Heidegger's position in the early twenties is that ontology can provide ethics, politics, and theology only with formal indications of the general characteristics of human existence. In turn, the practical disciplines can be of help to human action only indirectly by providing a rough outline of the practical sphere in question that has to be interpretively concretized in the historical situation of one's own existence. Ontology and the practical disciplines can be of assistance to the actual living of life, but they can never usurp the role of individual "conscience" (AJ 33). As Heidegger expressed this in 1919, philosophy conducts itself "neither as sport nor as prophetic pageantry that brings world-historical salvation" (AJ 6). When rightly conducted, philosophy "attains noninterference in personal decision making and so frees the individual for his self-reflection" (AJ 42). Philosophy is supposed to make matters not easier for human action by providing it with answers, techniques, and epochal visions, but rather more difficult by leading it back into the original difficulty of its fulfillment within the concrete situation of the individual. Thus Heidegger quotes from Aristotle's *Nichomachean Ethics* (1106b): "It is easy to miss the target, difficult to hit it" (PA 108).

Heidegger did not himself follow up his indications for rethinking ethical and political theory; these were taken up by others such as Hannah Arendt and Hans-Georg Gadamer, just as Rudolf Bultmann and other theologians took up Heidegger's early interest in finding a new language for Christian theology. In fact, Heidegger soon distanced himself from his youthful fusion of horizons with

Aristotle. What marked his 1927 *Being and Time* as a departure from his earlier identification with Aristotle was his newly emerging preoccupation with the transcendental thought of Kant, primarily the analysis of time in Kant's doctrine of schematism. His appropriation of the Kantian doctrine of schematism entered into his analysis of time in the second division of *Being and Time* and colored the whole work with the language of modern transcendental thought. Although risking violent oversimplification, one can still say that what happened in Heidegger's *Being and Time*, which is a later draft of his program from the early twenties, was that the three intentional moments of his earlier version of the sense of being—world, care, and temporal fulfillment—were transformed into the quasi-Kantian version of content-sense as the transcendental "structures" of "worldhood," relational sense as the transcendental structure of "Dasein," and temporalizing-sense as temporal "schemata." In the 1930s, Heidegger turned to still other dialogue partners, primarily the early Greek thinkers, Hölderlin, and Nietzsche. Again at the cost of oversimplifying, one can say that in his later writings the three intentional moments of his youthful version of the sense of being were transformed into the somewhat speculative and mythopoetic version of content-sense as the "fourfold" of earth and sky, gods and mortals; relational sense as "dwelling poetically"; and temporalizing-sense as the "destiny of being." One can legitimately ask whether his later thought is not a creative return to the early speculative, religious concerns and language of his 1916 habilitation writing on Duns Scotus, which were later pursued within a radically historical context.[19] In Heidegger's later writings, Aristotle, along with Kierkegaard and Husserl, was fitted into his schema of the history of the "forgetfulness of being" which effectively began after the golden age of early Greek thinking. Thus Heidegger could write in his "Letter on Humanism" that "the tragedies of Sophocles—provided such a comparison is at all permissible—preserve the *ethos* in their sagas more primordially than Aristotle's lectures on 'ethics'."[20]

There are a number of tendencies in the later Heidegger's distancing from his youthful formulation of the being-question and from his fusion of horizons with Aristotle, Husserl, and Kierkegaard. His shift of emphasis from the human fulfillment of being to being as the impersonal, determining element in human existence is perhaps not per se the decisive factor in this distancing, since the young Heidegger was not pursuing a form of subjectivism, had not yet adopted the transcendental-subjective language of *Being and Time*, had already pointed to the determining element of destiny

(PA 84) in human experience, and had emphasized the "it-worlds" and appropriating event of being in which there is no transcendental ego. In his letter to William Richardson, Heidegger indicated that his later writings are not so much a miraculous turn (*Kehre*) from an earlier intention as rather a bend (*Wendung*) in the realization of a unified intention, namely, the question of being.[21] Over and above what Heidegger meant by this notion of a bend in the development of his thought, one can pursue it in terms of a number of identifiable bents or tendencies in his later concern with being that, over and above his more attentive concern to the impersonal determining elements of being, aggravate this shift of emphasis and more seriously distance his thought from his youthful phenomenological ontology and from his fusion of horizons with Aristotle, Husserl, and Kierkegaard.

One can point to the later Heidegger's speculative bent, which does not merely acknowledge and explore the determining elements in experience but rather often tends to hypostatize being into an autonomous quasi-agent of world history (his notion of an "It" [*Es*] behind the "it gives" [*es gibt*] of being), almost eclipsing what he earlier stressed as the personal relational sense and fulfillment-sense of being in human life. Heidegger's related mythopoetic bent, in contrast to his youthful phenomenological language, portrays the sense of being in a mythopoetic language that derives from his dialogues with pre-Socratic thought, Hölderlin, and Nietzsche. His eschatological-utopian bent, in contrast to his youthful fusions of horizon with humanistic traditions, focuses on a radical forgetfulness of being and a world-night of contemporary technology, imaginatively projecting philosophy into the distant futural utopia of an other beginning.

Finally, the later Heidegger's autocratic bent, in contrast to his youthful insistence on the autonomy of the individual and aversion to Führers, prophecy, and cultural missions,[22] stresses the autocracy of the philosopher, the poet, the statesman, and even an entire nation, insofar as these are supposed to have privileged insight into the world-historical truth and epochal law (*nomos*) of being. "The *Führer* himself and he alone *is* German reality and its law, today and for the future," declared Heidegger in 1933 during his involvement with National Socialism.[23] "The individual, wherever he may stand, counts for nothing. The destiny of our people in its state counts for everything."[24] Contrast this with his statement in 1919 that "the self is in a way the ultimate issue in philosophy" (AJ 35). The later Heidegger's thought often looks like an epochalized version of the "absolute ethics" that he criticized in the early twenties.

These tendencies also distance Heidegger's later thought from many of his own readers who have tried to follow and make sense of it, but who have still called for "demythologizing" Heidegger or, as Habermas expressed this, "urbanizing the Heideggerian province."[25] Today we face Heidegger's thought in a hermeneutical situation similar to that in which Socrates faced the enigmatic mythopoetic thought of the early Greek thinkers. In both cases, there is a hermeneutical problem of coping with something foreign that has a hold over us and will not go away. But we do not really need to give a revolutionary cry to start demythologizing Heidegger, since this has already been underway for decades in hermeneutics, narrative theory, critical theory, post-structuralism, American neo-pragmatism, and the rehabilitation of practical philosophy.[26] These movements constitute creative effective histories (in Gadamer's sense) of the young Heidegger's fusion of horizons with Aristotle, Kierkegaard, and Husserl. The tendency has been to undercut the excesses of the later Heidegger's mythopoetic language, cultural pessimism, prophecy, and bad speculative politics in order to appropriate his rich phenomenological analyses of such matters as technology, the history of philosophy, art, science, being-in-the-world, history, and language, and to explore the significance of these analyses for concrete ethical and political thought, even when this goes "much against Heidegger's intentions."[27] The ongoing publication of his youthful writings provides us with a hermeneutical Rosetta stone for just this kind of interpretive reading of the later Heidegger.

Notes

1. Hannah Arendt, "Martin Heidegger at Eighty," in Michael Murray, ed., *Heidegger and Modern Philosophy* (New Haven: Yale Univ. Press, 1978), 293–303, pp. 293–94.

2. The following is a list of Heidegger's published youthful works from 1919 and the early twenties in the *Gesamtausgabe*: "Anmerkungen zu Karl Jaspers 'Psychologie der Weltanschauungen'," GA 9 (1976), 1–44 (abbreviated "AJ"); *Prolegomena zur Geschichte des Zeitbegriffs*, GA 20 (1979) ("GZ"), translated as *History of the Concept of Time: Prolegomena*, trans. Theodore Kisiel (Bloomington: Indiana Univ. Press, 1985); *Ontologie (Hermeneutik der Faktizität)*, GA 63 (1988) ("HF"): "Die Idee der Philosophie und das Weltanschauungsproblem," GA 56/57 (1987), 1–117 ("IP"): *Logik: Die Frage Nach der Wahrheit*, GA 21 (1976) ("LW"); *Phänomenologische Interpretationen zu Aristoteles*, GA 61 (1985) ("PA"); "Phänomenologie und

transzendentale Wertphilosophie," GA 56/57:119–203 ("PW"); "Über das Wesen der Universität und des akademischen Studiums," GA 56/57:205–14 ("WU"). Translations are my own, except in the case of GZ; after full citation, subsequent references to page numbers in existing English translations of Heidegger's works will appear after a slash immediately following the reference to the German edition. Since the writing of this essay two other important works from Heidegger's youthful period have been published: his *Der Begriff der Zeit* (Tübingen: Max Niemeyer Verlag, 1989) and his "Phänomenologische Interpretationen zu Aristoteles (Anzeige der hermeneutischen Situation)," *Dilthey Jahrbuch für Philosophie und Geschichte der Geisteswissenschaften* 6 (1989): 235–74. For Heidegger's forthcoming youthful works, see the prospectus of Martin Heidegger, *Gesamtausgabe*, announced by the publisher Vittorio Klostermann in June 1989.

3. Hans-Georg Gadamer, *Heideggers Wege* (Tübingen: J. C. B. Mohr, 1983), 82.

4. See John van Buren, *The Young Heidegger*, forthcoming from Indiana University Press.

5. See appendix, "Courses, Seminars, and Lectures of Martin Heidegger," in William J. Richardson, *Heidegger: Through Phenomenology to Thought* (The Hague: Martinus Nijhoff, 1963), 663–65; and Theodore J. Kisiel, "Heidegger's Early Lecture Courses," in Joseph J. Kockelmans, *A Companion to Martin Heidegger's* Being and Time (Washington, D.C.: Center for Advanced Research in Phenomenology, and University Press of America, 1986).

6. Edmund Husserl, *Briefe an Roman Ingarden* (The Hague: Martinus Nijhoff, 1968), 25. The introduction to Heidegger's planned work on Aristotle has been published under the title "Phänomenologische Interpretationen zu Aristoteles (Anzeige der hermeneutischen Situation)" (see note 2 above).

7. IP 89; GZ 301/219; LW 123, 191.

8. HF 14; AJ 3–4, 34; PA 41–52, 91–92.

9. Heidegger's interpretation of Aristotle in the early 1920s was a deconstruction of his own earlier approach in his 1913 doctoral dissertation and in his 1915 habilitation writing, where he followed the neo-Scholastic interpretation of Aristotle given by Franz Brentano and Carl Braig, and used Aristotle's being-question in the form of the doctrine of categories for his own metaphysical "onto-logic," as he later called it. See Heidegger, "Vorwort zur ersten Ausgabe der 'Frühen Schriften'," *Frühe Schriften*, GA 1 (1978), 55.

10. PA 93, 108, 112, 117; HF 10–11, 26–27, 70; GZ 365/264, 380/275, 393/284, 419/303; LW 1–2, 127–95.

11. Hans-Georg Gadamer, *Heidegger's Wege*, 118, 130; *Gesammelte Werke*, Bd. 2 (Tübingen: J. C. B. Mohr, 1986), 484.

12. Concerning the relation between ontology and ethics, see *Sein und Zeit* ("SZ"), GA 2 (1977), 22, 380, 389; translated as *Being and Time*, trans. John Macquarrie and Edward Robinson (New York: Harper & Row, 1962), 37, 332, 339. Concerning theology, see PA 197 and Heidegger's 1927 lecture, "Phänomenologie und Theologie," *Wegmarken*, GA 9 (1978), 45–78; translated as "Phenomenology and Theology," trans. James G. Hart and John C. Maraldo, in James G. Hart and John C. Maraldo, eds., *The Piety of Thinking* (Bloomington: Indiana Univ. Press, 1976), 5–21.

13. LW 52–53. Compare Gary E. Overvold, "Husserl on Reason and Justification in Ethics," in D. Ihde and H. J. Silverman, eds., *Descriptions* (New York: State Univ. of New York Press, 1985), 248–55.

14. LW 53. Compare Parvis Emad, *Heidegger and the Phenomenology of Values: His Critique of Intentionality* (Glen Ellyn, Ill.: Torey Press, 1981); "Heidegger's Value-Criticism and Its Bearing on the Phenomenology of Values," in J. Sallis, ed., *Radical Phenomenology* (Atlantic Highlands, N.J.: Humanities Press, 1978), 190–208.

15. See Beat Sitter, "Zur Möglichkeit Dezisionistischer Auslegung von Heideggers Ersten Schriften," *Zeitschrift für Philosophische Forschung* 24 (1970): 516–35.

16. PA 84; AJ 31. Compare SZ 507/435, 382/334, 389–90/339–40; GZ 441/319.

17. Martin Heidegger, "Drei Briefe Heideggers an Karl Löwith," in Dietrich Papenfuss and Otto Pöggeler, eds., *Zur philosophischen Aktualität Heideggers*, vol. 2: *Im Gespräch der Zeit* (Frankfurt am Main: Vittorio Klostermann, 1990), 27–39, p. 29.

18. See also SZ 222/211 where Heidegger states that ontology has nothing to do with "moralizing critique" and "philosophy of culture."

19. Cf. Karl Löwith, *Heidegger: Denker in Dürftiger Zeit*, 2. Aufl. (Göttingen: Vandenhoeck & Ruprecht, 1960), p. 20 n. 1.

20. Martin Heidegger, "Brief über den Humanismus," in *Wegmarken*, GA 9 (1978), 313–64, p. 354; translated as "Letter on Humanism," trans. Frank A. Capuzzi, in Martin Heidegger, *Basic Writings*, ed. David Farrell Krell (New York: Harper & Row, 1977), 193–242, pp. 232–33.

21. Martin Heidegger, Letter to William Richardson, in Richardson, *Heidegger: Through Phenomenology to Thought*, xvii. Compare Hans-Georg Gadamer, "Der Eine Weg Martin Heideggers," in Gadamer, *Gesammelte Werke*, Bd. 3 (Tübingen: J. C. B. Mohr, 1987); David Farrell Krell, *Intimations*

of Mortality: Time, Truth, and Finitude in Heidegger's Thinking of Being (University Park: Pennsylvania State Univ. Press, 1986), p. 180 n. 3.

22. For discussion of aspects of Heidegger's thought in the early twenties that foreshadowed his later involvement in National Socialism, see Theodore Kisiel, "Heidegger's Apology: Biography as Philosophy and Ideology," *Graduate Faculty Philosophy Journal* 14:2–15:1 (1991): 363–404; Michael E. Zimmerman, *Heidegger's Confrontation with Modernity: Technology, Politics, Art* (Bloomington: Indiana Univ. Press, 1990), 17–33; Victor Farías, *Heidegger and Nazism*, ed. J. Margolis and T. Rockmore, trans. P. Burrell and G. R. Ricci (Philadelphia: Temple Univ. Press, 1989), 38–47.

23. In Guido Schneeberger, *Nachlese zu Heidegger: Dokumente zu seinem Leben und Denken* (Bern: Suhr, 1962), 136.

24. In Hugo Ott, "Martin Heidegger als Rektor der Universität Freiburg i. Br. 1933/34," *Zeitschrift des Breisgau-Geschichtsvereins* 103 (1984): 117. Compare Thomas Sheehan, "Heidegger and the Nazis," *New York Review of Books*, June 16, 1988, pp. 38–47; Farías, *Heidegger and Nazism*; Hugo Ott, *Martin Heidegger: Unterwegs zu seiner Biographie* (Frankfurt am Main: Campus, 1988).

25. Sheehan, "Heidegger and the Nazis," 47; John D. Caputo, "Demythologizing Heidegger: Alētheia and the History of Being," *Review of Metaphysics* 41 (1987–88): 519–46; Jürgen Habermas, "Hans-Georg Gadamer: Urbanizing the Heideggerian Province," in Habermas, *Philosophical-Political Profiles*, trans. Frederick G. Lawrence (Cambridge, Mass.: MIT Press, 1983), 191–99.

26. Manfred Riedel, ed., *Rehabilitierung der praktischen Philosophie*, 2 vols. (Freiburg: Rombach, 1972, 1974). For the vast scholarship on Aristotle that the early Heidegger inspired, see the sampling of works cited in Thomas J. Sheehan, "On the Way to *Ereignis*: Heidegger's Interpretation of *Physis*," in Hugh J. Silverman, John Sallis, and Thomas M. Seebohm, eds., *Continental Philosophy in America* (Pittsburgh, Pa.: Duquesne Univ. Press, 1983), p. 136 n. 11; Franco Volpi, "Heidegger in Marburg: Die Auseinandersetzung mit Aristoteles," *Philosophischer Literaturanzeiger* 37 (1984): 173 n. 3. The appropriation of Aristotle's notion of *phronēsis* in Gadamer's hermeneutics, Arendt's practical philosophy, Habermas's critical theory, and Rorty's neo-pragmatism also derives from Heidegger's interpretations of Aristotle in the twenties. See Hans-Georg Gadamer, *Truth and Method*, 2nd. rev. ed., trans. rev. J. Weinsheimer and D. G. Marshall (New York: Crossroad, 1989), 312–24, 540; Hannah Arendt, *The Human Condition* (Chicago: Univ. of Chicago Press, 1958); Jürgen Habermas, "The Classical Doctrine of Politics in Relation to Social Philosophy," in Habermas, *Theory and Praxis*, trans. J. Viertel (Boston: Beacon Press, 1973), 41–81, esp. p. 42 n. 4; Richard Rorty, *Philosophy and the Mirror of Nature* (Princeton,

N.J.: Princeton Univ. Press, 1980), p. 319 and chapter 8; Richard J. Bernstein, *Beyond Objectivism and Relativism* (Philadelphia: Univ. of Pennsylvania Press, 1983), part 3.

27. Hans-Georg Gadamer, in Leo Strauss and H.-G. Gadamer, "Correspondence concerning *Wahrheit und Methode*," *The Independent Journal of Philosophy* 2 (1978): 5–12, p. 10. In spite of repeated requests, Heidegger for decades stood by his decision against publishing his writings from the early twenties. Before his death in 1976, he made no plans to have his early Freiburg lectures (1919–23) included in the edition of his collected writings. He himself destroyed his lecture course manuscripts from 1915 and 1916; see Friedrich-Wilhelm von Herrmann, "Die Edition der Vorlesungen Heideggers in seiner Gesamtausgabe letzter Hand," *Heidegger Studies* 2 (1986): 154. He believed that his "thoughtpath" began only around the time of his move to Marburg in 1923–24 and thus comprises only three phases, which he called the "sense of being" (*Being and Time*), the "truth of being" (1930s and 1940s), and the "topos of being" (1940s onward); see his *Seminare*, GA 15 (1986), 344. He viewed his early Freiburg and Marburg writings as "youthful leaps" and inferior anticipations of what was to come later; see his *Unterweg zur Sprache*, GA 12 (1985), 121, translated as *On the Way to Language*, trans. Peter D. Hertz (New York: Harper & Row, 1971), 35.

12

The Finitude of the World:
Phenomenology in Transition from Husserl to Heidegger

Klaus Held
(translated by Anthony J. Steinbock)

In the following reflections I would like to offer a reply to a question frequently posed: since *Being and Time*, has Heidegger's thought steadily developed the approach to phenomenology as founded by Husserl? Or does one find with Heidegger decisive motives outside phenomenology, such that one is forced to speak of a philosophical break between Heidegger and Husserl?

As my point of departure, I will tender the thesis that the world is the actual subject matter of phenomenology; it follows, then, that how we answer the question concerning the relationship between Heidegger and Husserl will have to be decided by a comparative analysis of their respective conceptions of the world. I will argue that Heidegger's treatment of the world carries on and radicalizes the fundamental problematic of Husserlian phenomenology.[1] This should not obscure the profound difference between these two thinkers. To the contrary—the difference shows up precisely in their understandings of world. The fundamental determination of world in Husserl is infinity; in Heidegger, finitude. These two determinations, however, do not exclude one another. Finitude of the world, understood in Heidegger's sense, makes its infinity in Husserl's sense possible. The following reflections are offered in substantiation of this thesis.

The novelty of phenomenological thought consists in a radical change in attitude. Every attitude is an attitude-towards-something: it has a correlate. The *tertium comparationis* of the prephenomenological attitude, which Husserl characterizes as the "natural attitude," and of the phenomenological attitude, is their common correlate. This correlate is the world. The difference between the two attitudes lies in how they are related to this correlate.² As a form of thought, phenomenology makes the world thematic, makes it an object of its analyses. The natural attitude is characterized by the fact that the world is not yet thematic in it. Essential to the natural attitude is its relatedness to the world, but precisely in such a way that the world cannot be made thematic.

Phenomenology can make the world thematic for the first time because it rigorously observes each being, in all its determinations, with respect to *how* human beings encounter it. Phenomenology occupies itself exclusively with this *How*, with the correlation between the being that appears to human beings and the way of this appearing. This is the indispensable methodical principle of phenomenology, the principle of correlation, which Husserl, looking back in his last work, "The Crisis of European Sciences," called the basis of the whole work of his life.³

"To appear" means to emerge and to come to light from an unlit background. Therefore the fundamental idea of a concrete analysis of correlation is that all appearances have something in common. Human beings never encounter anything totally isolated, no matter what type of being they may deal with; rather, the being stands out in relief from an unlit background, due to which in each case a diversity of beings belong together with regard to their appearing. This background is an open range of possibilities in which one can attend to other beings, forming in this way a "field of vision" (*Gesichtskreis*), a horizon for such possibilities. Since the possibilities refer to one another in a regulated manner, every such horizon is an indicated and indicating referential context (*Verweisungszusammenhang*). Every horizon also contains indications to other horizons. Thus, they are all bound together in a single nexus of indicating implications for all conceivable horizons, that is, in the world.

The How—the manner—of appearing for every being is its embeddedness in the latent universal horizon, "world," its worldliness. Because worldliness forms the background in every appearing as How, the human being is also already able in some way to speak prephilosophically of the world in which the appearing being belongs. But the world as the whole of beings, or as the dimension for this whole, belongs to beings and is not the How of its appearing, the universal horizon. The world is in play in the natural attitude as this How in every encounter with beings; and as such it is the correlate of this attitude. But the natural attitude is defined by its inability to enter expressly into a relationship with its correlate. The human being takes up a relation to this correlate for the first time in making it, as the univeral horizon, the theme of thought. This step is the transition to the phenomenological attitude.

Prior to this step, the world background of appearing stands open to the human being in a nonrelational way. It determines human existence as nonrelational worldliness, which Heidegger calls "being-in-the-world." In the natural attitude, the world as universal horizon remains as such unthematized. Phenomenology is the very discovery of this unthematicity. Accordingly, the phenomenological attitude places thought in a peculiar relation to the nonrelational worldliness of natural life. The task incumbent upon thought is to render the world thematic but without falsifying its horizonal character, which makes it insuperably unthematizable for the natural attitude. The fundamental task of phenomenology is to thematize the world horizon *as* what is unthematizable as such. The question whether and to what extent Heidegger is still a phenomenologist after *Being and Time* therefore turns on whether he contributed to the solution of this task.

Phenomenology has to explain, first, why the universal horizon cannot be made thematic in the natural attitude. Human beings are open to the universal horizon without taking up a relation to it. There are conscious relations, not with the horizon itself but merely with beings, each of which steps forward from the unthematized background. The relation is conscious in the sense that the human being grasps what appears as an identical object, in the knowledge that it can be encountered in a multitude of ways of appearing.

The human being is familiar with a difference in the ways of appearance that belongs to this consciousness of objects. The ways of appearance can be more or less suitable for making accessible to the human being a *full determination*, that is, the determination that gives the respective object its identity. Consciousness of the object harbors the tendency to make the ways of appearance in this sense optimal. Husserl calls this tendency *intentionality*, and the desired optimal appearance *evidence*. Thus, the conscious relation to beings in the natural attitude is characterized by an interest that pervades everything, namely, the aspiration of intentional consciousness toward bringing objective identity to the fore with evidence. This interest fixates the natural attitude on objects and prevents it from attending to the How of their appearing, to the world horizon.

In order to fulfill its intentional aspiration toward evidence, intentional consciousness must let objects appear in horizons; for only horizons, as nexus of indicating implications, hold in store the possibilities through which what appears can be further explicated in its determinateness. Consciousness is motivated by its interest in determinate objects to posit corresponding goals. Every particular horizon is a field of vision arising when intentional consciousness forms nexus of indicating implications which are related to such goals. Accordingly, it must give priority to certain nexus of indicating implications and screen out others. Because of this limitation, particular horizons are only excerpts of the universal horizon; they are finite. For this reason Husserl occasionally calls them "special worlds" (*Sondernwelten*) in his late period.[4]

Similar to the way in which we have an explicit consciousness of appearing objects, we likewise can occasionally become conscious of special worlds, each of which forms the objects' surroundings, as it were. This is the case, for example, when one becomes aware that one's horizon differs from that of others by virtue of profession, age, nationality, etc. Such differences are possible because horizons are conditioned by determinate interests in objects. Since intentional interestedness in the natural attitude ties us to special worlds, it prevents us from being able to enter expressly into a relation with the universal horizon, "world."

Nevertheless, we are familiar with the universal horizon unthematically. Intentional consciousness is an "I can," as Husserl appropriately writes. I can, as it were, inquire regarding every object appearing in a special world as to the indications lying implicit in it. In the process of explicating these implications, the special world does not post untrespassable boundaries for my "I can": I can also seize upon those indicating possibilities that go beyond the special world in question. Consciousness of ever repeatable implications belongs to the How—the manner—of appearing. The inexhaustibility of the nexus of indicating implications is a potential infinity, and is the main characteristic of the world as universal horizon.

This is the fundamental determination of the world in the natural attitude which Husserl discovered. This determination cannot be false even if it turns out to be the case (as with Heidegger) that the same unthematic world horizon can also be determined to be finite. Both characteristics must be valid in different respects. Up to now, concern with the universal horizon has been focused on the interestedness of the natural attitude. Intentional consciousness's interest in objective identity motivates it to transcend special-worldly limitedness in the inexhaustible nexus of indicating implications and to open up ever new horizons. If the world horizon can also be determined to be finite, this can only be due to yet something more that is in play in the nonrelational worldliness of the natural attitude, something other than intentional interestedness.

Intentional interestedness is a will, a will directed towards the formation and preservation of objective identity. It fixates our intentional consciousness in the natural attitude on objects or on their surroundings, the horizons. In order to be able to thematize the world horizon, we must therefore free ourselves from this will. "Suspending" (in Greek, *epechein*), in connection with the aspiration towards identity, makes the transition to the phenomenological attitude possible. For this reason Husserl characterizes the posture free from interestedness, upon which this attitude is based, as *epochē*. It arises through a decision, that is, an act of will, namely, the act by which we free ourselves precisely from willing an identity. The question before us now is, does this liberation from willing an identity first arise only through the *epochē*? Or does the *epochē* only bring to light an already existing freedom from willing an identity which, however, until that time remained concealed?

Husserl did not notice this alternative at all. Had he noticed it, he would probably have decided in favor of the former alternative. Nevertheless, we have to emphasize that only this second possibility comes into consideration phenomenologically. When the freedom from willing an identity is engendered through the *epochē*, it is not a real freedom from willing; for the existence of the *epochē*, taken up as a lasting attitude, is dependent upon the effort of willing (to which it owes its existence) for its entire duration. The effort of willing that persists in this way within the *epochē* must assume the form of an interest directed towards an object.[5] For the *epochē* this object can only be the world. Thus, the *epochē* replaces the old interest in objects with a new one. The new object, "world as universal horizon," takes the place of the objects that interest us in the natural attitude.

The phenomenologist arrives now at an inevitable succession of ideas. One can do nothing else than make one's conscious relation to the object "world" the paradigm of interpretation of the non-relational worldliness of the natural attitude. The unthematic correlation between this attitude and the world horizon, which is not an intentional relation attached to interests (which is to say, is not a relationship of consciousness *to* something), must be reinterpreted as an intentional relation by the phenomenologist. The relation of intentional consciousness to the special worlds offers itself as a model for this reinterpretation; for, as mentioned, in the natural attitude we can already occasionally have an express consciousness of the special worlds.

Consciousness of a special world is made possible by the interest in objects for which the special world forms the surroundings, so to speak. Through objectification, intentional consciousness renders identifiable what appears to it. With every objectification there arises a new potential of indicating possibilities which consciousness has at its disposal, not only at the moment of objectification, but from then on, lastingly. Consciousness "habitualizes" the new possibilities, as Husserl says. In principle, we can become conscious again and again of the habitualities and of the special worlds which are thereby accessible to us.

Once the correlation between the natural attitude and world is interpreted as an intentional relation, the formation of special worlds through habitualization can serve as a model for this relation. The universal nexus of indicating implications which is "world," is built up out of—becomes "constituted" by—the special-worldly "space" of indications, similar to the way in which these arise from the habitualization of new possibilities of the appearing of objects. In contrast to the genesis of special worlds in the natural attitude, the process of constitution through which the universal horizon is formed, falls into an insuperable forgetfulness because the interestedness in objects fetters intentional consciousness to the special worlds. Phenomenological analysis of world constitution is the transcendental recollection that frees us from these shackles.

At root, the world problematic in Husserl amounts to this understanding. It explains why, in Husserl, world-constituting consciousness takes the place of the world as the subject matter of phenomenology. The decisive mistake in this understanding, however, lies in the reinterpretation of preintentional nonrelational worldliness as an intentional relation to the world. The hidden reason for this is the misinterpretation of the *epochē*. When the liberation from willing an identity is first produced through the *epochē*, it is not really free from this willing. Accordingly, there must already be a freedom from willing an identity prior to the decision to execute the *epochē*, that is, within the natural attitude. Since the relation to appearing objects is based on this willing, it can only be the How of appearing whose character is determined by being free from willing an identity. Human being does not stand in an intentional relation towards the world as horizon, but, rather, the world stands open to human being, prior to all intentional interest in objects. But from the very beginning, this world openness is covered up by the relation determined by interest in objects and by the restriction to particular special worlds which form their surroundings. The *epochē* is the process of lifting this veil.

The preintentional world horizon has a lead on the constitution of special worlds (which allow of being explained by intentional interestedness), a lead that can never be outstripped. It is an a priori which therefore can also never be explained entirely by tracing back the accomplishments of constitution in transcendental memory. But the a priori world openness, which the *epochē* lays bare, has only been characterized in a negative manner: it is free from the willing an identity that dominates intentional-interested consciousness. How can it be characterized in a positive manner?

Willing an identity governs intentional consciousness in the formation of new horizons. Finding itself within a certain nexus of indicating implications, consciousness pursues a determinate indicated direction and thereby expands the present horizon or constructs a new one. The choice of the course of indication is an intentional, willing action, an activity. Here, the access to preintentional world openness presents itself for phenomenological analysis. The description just offered is, of course, one-sided. The choice of the course of indication is not only an action but also an affection: consciousness *lets* itself be guided in the horizon, in this or that direction. When it gives in to a direction, it follows an interest, to be sure. But this interest is aroused for its part by motives of which consciousness is not the master. The philosophical tradition characterizes these motives, which are not at the disposal of consciousness, as *pathos* or affect.

The obverse active intentional orientation in the nexus of indicating implications has the passive reverse of affectivity. Husserl always interprets this passivity fundamentally as a weakened activity, as a preliminary stage to being-intentionally-directed-towards-something. In so doing, he presupposes, without admitting it, that consciousness could univocally locate the origin and direction of indication in which consciousness comes across an affection. But affections are ambiguous. The course of indication along which we are guided by affections does not ultimately depend upon what affects us but rather upon a preceding readiness to be affected in one way or another. We are familiar with this readiness from life in the natural attitude as mood, as being attuned (*Stimmung*). It cannot be localized on either side of the correlation, "consciousness—appearing object"; rather, it determines the How of the appearing as a whole that occurs in this correlation. Thus, it is nothing other than the way in which the nonrelational world openness itself takes place at any one time. This insight seems to me to be one of Heidegger's greatest discoveries in *Being and Time*.[6] In this work, human being as the place of the original mood-related openness is called *Dasein*.

Dasein is dependent upon what the taciturn mood says to it in order to find out how it is doing with respect to its nonrelational worldliness, with respect to its being-in-the-world. How preintentional world openness occurs and becomes revealed in moods withdraws itself from Dasein's power of volition. It remains insuperably contingent—an accident. We are dependent upon it for the orientation in nexus of indicating implications and for the formation of horizons. The "I can" which opens up the universal horizon, world, to us is in itself limited through this dependency. But with this we see that the world horizon is finite and in what sense it is finite. It is finite as a How of appearing which precedes interest. A movement running counter to the intentional willing which objectifies, lies in the event of this How. It is a countermovement that we originally experience in being overcome by moods and in the dependency upon its taciturn voice. In the development following *Being and Time*, Heidegger will characterize this countermovement as withdrawal (*Entzug*). We respond intentionally to the withdrawal that we experience in moods by letting ourselves be guided in a certain direction and thereby renounce seizing upon other possibilities. As action, this is a commitment to the respective direction of interest by which we are bound to the special world forming our present field of vision. The dominating interest limits this field of vision by renouncing other indicated possibilities. The renunciation grants the character of finitude to the special world concerned. In the sphere of intentional activity of horizon formation, this finitude of renunciation manifests the cryptic concealed finitude unique to the preintentional world which reveals itself in moods through the withdrawal.

The world is the subject matter of phenomenology because the *epochē*, the main gate to phenomenology, lays bare the prevolitional worldliness which precedes interest, forming the a priori of the interest-governed intentional relation to the world. If the prevolitional world openness has the character of mood, and the *epochē* is only the exposure of this world openness, then it must also be by virtue of a mood that there is a decision to execute the *epochē*. In his late work, Husserl regarded phenomenology as the critical renewal of the first thematization of the world—the *kosmos*—through which the Greeks founded philosophy and science. According to the self-interpretation of Greek philosophy in Plato and Aristotle (both of whom were appropriated by Husserl and Heidegger),[7] philosophical and scientific thought arose from wonder (in Greek, *thaumazein*). But wonder is a mood. The fundamental trait of this mood is the astonishment with which we become aware of the world *as* world. This astonishment arises through the "miracle" that what is unthematic can indeed become thematic. The genesis of philosophy and science was an unpredictable accident—the accident that a mood appeared on the scene which motivated making the world itself thematic, that is, thematizing the world which reveals itself in moods and which remained, up to that time, unthematic.

Interpreting the world as an infinite nexus of indicating implications for the many finite special worlds was a tendency inherent in this thematization from the very beginning. This can be seen, for example, in Greek science, which from the start took a plurality (perhaps an unending plurality) of *kosmoi* into consideration. This tendency shows up still more clearly in the Ionic *historiē*—for us, the first concrete form of empirical science. It understands itself to be "gathering knowledge" of the wealth of the one world. As one can observe with Herodotus, the master of *historiē*, gathering knowledge does not mean the aimless accumulation of information. Rather, the thrust of this *historiē* was that customs, ideas of God, and institutions of differing cultural special worlds should be interpreted as adumbrations of intercultural identities. In this way, an infinite universal horizon appears to the human being as nexus of indicating implications of finite special worlds. Wonder becomes theoretical curiosity that marvels at the infinite wealth of special-worldly multiplicity. But, at the same time, it strives to refer this wealth back to the unity of the one world.

Heidegger recognizes curiosity in *Being and Time* as only one aspect of inauthenticity, the flight in the face of oneself. In his later ontohistorical thought, it belongs to the forgetfulness of Being. The metaphysical will, which only admits of what can be brought into presence, reaches its extreme form in the attempt to hold everything at one's disposal through unlimited information. This will is characterized by the fact that in it the withdrawal itself withdraws in an abysmal concealedness. This forgetfulness of the withdrawal, according to Heidegger, also dominates in the curiosity of science; it begins with "wanting to know everything," a criticism of the "polymath" that Heraclitus, as contemporary of *historiē*, had already made.[8] Heidegger never seriously considered the possibility that there could be a theoretical curiosity for the infinity of the world in the mode of authenticity, a science not forgetful of the withdrawal.

But this possibility exists from the beginning of the history of science up to the present. Authentic theoretical curiosity responds to the withdrawal, which, in philosophically and scientifically motivated wonder, is experienced as mood. As explained, the withdrawal manifests itself on the level of intentionality in the renunciation through which the special worlds are alone constituted in their finitude. But the withdrawal also gives the impetus for transcending the finitude of the special worlds in the universal horizon; for the mood, the experience of the withdrawal, makes the affections possible through which all latent indicated possibilities (even the possibilities beyond the particular special world) can be awakened passively in the first place and thereby seized upon actively. Laying bare the relation between the one universal horizon and the many special worlds, that is, a relation whose relata can only be separated through the withdrawal, is the motive for authentic curiosity.

Indeed, the danger accompanying theoretical curiosity is a forgetfulness. Philosophical-scientific thought threatens to forget finitude once it encounters the infinity of the universal horizon. Finitude characterizes fundamentally the world horizon insofar as this horizon precedes all special-worldly differentiation as an a priori that remains open to us in moods. This differentiation arises from willing an identity and intentional consciousness's interest in objects. The more firmly the unthematic world horizon is fastened to the Procrustean bed of objectification by thematizing it in philosophical and scientific thought, the more ostensibly the infinity of the world juts out into the foreground over against its finitude.

In ancient thinking the belief that the world is finite was prevalent; in this respect, that thinking indirectly had a presentiment of the withdrawal. Not until the modern period does there emerge, through philosophical-scientific thought, an extreme intensification of its pathos for infinity. Despite his sympathy for this pathos of curiosity, it was Husserl who first clearly described the connection between the objectification of the world in the modern period and the domination of the thought of infinity.[9] The world is objectified in its infinity by modern specialized sciences in a peculiar way. The world appears in these sciences as the pole which lies in infinity; through its never-ending work, specialized scientific research approaches the world without ever reaching it. We pay for this objectification with a profound forgetfulness of the horizonal character of the world. Husserl calls such forgetfulness *objectivism*.

The tendency of Husserl's criticism of the objectivistic forgetfulness of the world is towards a thoughtful reflection on the finitude of the world. But, in the end, this thoughtful reflection lacks efficacy because Husserl's theory of the constitution of the universal horizon, which remains fixated on the infinity of this horizonal character, thereby still remains attached to the spirit of objectivism. The finitude of the special worlds is submerged in the infinity of the universal horizon. This finitude comes into its own when it is first interpreted from the perspective of the withdrawal. Heidegger paved the way for this by having broken through to the preintentional world openness and by having laid bare its mood character.

Notes

1. This was already the original idea of Eugen Fink, whose outstanding early efforts concerning the tension between Husserl and Heidegger are most worthy of further attention; see his essays in Eugen Fink, *Studien zur Phänomenologie, 1930–1939* (The Hague: M. Nijhoff, 1966); and *Nähe und Distanz: Phänomenologische Vorträge und Aufsätze*, ed. F. A. Schwartz (Freiburg, München: Alber, 1976). The world as proper theme of phenomenology also forms the subject matter of my investigation, "Husserls neue Einführung in die Philosophie: Der Begriff der Lebenswelt," in C. F. Gethmann, ed., *Lebenswelt und Wissenschaft* (Frankfurt am Main: Suhrkamp, 1990).

2. Therefore phenomenology has its "matter" in common with prephilosophical life, but it considers this matter in a radical, new manner. In this sense phenomenology appears originally as method, as Heidegger correctly emphasized in *Being and Time*, section 7.

3. Edmund Husserl, *Die Krisis der europäischen Wissenschaften und die transzendentale Phänomenologie*, ed. W. Biemel (The Hague: M. Nijhoff, 1954), 168–69 note. Compare *The Crisis of European Sciences and Transcendental Phenomenology: An Introduction to Phenomenological Philosophy*, trans. D. Carr (Evanston, Ill.: Northwestern Univ. Press, 1970), 166–67 note.

4. On the differentiation of the notion of special world in the later Husserl see Klaus Held, "Heimwelt, Fremdwelt, die eine Welt." This essay is available in French as "Le monde natal, le monde étranger, le monde un," in vol. 115 of the Phaenomenologica series, *Husserl-Ausgabe und Husserl-Forschung*, ed. S. IJsseling (Dordrecht, Boston: Kluwer Academic Publ., 1990). It will appear in German in vol. 24 of the Phänomenologische Forschungen series, forthcoming from K. Alber.

5. On the relation between *epochē* and effort of willing (*Willentlichkeit*) see Klaus Held, "Husserls Rückgang auf das Phainomenon und die geschichtliche Stellung der Phänomenologie," in *Dialektik und Genesis in der Phänomenologie*, Phänomenologische Forschungen 10 (Freiburg, München: Alber, 1980); and "Husserl und die Griechen," in *Profile der Phänomenologie*, Phänomenologische Forschungen 22 (Freiburg, München: Alber, 1989).

6. I have tried to establish that Heidegger's point of departure (*Ansatz*) is to be interpreted primarily as a phenomenology of world openness in the following essays: "Heidegger und das Prinzip der Phänomenologie," in A. Gethmann-Siefert and O. Pöggeler, eds., *Heidegger und die praktische Philosophie* (Frankfurt am Main: Suhrkamp, 1988); and "Grundstimmung und Zeitkritik bei Heidegger," forthcoming from Klostermann in a collection of essays on Heidegger.

7. See Husserl, *Krisis der europäischen Wissenschaften*, pp. 331 ff.; and Martin Heidegger, *Grundfragen der Philosophie*, ed. F.-W. von Hermann, GA 45 (1984), 115–57, 197–98.

8. I refer to the phenomenological interpretation of Heraclitus in Klaus Held, *Heraklit, Parmenides und Anfang von Philosophie und Wissenschaft: Eine phänomenologische Besinnung* (Berlin: De Gruyter, 1980), part 2; on *historiē*, see esp. pp. 73ff. and 187ff.

9. I treat of the discord in Husserl's thinking—between the pathos for infinity in the modern period and reflection on finitude—in another perspective in the following essays: Held, "Husserl und die Griechen"; and "Husserls These von der Europäisierung der Menschheit," in C. Jamme and O. Pöggeler, eds., *Phänomenologie im Widerstreit* (Frankfurt am Main: Suhrkamp, 1989).

13

Hegel, Heidegger, Derrida: Retrieval as Reconstruction, Destruction, Deconstruction

Joseph C. Flay

There are obvious ways in which Heidegger and Derrida can simply be opposed to Hegel. For example, Heidegger, on the one hand, takes as a major theme that of the forgetting of the original question of Being, whereas Hegel clearly thinks that there was no forgetting of anything. Derrida, on the other hand, has taken up Hegel as a primary thinker to be deconstructed, finding time and again in Hegel's devotion to *Aufhebungen* an unjustified commitment to thought bound in an unthought economy, while Hegel claims to have achieved self-comprehension. Yet for both of these twentieth-century thinkers it became increasingly clear that their respective relations to Hegel were more complex than they had at first believed. In my view, neither Heidegger nor Derrida adequately grasps Hegel's philosophy. In the case of Heidegger, a destruction of Hegel's thought was not successfully carried out, although such a project would have been necessary for Heidegger's thought. In the case of Derrida, although Hegel's exclusionary principles are made clear, there is a relation to metaphysics that Derrida has not seen.

One consequence of this failure by Heidegger and Derrida fully to confront Hegel was the tendency to move "the end of metaphysics," first attributed to Hegel, closer and closer to the present time. This, I think, is due to their failure to understand precisely in what manner Hegel did claim to bring the tradition to an end.[1] My intention in this paper is to understand Hegel's thought as a *reconstructive retrieval* of the tradition, a retrieval that not only completed metaphysics governed on the whole by an ontotheological perspective, but also, when correctly understood, will necessitate a critical rethinking of Heidegger's destructive retrieval of the tradition and of the deconstructive retrieval of Derrida.

I will begin my discussion with the observation that if anything is to be retrieved, it must first be there in a form in which it can be retrieved. Previous to Hegel, however, the tradition did not exist as *the* tradition; metaphysics did not exist as *the* metaphysics of *the* tradition. Since the tradition of metaphysics is in part what is thematized by Heidegger and Derrida, its existence as such is a precondition for these thinkers. I will then show that Hegel was able to retrieve metaphysics by a systematic reconstruction because he employed a method open to dialectic and governed rhetorically by irony,[2] and that this irony brings about the revelation of the ontological difference and Being as such, and does so precisely in the most extreme oblivion of the question of Being, that is, precisely in Hegel's oblivion to the question of Being.[3] Finally, I will argue that in this opening of a "beyond" of metaphysics, we also have the possibility of distancing from any economy, and thus the possibility of deconstruction. And, again, as in the case of the laying of the ground for Heidegger, this possibility of distancing is accomplished in Hegel's oblivion to the questions to be posed by deconstruction.

THE ORIGIN AND TASK OF HEGEL'S RETRIEVAL

Heidegger carries out his destruction and reveals the unhiding of the hidden by addressing the tradition as metaphysics. If Heidegger is to retrieve the tradition, and in particular if he is to address metaphysics as such—for example, in order to grasp the ontotheological nature of metaphysics—then metaphysics as a whole must already be present for thematization. It will not suffice that it be there as the metaphysics propounded by this or that thinker; it must be there as metaphysics as such.

Thinkers before Hegel never thematized *the* tradition. They may have addressed one or another problem in terms of one or another philosopher in order to lay the problematic for their own thought, but this did not give us the thematization of metaphysics as such. Hegel, however, identified philosophy with the history of philosophy and saw it as his task to bring this history of philosophy into a systematic whole. For Hegel the history of philosophy did not consist in various philosophies but in only one philosophy which had been set on its way by the pre-Socratics and, through the historical-philosophical dialogue, had been given to him.[4] To Hegel this meant that he was only a participant in this dialogue, a participant to whom the task had been given to bring the dialogue to completion. Consequently, this did not mean that he was to make the tradition fit his own philosophy; it meant, rather, that he was to make his own thought conform to the tradition with which he was in dialogue.[5]

To grasp Hegel's project, we cannot simply turn to his *Lectures on the History of Philosophy*; for at that level one is governed by a mere chronological, diachronic succession of positions which are developing into the metaphysics which Hegel seeks eventually to capture. What is demanded if one is to have at hand the metaphysics of the tradition is the thematization of this tradition as a systematic metaphysics, giving us thereby a synchronous structuring of the whole of the temporal development.[6] It is, then, rather to his *Science of Logic* that we must turn, for there he reconstructs the historical-philosophical dialogue and transforms, *for the first time*, the metaphysical discussions of the dialogue into a single, coherent system of metaphysics.[7] For the first time we have *the* metaphysics of *the* tradition: metaphysics as such is made fully present.

Given this claim, the question arises: How can Hegel bring the tradition to completion and not be simply another voice *in* the tradition? This question must be answered because, among other things, it is clear that Hegel's system does violence to the thinkers of the tradition not only in his historical accounts but as well in his discussion of the categories of metaphysics in the *Science of Logic*, and thus that he is not, in any straightforward way, simply retrieving that tradition. How can he claim to have completed the quest for the nature of the Being of beings if he seems to be voicing just another view in conflict with his predecessors?

The answer lies in Hegel's method, a method I am calling a reconstructive retrieval.[8] First, it is a retrieval because it is an approach to the tradition that aims to uncover what was not said in what was said. But it differs from the retrieval by Heidegger and others writing in the latter part of the twentieth century because it accepts *as a given* the correctness of the tradition conceived as the task of articulating the nature of the Being of beings. That is to say, in contrast to a destructive retrieval, it involves a positive attitude toward the self-conscious thematics of the tradition. Second, the retrieval is reconstructive, and not destructive, because Hegel's intention is to complete the tradition by authentically bringing the historical-philosophical dialogue into a single system, into the system that had been sought from the beginning.[9]

What makes this reconstructive retrieval not simply a recapitulation of what was said—what allows for *re*construction in retrieval—has two aspects, one logical and one rhetorical. Logically, Hegel proceeds dialectically. That is to say, he proceeds by accepting as true what has been said and then, holding strictly to what has been said, acts as "midwife." The *negative* outcome of the dialectic is that what has been said proves unacceptable to the one who made the original claim. Consequently the original claim in its original form must either be given up or modified in such a way that it would have been acceptable. The *positive* outcome of the dialectic is that, intent on saving the truth of what was said in the tradition, a "remedy" is sought so that what was said is modified in such a way that it will be acceptable.

Rhetorically—and it is in the rhetorical component that the necessity of the progress of the system of metaphysics lies—the dialectical exchange is governed by irony.[10] First, both Hegel and his "interlocutors" are engaged in and committed to the project of articulating the nature of the Being of beings. Without this engagement and commitment, irony would not have the "bite" it must have. What happens in the process of the dialogue really matters, both to Hegel and to others committed to the tradition.[11] Second, in the respective theses examined concerning the categories there are excesses, surpluses, something which not only makes of the thesis something it was not and was not intended to be, but more specifically makes of it something that is inconsistent with what it was originally taken and intended to be. In these unintended, unforeseen, and unacceptable consequences of what had been said—and the heart of irony lies here—the project is threatened with self-destruction founded on the emergent self-contradiction. This negative form of irony—the form that irony usually takes—forces one to distance oneself from the original acceptance of what was said, while at the same time remaining engaged in the original project. In an effort to save the dialogue and its project, a positive irony emerges and it is discovered that, if one accepts something originally thought unacceptable, one can save the project from self-destruction. But what one must accept ironically involves a constructive contradiction. One is saved from a self-destructive contradiction by embracing a constructive one. This takes us beyond anything that Plato or Plato's Socrates envisioned for their *dialegesthai dia tou logou*, and this is what distinguishes Hegel from the earlier dialectical thinkers.

THE RETRIEVAL OF THE METAPHYSICS OF THE TRADITION

It might be useful to make concrete this sketch of a reconstructive retrieval by looking at the categories most familiar and, in a way, most problematic: Being, Nothing (or Non-being), and Becoming. This more detailed account is necessary if one is to understand how Hegel's retrieval lays the groundwork for later thought. What I will show here holds for the whole of the *Logic*, not in the sense that there is a robotic repetition such as was envisioned in the putative and erroneous paradigm of thesis, antithesis, and synthesis, but in the sense of different and specific contents revealing, respectively, different and specific self-contradictions.[12]

The Being to which we refer here is, of course, the Being of beings.[13] The general claim of this category when it is understood as the absolute is that it is true of everything without qualification. As Parmenides' goddess puts it: "It is" (*esti*) is to be said of everything and is the only way to truth. The way of Non-being or *ouk esti* is impossible, and the two are to be absolutely separated. Furthermore, the way of Becoming is also unacceptable and represents at best mere seeming, illusion, and the like. Being is one, undifferentiated, and absolutely and uniquely equal to itself. It is eternally what it is; it is the Being of all beings whatsoever.[14]

What is discovered is that, ironically, Being is thereby indistinguishable from that from which it was to be absolutely distinguished, namely, from Non-being or Nothing. Now this is not Hegel's view in the sense that it is a position posited by him and to be opposed to the view that Being is ultimate; it is, on the contrary, a result that emerges *of necessity* from the original position. Because both Hegel and those who would hold this position about Being are fully committed to the quest for the Being of beings, and because, for the "thinkers of the understanding" whom Hegel is addressing, contradiction of any sort signifies unintelligibility and untruth, this original position is self-destructive because it is self-contradictory.[15] The violence visited upon this traditional characterization of pure Being is therefore a violence which it brings on itself. But how can one now continue and yet retain the original intention of comprehending Being as the ultimate category? How can the category be reconstructively retrieved from this self-destructive result of its own positing?

The answer lies in an examination of the way the contradiction arose in the first place. It arose due to the denial of any difference whatsoever in the nature of Being, namely, in the claim that "it is" can be said *indifferently* of everything. It was also due to the demand that Being and Non-being must be absolutely separated, not related in any way. Out of these claims of the indifference in Being and of the absolute separation of Being from Non-being ironically arose the situation that they could not be separated at all but were, rather, identical to each other.

The solution to this *aporia* comes from the tradition itself; for we have been given, in the process of specifying what pure Being is, a category—the category of Becoming—that will allow us to define Being and at the same time distinguish Being from Non-being. If Being is understood as Becoming in such a way that in Being itself there is a distinction between Being and Non-being—that is, if Being is understood as the movement from Non-being to Being (generation and sustenance) and from Being to Non-being (degeneration and destruction)—then we can "save" Being. Being is then present in two forms: first, Being as Becoming, that is, as the constant and eternal presence of what-is as generation and destruction, with Becoming itself neither coming to be nor ceasing to be (for example, the *logos* of Heraclitus) and, second, Being as an element of Becoming. Again, this is not a private view of Hegel's. Through a positive, constructive irony that enframes the dialectic, the *aporia* to which we had been led is overcome.

The reconstructive retrieval of the category of Being can be summed up in this way. If Being is characterized as Becoming and is understood to be related to Non-being in the ways in which it is so related in Becoming, then the indeterminacy of Being can be preserved as the ultimate foundation of all else, while at the same time making Being determinate and distinguishable from Non-being. Contradiction, therefore, is at the heart of the nature of the Being of beings. If, however, what was said concerning an absolute difference between Being, Non-being, and Becoming is insisted upon, then one cannot say what one intended to say. Only by means of the reconstruction given here in the dialectic can the original intention be preserved and pursued further.[16]

Given this example of the nature of a reconstructive retrieval, we can turn to a sketch of what follows in the *Science of Logic* and come to an understanding of how it is that what is hidden, in Heidegger's sense, reveals itself in its own hiddenness. Hegel's retrieval in the course of the *Logic* can be summarized as follows: First, the "Doctrine of Being," the account of what-is in its pure happening, leads us to the conclusion that there are only beings. The ultimate presupposition and ground of what-is in its Being is beings themselves, mutually and reciprocally conditioning the existence, presence, and nature of each other. Since the beginning of philosophy it has been recognized that everything must have its measure which, in turn, gives us its essence. Hegel's retrieval shares in this recognition; but the retrieval also shows that there is no ultimate measure for all measures, no being that transcends other beings and is the measure of all measures.

If one turns then, as the tradition did, to a sense of the ultimate understood as Essence rather than as Being—"Essence" meaning that which stands behind, above, below what-is in its being—the reconstructive retrieval shows again that, necessarily, there is no beyond or behind; rather, there is only "the absolute relation" (the last category of the Doctrine of Essence), which is the relating of beings to each other through their own reciprocally determined and determining measures. There is, ironically, something like traditional Essence only if one identifies Essence with Being, locating it not in some transcendent being, as the tradition did, but in the very Being of beings themselves. What-is is *itself* totally self-determining and thus both absolutely necessary and absolutely free as *causa sui*.

Finally, if one turns to the Concept, as distinguished from Being and Essence, in order to find some transcendent which gives a ground to the Being of beings, one finds that only the Absolute Idea, *understood as dialectic in general*, can give us the completion of the task of metaphysics. Hegel's discussion of the Absolute Idea, traditionally interpreted to be a final destruction of finitude and a full immersion of all in an undifferentiated identity, is in fact only the dialectic itself, an ontological process of self-differentiation such that identity is identity only on the grounds of difference, that is, that the identity of anything is a function only of its differences both in relation to itself and in relation to what is other to it. The philosophies of the understanding are thus forced to find, again ironically, that only if their linear logics and their rejection of contradiction are surrendered and dialectic is embraced can we have the completion of the task of metaphysics.

THE UNHIDING OF THE HIDDENNESS OF BEING

This outcome gives us the ground for the unhiding of the hiddenness. Where most thinkers, including Heidegger and Derrida themselves, have argued for a break between Hegel and his successors, I would argue for continuity.[17] Hegel's conclusion focuses us *entirely and exclusively* on the Being of beings understood as the mutual determination and redetermination of beings by each other. All forms of transcendence, which prior to this have made metaphysics ontotheological, have been shown in fact to prohibit the completion of metaphysics. Everything, in its full finitude and contingency, has been brought to transparent presence *on the same level of being.*

According to Hegel's view of the tradition, a transcendent presence, the presence of the transcendent Being, had hidden Being as such.[18] That is to say, when Being as such was thematized as transcendent presence in the tradition, it was thematized only in the form of a transcendent Being, giving us ontotheology. With Hegel's reconstructive retrieval ontotheology is banished for the first time, and the hiddenness of Being reveals itself when the dialectic of the Absolute Idea removes all possibility of transcendence in the traditional sense. What-is is now enframed within itself, by itself, and is both cause and effect of itself. Thus, where before there was some kind of presence, the presence of the transcendent Being, now there is emptiness. The unhiding of the hiddenness comes with Hegel's destruction of ontotheology, or rather, in Hegel's terms, with the tradition's own rejection of ontotheology. The place, that is, the space-time complexus referred to as "eternity," hitherto hidden by *a* being, was opened, and Heidegger could take his step back.[19]

The consequence of the opening of this place is seen as nihilism or atheism by those still submerged in the unreconstructed tradition. If the term is retained as used by the tradition—and dialectically it must be—then Hegel is saying that only the acceptance of nihilism can save us from nihilism, only the acceptance of the absence of a transcendent, nonrelative ground can give us any ground at all. Hegel ends ontotheology not by opposing it, but by employing dialectic; and he finalizes the closure of the economy of philosophical thought by giving a complete, discursive account of being, essence, and concept.

But this closure has in it a fissure, and the irony continues. Hegel himself did not enter the Open to think it, but he created it by opening it for the first time. The mere possibility of entering the place previously inhabited by a highest being constitutes the fissure. Metaphysics and the tradition as a whole have finally been thematized and realized as a whole in a single philosophical position that has shown itself to be the *only* possible position *if* what-is is to be made completely intelligible. At the same time that the transcendent is removed from consideration, however, thus leaving empty that place, Hegel was prohibited by the economy of his own thought from thematizing what had been opened; for the opening was to him only the opening in which the dialectic takes place.

HEGEL'S RETRIEVAL AND THE OPEN

This place opened by Hegel and which Heidegger explored as the Open is the origin of all economies of thought and action. It is for this reason that within this Open the dialectic takes place and rationality is restricted and defined. But it is also, as origin, the place of the fissure, of the rupture that allows us to step back and to undertake the deconstruction of those economies.[20] In the deconstructive retrieval of those economies, we not only think the nondialectical difference, but we free thought from those presuppositions which, previously unthematized and hidden, subordinated the philosopher to the demands of a particular economy. Deconstruction, therefore, standing in the place opened by Hegel, completes the task that Hegel began; for what had been "naturally" excluded by the tradition of ontotheology is reconsidered in its relation to what had been "naturally" included. The connection of an acceptable economy to the transcendent being is brought into question precisely because the transcendent being is no longer there. We stand before an economy without anchor, a naked economy, an economy founded only by the decisionary inclusion/exclusion at the basis of the reciprocating constitution of beings by beings.

This reconsideration gives us the "dependency" on metaphysics of which Derrida is constantly aware.[21] But it also shows us that this dependency does not imply a vicious circle or a debilitating relation to what is to be deconstructed. The dependency is not one that encases the thinker of deconstruction within the indicated economy; for the thinker—if I am right about what Hegel has accomplished—"stands" in the ambiguous originary place opened by Hegel's reconstructive retrieval of ontotheological metaphysics.

In view of this conclusion, exactly what can we claim to be the subsequent results of a destructive or a deconstructive retrieval? Better yet, what can we expect? How should we look at the way in which the destructive and deconstructive retrieval of (ontotheological) metaphysics will affect thinking?

In absolute idealism and its reconstructive retrieval of the tradition, humans and their world are shown to be joined in their respective differences. This conjunction is founded on the relation that humans have to beings. Being and thinking belong together; together they form "the same." Given this relation, metaphysics is possible. But it is a metaphysics separated now from ontotheology. The final ground is just the Being of beings.

In the space that has been opened up, Being as such is revealed to be an origin out of the emptiness of the place formerly inhabited by a transcendent being. When Heidegger sets out to accomplish his destruction of metaphysics through a repetition, he is in turn asking for the ground which lays the ground of metaphysics, that is, he is asking for the possibility of the possibility of metaphysics, for the relation of finite human beings to Being as such, understood now as this Open. He therefore retains as presupposition the connection of thinking and Being at the level of metaphysics. In section 41 of *Kant and the Problem of Metaphysics* he writes, "That we, as men, have a comportment [*Verhalten*] to beings is evident."[22] This comportment is constitutive of Dasein in Heidegger's sense, and it is through Dasein that we gain access to the Open. So Heidegger's step back from the economy of metaphysics does not destroy metaphysics any more than did Hegel's opening of the Open. Rather, it gives us the possibility of examining, from the place which is the Open, not only that economy, but all economies, including those various economies that constitute systems of mores and of ethics.

What, exactly, does this step back allow us to think? When Derrida's deconstructive retrieval allows us to examine the "prime-ordial" decisions made in conjunction with an ontotheological metaphysics—the decisions about what is to be excluded and what is to be included—we are moved to think two things: First, we think the difference that is not dialectical difference, that is not bound up within an already given economy. Second, we rethink the decision—the prime-ordial decision—made previously in the night of onto-theological metaphysics, but now remade in the daylight of the Open. There is no claim that any economy can be founded without the decisions of exclusion and inclusion. The only claim justified is that a decision was made.

What this means can be understood in light of the following considerations. The place occupied by Heidegger and Derrida is not an origin in the sense of a cause or a founding. It is an origin that has no effect; it is simply the Open. Nothing is determined by it, not even the nature of metaphysics. In other terms, metahistories are not abolished by the authority of the Open; there is no authority, no author. Rather, standing in the Open we come to know the authentic mode of being of metaphysics and of all metahistory, a mode of being that "eternally" originates in this origin which is a nonorigin. We are made aware of the authentic condition of being itself.

The economies and their respective prime-ordial presuppositions are therefore not abolished; they are simply understood for what they are: structures in the happening of what-is.[23] But in that happening of what-is there is a twofold relation: that of thinking to beings and to the Being of beings, and that of thinking to Being as such, to the Open. And the relation is literally twofold; for each folds into and out of the other.[24] As we stand in this relation, we find our own prime-ordial presuppositions in force, presuppositions which perhaps are minimal and cannot be escaped. The twofold relation must be presupposed *if* one is to speak of anything.

Here the thought of Heidegger and Derrida, standing in the place opened by Hegel, reveals the decisionistic nature of metaphysics and of all other economies of thought and action, as well as of retrieval itself. Our prime-ordial relations are decisionistic in nature. This opens us to the question of the relation between that decisionistic act—seemingly necessary—and metaphysics or philosophical thought in general. But this is precisely the question of the relation of nonphilosophy to philosophy, which is, after all, the relation opened to us when Socrates' prisoner in the cave arises, *hupo anangkēs* (by necessity), and begins his ascent from the cave; or when Parmenides is, of a sudden, taken up in the chariot that eventually carries him to the goddess and to truth.[25]

Notes

1. Compare Adriaan Peperzak's "Einige Fragen zum Thema 'Hegel und Heidegger'," in Marcel F. Fresco, Rob J. A. van Dijk, and H. W. Peter Vijgeboom, eds. *Heideggers These vom Ende der Philosophie*, Verhandlungen des Leidener Heidegger-Symposiums April 1984 (Bonn: Bouvier Verlag, 1989), 49–74. This essay was brought to my attention after the present paper was finished. Although I rely on the concept of "the tradition" here, I do not disagree with Peperzak on his point that this concept is highly questionable. For the purposes of this paper, since Hegel claimed to have completed "the tradition," and since I want to understand how this governing thought plays a part in philosophy, the question of whether or not such a unitary tradition exists is not relevant. See also note 16 below.

2. This can be taken as my response to David Krell's question in *Intimations of Mortality: Time, Truth, and Finitude in Heidegger's Thinking of Being* (University Park, Pa.: Pennsylvania State Univ. Press, 1986), 122: "How can one claim to have achieved a decisive grasp on the essence and source of the metaphysical tradition as a whole and yet allow thinkers within that tradition to be heard?" Put another way, Hegel's retrieval is a necessary condition for the "loosening up of the tradition" to which Heidegger refers

in, among other writings, *Sein und Zeit* (Tübingen: M. Niemeyer, 1953), sec.
1. For the English translation see *Being and Time*, trans. John Macquarrie
and Edward Robinson (New York: Harper & Row, 1962), sec. 1.

Richardson gives a good account of Heidegger's various attempts to face
the problem of justifying the "violence" of a retrieval. See William J.
Richardson, *Heidegger: Through Phenomenology to Thought* (The Hague:
Martinus Nijhoff, 1967), 158–60, 294–95, 442, 498–500, 545–46, 611–12, and
614–15. See also Michael Allen Gillespie, *Hegel, Heidegger, and the Ground
of History* (Chicago: Univ. of Chicago Press, 1984), 17.

3. On this and Heidegger's "step back," see David Kolb, *The Critique
of Pure Modernity* (Chicago: Univ. of Chicago Press, 1986). It is a much more
complicated affair than, for example, John Caputo makes it out to be in
Radical Hermeneutics: Repetition, Deconstruction, and the Hermeneutic Project
(Bloomington: Indiana Univ. Press, 1987). Caputo, in a discussion of Hans-
Georg Gadamer, writes there that "Gadamer, like Hegel, is interested in the
Auf-hebung, the step up—let us say here the step-forward, the progress of
the tradition in the sense of its progressive, albeit finite, elaboration and
unfolding—and not the step back, the regressive return to that which gives
the tradition, which both reveals and conceals itself in the various epochal
sendings" (p. 114). David Kolb, *Critique of Pure Modernity*, pp. 133–37, comes
closer to my position.

4. The most explicit statement of this is to be found in his Introduction
to the *Lectures on the History of Philosophy*. See Hegel, *Werke*, vol. 18,
Vorlesungen über die Geschichte der Philosophie (Frankfurt am Main:
Suhrkamp Verlag, 1971), Bd. 1, esp. pp. 18–19, 46–55; *Lectures on the History
of Philosophy*, trans. E. S. Haldane (London: Routledge & Kegan Paul, 1955),
1:6, 28–36.

5. It is improper to construe Hegel to be fitting the tradition to his own
philosophy. He is engaged in dialectics. The same mistake is often made in
insisting that Socrates argues until the interlocutor says what he wants him
to say.

6. For a partial account of the part played by the *Lectures on the History
of Philosophy* and that history as *res gestae*, see Joseph C. Flay, "The History
of Philosophy and the *Phenomenology of Spirit*," in Joseph O'Malley, *et al.*,
eds., *Hegel and the History of Philosophy* (The Hague: Martinus Nijhoff, 1975),
47–67; and "Hegel's *Logic*: Ironies of the Understanding," in George
DiGiovanni, ed., *Essays on Hegel's Logic* (Albany: State Univ. of New York
Press, 1990), 153–69.

7. It is true that Hegel's metaphysics in the most general sense is
constituted only by the whole of his system. However, for present purposes
it is sufficient to concentrate on the *Logic* since it is there that the end of
the tradition is established. The philosophical sciences of nature and spirit
complete this finalization but do not change its essential character.

8. The rejection of the traditional view of Hegel's method has now been established in serious Hegel scholarship, but unfortunately still continues to be held by many other philosophers. Exactly how one should understand Hegel is now a new question. The interpretation to follow is, of course, not without problems. It has been worked out in other essays and will soon be developed in a complete interpretation of his *Science of Logic*. It also has a clear relation to what I proposed in my *Hegel's Quest for Certainty* (Albany: State Univ. of New York Press, 1984). See also, for example, Dennis Schmidt, *The Ubiquity of the Finite: Hegel, Heidegger, and the Entitlements of Philosophy* (Cambridge, Mass.: MIT Press, 1988), pp. 153–54, where he characterizes Hegel as being involved in "construction," in contrast to Heidegger's "deconstruction." Schmidt and I go in different directions, although we have much in common.

9. Thus, Hegel has no "new" categories in his system, only the categories of his predecessors.

10. For a more detailed analysis of this and matters relating to the connection of rhetoric and logic, irony and dialectic, see my "Hegel's *Logic*: Ironies of the Understanding."

11. This is the great strength of irony when combined with dialectic. No other form of philosophical discussion can avoid the problems of discourse arising in the simple confrontation of positions or in the dominance of either participation or distancing. On the problem of participation and distancing see Ronald Beiner, "Do We Need a Philosophical Ethics?: Theory, Prudence, and the Primacy of *Ethos*," *Philosophical Forum* 20 (1989): 230–43, p. 234. The direct reference is to Gadamer, but what Beiner says is generally applicable to any problem of interpretation.

12. I hope soon to complete a "companion to Hegel's *Logic*" in which the whole of the *Science of Logic* is explicated in terms of this methodology of reconstructive retrieval. For a more detailed account of what follows concerning these four categories, see my "Hegel's *Logic*: Ironies of the Understanding."

13. This is important to note here, for there are some who would identify Hegel's beginning with Being and the negation that comes out of it with Heidegger's discussion of Nothing. But this simply is not the case; for Hegel never reaches in a thematized way the level of Heidegger's discussion.

14. See, for example, Parmenides' strict connection, in fragment 8, of the question of the "it is" with beings or things. The goddess offers us a reason for her claim in fragments 3, 6, and 8 about the relationship of thinking to being (*to gar auto noein estin te kai einai*, to use the formulation in fragment 3), by arguing that one "will not find thought without what is, in relation to which it is uttered; for there is not, nor shall be, anything else besides

what is, since fate fettered it to be entire and immovable [*ou gar aneu tou eontos, en ho pephatismenon estin, eureseis to noein; ouden gar estin e estai allo parex tou eontos, epei to ge Moir' epedesen oulon akineton t' emenai*]," meaning that it is definitely and only the Being of beings to which one can refer. For these texts both in Greek and in translation see G. S. Kirk and J. E. Raven, *The Presocratic Philosophers* (Cambridge: Cambridge Univ. Press, 1960). The translations used throughout the present chapter are those given by Kirk and Raven.

15. Hegel counts as philosophies of the understanding the positions of all of his predecessors. Some approached to a lesser or greater degree the position of reason, Hegel's position; but in the end they remained philosophers of the understanding. One of the primary marks of such a philosophy is the total rejection of contradiction and thereby of self-contradiction.

16. This is not to say that other positions are impossible; but if there are others, they will not be governed by the irony that alone gives necessity to Hegel's dialogue with the tradition. That is to say, Hegel cannot and has no desire to claim that positions outside of the tradition as he conceives it are not possible. They are simply irrelevant for one committed to the self-conscious truth of the tradition. For us, then, they are irrelevant to the grounding of the possibility of destructive and deconstructive retrieval.

17. Among those most recently holding such a position are Joseph Kockelmans, *On the Truth of Being* (Bloomington: Indiana Univ. Press, 1984); David Krell, *Intimations of Mortality*; John Caputo, *Radical Hermeneutics*; and David Kolb, *The Critique of Pure Modernity*.

18. Spinoza is an exception to this, and that is why Hegel characterizes the category of "the Absolute" in terms of Spinoza's philosophy.

19. Compare this with Kolb's view, *The Critique of Pure Modernity*, pp. 133–37, 210–22. My view (in disagreement with Kolb, whose view, however, I find close to mine) is that Hegel *did* achieve the "overarching totality," and because of this ironically opened the fissure that would "destroy" it. See Kolb, *The Critique of Pure Modernity*, p. 237. Compare also Peperzak, "Einige Fragen zum Thema 'Hegel und Heidegger'."

20. The most radical form of this step back is Georges Bataille's "laughter." See the discussion of Bataille by Jacques Derrida in his "De l'économie restreinte à l'économie générale: Un hegelianisme sans réserve," in *L'ecriture et la différence* (Paris: Éditions du Seuil, 1967), 369–407. This originally appeared in *L'arc* 32:24–44, and can be found in English translation as "From Restricted to General Economy: A Hegelianism without Reserve," in *Writing and Difference*, trans. Alan Bass (Chicago: Univ. of Chicago Press, 1978), 251–77.

21. On this see Irene Harvey, "Derrida and the Concept of Metaphysics," *Research in Phenomenology* 13 (1983): 113–48, as well as her treatment of this in *Derrida and the Economy of Différance* (Bloomington: Indiana Univ. Press, 1986).

22. Martin Heidegger, *Kant und das Probleme der Metaphysik* (Frankfurt am Main: Klostermann, 1950), 204. For the English translation see *Kant and the Problem of Metaphysics*, trans. James S. Churchill (Bloomington: Indiana Univ. Press, 1962), 233.

23. Talk of a *Geschick* is therefore misleading. There is only a *Geschehen*.

24. To speak of *Ereignis* is to make a beginning, but only a beginning.

25. I refer here to the essentially unexplained beginning of philosophy in Parmenides and Plato. If one asks why the prisoner arises in the cave, there is no answer except that he does so *physei* (by nature) or by necessity, which latter is shown in a series of compounded words beginning with *anangkē*: e.g., *anangkazoito, anangkazoi* (*Republic* 515c–517b). If one asks for the origin of Parmenides' journey, we begin *in medias res*: "The steeds that carry me took me as far as my heart could desire..." (Parmenides, fragment 1).

14

Architecture as Properly Useful Opening

Robert Mugerauer

INTRODUCTION

At the Mission San José in San Antonio, Texas, the December afternoon's light passes over the western wall of the compound, between the old live oak trees, to fall across the ruined limestone arches of the *convento,* casting strong and dramatic shadows against the walls and floor of what once were the priests' living quarters and offices. These shadows and the movements of passersby among them seem as much a part of the place as the texture of the walls, the contrast of cool winter air and bright light, the memories and meanings evoked by the place. But what of it? Do we have here merely the experience of a tourist encountering a curiosity, perhaps a nostalgic lingering? Of what relevance is this experience to architecture today?

Answering this question presupposes an understanding of what architecture is to be. Clearly, the traditional view that architecture is the art of building beautifully is challenged in the postmodern era. For hundreds of years, buildings have been understood to be objects that should have aesthetic quality and the design process to be the architect's subjective, artistic contribution. In the emerging technological world, however, buildings and the entire built environment are conceived as a system of networks—interior heating and cooling, electronics and communication, transportation and delivery networks. The power of this technological sphere, in which the aesthetic object has disappeared, is unquestioned; its power is evident in the spread of systemic architecture across the globe.[1]

This current shift in conceptual paradigms is not without problems. With the passing of the traditional forms and values of Western architecture, many people are experiencing a loss of genuine dwelling and a sense of place. Without arguing about whether such losses are more imagined than actual or whether the new is either inevitable or preferable, this chapter seeks to examine an alternative to rootlessness and the loss of place by exploring the new interpretation of architecture inherent in the work of Martin Heidegger.[2]

Heidegger, who as much as anyone in our century may show us what an alternative might look like, held that it would be naive and nostalgic to think we could replace the technological realm or go back to an earlier, better way of living. Rather, the task is to work out an understanding of architecture appropriate for our new epoch, that is, an architecture that would be a viable option, or vital complement to the systemically technological.

Heidegger's way of thinking and his language are full of implications for the changes that would accompany the language of a no-longer-technological architecture. The "language" of architecture has two meanings: (1) in the broadest sense, "language" means that by which we understand the discipline and practice of architecture; (2) in a delimited sense, it constitutes what we call the architectural vocabulary. Hence, we need to think, respectively, both about what architecture itself would be and about roofs, columns, arches, doorways, and windows. A new architectural vocabulary begins to appear in some of Heidegger's key words: "opening," "listening," "joining," "use," "between," "measure," "gift," and "admittance."[3]

ARCHITECTURE AS OPENING

According to Heidegger, architecture would have the task and possibility of *opening* a world. He points out that before anything can happen, an opening must occur. For example, the story of our becoming human is, in significant part, the story of our gathering together in settlements, a mode that simultaneously changes, and renders newly problematic, the relation of humans to the natural world.[4] But for us to "have a city" at all, there first must be a clearing.

When a city is founded, a clearing is made by clearing away brush or rocks, by removing undesirable or unclean elements, by evoking protective gods or the secular values of progress and commerce so that the place may prosper. It is within the site established—and sustained—by such physical and symbolic opening that the city and its buildings can be built. The mutual articulation of city, surrounding landscape, and human culture happen all at once where opening already occurs as the site, or it does not happen at all.

Architecture, then, following Heidegger, would be a mode of opening. It would be the primary mode of opening, prior to the building of particular buildings and the fabric of the town and city. How is such an opening created practically? According to Heidegger, the opening is not something we can accomplish by willful exertion. It is *not* something we can *create* all by ourselves. In the founding of a city, the natural site, local environment, and either an encompassing sacred or secular realm are contexts within which the specific event of founding either succeeds or fails.

Humans promote the opening necessary and appropriate to architecture by "letting it occur." Letting something occur is not a merely passive inactivity, but the active participation of discovery. Heidegger teaches that we can learn to help let an opening occur by, first, holding ourselves back. This is very different from our usual understanding of the architectural task, where the architect, as self, creates the original design or idea, and eventually is responsible for the real building and its use. In holding oneself back, the architect would no longer function as an ego or artistic subjectivity, artistically creating aesthetic works; architecture would no longer be a set of products for consumption or aesthetic experience.

Holding oneself back requires, before all else, a *patient listening,* according to Heidegger. Initially, such a listening is a preliminary opening in that it is an opening to something other than one's self. Here is a first putting of the self or ego aside. The architect needs to attend to the spirit of the place where the building is to be placed— to the physical and cultural context that will receive, surround, and animate the new building— and to what it is that the building is called on to provide. The architect begins listening by being open to the client, the site, the surrounding buildings and customs, and the specific social need. In this style of listening, one works to become attuned and responsive to what is given. Clearly, the listening must abide with the listened-to for a long time. That would mean that architects could not adequately design projects for sites they had not visited or for places of which they had only a superficial familiarity.

The architect would listen. To what? The requisite listening presupposes that there is something distinctive and enduring to be heard. For the listening to be possible, what we traditionally term the character of things must, more fundamentally, be given; that is, the basic dimensions of reality (the human and natural worlds, and, some would claim, the sacred, which, if not efficacious today, at least remains in its telling "absence") call to us. This given, to be listened to, also has its own history and prior interpretation. This means that in listening to the natural, human, and present or lost sacred realms, we unavoidably encounter our own traditions.

We would have to listen to the manner in which architects and architecture of the past responded to the natural, human, and sacred realms. The way a traditional, often regional, set of architectural customs and design elements themselves succeeded or failed to be attuned to their world is a body of knowledge that needs to be kept in memory and listened to today. The discipline of architecture would need to retrieve and hold on to its historical responses, in order to adapt them appropriately.

To refocus, let us ask: Why would we need to know about, and thus need to listen to, such things? Because, according to Heidegger, the task before us—since it is not the willful creation of new aesthetic objects—is to let the fundamental things in question fulfill themselves; that is, generally, it is to let the natural, human, and sacred realms together come into their own, in a specific mode and place.

A PLACE FOR LIGHT

As an example of how architecture lets cultural and natural spheres come forward, think of the relation of *buildings and light*. How would Heidegger's approach help us understand what we might call architecture's providing an opening for light to come forth into its own nature? Of course, all buildings are connected to light. All buildings appear in the light, cast shadows, and have cooler and warmer areas. Windows and skylights let light in so that it can illuminate activities and objects inside the building. We have artificial light inside buildings and sometimes outside, to display them. But in these cases buildings and light appear in a reduced sense: light is nothing more than the taken-for-granted means for seeing something else that we take to be important. Light and windows, too, are experienced as transparencies, disappearing in the presentation of that to which we attend. Similarly, the buildings disappear in themselves insofar as they function efficiently. Light and buildings normally appear as mere instruments, facilitating interactions with the objects we produce and use. But what of the nature of light itself or the fuller character and power of a building?

In Texas, out in the open, light beats down upon the earth much of the time. Often there is no chance for light to show itself subtly, so dominant is the fierce summer light and heat or so dramatic the winter wind and cold. Living in the direct light of the sun is uncomfortable, if not intolerable. Buildings, too, must endure it. Architecture that ignores this fierce light will likely fail; certainly its use will be diminished, as is the case with well-intended but unshaded urban plazas exposed to July's sun. But endurance and shelter are not the only needs. To evoke a richer, more satisfying environment, to attend to light, architecture needs to let light play, to show itself in its variety.

In the regions of the Southwest there are numerous traditional responses to the sunlight; that is, there are forms that modulate the relationship of light and earth, of light and buildings and the people who live and work in them. The forms that do this sometimes have been architecturally designed and sometimes are vernacular. The best regional buildings already are the setting-to-work (*sich-ins-Werk-setzen*) of the manner in which a people's mode of life interprets its place and tradition. The regional buildings, then, are a mode of responding to light, a way of joining light to earth and to its inhabitants' patterns of life.

The missions of Texas inaugurated one mode of opening, one way in which light is allowed to play out its variations. At the Mission San José, mentioned at the beginning of this essay, light has long shown itself in golden tones on the adobe and limestone facade and tower of the church, and in muted form inside the single nave after passing through Pedro Huizar's famous rose window. At one time it also reflected brightly from the water in a canal that irrigated the crops and orchard and provided for fishing, and from the separate swimming pools inside the compound for soldiers and neophytes. In these ways, light entered this architectural opening to be joined with the rhythms of residents in their work and prayer.

Today, in the same region, drawing on the Spanish heritage and the still radiant light, Plaza Guadalupe in San Antonio also lets light play. Through the vault of the slatted roofs, light joins in the shout of color and festive social events. The light and shadows, the colors of walls and tiles, the smells of food from the booths, the cool of the grass, the sound from the churchyard bell across the street, the people celebrating: all enter into the site opened by the architecture of the Plaza. As the sun above San Antonio simultaneously floods both Mission San José (1720 and 1768) and Plaza Guadalupe (1985), setting at play the dance of strong light and neighboring shadows, two-and-a-half centuries of the regional gathering together of earth, sky, and human life, as accomplished by architecture and open space, are spanned and continued.

In Fort Worth, 270 miles to the northwest, an exemplary opening to light occurs in the Kimbell Art Museum. The building lets light play out more subtle variations than usual in this part of Texas. The light is strong in some places, so that sharply demarcated shadows alternate with bands of light; elsewhere it dapples downward through the rustling trees or reflects off water; yet again, it comes and goes intriguingly as the shadows of clouds trace their way across the building's vaults. The Kimbell, however, is not merely a canvas on which light paints its effects; the museum lets light play appropriately, as measured by its context and the need addressed by the building. This accomplishment shapes our experience and joins us with light's occurrence.

Figure 1. "The building lets light play"
Kimbell Art Museum, Louis Kahn, 1966 (exterior)

Coming down the hill from the nearby Amon Carter Museum, you move through the strong Texas light, across a park, toward the strong, simple vaulted forms of the Kimbell Art Museum and its garden. It is not an exaggeration to say that you are drawn to the building. The simple and powerful horizontal forms pull you toward it. As you approach, you hear, then see, splashing water in the garden's pool, lined with Andes black granite. The loose marble crunches beneath your feet as you move through the grove of Yaupon holly trees up to the porch. These elements are at once familiar and yet distinctive. The gathering of trees, stone, and water occurs in a simple, archetypal mode. At the same time, the sophisticated combination of these elements with the travertine, concrete, metal, and glass of the building constitutes an atmosphere quite different from that of the surrounding city, cultural complex, and parking areas. These built features are experienced neither as mere background nor as part of a continuous, undifferentiated landscape. Rather, the Kimbell presents itself as a focal, figural place that does seem to call one to attend to it, to regard it with care. Here one feels invited to linger.

After sitting on a ledge, in the company of the garden and building, you will likely make a mental note to spend more time there before leaving. Then, you cross the porch, through its bands of shadow and bright light, and pass into the museum. On entering, you find yourself in a realm of light—light unfolding quietly and calmly as it does in an afternoon's sunbeams. Here light itself occurs, abiding in its moods and changes. This light does not appear as volume or space made visible; those are architectural or philosophical abstractions. The experience and disclosure is not at all that of air, space, or volume filled with light, but of light itself manifest in its own modalities. What emerges is neither the common contrast of white light and blackness or shadow, nor a reduction as the former overwhelms the latter. The museum's light is more diverse. The light unfolds its polyvalent appearance out of its own primal possibility. It scatters and regathers. It plays upon itself. This light is rich and saturated.

The awareness of the light intrigues: how does light appear this way? You note the slits at the top of the vaults. Light streams in or seeps in depending on the day's sun and clouds, and the time of year. The skylights are more complex: the oculus of the vault lets light enter, to be split by the aluminum reflectors. Bouncing back up to the ceiling, now silver-toned, the light reflects off the polished stone, to wall and floor. Light, modulated in hue and intensity by materials, becomes diffuse, a glow. This soft light—the stronger light from room's further end; light itself.

Figure 2. "A joining of crafted materials and modulated light"
Kimbell Art Museum, Louis Kahn, 1966 (interior)

What happens here? How is it done? As you walk closer to the walls and inspect the ceiling, the simple, elegant materials emerge as important in themselves: polished stone, glass, white oak, stainless steel, and aluminum. These are complexly *joined together*, yet with an ease of inevitability—as if there never was any doubt that this was the way they could, and should, fit together: the hallmark of craftsmanship.[5] And, in the precise joining of materials, light plays a part, as if another element, summoned by and interacting with the materials. It is not just that the technical assemblage of materials makes light possible (that is done by any window or opening to the outside); here the gathering of material creates a sort of site, where what matters is the ensemble of materials and the light's play as an integral part of the same phenomenon. Heidegger's key words *joining* (*fugen*), and *jointure* (*die Fuge*) name both the physical joint and the ontological coming together of the fundamental dimensions of reality.[6] *From the crafted joining of materials the building emerges; the*

joining—the building as a whole—enables the disclosure of light. The
Kimbell is a place for light. Light really is liberated and evoked by
the building. Light abides there.

Even more happens. Of course, you are not in a realm of pure
light. Looking across the museum, you see the progression of interior
spaces and paintings placed along the walls, with people passing, one
by one, before each of them. The movement seems natural, inevitable.
Given the focal character of the museum as the place where people
come to seek what the paintings can show them, the event of light
and the building's crafted body are not ends in themselves. In fact,
the powerful and intriguing building and the Texas sun both present
a great danger: they could overwhelm or obscure the paintings
sheltered and disclosed in the museum, frustrating the joining of art
works and visitors. To be successful, the building must let light come
in in the proper ways. For paintings and sculpture to come into their
own, they must be allowed to show their own colors and forms, their
own mood, to the people who come to see them.

Visitors can step into the autonomous worlds of the individual
art works, as modern Westerners have learned to do through the
course of metaphysical awareness. Each work may be perceived as
a world in itself, so that in the shelter of the museum, visitors are
free from reference to the immediately external realm, free to enter
imaginatively into the art work, and thence, through the work, into
the world it represents.[7] It seems so easy to enter the natural, cultural,
or religious realm held in the works; that is, people are joined with
their own cultural past, which involves ways of relating not only to
earlier and other cultures, but to nature and the gods. Light, then,
must be properly joined with the Texas landscape, with today's
viewers, with the heritage given through the still-vital paintings of
human, natural, and sacred realms.

Further, the inward spiral of seeing into past and imaginary
worlds by looking at and into the art works has a counterpart in the
openings in the building: courtyards inside the building bring light
in and let visitors look out (often to sculpture in the courtyard);
openings above visitors' heads connect them to the sky. People are
drawn back and forth, to the light and to the art works. In an
additionally appropriate manner—for example, through its great
horizontal vaults and quiet presence—the Kimbell resonates to the
Texan and Midwestern traditions, where public life and certainly the
arts have been developed more from our Roman rather than our Greek
heritage; that is, beyond the general Mediterranean influence in the
state, the specific attitudes and forms do not reflect the quick

brilliance of Athenian tragedy and comedy or of the plastic Hellenic temples but rather the dependability and organization displayed in Shakespeare's or Plutarch's moral accounts of life and citizenship and by Roman civic engineering and built forms.

The Kimbell has as one of its tasks the retrieval and adaptation of what is appropriate to the local, regional, and historical traditions. Such a calling does not require that the building, in "holding itself back" and thus allowing the natural and cultural environments to emerge and be gathered together, be bland or without meaning. The building becomes itself precisely through its mode of enabling this specific, complex opening to occur, and through the subsequent joining together of the dimensions of world. The Kimbell is a marvelous work of architecture because it fundamentally withdraws in favor of its responsibility to be the opening; that is, the museum is not so much an object as the occurrence of a site where other events—light and art works—are allowed to occur.

The Kimbell exemplifies what Heidegger means by *proper use* (*der Brauch; brauchen*).[8] To use something does not mean fundamentally to use it for humanly willful purposes, as a tool; nor does it mean to use something up as in our commodity culture. These common meanings of *to use,* according to Heidegger, are derivative. The original, and still efficacious, meaning of *to use* actually is: to let something come to its own nature, which involves letting the thing belong with human, natural, and perhaps sacred dimensions of reality. Proper use would be appropriate to its place, time, and mode of existence—thus the quiet spell of the Kimbell Museum. The building is a properly useful opening: it achieves the powerful gathering of visitors, art works, local place and cultural tradition, together with an experience of light itself.

CONCLUSION

Suppose, following Heidegger, that we accept this change in the language used to understand and practice architecture, so that architecture appears as the opening of sites—through listening that enables our making to be commensurate with the character and needs of things—and thus as essential for the gathering of world. In this case, architecture faces the initial and persistent question of the proper use of the human and natural. As noted, past ways of living may themselves be attuned to their given natural, cultural, and sacred realms—to the local spirit of place. Accordingly, Heidegger helps to articulate a new question and approach for the discipline of architecture: How can we appropriately attend to and respond to our traditional, often regional, modes of architecture and design elements in a manner that will allow us to turn toward, and provide an opening for, tomorrow's world?

Notes

1. Martin Heidegger, *The Question concerning Technology and Other Essays* (New York: Harper & Row, 1977); Robert Mugerauer, "Heidegger's Originary Dwelling." (Paper presented at the Society for Phenomenology and Human Sciences Annual Meeting, Northwestern University, 1981.)

2. The following characterization of architecture draws especially from Heidegger, *Early Greek Thinking*, trans. David F. Krell and Frank A. Capuzzi (New York: Harper & Row, 1975); "Letter on Humanism," trans. Frank A. Capuzzi with J. Glenn Gray, in *Basic Writings*, ed. David F. Krell (New York: Harper & Row, 1977), 189–242; *Poetry, Language, Thought*, trans. Albert Hofstadter (New York: Harper & Row, 1971); and *What Is Called Thinking?*, trans. J. Glenn Gray (New York: Harper & Row, 1968).

3. The specific exploration of this essay takes place within the larger project of working out a Heideggerian interpretation of the built environment. See, for example, Karsten Harries, "Thoughts on a Non-Arbitrary Architecture," *Perspecta* 20 (1983): 9–21; and "Space, Place, and Ethos," *Artibus et Historiae* no. 9 (1984): 159–65; Christian Norberg-Schulz, *Genius Loci* (New York: Rizzoli, 1980), and *The Concept of Dwelling* (New York: Rizzoli, 1985); Robert Mugerauer, "Toward an Architectural Vocabulary: Porch as Between," in *Dwelling, Seeing, Building*, ed. David Seamon (forthcoming); R. Lang, "The Dwelling Door: Towards a Phenomenology of Transition," in *Dwelling, Place, and Environment*, ed. D. Seamon and R. Mugerauer (Dordrecht: Martinus Nijhoff, 1985), 201–14.

4. See Norberg-Schulz, *Genius Loci*, pp. 6–22, 50–189; *Concept of Dwelling*, 13–110.

5. See Michael Benedikt, "Craftsmanship," *Texas Architect* 30:55 (Sept./Oct. 1980): 26–37. *Light Is the Theme* (Fort Worth, Tex.: Kimbell Art Museum, 1975).

6. See especially Heidegger, "The Anaximander Fragment," in *Early Greek Thinking*, 52–58.

7. Of course, other relationships to the art works and the world are possible; but, in the culture of contemporary American museum curators and visitors the modern Western metaphysical modes of representation still dominate, preventing the possibility of the originary retrieval of meaning. A full treatment of the Kimbell Art Museum would need to describe how it actually joins together (1) a technological mode of building (for example, in its modular vaults), (2) a metaphysical architecture and aesthetics of presence, and (3) an originary dimension.

8. See, for example, Heidegger, *What Is Called Thinking?*, lecture 7, pp. 182–93; and Robert Mugerauer, *Heidegger's Language and Thinking* (Atlantic Highlands, N.J.: Humanities Press, 1989), 5, 97, 132–33, 233–34.

Part 3

Ethical Currents in Continental Thought

15

Does Continental Ethics Have a Future?

Edith Wyschogrod

Instead of considering the question, is there a tradition of ethics in continental philosophy?, I propose to ask: Is there a future for continental ethics and, if so, what direction might this future take? What elements of preceding thought are likely to be preserved and in what shape will they reappear? Conversely, what will drop away and why? By "preceding thought" I mean principally Husserlian phenomenology but also dialogical philosophy and neo-Kantianism. The historical and speculative questions—inquiry into both the past and the future of this thought—are more intimately linked than may at first be apparent in that an investigation of tendencies that are promising for the future are parasitic upon an anterior conceptual language. Think of Marx's celebrated remark in the *Eighteenth Brumaire* about political history: "Men make their own history, but they do not make it just as they please: they do not make it under circumstances chosen by themselves, but under circumstances directly encountered, given and transmitted from the past."[1] If there are to be novel developments in continental ethics, there must be a conceptual repertoire from which they derive; there must be accounts of self, time, and language that, accepted or rejected, constitute the backdrop against which the new tendencies are articulated.

At the same time, it is worth pondering the second part of Marx's remark: "The tradition of all the dead generations weighs like a nightmare on the brain of the living." In attempting to sketch an

answer to the question, whither continental ethics?, I confine myself
to three revolutionary, as it were, developments. First, I consider the
revolt against the epistemological subject and the emergence of an
ethics of alterity or otherness. Second, I take up the revolt against
the subject as knower and show the importance of the corporeal
subject. (These two foci are related in that ethical subjectivity as a
primordial responsiveness to the other takes for granted the corporeal
being of others.) Third, I discuss the revolt against ethical theory that
has occurred both in continental and analytic philosophy and suggest
that recent analyses of narrative, especially in France, provide an
entering wedge for an ethics of story, an approach employed in recent
Anglo-American ethics but not yet explored in continental thought.

LEVINAS AND THE INCURSION OF THE OTHER

The subject as the consciousness that knows has been criticized
in recent French thought from a variety of perspectives: that of the
historical relativity of knowledge (Foucault), that of knowledge as
a power constellation (Lyotard, Baudrillard, Castoriadis), and that
of the repressiveness of epistemological consciousness (Lacan, Deleuze
and Guattari, Kristeva). But the specifically ethical challenge
(especially by Levinas, Blanchot, and Lyotard) to the epistemological
subject as conceived in classical phenomenology focuses upon the
intentional character of consciousness and upon intentionality as a
quasi conatus that subordinates all content to itself by subjecting this
content to its own meaning-bestowing acts. Thus the phenomenological apparatus of intentionality, transcendental constitution, and
the various modes of bracketing as conceived by Husserl are
interpreted as so many means for subordinating the world's otherness
to an egoity without egress. On this view, conferring significations
upon the other without prior recognition of the other's claim on the
self is tantamount to an act of primordial violence that serves as a
springboard for actual violence or, in older Kantian terms, constitutes
an offense against the dignity of the other.

Recent French thought has sought to undermine the primacy
of consciousness; first, by demonstrating that cognition is not the
subject's most primitive encounter with the other and, second, by
showing that Husserl's view of cognition is based upon a flawed model,
that of knowledge as representation. The first tactic, deployed in the
ethics of Emmanuel Levinas, uncovers an impingement or weighing

down of the other upon the self anterior to representation; the second, Jacques Derrida's tactic, undermines representation by showing that it cannot deliver what it promises, the making present of some truth. Thus, a covert immorality, implied but not stated, is attributed to representation: it always already delivers a lie. This lie covers up no original truth, yet the account itself of the disingenuousness of representation functions, so to speak, as a restoration of metaphysical "honesty."

Consider first Levinas's analysis of how alterity or otherness breaks into the field of experience, bypasses intentionality, and yields ethical signification. According to Levinas, Husserl argues that consciousness is intentional and serves to bestow a unitary meaning upon its objects, a meaning that is sustained through their multiple and vanishing appearances. To confer a meaning is to understand something as X. What is more, if designating some object as X counts as an act of attributing signification, then meaning is bound up with language in the form of a judgment: this is X. Language is not merely incidental to experiencing phenomena: the phenomenon is already a fragment of discourse. Language, inextricable from meaningful experience, can confer universality on what is apprehended so that discourse opens up phenomena to all.[2]

Absent from this approach to truth and language is the interlocutor, the speaker her- or himself who, on this view, can only appear as a particular discursive content, an object of cognition. But, according to Levinas, there is an access route to the other that does not reduce the other's exteriority by making the other a content of consciousness. This approach to alterity is proximity, the proximity of interlocutor and self. "The hypothesis that the relationship with an interlocutor would still be a knowing reduces speech to the solitary or impersonal exercise of a thought, whereas [communication is already] a proximity between me and the interlocutor, and not our participation in a transparent universality," Levinas avers (LP 115). The meaning of the other who cannot be thematized must be seen to be beyond ontology. Proximity is thus not a supplement to intentionality, the handmaiden of a consciousness interpreted in Husserlian terms, but a revolt against the primacy of consciousness as will and spontaneity.

It is through proximity that, for Levinas, the ethical datum of the face emerges and what is essentially a form or shape is transformed into a moral imperative. The revelation of the face constitutes a new stratum within sensibility itself. Once the face is apprehended, it addresses and solicits a relationship with the perceiver an-iconically, not as an image, but as weight or pressure that compels one to see the other as destitute. This is not to say that the other's destitution is an empirical matter, for the other may not actually be in need. It is rather to insist that the face is to be read as an overturning of power relations, a solicitation to an agent to refrain from the exercise of power which, in its most extreme form, consists in the annihilation of the other. By accepting responsibility for the other, the subject becomes what she or he always already is, an *ethical* subject. She or he must be willing to become hostage for the other. In short, what is demanded by the face of the other is a radical altruism (even if Levinas does not use this term), an altruism that cannot be refused if the face is genuinely apprehended in proximity.[3] Gilles Deleuze's recent critique of faces as stylizations of social roles misses the point in that faces are always already "nude" and cannot be further deconstructed.[4]

Levinas's critique of the subject of knowledge from the standpoint of the primordiality of altruism was preceded by Heidegger's and Sartre's criticisms of the monadic character of the subject, attacks that helped to lay the groundwork for an ethics of responsibility. In interpreting the existing individual as consciousness, classical phenomenology was seen as having failed to consider the world of others to be intrinsic to the formation of the subject. Heidegger (and later Sartre) shows that the subject is not only enmeshed in a nexus of things but also and equiprimordially engaged in social transactions.

Behind the development of these social ontologies lies a disagreement with Husserl's description of the other in the well-known fifth of the *Cartesian Meditations*. There Husserl explains that the other can never be given in an original way but only through analogical appresentation, a mode of apprehension through which the seen aspect of a thing allows one to imagine or "appresent" its unseen aspect, much as from the perceived side of a cube one can configure its invisible sides. It is through a material representation, the body of the other, that I come to configure along with it the existence of an alien subjectivity. What justifies this assumption is a presumed analogy between the relation of the other's body to her or his ego and the relation of my body to my ego.[5] Describing analogical appresentation in Husserl's thought, Michael Theunissen writes:

> As a purified analogical apperception [the alter ego] must be allowed to proceed from my ego. Just as my body, as mediator of all alien embodiment, plays the "role of the originary body," so my I, as the mediator of all alien I-ness, takes on the meaning

of an "originary norm."... Everything alien in the sense of belonging to the Other...is "only thinkable as the analogue of that which is characteristically [one's] own."[6]

Theunissen goes on to say: "I have indeed already degraded the Other in that I degrade that I that is constituted by him to a derivative mode of myself and affirm him over against myself as an originary I."

Although Heidegger and Sartre go part of the way toward establishing the primordiality of the other in the formation of the individual and in overcoming the solipsistic aspects of Husserl's phenomenology, neither is willing to relate the sociality of the subject to ethics. What is lacking, especially for Levinas but also for Maurice Blanchot and Jean-François Lyotard, is the authority of imperatives, that is, the command function that militates the restraint of violence against the other. Commands cannot be derived from ontology any more than from intentional consciousness. For Heidegger this constitutes an advantage in that commands would be, for him, a form of willing, the last fruit of a Kantian interpretation of being as subjectness. But for Levinas, without the ballast of the ought structure of commands, there can be no restraints upon violence. Yet Levinas seeks no more than Heidegger to return to a straightforwardly Kantian position: the interpretation of the subject as will. For Levinas, therefore, the other is an anchorage for the command, rather than the command an anchorage for otherness. Yet the other cannot anchor in *sensu strictu* because the other can never present her- or himself, never be delivered as full presence; consequently the other remains extraontological. In sum, an ethics whose starting point is consciousness—for example, one that is based on a mental intuiting of values, or an ethics that begins with the meaning of being—cannot (as Heidegger saw) legislate restraints upon agency.[7]

Derrida's criticism of cognitive consciousness, although lacking any obvious moral agenda, has implications for ethics in that a promise by the consciousness-that-represents to deliver truth and certainty is shown to be unredeemable. According to Derrida (following Heidegger) a specific character is attributed to being and time in traditional accounts of knowledge: that which is, is divided, on the one hand, into what presents itself before a subject, what that subject can sensibly intuit or rationally conceive, and, on the other, into the consciousness of the subject, what is constantly present from moment to moment in sensible or rational intuition in the form of a self. Because the content of consciousness is delivered as what is now before a subject, the primacy of present time is taken for granted by traditional (including phenomenological) epistemologies.

But, Derrida contends, this notion of originary apprehension cannot be sustained, because what is allegedly original is the product of a temporally distended act. Husserl, he shows, divides language into an indicative and an expressive layer. The indicative layer lacks meaning because meaning arises only later when a linguistic expression confers signification upon this unorganized content. The so-called original moment of presentation is actually characterized by an unacknowledged temporal spread.[8] The claim of a purely presentational meaning is a lie, one that does not negate some prior truth (because there is no original to negate) but instead resembles the unconscious dissimulations that psychoanalysts attribute to patients who repress painful experiences. Like sincerity in Sartre's account of it, truth for Derrida is an impossible ideal.

In sum, recent French thought rejects Husserlian phenomenology as a starting point for ethics on the grounds that it fails to notice that, in its interpretation of consciousness, otherness is sacrificed to a spurious ideal of truth and certainty. For Levinas, the other in Husserl's thought is grounded in egoity and, as such, subordinate to it. For Blanchot, the problem of the other is bound up with the question of how the other's exteriority—an outside that is at once inside and outside the familiar world—is to be described without traducing this exteriority. For Lyotard, the other is a social phenomenon, the powerless, voiceless group silenced by a dominant "we." The development of non-reductive strategies for analyzing the claims of the other or others upon the self is an important tendency in present-day continental ethics and is likely to continue.

THE BODY SUBJECT

The Cartesian mind-body distinction, already called into question by social ontologies, is further eroded by the understanding of the subject as corporeal, a feature of the subject that emerges within Husserlian phenomenology itself. If the new ethics is a revolt against Husserl's philosophy of consciousness, Husserl's articulation of the concept of the body as subject and its later refining by Edith Stein and especially by Maurice Merleau-Ponty have a crucial role to play in the new ethics. Levinas's view of the face as proscribing violence is parasitic upon an anterior view of the other as the body against which this violence is directed and of one's self, offered as hostage for the other, as one's own body. On this reading the body, both of self and other, is apprehended as sheer vulnerability, as subject to pain, mortification, and death.

But the body is not simply susceptibility or vulnerability. Just as non-corporeal subjectivity was shown to be bipolar—on the one hand, an anterior ethical inwardness, the subject of responsibility and, on the other, egoity, the subject of knowledge and agency—so, too, the body subject replicates these distinctions. Consider first the body as a precondition for world apprehension, as an indispensable pre-requisite for the coming-to-be of objects for me. Merleau-Ponty writes: "If we want to describe it, we must say that my experience breaks forth into things and transcends itself in them, because it always comes into being within the framework of a certain setting in relation to the world which is the definition of my body."[9] According to Edith Stein, the body's emplacement determines location: proximity to it defines "here," remoteness from it, "there." But if what is sensed is distanced from me, where is the "I" from which it is at a remove? Edith Stein writes:

> Since sensation is always spatially localized "somewhere" at a distance from the "I" (perhaps very near to it but never in it), I can never find the "I" in it by reflection. And this "somewhere" is not an empty point in space, but something filling up space. All these entities from which my sensations arise are amalgamated into a unity, the unity of my living body, and they are themselves places in the living body.[10]

The body as the condition for world transactions does not, however, explain the ethical functions of corporeality. What is more, when the body subject is taken into account, there is a multiplication of subjects fissuring individuality in multiple ways: there are the subject-as-ego and the ethical subject on the one hand and the body as world-orienting subject and the body of pain and vulnerability on the other. In his *Otherwise than Being; Or, Beyond Essence*,[11] Levinas sidesteps the vestiges of the dualisms inherent in the persistence of both corporeal and non-corporeal subjectivity by attending to the process of sensation which folds into itself cognitive meaning on the one hand and vulnerability on the other.

In his analysis of sensation, Levinas argues for a built-in ambiguity in its structure: first, sensation or sensibility is bound up with meaning; second, it is also the capacity to be affected, an irreducible noncognitive dimension of sheer sensory input, for example, the blue of the water or the loudness of the crash. Between the lived and the meaningful sensed, there is an "open chasm of meaning." The pure flow of experience, the being-affected property of a sensation, is subject to meaning bestowal by consciousness across the split within the sense impression itself. This differing within the impression is expressed as time, the time in which the impression's fulfillment is awaited or has already occurred. The important point is that the impression always catches up with itself so that nothing is lost through the original "scissiparity" or splitting (OB 14–15, 61–64).

The advance of Levinas's formulation for ethics lies in the positing of a purely affective dimension of sensing that can be experienced as vulnerability: what is other than the self can affect the self through pain and wounding. Being affected means exposure to another without a coming to fruition in linguistic meaning or in sense content. Such exposure is possible because the body is a sensorium and because sense is as much susceptibility as it is a cognitive channelling of the world. In sum, classical phenomenology's account of the body subject is recontextualized so as to highlight the body's receptive capacities, its vulnerability, its patience; it is thus replete with ethical significations. Blanchot is moved to write: "The word 'body,' how easily it gives one the illusory impression of being outside of meaning.... The body does not belong; it is mortal immortal; it is unreal, imaginary, fragmentary."[12]

THE REVOLT AGAINST THEORY

The revolt against moral theory has occurred in many quarters in no small measure because moral theories have failed to produce moral lives. Some analytic philosophers such as Bernard Williams argue that ethical theories are generally thought to be like theories in science. This assumption has led to the mistaken notion that just as agreement can be secured about the result of scientific inquiry, so too it is possible to reach an accord about how moral lives are to be lived.[13] Alasdair MacIntyre contends that the discord is deeper than disagreement about moral action in that the heterogeneous background claims of the disputants preclude agreement about the terms in which moral disputes are framed. Moral theories, he contends, fail to produce moral dispositions without which human beings cannot lead moral lives.[14]

But it is not enough simply to bring this failure to attention. The question about whether moral theory is necessary for leading a moral life cannot be determined without deciding first what is at issue when the notion of theory is invoked. The model of scientific understanding has helped to fix the word's meaning in ordinary usage: the systematizing of material that is not yet organized, the application of the results of this procedure to other phenomena and the prediction of future behavior of phenomena based on the outcomes of what has thus been securely acquired. In Heidegger's *Metaphysical Foundations of Logic* the structures of reality implied by a view of theory grounded in modern science are brought to the fore.[15] "Science in general," Heidegger asserts in *Being and Time*, "may be defined as the totality established through an interconnection of true propositions."[16] For Heidegger, the view of knowledge integral to modern philosophy is grounded in the notion of judgment. The idea of judgment is already embedded in Aristotle's contention that the primitive constituents of the *logos* are concepts subsequently linked into propositions which, in turn, are connected with one another by thinking. Because truth and falsity are attributes of propositions, and their inferential relations are logical relations, the inquiry into theory must take logic understood in terms of the judgment as its starting point. Truth in every sphere of being has become propositional truth (MF 100–101).

Heidegger contrasts his own position—that logic has metaphysical foundations—with the view that "logic is free-floating, something ultimate" to be identified with thinking itself. Grounded in the latter and misleading assumption is the related view that logic presides over the sciences. Posing as common sense, this position takes for granted that without rules of thought thinking could not take place at all. Moreover, it is alleged that in the absence of the science of logic, all argument, including Heidegger's own, is precluded. Heidegger acknowledges the inescapability of rule-bound reasoning but denies that this admission entails the primordiality of logic. This denial is based on the view that logic as the systematic laying out of the conditions for truth is itself the product of a tradition. If it is foundational, it must justify and account for this tradition, a task that can only be undertaken by a metaphysics of truth. To maintain the primacy of the science of logic is sophistical because such an assumption feigns an ultimacy for which it cannot provide the warrant (MF 102).

In sum, the claim of logic to be paradigmatic for theory as such cannot be sustained because the alleged independence or free-floating character of logic reflects a neglect of its ontological ground. This ground remains invisible so long as it is maintained that logic is identical with thinking *tout court*. If it is argued that the rules of thought can be grounded by creating metalanguages with more reflexive properties, a Heideggerian response must note that additional complexity only multiplies the levels of analysis and moves the rules of thought further from self-understanding.

So long as an appeal is made to theoreticity, the results of thinking, including thinking that takes human conduct as its problematic, falls under the sway of the science of logic. This can only reduce the other to a calculable unit in accordance with the structure of thinking in the present epoch.

NARRATED LIVES

If moral theories fail, it is still possible to appeal to the concrete life that displays in language and action its attentiveness to the interests of others and which by its very existence issues an appeal to live in the same way. If the answers to the question, what is the good according to which these lives are lived and why is that good worth pursuing?, determine the selection of a life path, there is a covert return to moral theory, a theory about the good. But the life of another can also be apprehended as a narrative that solicits following in its footsteps. Some Anglo-American philosophers have already taken the life story as significant for encouraging moral lives. But the rich resources of continental thought for understanding lives as stories have yet to be explored.

Narrative refers to a discursive form in which the facts about a life are brought to light. Derrida notes that narrative is in part a juridical discourse: "Someone demands the narrative of another, seeks to extort from him. . .something they call the truth of what has taken place: 'Tell us exactly what happened.' "[17] This view would, on the face of it, appear to support a description of narrative as representation, as a mirroring of the events that are the story's referents. But before a narrative comes into being, events are nothing more than a shapeless flux, an an-archic inchoate nonground. Only through narrative articulation are events disclosed as such. Maurice Blanchot insists:

> If we regard the tale [*le recit*] as the true telling of an exceptional event which has taken place and which someone is trying to report, then we have not come close to the true nature of the

tale. The tale is not the narration of an event but the event itself, the approach to that event, the place where that event is made to happen—an event which is yet to come and through whose power of attraction the tale can hope to come into being too.[18]

It could be argued, as Lyotard has done, that narrative is "the quintessential form of customary knowledge" and thereby insures the transmission of existing values.[19] But narrative may articulate various voices, each contesting the multiple voices of others. Thus institutional or conventional claims can be opposed by idiosyncratic or opposing voices. The validating rules for the socially disruptive and institutionally destabilizing features of ethical lives are not to be looked for outside life stories but are immanent to them. Such rules are rules of thumb that are established in the context-specific local determinations of the lives themselves.

In sum, as a result of a many-faceted critique of classical phenomenology's understanding of the subject of knowledge, continental ethical thought—specifically the work of Levinas and Blanchot—posits a primordial ethical subject. It is likely, however, that the Husserlian account of the body as subject will be retained and further developed to avoid what in Husserl and Sartre remains the residual dualism of consciousness and body subject. Levinas's position is built upon these inquiries, even if indirectly, in that he stresses the other's corporeal vulnerability as soliciting one's generosity.

Recent attacks on the character of theory, especially Heidegger's analysis of the primacy of logic in the understanding of ontology in the present epoch, indicate that continental philosophy may strive to bypass theory as a mode of reflection upon moral life. This does not mean that continental philosophy will become thoughtless but that new avenues of approach are to be developed. I suggest that narrative ethics, a tack pursued by certain analytic philosophers, would repay investigation by continental philosophy because of extensive work in the understanding of narrative by such thinkers as Derrida, Blanchot, Lyotard, Paul Ricoeur, and Julia Kristeva. Although prophecy is perilous, the trends described are sufficiently developed to suggest their persistence and future refinement.

Notes

1. Karl Marx and Frederic Engels, *Selected Works*, n. t., 2 vols. (Moscow: Foreign Language Publishing House, 1962), 1:247.

2. Emmanuel Levinas, "Language and Proximity" ("LP"), *Collected Philosophical Papers*, trans. Alphonso Lingis (Dordrecht: Martinus Nijhoff, 1987), 109–26, pp. 109–13; collection abbreviated "CP."

3. Emmanuel Levinas, *Totality and Infinity: An Essay on Exteriority*, trans. Alphonso Lingis (Pittsburgh, Pa.: Duquesne Univ. Press, 1969), 197–201.

4. Gilles Deleuze and Félix Guattari, *A Thousand Plateaus: Capitalism and Schizophrenia*, trans. Brian Massumi (Minneapolis: Univ. of Minnesota Press, 1987), 181.

5. Edmund Husserl, *Cartesian Meditations: An Introduction to Phenomenology*, trans. Dorion Cairns (The Hague: Martinus Nijhoff, 1960), 113–20.

6. Michael Theunissen, *The Other: Studies in the Social Ontology of Husserl, Heidegger, Sartre, and Buber*, trans. Christopher Macann (Cambridge, Mass.: MIT Press, 1984), 184; following quote is from p. 162.

7. Emmanuel Levinas, "No Identity," CP 141–51, pp. 143–48.

8. Jacques Derrida, "Differance," *Speech and Phenomena, and Other Essays on Husserl's Theory of Signs*, trans. David Allison (Evanston, Ill.: Northwestern Univ. Press, 1973), 129–60, esp. pp. 129–49.

9. Maurice Merleau-Ponty, *The Phenomenology of Perception*, trans. Colin Smith (London: Routledge & Kegan Paul, 1962), 303.

10. Edith Stein, *On the Problem of Empathy*, trans. Waltrout Stein (The Hague: Martinus Nijhoff, 1964), 39–40.

11. Emmanuel Levinas, *Otherwise than Being; Or, Beyond Essence*, trans. Alphonso Lingis (The Hague: Martinus Nijhoff, 1981); abbreviated "OB."

12. Maurice Blanchot, *The Writing of the Disaster*, trans. Ann Smock (Lincoln: Univ. of Nebraska Press, 1986), 45.

13. See Bernard Williams, *Ethics and the Limits of Philosophy* (Cambridge: Cambridge Univ. Press, 1985), 200–201.

14. Alasdair MacIntyre, *After Virtue: A Study in Moral Theory* (Notre Dame, Ind.: Univ. of Notre Dame Press, 1981), 10.

15. Martin Heidegger, *The Metaphysical Foundations of Logic*, trans. Michael Heim (Bloomington: Indiana Univ. Press, 1984); abbreviated "MF."

16. Martin Heidegger, *Being and Time*, trans. John Macquarrie and Edward Robinson (New York: Harper & Row, 1962), sec. 4, p. 32.

17. Jacques Derrida, "Living On: Border Lines," in Harold Bloom et al., *Deconstruction and Criticism* (New York: Seabury, 1979), 75–176, p. 109.

18. Maurice Blanchot, "Song of the Sirens," *The Gaze of Orpheus and Other Literary Essays*, trans. Lydia Davis (Barrytown, N.Y.: Station Hill, 1981), 105–13, p. 109.

19. Jean-François Lyotard, *The Postmodern Condition: A Report on Knowledge*, trans. Geoff Bennington and Brian Massumi (Minneapolis: Univ. of Minnesota Press, 1984), 19.

16

Asceticism/Askēsis:
Foucault's Thinking Historical Subjectivity

Ladelle McWhorter

In the Introduction to *The Use of Pleasure* Foucault calls his work an *askēsis*, "an exercise of oneself in the activity of thought." The "living substance of philosophy," Foucault writes, is the essay, "which should be understood as the assay or test by which, in the game of truth, one undergoes changes, and not as the simplistic appropriation of others for the purpose of communication."[1] Foucault's work, then, does not simply report to us his conclusions or theories. Foucault is not primarily interested in imparting information. What he offers instead is a kind of exercise book.

Hence, if we are to think through Foucault's work, we need first to think the meaning of the word *exercise*. An exercise, of course, is a kind of practice, a practice designed to change the one who undergoes it. We undertake various programs of exercise in order to alter ourselves in some way. We engage in physical exercises to change the contours of our bodies or magnify their strength, to clear our minds of anger or depression, or to stimulate ourselves for intellectual work. We engage in mathematical or logic exercises in order to train ourselves in the patterns of mathematical or logical thought, as we engage in grammatical exercises in order to discipline our writing and speech. Exercises are transforming practices, practices "by which...one undergoes changes."

243

An exercise book, then, requires an approach quite different from most works of professional scholarship. *If* a typical work of scholarship is to be understood as simply a report of its author's conclusions, suggestions, and perhaps still-embryonic ideas, then it may be taken as a product, the result of an agent's or a subject's having acted to produce it. As such it is an object to be perceived and judged and thought about, an object external to and separable from us subjects who read and judge it. But an exercise book demands to be treated as a very different kind of thing. If it is the case that exercise, *askēsis*, is a transformative practice, then Foucault's exercise books cannot be adequately comprehended by the notion 'object'. They cannot be perceived and read and judged by a subject whose being is wholly external to them. As we have noted, an exercise is a practice whose very nature it is to alter the practitioner. And that means that the practitioner (the writer, the reader) and the practice are not external to one another. As the *askēsis* plays out, the boundaries necessary for maintaining subjective and objective identities shift and may even erode.

Exercises are often empowering and enlightening. There may be very good reasons for engaging in them. However, we who have Nietzsche's works as part of our heritage have reason to hesitate. In the wake of the third essay in *On the Genealogy of Morals*, Foucault's use of the word *askēsis*, from which we get *asceticism*, cannot help but make us wince. We cannot help but notice that asceticism, like Foucault's *askēsis*, denotes self-transforming practice; asceticism, too, changes the subject who undergoes it. Foucault's use of such a closely related word forces us to ask the question: Is it possible that Foucault the neo-Nietzschean in some sneaky or occluded way embraces the ascetic ideal after all? Is Foucault's *askēsis* just a new twist in the history of asceticism? Or does it bring with it a possibility for difference? In pursuit of that question we first need to examine Nietzsche's genealogy of asceticism.

In *On the Genealogy of Morals* Nietzsche locates the beginning of the modern self—a being with interiority, memory, conscience, the ability to make promises—in a certain fastidiousness, a certain desire for keeping clean.[2] Modern selfhood begins in a dream of purity, of the putting aside, the exclusion of whatever appears extraneous, unnecessary, in excess. Perhaps it begins innocuously enough. This abstinence is empowering, self-affirming; it breeds more of itself. And so a sorting process begins. As this complex of self-affirming drives intensifies itself, it discounts, excludes, perhaps in some cases denies that which it now names *other*.

Thus modern selfhood is born, and at the same time modern morality. By a process of sorting out and refusing there comes to be constituted a world, an "external world," an "evil world" from which the self rebounds and turns inward, relentlessly seeking that world's pure opposition, seeking to affirm itself. The modern self's drive for self-affirmation *is* an ascetic drive. What are we modern ascetic selves seeking? That which is truly ourselves, the pure kernel, the self-identical core. How shall we find it? Exclude all that merely adorns, all that clings, all that soils, all that corrupts. Thus asceticism begets the will to constancy, clarity, reliability, integrity, certainty, eternality, identity, the Selfsame. Thus asceticism begets the will to truth.

Nietzsche pulls no punches. It is out of fear that asceticism begets this will to true identity. In order to perpetuate itself it must deny its origins in dispersed drives; it must insist upon the existence of a perfect unity at the heart of things, underlying all that differs and dies, all that wrecks itself in the winds of change. It must insist on the persistence of its self-identity in order to continue being what it is—the drive to purify. To do otherwise is to endanger itself, to risk itself. And that it will not do; that it is too fearful to do.

Now, we could sit in judgment of Nietzsche's discourse; we could criticize his logic or his sense of history. We could even out-Nietzsche him and fault him for reading too much simplicity into things. But none of that would change the fact that Nietzsche's discourse disturbs, and we undergo that disturbance, regardless of how we appropriate it. The discourse appropriates us. We find ourselves within its lineage. It gives rise to us.

We ascetic selves probably will live out Nietzsche's attack on the ascetic ideal in embarrassment. It is embarrassing to find oneself in a discourse whose own fearful, timid lineage is laid bare. Through Nietzsche's discourse the ascetic ideal inspires us with disgust. We smell ourselves and hurry to hold our noses. But that does not help, for the very gesture of nose-holding itself is an ascetic response, a rejection of impurity, a refusal of the corrupt. So, despite ourselves, the ascetic ideal plays itself out first in our embarrassment and then in our frustration within its tenacious grip.

Therefore, when Foucault calls us to *askēsis* unapologetically and without so much as a blush, we have every reason to be surprised, and somewhat suspicious as well. Just what is Foucault asking us to submit to? It would seem that he is asking us to participate in the perpetuation of asceticism's ugly history, a perpetuation all the worse for its apparent forgetfulness of Nietzsche's thought. But Foucault's *askēsis* purports to be other than an insistence upon ascetic submission to rigid identity structures. It purports to be the very opposite, in fact—an attempt to think subjectivity in the absence of transhistorical structure, the pure kernel of the ascetic dream. However, if this claim to otherness is true, Foucault is engaged in an apparent paradox. He—a subject, a self, a person with a particular identity, that man Michel Foucault—is trying to exercise himself in the thinking of his own contingency, his own optionality. He is attempting to put himself through an exercise that would constitute the undergoing of his own dispersal. What are we to make of even the thought of that?

Cynicism snaps: This call of his for inwardness, selfhood, and subjectivity to think its historical emergence out of disparate forces and shameful heterogeneous unions could not possibly emerge from within the ascetic complex that is modern subjectivity, unless— *unless*—it is some new ploy, some new strategy for purification. Perhaps in Foucault's discourse the ascetic will is attempting to subject itself to a rigid identity in yet a new way; perhaps it is attempting to think dissension as—its truth.

Foucault has been read that way, as Nietzsche has. Foucault's *askēsis* can be read as a kind of vengeful attempt to humiliate the ascetically produced self-identical self by bringing it up against its *real* genealogical past. If we were to read Foucault this way we would understand him to be perpetuating and perhaps developing asceticism in at least two ways. First, he would be maintaining the notion of a pure, self-identical truth of the self. In other words, he would still be positing a constant core, but in this case the core would be something like the Freudian id, a petty, infantile, frightened little thing. Second, in addition to positing this pure center of being, Foucault's discourse would be a perpetuation of asceticism in the sense that he would be forcing himself, and us, to turn around and face this puny, ugly little truth that is ourselves; he would be forcing us to strip away our delusions of grandeur and our pride in order to *be* that which we *really* are; he would be imposing, once again, and in yet a new and more repulsive way, the rigid standard of absolute identity. He would be calling us to an ever more honest ownership of ourselves. (But lest this sound too cruel, let us hasten to add that in such debasement there is, we must admit, a certain ascetic appeal.)

It would be unwise to discount this reading out of hand—as though we had some standard of truth against which it failed to measure up—so we will allow it to stand as a possible reading of Foucault's text. But there is an instability at the center of that reading, an instability that is the reader him- or herself. In order to read Foucault's discourse as *nothing but* a perverse perpetuation of the ascetic ideal we must engage in a bit of ascetic refusal ourselves; we must insist that a discourse is the product of an author, a subject who acts. We must reject the possibility that Foucault's *discourse itself* might move us beyond the control of the ascetic self who produced or reads it. In other words, we must insist that there exist logically separable subjects and objects that stand in relation to each other as external causes and effects and maintain their identities regardless of change. But, if we pay careful attention to the transformative processes of *askēsis*, we realize that that insistence is optional, and we can begin to undergo the possibility that there are other powers in this discourse of Foucault's, other voices besides the active, other grammars besides our Latinate substantive. The only way to find out is to engage the *askēsis* and allow ourselves to undergo.

We cannot reproduce Foucault's *askēsis* here. However, some remarks may help us get a feel for some of the directions such an exercise might begin to take. Foucault's tool is genealogy, the patient, meticulous tracing of relations of force. In Foucault's texts—*Discipline and Punish*, for example, as well as the sexuality series—what emerges are coherent, plausible accounts of the gradual manufacture of human selves—sexual selves, law-abiding selves, delinquent selves, moral selves, beings whose births bear great resemblance to the births of institutions, practices, and discourses of all kinds.

In Foucault's discourse, a self—like an institution such as a legal system or a state—is not best understood as something substantial and enduring. In a certain sense neither a self nor an institution is a thing at all. Both are better thought as occurrings, innumerable indiscrete events. Some analogies may be of help.

If one were to make a film of an immobile object stationed in a windowless room and then were to project that film for an audience, what the audience would see would be a still image. But the image would be sustained not by some enduring substance manifesting itself or deigning to appear. Rather, the image would be sustained by dozens and perhaps hundreds or thousands of bursts of patterned light. The apparently stable image would continually occur rather than subsist. Perhaps a better example is the shape formed when water rushes down a circular drain. Despite its visibility and regularity, this funnel shape is not a subsisting thing; it is simply the sensible tension of a set of forces in play. It exists only as long as those forces maintain a certain equilibrium.[3]

For Foucault, the world occurs, as the film image and the water funnel occur, as always changeable sets of repeated force events clashing against each other or holding each other in tension. We need posit no subsisting things. We may think among events, as ourselves events, of the eventful character of seemingly subsistent things. Does this mean we have thought those things in their truth? Not in this discourse, if by truth we mean some constant reality, some subsisting thing. The ascetic insistent upon constancy finds itself in continual frustration here. There is no constant truth of the ascetic self, not even an ugly one.

Self, then, as part of the eventful world, is itself eventful. It is to be thought as a nexus of repeating force events remaining more or less steady through time. Selves take many different shapes, as it were, as force events shift, are unable to repeat, or occur at a reduced level of energy *vis-à-vis* one another. Nevertheless, the shifts are usually minor; selves remain identifiable most of the time. This is to be expected, unless there is some relatively cataclysmic change in the sustaining patterns of force events. But what if there is? Well, then, selves may be dramatically altered. Some may die. New forms may be born.

Postcataclysmic arrangements are not predictable; for, in an eventful world, there are no underlying, hidden laws or structures that govern change. However, the emergings of arrangements are often traceable in retrospect. Certain sorts of force networks might come to show themselves as essential to the maintenance of a given equilibrium. One might interrogate such a network with regard to its structure and emergence and so begin to think the history of its becoming the essence of a particular arrangement or current equilibric form.[4]

Selves, then, have histories, of course, but they also *are* historical. They are not subsisting entities to which things happen, around which events occur; not enduring substances whose manifestations are sometimes deformed or incomplete; selves occur at every instant, and at every instant their occurring interacts with or conflicts with, reinforces or disrupts all sorts of other occurrings "in" the matrices of world-event. Analyses will accordingly be multiple and complex. Hence genealogy as opposed to a quest for truth.

But back to our first question: must we read Foucault's discourse as a new and more insidious ascetic trap? As long as *we* insist upon *reading it*-as-an-object, protecting ourselves from its action, remaining in tight control, perhaps that is all that it can be. Perhaps we will never read it as anything but a fanciful report on the contents of

Michel Foucault's mind. But when the discourse begins to stir us, when the *askēsis* gets underway, something else may very well occur.

A first sign that something else is occurring is the appearance of fear. Very often, and as Nietzsche no doubt would have predicted, this fear expresses itself as a desire to maintain social or moral order. Time after time students and colleagues have voiced to me their fear that if we cease to hold to the notion that selves have self-identical, transhistorical cores, we will no longer be able to hold people responsible for what they do. And, if people cannot be held responsible, order cannot be maintained. Might will equal right, and society will degenerate into a war of all against all.

One response to that fear might be: what makes you think that that is not how things are now? But as an initial answer, such would be a frivolous response. A second, less frivolous response might be to question the logic of the fear. Does the absence of transhistorical subjectivity necessarily result in the preclusion of personal responsibility? The answer to that question is, I think, no, but eventually, as we undergo Foucault's discourse, the question itself comes to seem strange and answering it comes to seem beside the point. Nonetheless it will be instructive to pursue this issue briefly here.

First, we need a better account of the allegedly threatened link between constant self-identity and personal responsibility. A little social observation can give us that. Apparently one of the rules of the game of responsibility assignments is that one should not hold someone responsible for a situation if that person is *other* than the person who brought it about. For example, most people would not be likely to consent to holding the grandchildren of a murderer responsible for the murderer's crimes. (Of course, as we know, people really do hold relatives responsible for the wrongdoing of others. Entire families are treated with contempt when one family member offends the public taste. And, without doubt, there are times when outrage over one incident turns into violence against whoever happens to get in the injured one's way. But these cases, most would insist, are regrettable reminders of the imperfections of human beings, not true exemplars of justice well wrought.) Likewise, many people would argue that one cannot hold a person responsible for an act if the person has changed significantly since its commission. When a prisoner pleads that he was temporarily insane at the time of the act, he may be understood in part to be claiming that he is not the same man in some important way, so that to punish him now would be unjust. We might also understand the sentiment "he has suffered enough" to mean in part "because of what he has undergone he has changed since the time of the egregious act, so it is not appropriate to hold the person he is now responsible for it." At any rate, it seems clear that we typically require a person who is to be held responsible for something to have a fairly stable identity through time. Therefore, anything we do to undermine our ordinary belief in stable personal identity cores threatens our ability to hold people responsible for whatever occurs.

Of course, stability of identity is not the only official prerequisite for holding someone responsible. In order for us legitimately to hold a person responsible for something, he or she must be related to it as its cause. It is officially illicit to blame, for example, the bearer of bad news. We should reserve our wrath for the person who actually brought the bad situation about.

Now, some claim that Foucault's historicization of the subject places in question the notion that there is any stable core, any identity that would unify the undergoing of punishment with the commitment of an act. If the transhistorical self is merely a dream of Western man, then subjective duration is just an illusion, too. Foucault has destroyed the responsible self.

This, however, is simply not the case. Foucault is not attempting (primarily, or even necessarily) to dismantle the responsible self; he is attempting to understand how it came to be, a task whose presuppositions obviously include a conviction that there do exist such selves. Foucault's work does not suggest that no one is ever *really* responsible for anything; it does suggest that responsibility is historically formed and its necessary preconditions are maintained by relations of force. Foucault's primary question is not, how can we expose and dispose of an illusion?, but rather, how did the real phenomenon of self-identity come to be and how is it sustained in a given discursive region? His genealogical analyses of sexuality and desire are examples of his attempts to understand how forms of self-identity are constructed and how they are reproduced within networks of power relations that themselves are unstable and shifting. As we said before, Foucault's understanding of the self-identical self is that it is not a persisting entity so much as it is a steady repeating of relations or events, like the film image or the water funnel.

Of course, even if Foucault leaves us with some shimmering alternative to the *stable* responsible self, he may still threaten the game of responsibility assignments on some other front. If we are to be able to hold people responsible in the usual ways, we also need to be able to understand a self as a cause and, furthermore, as a cause that is not itself totally caused.

If self is impinged upon by social, historical, or linguistic forces, then self is not an uncaused cause. Little will eliminate our desire to hold someone responsible faster than our deciding that the person was absolutely unable to behave otherwise than he or she did.

Foucault's view *seems* to eliminate the possibility that selves are not completely determined by social forces. For, if selves are maintained at every moment by power networks, then each self must be at the mercy of the networks that hold it together and make it up. Therefore the self itself is not responsible for what it does.

However, this way of thinking is not Foucault's. This way of thinking still assumes that self is somehow independent of the forces in question. On Foucault's view, self is precisely not some*thing* upon which historical forces act. Self *is* the networks of forces themselves. These forces are not causes external to the product they create. Self simply *is* those forces in tension with themselves. The analytic dichotomy inside/outside just breaks down.[5]

To reiterate, in order to understand self as not responsible for any of its acts, we must assume self to be a kind of thing preexisting the forces that act upon it and external to them. But if self *is* those forces or some subset of them, it is not merely being acted upon. Therefore, while it is true that in Foucault's discourse it is not the case that self is an uncaused cause, the pure origin of its a posteriori acts, neither is it the case that self is nothing but the middle billiard ball in a combination shot. Personal responsibility does not necessarily go out the window; but it does need to be rethought. (And I would like to suggest that that might be part of what Foucault was doing the last years of his life.)

But far more interesting than the idea that Foucault could answer his critics on more or less their own terms—that he can perhaps reassure them that the game of responsibility assignments need not be stopped or lost—is the existence of this threatened posture itself. We may take this as a clue that, while on some levels Foucault's discourse may be a perpetuation and development of the power of ascetic drives, on some level those drives are also threatened with erosion and possibly undermined. Let us look again at asceticism as self-transformative practice.

It is the case, within Nietzsche's account, that asceticism transforms itself as it affirms itself and extends its strength. Ascetic drives refine themselves, produce ever finer points of distinction as the sorting process of self and other plays itself out. The ascetic self, then, undergoes changes as the process intensifies, becoming more powerful perhaps and ever more rigidly defined. The ascetic self is subjected and subjectified by the processes of purification that posit its ever more carefully delineated identity core. The ascetic self en-selfs itself by enforcing the continued stability of the identity it seeks to *be*. Asceticism is a powerfully paradoxical drive for constant self-transformation toward a perfect stasis in a pure unity of self-identical repose.

Foucault's *askēsis* bears great resemblance to the movement of self-transformative ascetic drives. The ascetic self's drive to *know* itself is certainly apparent in Foucault. And there is a sense in which in Foucault we encounter a kind of truth, a truth that the self is not self-identical but rather that it is an amalgamation of disparate forms. The ascetic self, upon encountering that "truth," upon acceding to the plausibility of genealogical accounts, begins, predictably enough, to discipline itself to that self-knowledge, to bring itself into intellectual conformity with that truth.

But when the drive to purify confronts the "truth" of its own impurity, when it runs headlong into the contradictory project of attempting to pare itself down to its fundamental multiplicity, ascetic selfhood begins to undergo the self-transforming power of Foucault's discourse, and the valences that held themselves in tension to produce the notion of a perfect unity, of some enduring Same, must necessarily shift. The thought of self in the center of Foucault's discourse is the thought of transgression, a reversal of forces, a gradual or perhaps violent turning outward of the valences before turned in, like fingers pulling loose from a stone they have gripped too hard for too long. It will be necessary to find a different way to speak: *When there occurs the undergoing* of the genealogical stripping away of the argumentative and commonsense forces sustaining belief in the unitary self, when there occurs the undergoing of the exposure of the fearful and nonrational drives that put those beliefs in place, there may occur a kind of death of the ahistorical self, just as, in Nietzsche's discourse, when there occurs the undergoing of the exposure of the ungodliness that supported gods, there occurs a kind of death of the ahistorical God. As the thought of God loses its power to shape a world, the thought of a unitary self-identity begins to lose its power to shape a life.

And what then? Will human being simply fly apart? Will we all go stark raving mad? Will might equal right and society degenerate into a war of all against all? Perhaps. But why should it come that? Selfishness would be a strange thing in a discourse that did not insist upon the unity of self-identical selves. Perhaps, as Nietzsche says, morality and evil are Siamese twins.

Foucault's discourse, then, like ascetic discourses, is a self-transformative exercise. It is an *askēsis* that allows the powers of ascetic selfhood to bring themselves to bear in characteristic ways. But because Foucault's discourse draws asceticism to focus its self-transformative power on the drive for purification itself, ascetic selfhood finds itself in question. Not only does self-transformation occur here, but there is within the discourse an awareness of this transformative power and an allowance of it as opposed to a denial or an attempt at masterful control. Thus, like ascetic discourses, Foucault's is a discourse that transforms itself; but it transforms itself from an active production of an agent-subject to a process of self-overcoming that opens possibilities for movements of differing rather than the continued movement of purification that is an insistence upon the identity of the same.

Yes, Foucault's discourse begins as and in some ways may be read as remaining an ascetic discourse. It draws its energy from its ascetic lineage and past. But within Foucault's discourse ascetic selfhood cannot maintain control of the direction of its own forceful drives. Thus, as Foucault's discourse operates upon the forces at its own discursive center, something other to asceticism may begin to emerge, something we ascetic selves are not able to name, something that will resist the ascetic drive to label and identify, but something the undergoing of which may be either beautiful or terrible or both but which will definitely be—to use a Nietzschean word—interesting.

Notes

1. Michel Foucault, *The Use of Pleasure*, trans. Robert Hurley, vol. 2 of *The History of Sexuality* (New York: Pantheon Books, 1985), 9.

2. Friedrich Nietzsche, *On the Genealogy of Morals and Ecce Homo*, trans. Walter Kaufmann and R. J. Hollingdale (New York: Vintage Books, 1967), First Essay, section 6, p. 32. It is doubtful that this account of the ascetic ideal would have emerged for me had it not been for the work of Charles Scott of Vanderbilt University; in particular, see *The* Question *of Ethics* (Bloomington: Indiana Univ. Press, 1990), chap. 2.

3. After this paper was written I happened to be reading J. Baird Callicott's *In Defense of the Land Ethic: Essays in Environmental Philosophy* (Albany: State Univ. of New York Press, 1989), when I ran across the following quotation from Yale biophysicist Harold Morowitz: "Viewed from the point of view of modern [ecology], each living thing...is a dissipative structure,

that is it does not endure in and of itself but only as a result of the continual flow of energy in the system. An example might be instructive. Consider a vortex in a stream of flowing water. The vortex is a structure made of an ever-changing group of water molecules. It does not exist as an entity in the classical Western sense; it exists only because of the flow of water through the stream. In the same sense, the structures out of which biological entities are made are transient, unstable entities with constantly changing molecules, dependent on a constant flow of energy from food in order to maintain form and structure....From this point of view the reality of individuals is problematic because they do not exist per se but only as local perturbations in this universal flow." Callicott cites this from Morowitz's "Biology as a Cosmological Science," in *Main Currents in Modern Thought* 28 (1972): 156.

4. It is important to notice how very differently the word *essence* functions in this context from the way it seems to function in classical contexts. *Essence* here is the name of whatever historically emerging forces function to maintain a particular structure and protect it from perversion or disintegration. *Essence* does not name the truth of any set of structures or forces.

5. The breakdown of the dichotomy inside/outside occurs here much as it does in ecological discourse (compare note 3). Once thinking begins to occur in the absence of the classical liberal notion of atomic individuality, the rigid distinction between what is *I* and what is *not-I* (or what is here inside and what is there outside) carries little force. Perhaps what we are moving toward is an ecological understanding of human being.

17

Foucault and the Problem of Agency;
Or, Toward a Practical Philosophy

Mario Moussa

Every discourse on social matters boils down, of course, to the issue of free will. This is something of a paradox, however, since regardless of whether the will is free or not, in any outcome of such discourse it will be curbed. One's curiosity regarding the nature of the will is therefore either sadistic or academic or both.
—Joseph Brodsky

AGENCY, THEORY, AND PRACTICE

Recent academic philosophy appears to have become increasingly political, in a very distinct way. Reflection on politics itself is nothing new; ever since the Greeks, obviously enough, philosophers in the West have argued, moralized, and hectored about the ideal (or at least the most rational) forms of collective life human beings can achieve. But in the wake of postmodern critiques of subjectivity, philosophical discussion concerning politics has focused on a particular and distinctive issue: the very possibility of political action or, more precisely, *revolutionary* political action.[1] Generally speaking, this discussion begins with the following problem: if it is true that social forces crisscross and shape the human subject, and

255

if it is therefore true that nothing like an autonomous Cartesian "I" exists, then how is it possible for the political agent to instigate action? This has come to be called the problem of agency. As Paul Smith asks, reflecting on the various theoretical de-centerings and deconstructions of the subject, do people simply suffer history, or can active political agents change it?[2]

Michel Foucault has come in for much criticism on this score because of his genealogies, especially *Discipline and Punish*, which hammers away at the putative link between subjectivity and subjection. Charles Taylor, for example, charges Foucault with an unrelenting negativism, that is, with exposing the evil and oppression embedded in the institutions governing everyday life, but not affirming any effective political program that would make for greater freedom. According to Taylor, Foucault's notion of power amounts to "a kind of Schopenhauerian will, ungrounded in human action," and from which there is "no escape." Similarly, Michael Walzer claims that, Foucault leaves no room for "the free human subject," and Jürgen Habermas has described Foucault's history as "a senseless back-and-forth of anonymous processes of subjugation in which power and nothing but power appears in ever-changing guises."[3] Related criticisms abound, varied in their insightfulness, and all touching on Foucault's apparent failure to provide an account of freedom and effective political resistance.[4]

These criticisms, I argue in the following sections, misunderstand the nature of Foucault's genealogies and, earlier, the verbal experiments undertaken during his "archaeological" period.[5] Throughout his life Foucault urged intellectuals to stop thinking of theory and practice as somehow opposed: to see, instead, the one as a reflection of the other; or even simply to drop the problem of theory and practice.[6] His work from *Madness and Civilization* (1961) up to *Discipline and Punish* (1975) and possibly *The Will to Truth* (1976) should be understood as an attempt to show what philosophy becomes after the debate over theory and practice has been shelved. What it becomes—or what it *recovers*, to borrow an idea from Stephen Toulmin—is practical philosophy.[7] That Foucault offers no account of political resistance is not a shortcoming; it merely follows, as I hope to show, from his own particular political engagements. This is not a defense of Foucault, although at times it might appear to take the form of one, but rather an exploration of the philosophical and political possibilities raised by his work.

PHILOSOPHY AS CULTURAL DIAGNOSIS

Foucault's genealogies have often been described as postmodern, but in fact the postmodern tag applies to Foucault only in a very limited and perhaps trivial sense.[8] If it is true, as Foucault himself suggested, that the modern period ended sometime around 1950, then Foucault's genealogies are obviously, from the standpoint of historical eras, *post*modern.[9] To be sure, parsing out the past into distinct eras in order to assign authors their proper categories is in itself a meaningless activity, unless Toynbee has seen the nature of history more clearly than anyone else. But the point is that Foucault can be grouped together with other so-called postmoderns—Jacques Derrida, Jean-François Lyotard, Jean Baudrillard, among others—only in this rather meaningless way. Of course *postmodern* in its common critical usage carries another meaning: it refers to a loosely defined philosophical program or movement, and when commentators label Foucault "postmodern," intentionally or not they associate him with that movement. So, it seems to me, largely because Foucault shares with the postmoderns a particular historical place, he has also been assumed (but mistakenly) to share their philosophical aims; strange to say, geographical place (that Foucault studied and lived in Paris) might have something to do with it, too.[10] In any case all this has caused a great deal of confusion.

True, all along Foucault aimed to unsettle the Modernist assumption that subjectivity provided an adequate standard against which claims to truth could be evaluated, and he therefore helped to "de-center" subjectivity just as much as, say, Derrida did. But when Arthur Kroker, for example, declares, "The Cartesian self no longer exists"—ignore for the moment the question of exactly how that might be determined, much less whether the declaration is true—and invokes Foucault's name as one among many postmoderns who have argued to this effect, he makes a common error.[11] The only sense in which the Cartesian self no longer exists is that a certain theoretical account of human experience and knowledge has been challenged by critics with conflicting and equally theoretical accounts, and it may be that those critics have had far less impact than they imagine.[12] For the most part, however, Foucault was not concerned to provide a philosophical alternative to the Cartesian-Kantian subject nor even (a less ambitious project) to expose its pretensions as hopelessly grandiose.

What Foucault attempted—and this might provide the proper tag for him, if one is needed—was a cultural diagnosis. Foucault himself often labelled his work, as he did in the frequently quoted line from *Discipline and Punish*, a "history of the present"; with equal justification it could be described as an ethnology, an anthropology done by somewhat unusual means. (That an anthropologist such as Paul Rabinow continues to be interested in Foucault is not surprising.) In fact, Foucault made an explicit comparison between ethnological studies and his own historical research, calling it "an internal ethnology of our culture and of our rationality."[13] Even *The Order of Things*, which seems so textually thick and dizzyingly abstract, is not primarily concerned with debunking philosophical theories; nor does it represent, as some commentators have suggested, a quasi-Kantianism, Foucault's *epistemes* being in some way comparable to Kant's categories. So great is the misunderstanding here that one commentator, referring to the very pages in *The Archaeology of Knowledge* where Foucault explains the archaeological method, summarizes it as the "determination of the historical *a priori* for the appearance of ideas, sciences, philosophies, etc." Somehow, according to this reading, the *episteme* "gives rise" to formalized systems.[14]

Hence, Foucault the neo-Kantian, the mandarian theoretician par excellence.[15] Even so sensitive a reader as Ian Hacking characterizes the Foucault of the middle to late sixties in this way.[16] But Foucault himself, in *The Archaeology of Knowledge*, carefully dissociates his analyses from any project that aims to establish "conditions of possibility," whether Kantian or discursive. Archaeology, he says, "is nothing more than a rewriting: that is, in the preserved form of exteriority, a regulated transformation of what has already been written. It is not a return to the innermost secret of the origin; it is the systematic description of a discourse-object."[17] What Foucault took from phenomenology—systematic description— is obvious. As this passage indicates, however, his archaeology was more than description, too; the phrase "a regulated transformation" carries a tendentious freight. Clearly, then, Foucault had an agenda. The problem is that its specifics were far from clear.

At least, that is to say, his books left the agenda unclear, or were confusing; in his interviews, however, Foucault managed to clarify his aims. Whether or not he actually achieved those aims in his books is, of course, a valid question in its own right. But the answer to that question does not affect my argument here, since this is not a defense of Foucault and his writings. Everyone, in fact, and especially the "Foucauldians," would do well to follow Baudrillard's advice and "forget Foucault," but not for the reasons Baudrillard offers.[18] Again and again, Foucault denied that his work was terribly original and disavowed any wish "to say it all," so to speak, or "to tell others what they must do," as he put it near the end of his life.[19] Hardly a system, hardly an epistemological project, his work represented a possibility, and that is probably its greatest value.

So what did Foucault say he wanted to do? How did he understand the possibilities contained in his work?[20]

CRITICAL HISTORY, POLITICAL COMMITMENT, AND ACTIVISM

In a 1966 interview given soon after the publication of *The Order of Things*, Foucault characterized the appeal of what he called his archaeological method, and the words he used are very suggestive: "It permits me to *avoid* every problem concerning the anteriority of theory in relation to practice, and the inverse."[21] In contrast to Sartre, says Foucault, he writes from the position of the "theoretico-active." Theories, practices, institutions: for the archaeologist, they are all traces, among which are "common traits." The archaeologist, Foucault continues, then organizes these traits into classes, forms, or—and this word has led to many misunderstandings—structures, which collectively define an era. But it would be wrong to fixate on the notion of structures, as many readers did at that time, and risk overlooking what might be the most interesting aspect of what Foucault was attempting in *The Order of Things*, namely, to avoid the problem of theory and practice. This is not to say that he solved the problem. Rather, he chose a style of analysis that allowed him to shelve it.

Placed against the backdrop of late-fifties, early-sixties French politics and the omnipresence of Marxism in intellectual circles, this choice appears in its fullest significance.[22] Without question, there is something very different about *The Order of Things* in comparison with the rest of Foucault's books, before and after. *The Order of Things* was clearly an experiment, designed to answer the question: What would be the result of a cultural analysis that treats discourse neither as Marxist superstructure nor as the eternal dialogue of Truth with itself? So, here in an unexpected place, in what many took to be an idealist discursive analysis, Foucault was responding to political concerns in the most general sense.

Even at that time, then, the "agency" critique would have been in the position of talking past Foucault's aims. The question of whether or not political action is possible, or what relationship political theory bears to practice, was simply not Foucault's question. To put it more strongly, Foucault was urging that these kinds of questions be *avoided*. As he said preemptorily five years later, in 1971: "Reject theory and all forms of general discourse."[23] He argued that the need for theory was part of the system he and other activists were rejecting—and here, it should be stressed, he meant not only a philosophical system, though he certainly had that in mind, but as well a system of institutions and practices that interlock to form a totalizing social entity. Yet the fact is that Foucault continued to write books even after this denunciation of theory. He might well have appeared hypocritical, or intoxicated with an anarchic exuberance, and some have argued he was both.[24] But Foucault was not hypocritical in his continued philosophizing, while Foucault the anarchist is largely a caricature.

To take the question of his anarchist tendencies first: Foucault's critics have often portrayed him as more of an anarchist than he really was, though admittedly he had a penchant for oracular and even apocalyptic pronouncements, the most extreme of which seem increasingly pompous and quaint with the passage of time. As an example, take the famous one at the end of *The Order of Things*: "As the archaeology of our thought easily shows, man is an invention of recent date. And one perhaps nearing its end."[25] True, the "easily" is clearly ironic, coming as it does after hundreds of prose-tangled pages, and the "perhaps" mollifies the prediction. Still, Foucault is playing the apocalyptic prophet or jokester here. In all, if the pronouncement can be taken seriously—as, say, a cultural diagnosis— then it was wrong. But mostly, as noted before, Foucault sought to limit the expectations concerning his work.

Consider his response when told of an odd quasi criticism of *Discipline and Punish*—that because of its "implacable logic," it left "no possible room for initiative":

> I don't feel myself capable of effecting the "subversion of all codes," "dislocation of all orders of knowledge," "revolutionary affirmation of violence," these hopes and prospectuses that currently underpin all those brilliant intellectual ventures that I admire all the more because the worth and previous achievement of those who undertake them guarantee an appropriate outcome.[26]

His project, he says, "is far from being of comparable scope." He claims, and "agency" theorists should take note, to be capable only of participating in the "difficult displacement of forms of sensibility and thresholds of tolerance." His project is "precisely to bring it about that they [e.g., social workers and prison administrators] 'no longer know what to do'." As for action itself: "It seems to me that 'what is to be done' ought not to be determined from above by reformers, be they prophetic or legislative, but by a long work of comings and goings, of exchanges, reflections, trials, different analyses." This last remark would probably have been the core of Foucault's answer to the "agency" critics, if he had ever addressed them directly (he did not, so far as I know). But perhaps as it stands it needs some explanation.

Sometimes identifying himself as a historian, sometimes distancing himself from historians, Foucault unquestionably used history in his archaeologies and genealogies. From *Madness and Civilization* up to the unfinished work on sexuality, history of one sort or another always figured in his "theoretico-active" endeavors. But naturally his interest in history was never solely contemplative, never linked to a desire merely to behold the spectacle of the past. As Foucault put it in 1983, "the return to history makes sense in the respect that history shows that that which is was not always so. . . . What reason considers its necessity or much more what various forms of rationality claim to be their necessary existence, has a history."[27] Sensitive to the charge of being an antirationalist, he adds: "But this doesn't mean that these forms of rationality are irrational. They rest upon a foundation of human practices and human faces; because they are made they can be unmade—of course, assuming we know how they were made." Foucault should be taken literally when he refers to "human practices" and forms of rationality being "made" and possibly "unmade." The concern with explicit practices is obvious in *Discipline and Punish*, for example, where he discusses particular timetables (such as Leon Faucher's rules for the young Parisian prisoners) and detailed methods for "making" soldiers (such as the ordinance of 1764).[28] The same goes for his later analyses of self-forming practices among the Greeks and Romans. As he stresses time and again, the "care of the self" was not merely an "attitude of consciousness or a form of attention," but also a "form of activity."[29] These self-forming practices constituted an important part of the day, much the way meditation, prayer, or even exercise does among other cultures and peoples in other times. Literally working upon the body, in explicit and often meticulous ways, the practices Foucault analyzed throughout his career (from the incarceration of the mad to the self-scrutiny of the Stoic) had a hand in creating the notions of rationality, truth, self-evidence, and so on, that define the boundaries of intellectual discourse. The possibility Foucault envisioned, and it is an exciting one, is that by exposing and then helping to dismantle (if necessary) those practices, intellectuals might help in the "formation of a political will," as he described it.[30]

This might be thought of as Foucault's "solution" to the problem of theory and practice. There is, on the one hand, the unsettling of accepted truths, which represents the intellectual's work and corresponds to theory; and then, on the other hand, there is the formation of a political will, which any citizen may take up as a commitment and corresponds to practice. Satisfying or not, not much more can be expected than this solution—from Foucault, at any rate. In this sense, Foucault's politics—at least one aspect of it, the discursive aspect—could be justifiably described as Nietzschean. In *On the Advantage and Disadvantage of History for Life*, for example, Nietzsche claims that everyone "must have the strength, and use it from time to time, to shatter and dissolve something to enable him to live." This is done "by dragging [the past] to the bar of judgment." So that no age assumes its past to be pure, Nietzsche adds that "every past . . . is worth condemning," human affairs always being built upon violence, weakness, and pettiness. Calling this judgment on the past "critical history," Nietzsche describes its operation in harsh terms: "one puts a knife to [history's] roots, then one cruelly treads all pieties underfoot."[31] Ironically though, what is critical history today becomes pieties tomorrow. And then tomorrow's historians have the task of unsettling today's critical insights.

In one of his last interviews, responding to the oft-repeated charge of pessimism, Foucault makes a similar point:

> I would like to do a genealogy of problems, of *problematiques*. My point is not that everything is bad, but that everything is dangerous, which is not exactly the same as bad. If everything is dangerous then we always have something to do. So my position leads not to apathy but to a hyper- and pessimistic activism.[32]

With or without good philosophical reasons, Foucault did not worry himself about "agency"—there was "always something to do." But then why is it that Foucault was saddled with the charge of producing a stunned quietism, supposedly an unfortunate result of his genealogies' "implacable logic"?

What a paradox it would be if Foucault, who was himself a political activist, had stymied other activists with his geneaologies. Far from conceiving of "agency" as a problem for his varied analyses of subjection and oppression—and notice that it is possible, on Foucault's terms, to speak of oppression straightforwardly and without deconstructive apologies[33]—Foucault himself considered them "enabling," as the "agency" theorists say. True, power is everywhere, even in the minutest gesture, even in private moments of self-reflection, but power does not therefore cripple those who oppose it. Antaeus-like, resistance gains its strength from the ground of power itself. As Foucault argued, the various forms of resistance "are all the more real and effective to the extent that they are formed there where the relations of power are exercised; resistance to power doesn't have to come from elsewhere in order to be real. . . . It is, therefore, like power, multiple and integratable into global strategies."[34] What Foucault did in *Discipline and Punish*, for example, was to ferret out power as it insidiously worked its effects on the body. Once the site of its activity was identified and located, then power could be resisted. (The feminists' declaration in the sixties that "sex is a political act" resulted from a similar reconnaissance operation.) And that Foucault's analysis of body-subjection spurred action—rather than anaesthetizing it—is demonstrated by, among other things, the many feminist analyses that have set off from *Discipline and Punish* and taken a knife to the roots of eating disorders, medical biases against women, discrimination in the workplace, and many other forms of subjection and domination.[35] These analyses, in turn, promise to have real liberating effects.

Foucault should be taken seriously—and quite literally—when he describes history as a "curative science."[36] In a passage that might have inspired Habermas's remark about "a senseless back-and-forth of anonymous processes of subjugation," Foucault offers what could serve as a description of his own discursive activism:

> Humanity does not gradually progress from combat to combat until it arrives at universal reciprocity, where the rule of law finally replaces warfare; humanity installs each of its violences in a system of rules and thus proceeds from domination to domination. . . . The successes of history belong to those who are capable of seizing those rules, to replace those who had used them, to disguise themselves so as to pervert them, invert their meaning, and redirect them against those who had initially imposed them.[37]

Does this envision endless subjugation? Yes, it clearly does, yet it also envisions endless activism—or hyperactivism—which Foucault held out as the goal of his genealogies. The agency critics, however, treat Foucault's genealogies as though they were attempts at constructing tightly interlocked and crushing systems, as though they were participants in the hoary philosophical discussion concerning the nature of the human will and sought to demonstrate the illusoriness of its freedom. Or, alternatively, Foucault is lumped together with the so-called postmodern writers, with their fascination over the seemingly endless play of meanings and interpretations and the impossibility of assigning guilt or responsibility to anyone or anything.

It seems that both the agency critics and the followers of postmodernism who want to conscript Foucault into their ranks misunderstand the nature of Foucault's historical enterprise and, more generally, the nature of any historical writing. Consider, first, those attempting to "theorize resistance," or, in other words, to provide a theoretical account of radical political action: from their point of view Foucault appears to leave no room in his genealogies for the free human subject. Take Paul Smith's dismissal of Foucault as an example:

> It may sound surprising to say this, especially since Foucault is frequently praised for emphasizing both the dominatory and the enabling function of power. However, it seems that *Foucault's "subject" is more incapable than not of becoming an agent of large social change* and that the supposedly enabling moments of power relations are subsumed under the "subject's" subjection.[38]

The odd thing about this passage—and the criticism found here represents a common one—is that it treats "Foucault's 'subject' " as though it were an actually existing entity or even a person, the way students in introductory literature courses often discuss literary characters as though they were real people. ("Ugh, Humbert Humbert is a *disgusting* person!") The criticism seems to be that Foucault, godlike, somehow *consigns* the subject to its subjection.

If, instead, Foucault is understood to be offering a cultural diagnosis, then his claims about the subject make much more sense. Although a frightening prospect, it may well be that in important respects the autonomous human subject has become extinct, killed off by increasingly effective technologies of control and normalization, or even that it is and has always been an illusion. Other cultural critics at least have made similar observations. Robert Musil, for instance, in *The Man without Qualities* (1930), has outlined the contours of a culture no longer able to sustain "individuality":

> In earlier times one could be an individual with a better con-
> science than one can today. . . . Today, responsibility's center
> of gravity lies not in the individual but in the relations between
> things. Who has not noticed how independent experiences have
> made themselves of humans. . . . Who today can still say that
> his anger is really his own anger, *with so many people butting
> in and knowing so much more about it than he does*?[39]

Musil's human being has become a mere placeholder within bureaucratic systems and knowledge schemes. No one would accuse Musil, however, of constructing a human being "incapable of becoming an agent of large social change," but for some reason the agency critics have taken Foucault to task on just these grounds. The reason seems to be that these critics assume that Foucault, as a historian, makes claims about the human subject that must be taken as objective in the crudest sense: that, for example, if Foucault assembles a genealogy according to which subjectivity is a product of repressive self-forming technologies, then the human being is nothing more than the product of those technologies. But very few historians, even the most traditional, would understand the activity of writing history in this way; history never says all there is to say. To put it differently, the historian is a writer faced with the problem of telling a story. What should be included and what should be left out?

Not that in *Madness and Civilization* or *Discipline and Punish* or in any of his other works about the human subject Foucault was actually fabricating fictions, despite the obviously provocative claim he made in an interview about *The Order of Things*: "My book is a pure and simple 'fiction'."[40] Rather, writing history is inevitably an interpretive enterprise, with many similarities to writing fiction—this is the most sober way of taking Foucault's claim. And it is a particularly defensible claim when applied to Foucault's genealogical studies, which set out to constitute historical objects (the history of madness, of incarceration, etc.) where before there were none. For such a philosophically sensitive historian as Paul Veyne, in fact, who describes himself as an "obsolete empiricist," it is only because history relates events that have actually happened does it differ at all from a novel, which deals largely with imaginary events.[41] Apart from that very significant difference, not much separates the activities of the historian and the novelist, especially since they both must pay attention to plot more than anything else; otherwise events would disperse into meaninglessness. In this sense, Foucault in his work before the studies on sexuality chose a very specific plot—the formation of subjectivity by hidden and unexpected means—and then the relevant facts fell into a pattern. *Madness and Civilization, The Birth of the Clinic*, and *Discipline and Punish* are not therefore installments of the Book of History, whose underlying structure is provided by an "implacable logic" that dwarfs the individual. If there were a Book of History, and Foucault were its Author, then perhaps political action or any freely chosen action at all would be impossible, and Foucault could be held responsible. As it is, however, Foucault wrote *histories*, not History; so to argue that "Foucault's 'subject' " cannot engage in political action is to invoke both odd and naive notions of history and of the historian's role in organizing it.[42]

It would be equally misguided to assume that Foucault, in acknowledging his work to be interpretive, abandons the idea of fidelity to the past as a standard against which to measure claims about history. Because the historian must interpret documents in order to construct an account of the past, and because there exists among historians no commonly agreed-upon intellectual procedure (as, for example, among most scientists in the natural sciences) by which they pursue their aims, it does not necessarily follow that history amounts to nothing more than naked ideology or, at best, ideology given the semblance of impartiality. Foucault might be criticized for distorting his sources, or selectively consulting sources, or failing to draw on a sufficient number of sources—and he has been criticized in all these ways—but he retained the belief in a historical record that constrains the possible interpretations of a given event. As he put it harshly not long before his death: "All those who say that for me the truth doesn't exist are simple-minded."[43] And he did not hesitate to speak of historical facts and to challenge those who disagreed with his historical claims to return to the sources and demonstrate exactly in what sense he was wrong.[44] For this reason, the metaphors and adjectives commonly found in postmodern writing—"dizzying," "radical," "shifting," "mobile," etc.—are inappropriate in a discussion of Foucault. Foucault was not a postmodern and, for that matter, explicitly distanced himself from the "movement."

If Foucault must be assigned a place in a philosophical tradition, then let it be the tradition of what Stephen Toulmin calls "practical philosophy." Since the seventeenth century, philosophy has for the most part set aside those problems that do not admit of solutions framed in eternal, universal terms; it ignores, in Toulmin's words, the "oral," the "particular," the "local," and the "timely"; it disdains to ask, for example, "*Who* addressed this argument to *whom*, in what *forum*, and using what *examples*?"; it seeks general principles at the expense of particularity; for most of modern philosophy, as Toulmin says, "the Permanent is In, the Transitory is Out."[45] The Aristotle of the *Nicomachean Ethics*, the Cicero of *On Duties*, the Seneca of the *Letters to Lucilius*—these are practical philosophers, and the Foucault of *Discipline and Punish* should be added to the list. When Foucault says, "My objective isn't to propose a global principle for analyzing society," or, "Reject theory and all forms of general discourse," he is not calling for an anarchist trashing of rationality; he is stepping away from, *avoiding* the sorry problems that inevitably limp along behind philosophical systems. But Foucault is still philosophical, or rational—in the nonsystematic style of Cicero, say, or Aristotle.

Is political action possible? This is not Foucault's question. But consider a question of a different order: what can be done to break up the discourse that has accreted on the walls of the prison? That, for instance, is Foucault's question in *Discipline and Punish*, and the book itself is his answer. But he was very clear that this "bookish act of participation," as he described his writing, was not a substitute for activism pure and simple. "The essence of being radical is physical," he said. "The essence of being radical is the radicalness of existence itself."[46] For better or worse, Foucault was radical; he took part in political movements; he never asked whether action was possible. Any philosopher and, for that matter, any citizen can decide to take part in political movements—to demonstrate for gay rights (as Foucault did), to garner support for reproductive freedom (as feminists do), to organize action groups for the homeless (as artists and writers do)—but it would be surprising if asking whether political action is possible could ever have an effect on today's most pressing and timely issues.

Notes

1. An exemplary text in this regard is Paul Smith, *Discerning the Subject* (Minneapolis: Univ. of Minnesota Press, 1988), one of the few book-length treatments, if not the only one, of the so-called problem of agency.

Summarizing Smith's aims, John Mowitt in the foreword to the book makes the extraordinary statement: "Paul Smith argues that a distinction between the subject and agency needs to be introduced within the critical theory of society *in order to sustain the historical possibility of the political resistance that is currently exemplified with international feminism*" (p. ix, emphasis added). What makes this statement extraordinary is that Smith, it seems, actually does believe that his theoretical venture will affect contemporary political activism in such a significant way—he believes it will "sustain its historical possibility." The italicized lines should be kept in mind throughout this chapter.

2. Concerning the point about agency, see Susan Bordo and Mario Moussa, "Rehabilitating the 'I'," forthcoming in Hugh Silverman, ed., *Questioning Foundations*, Continental Philosophy 5, from Routledge. In the final section of that paper, Bordo and Moussa offer an alternative to what might be called the "agential 'I'." For the question about deconstruction and political action, see Smith, *Discerning the Subject*, 168.

3. Charles Taylor, "Foucault on Freedom and Truth," in David Hoy, ed., *Foucault: A Critical Reader* (New York: Basil Blackwell, 1986), 69–102, pp. 88–89; and in the same volume, Michael Walzer, "The Politics of Michel Foucault," 51–68, p. 61, and Jürgen Habermas, "Taking Aim at the Heart of the Present," 103–8, p. 106.

4. The 1988 SPEP (Society for Phenomenology and Existential Philosophy) conference seemed to abound with papers critical of Foucault on this point. Linda Alcoff's paper was, to my mind, among the most sustained and perspicuous critiques of Foucault's lack of a theoretical account of resistance. In many ways this paper is a response to her critique. See Linda Alcoff, "Feminist Politics and Foucault: The Limits to a Collaboration," in A. B. Dallery, C. E. Scott, with P. H. Roberts, eds., *Crises in Continental Philosophy* (Albany: State Univ. of New York Press, 1990), 69–86.

5. Foucault himself suggests that he was experimenting (my word, not his) during the archaeological and genealogical periods. See, for example, the interview, "The Return of Morality," published in Michel Foucault, *Foucault Live (Interviews, 1966–84)*, trans. John Johnston, ed. Sylvère Lotringer (New York: Semiotext(e), 1989), 317–31; in particular, see pp. 318–19.

6. See, for example, the interview with Foucault and Gilles Deleuze originally published in *L'Arc* 49 as "Les Intellectual et Le Pouvoir," translated as "Intellectuals and Power," in Michel Foucault, *Language, Counter-Memory, Practice*, ed. Donald Bouchard (Ithaca, N.Y.: Cornell Univ. Press, 1977), 205–17.

7. Stephen Toulmin, "The Recovery of Practical Philosophy," *The American Scholar* 57 (Summer 1988): 337–52.

8. For descriptions of Foucault as a postmodern thinker, see, for example, Wilhelm S. Wurzer, "Postmodernism's Short Letter: Philosophy's Long Farewell..." in Hugh J. Silverman and Donn Welton, eds., *Postmodernism and Continental Philosophy* (Albany: State Univ. of New York Press, 1988), 243–50, and Arthur Kroker, "Panic Value: Bacon, Colville, Baudrillard and the Aesthetics of Deprivation," in John Fekete, ed., *Life after Postmodernism* (New York: St. Martin's Press, 1987), 181–93, esp. pp. 181–82. Wurzer places Foucault's genealogies between Derrida's "deconstructive strategies" and Deleuze's "schizo-analytic mode of thinking," while Kroker speaks melodramatically of Foucault's "tragic reflections on transgression."

9. Foucault made the comment about the end of modernism in the interview, "The Discourse of History," in *Foucault Live*, 11–33, p. 30. If there is any sense in which Foucault is postmodern, then it might be in the sense Jean-François Lyotard gives the term in *The Postmodern Condition: A Report on Knowledge*, trans. Geoff Bennington and Brian Massumi (Minneapolis: Univ. of Minnesota Press, 1984). It might be argued that, since Foucault questioned the authority of subjectivity and of totalizing theories and metadiscourses, he exemplified the pervasive postmodern scepticism concerning any intellectual enterprise that purports to account for all phenomena. But, as should become clear in this chapter, such an argument would probably obscure more in Foucault's work than it would illuminate.

10. It *is* strange to claim that geography might have something to do with the misinterpretations of Foucault, but I think the not-infrequent comments in the secondary literature about St. German des Prés, the *rive gauche*, and the Parisian intellectual scene bear out the claim. See, for example, J. G. Merquior, *Foucault* (Berkeley: Univ. of California Press, 1985), in which Foucault's supposed Parisian intellectual excesses form a leitmotif. Also consider Taylor's remarks ("Foucault on Freedom and Truth," 89) about the "death of subjectivity" having "its epicentre in Paris."

11. Kroker, "Panic Value," 183.

12. On the persistence of the Cartesian notion of the self, see Stephen Toulmin, "The Inwardness of Mental Life," *Critical Inquiry* 6 (Autumn 1979): 1–16.

13. Foucault, "The Discourse of History," in *Foucault Live*, 29–30. In "An Historian of Culture," also in *Foucault Live* (73–88), Foucault speaks of his work as producing "diagnostic knowledge"; see especially pp. 73–74.

14. Tony O'Connor, "Foucault and the Transgression of Limits," in Hugh Silverman, ed., *Philosophy and Non-Philosophy Since Merleau-Ponty*. Continental Philosophy 1 (New York: Routledge, 1988), 136–51, p. 137.

15. In various places Foucault does speak of "conditions of possibility," most notably in *The Birth of the Clinic*, trans. A. M. Sheridan (New York:

Vintage Books, 1975): "The research I am undertaking here . . . is concerned . . . with determining the conditions of possibility of medical experience in modern times" (xix). But careful attention to the contexts in which he uses this phrase reveals, I think, that Foucault was never arguing for a Kantianism of any sort. As Foucault puts it in *I, Pierre Riviere, having slaughtered my mother, my sister, and my brother. . . : A Case of Parricide in the Nineteenth Century*, ed. Michel Foucault, trans. Frank Jellinek (Lincoln: Univ. of Nebraska Press, 1975), he was always concerned with "historical fields" (209), and the reconstruction of such a field inevitably involves the work of a historian. When Foucault says his work has "nothing to do with the Kantian categories," he is thinking (it seems) of the specific historical analyses that he produced. See "An Historian of Culture" in *Foucault Live*, 76.

16. Ian Hacking, "The Archaeology of Foucault," in *Foucault: A Critical Reader*, 27–40, pp. 31–33.

17. Michel Foucault, *The Archaeology of Knowledge*, trans. A. M. Sheridan (New York: Pantheon, 1972), 140.

18. Jean Baudrillard, *Forget Foucault* (New York: Semiotext(e), 1987). Broadly speaking, Baudrillard's argument is that modern power is no longer operative, so that Foucault's analysis of power, specifically modern power, is outmoded. But still the injunction to forget Foucault—to forget his *texts*—has much to recommend it, and it is one this chapter follows in its own way.

19. Michel Foucault, "The Concern for Truth," in *Foucault Live*, 293–308, p. 305.

20. These questions represent a very specific methodological move, but not, as it may seem, in the direction of the intentionalist fallacy. Obviously Foucault's work might raise issues that have nothing with his intentions, but here I am suggesting that Foucault's work be read in light of his stated project, which has implications for philosophy as a whole. Again, whether or not he actually accomplished this project in his writings is a fair question.

21. Michel Foucault, "The Order of Things," in *Foucault Live*, 1–9, p. 2, emphasis added.

22. On this point, see Alan Sheridan, *Michel Foucault: The Will to Truth* (London: Tavistock, 1980), 211–13.

23. Michel Foucault, "Revolutionary Action: 'Until Now'," in *Language, Counter-Memory, Practice*, 218–33, p. 231.

24. See, for example, the chapter entitled "The Ironic Archive" in Merquior, *Foucault*. Also see Taylor's most recent discussion of Foucault in *Sources of the Self: The Making of Modern Identity* (Cambridge Mass.: Harvard Univ. Press, 1989), especially the chapter entitled "Epiphanies of Modernism."

25. Michel Foucault, *The Order of Things* (New York: Vintage, 1973), 387.

26. Michel Foucault, "Questions of Method: An Interview with Michel Foucault," in Kenneth Baynes, James Bohman, and Thomas McCarthy, eds., *After Philosophy: End or Transformation?* (Cambridge, Mass.: MIT Press, 1987), 100–117, p. 112. For following quotes, see pp. 112–14.

27. Michel Foucault, "How Much Does It Cost for Reason to Tell the Truth?" in *Foucault Live*, 233–56, p. 252.

28. Michel Foucault, *Discipline and Punish*, trans. Alan Sheridan (New York: Vintage, 1979), 6, 135–36.

29. Michel Foucault, "L'Herméneutique du Sujet," in *Michel Foucault: Resumé des Cours 1970–1982* (Paris: Juillard, 1989), 148.

30. Foucault, "The Concern for Truth," 306.

31. Friedrich Nietzsche, *On the Advantage and Disadvantage of History for Life*, trans. Peter Preuss (Indianapolis: Hackett, 1980), 21–22.

32. Michel Foucault, "On the Genealogy of Ethics: An Overview of Work in Progress," in Hubert L. Dreyfus and Paul Rabinow, *Michel Foucault: Beyond Structuralism and Hermeneutics* (Chicago: Univ. of Chicago Press, 1983), 229–52, p. 232.

33. There are many places in *Foucault Live*, for example, where Foucault speaks frankly of sexual repression and political oppression. See, for example, "The End of the Monarchy of Sex," 137–56.

34. Michel Foucault, "Powers and Strategies," in Meaghan Morris and Paul Patton, eds., *Power, Truth, Strategy* (Sydney: Feral Publications, 1979), 55.

35. See, for example, Irene Diamond and Lee Quinby, eds., *Feminism and Foucault: Reflections on Resistance* (Boston: Northeastern Univ. Press, 1988).

36. Foucault, "Nietzsche, Genealogy, History," in *Language, Counter-Memory, Practice*, 139–64, p. 154.

37. Foucault, "Nietzsche, Genealogy, History," 151.

38. Smith, *Discerning the Subject*, 168, emphasis added.

39. Robert Musil, *The Man without Qualities*, trans. Eithne Wilkins and Ernst Kaiser (New York: Perigree Books, 1953), 174–75, emphasis added.

40. Michel Foucault, "The Discourse of History," in *Foucault Live*, 20.

41. Paul Veyne, *Writing History*, trans. Mina Moore-Rinvolucri (Middletown, Conn.: Wesleyan Univ. Press, 1984), 11–12.

42. Veyne's distinction between *diegesis* and *mimesis* is very helpful in this connection. See *Writing History*, p. 5. History, Veyne argues, is inevitably an interpretive process; there is no History against which to check—to mirror—historical interpretations. What there is, however, is the historical archive.

43. Foucault, "The Concern for Truth," 295.

44. See, for example, Foucault, "The Concern for Truth," 294–95, and also "The Discourse of History," 19.

45. Toulmin, "The Recovery of Practical Philosophy," 333, 341.

46. Michel Foucault, "Clarifications on the Question of Power," in *Foucault Live*, 179–92, p. 191.

18

Partial Attachments:
A Deconstructive Model of Responsibility

Cynthia Willett

The revelation of Paul de Man's anti-Semitic writings in the early 1940s has intensified concerns over the ethical implications of deconstruction. The fact that de Man concealed his past seems to lend support to those critics who charge that deconstruction is only the latest form of academic quietism. This criticism draws its primary force from de Man's reading of Rousseau's *Confessions*.[1] There de Man locates a logic of undecidability that undermines any attempt to account for action. The consequence for ethics is as inexorable as it is notorious. "It is always possible," de Man concedes, to "excuse any guilt."[2] The intent of deconstruction is to expose moments of blindness that perforate insights into experience. De Man's past, however, would seem to give support to those who accuse the deconstructionist of blinking in the face of responsibility.

Nonetheless, I suspect that de Man's deconstruction of Rousseau's *Confessions* is less revealing as an attempt to conceal guilt than as an attempt to locate what binds oppressors to their victims. By way of irony, de Man demonstrates that before the law of the text, every author of word or deed is doomed to wander in exile. This wandering, or displacement, is not free. Authorship originates not in desire or obligation but in a necessity that dislocates both. De Man finds himself sentenced to labor on behalf of an arbitrary text-machine. Thus deconstruction does not so much detach de Man from

273

his past associations as solicit a law of inversion that renders every author *deplacé*, or Jew.

In a similar vein, the return to the unhuman *Abgrund*, or abyss, of reason and desire delimits Derrida's response to de Man's past. In the article, "Like the Sound of the Sea Deep within a Shell: Paul de Man's War," Derrida begins and ends with questions. "Unable to respond to the questions," Derrida writes, "to all the questions, I will ask myself instead whether responding is possible and what that would mean in such a situation. And I will risk in turn several questions prior to the definition of a responsibility."[3] Derrida proceeds to expose the futility of an ethics seeking clear solutions. As long as the "absolutely unforeseeable" crisscrosses the explanation of our action, Derrida continues, any account of responsibility will be "torn apart by tragedies, ruptures, dissociations, 'disjunctions' " (MW 594). The demand for solutions in the face of ethical ambiguity smacks of the very violence that circumscribes authoritarian politics.

In Derrida's effort to sustain difficult questions, however, even a tentative notion of ethical responsibility is still missing.[4] On the one hand, Derrida's patient reading of de Man's past does not include censure of de Man's early writings. On the other hand, it also does not "justify what does not deserve to be saved" (MW 651). Deconstruction continues to leave ethical judgment in suspension. The difficulty of establishing an ethics is clear, given that deconstruction traces an irremediable forgetting, an absolute unconscious that constitutes any action. Deconstruction's logic of an "on the one hand . . . , and on the other hand . . . ," however, would appear to leave every actor *equally* split between guilt or innocence before his or her crimes. It is this "equality" that I am questioning. If we are guilty and innocent of any charge, can deconstruction allow that for some acts we are more guilty than for others? What does deconstruction have to say to the "more or less"? Without some sense of greater or lesser responsibility, deconstruction leaves us able to affirm nothing more than the absurdity of acting before the "absolutely unforeseeable."

In order to disturb the paralyzing rhetoric of an "all and nothing," or "on the one hand, and on the other hand," I will trace asymmetrical and irreversible subtexts in deconstructive logic that weave together incomplete but significant associations, which I am calling "partial attachments." Partial associations can be used to develop a deconstructive notion of responsibility. At least some, perhaps random, textual associations bind; that is, some accidents fit a pattern of motivation, or a fabric of associations, which generates ethical judgment.

Constructing this pattern requires locating associations that survive the dissociation of de Manian irony. I will insist that an action performed ironically (in de Man's sense) nonetheless carries ethical implications. Ironic actions may never betray a hard and fast position, but they can and do testify to certain inclinations. These inclinations generate a locus of responsibility. Thus, while such a notion of responsibility exceeds ironic detachment, it also eludes rational determination.

WOMAN DISFIGURED: THE IMPLICATIONS OF DE MAN'S IRONY

De Man's article, "Excuses (Confessions)," focuses on an episode from Rousseau's *Confessions*. The episode concerns a crime that occurred during Rousseau's service in an aristocratic household. The young Rousseau steals a ribbon. Moreover, upon the crime's discovery he accuses an attractive young maidservant, Marion, with having given him the ribbon. Thus, Rousseau attempts to establish his own innocence at the girl's expense. The innocence and goodness of the maid appears in her response to Rousseau's false accusation: "Ah Rousseau! I took you to be a man of good character. You are making me very unhappy but I would hate to change places with you" (EX 279).

What motivates Rousseau's eventual confession? De Man observes that the purpose of confession is to excuse oneself. The excuse in turn erases the crime. This is because, de Man argues, the real crime is the lie that protects the crime. The confession corrects the misdeed by restating the truth. Something, however, disturbs the symmetry of the reversal, the return to truth, for, as de Man points out, Rousseau is compelled to repeat his confession in the *Fourth Reverie*.

This time the confession attributes significance to the ribbon, or to what otherwise, de Man insists, would be "devoid of meaning and function" and would "circulate symbolically as a pure signifier" (EX 283). It seems that Rousseau originally intended to present the ribbon as a gift to the young girl. Perhaps, then, de Man suggests, the ribbon is a trope that signifies Rousseau's love for Marion. So, the freely exchanged signifier, the ribbon, comes to stand for their freely exchanged love. The ribbon represents symmetrical reciprocity, which Rousseau envisions as the very condition of ideal love. De Man writes that the ribbon "stands for the substitutability of Rousseau for Marion and vice versa. Rousseau desires Marion as Marion desires Rousseau" (EX 283). Rousseau's love excuses his theft not because of the purity of his motive but, more importantly, because of the symmetry of ideal love. Inasmuch as Rousseau steals Marion's heart, he also shares her innocence. In love they become one. If crimes like theft and slander presuppose otherness, the symmetry of ideal love denies otherness and thereby cancels the possibility of violation.

De Man's reading of Rousseau's desire, however, does not end with Rousseau's second confession, that is, the confession of his secret love for Marion. The joy with which Rousseau confesses mounts evidence that Rousseau's theft as well as its repeated confession may stem from the desire for exposure rather than from love. "What Rousseau really wanted is neither the ribbon nor Marion," de Man writes, "but the public scene of exposure which he actually gets. . . . The more crime there is, . . . the better" (EX 285).

Here I would add that the desire for self-exposure might reveal the truth about ideal love. Ideal love, the love of another as oneself, renders the other a mere reflection of oneself. Ideal love turns out to be a form of narcissism. That is, we may interpret de Man's rereading of Rousseau's confession as an exposure of the vacuity of ideal love, or love based on symmetry.

Thus far, Rousseau's introduction of ever new and more incriminating revelations builds up to an ever more complicated story or narrative. If the metaphoric significance of the ribbon alters, and the crime of love turns into a tale of narcissism, metaphor—that flower of speech—remains intact. And should the account never end, repeating in countless reflections and reinterpretations, nonetheless we are assured of the relevance of desire and the utility of signifiers. The ribbon and its theft signify something, even if this meaning is never fully determinate. A second account does not deconstruct even if it reopens an earlier account; for "both converge towards a unified signification" (EX 286). The figure of woman—along with the ribbon that is somehow associated with her—remain maidservants of truth.

Irretrievable discord announces itself, de Man continues, with an unusual locution that mars Rousseau's stated confession: "I excused myself upon the first thing that offered itself." De Man argues that

> the use of a vocabulary of contingency . . . within an argument of causality is arresting and disruptive, for the sentence is phrased in such a way as to allow for a complete disjunction between Rousseau's desires and interests and the selection of

this particular name. Marion just happened to be the first thing that came to mind; any other name, any other word, any other sound or noise could have done just as well and Marion's entry into the discourse is a mere effect of chance. She is a free signifier, metonymically related to the part she is made to play. (EX 288–89)

Taken as a meaningless sound, the name of Marion unweaves narrative, blinds tropes, and eludes any explanation in terms of desire. The ultimate excuse for any crime, then, is the excuse of randomness, an excuse that slips gratuity into any system of truth and undoes any system of causality. When the reader perceives this randomness, he or she realizes the inconsequence of any action, the uselessness of any speech act, the harmlessness of any lie. To lie is not a crime, de Man urges, but a fiction, for it exceeds the economy of truth altogether.

If Rousseau's accusers had realized that all crimes are fictions, they would have recognized the innocence of both Rousseau and Marion. Crimes have a moment of randomness which strips them of decidable motivation. Thus, de Man utters his notorious conclusion: "The indecision makes it possible to excuse the bleakest of crimes because, as a fiction, it escapes from the constraints of guilt and innocence. On the other hand, it makes it equally possible to accuse fiction-making. . . of being the most cruel" (EX 293). Desires and the narratives or tropes that inform our desires—finally, all of our excuses—are the effects of a textual machine whose "implacable repetition" is insured by random disruptions. De Man concludes by fashioning the power of this machine in terms of irony. "Irony is no longer a trope but the undoing of the deconstructive allegory of all tropological cognitions, the systematic undoing, in other words, of understanding" (EX 301).

De Man's determination of crimes and their confessions in terms of fiction rests on a single piece of evidence. This evidence consists of the random nature in which the name of Marion appears in Rousseau's confession.

[Consider] how the name of Marion came to be uttered in the key sentence in the *Confessions*: *'je m'excusai sur le premier objet qui s'offrir'*. . . . Rousseau was making whatever noise happened to come into his head; he was saying nothing at all, least of all someone's name. (EX 292)

I find it troubling that de Man interprets a sentence whose referent might be a woman as one that should be read without anthropomorphic connotations. The distinctly feminine character of the stolen object, described as a "pink and silver colored ribbon," and the occurrence of theft at the threshold between innocence and self-knowledge predispose the reader to search for sexual connotations in Rousseau's crime. The scene is mythic. We are not surprised that a woman might be involved. Moreover, the noise that happened to come to mind is not in fact nonsense but a proper name, the name of a young woman. Events may occur in part by chance; but whatever the element of chance, there are also some textual motivations for the occurrence of Marion's name. De Man must strip the anthropomorphic connotations from a sentence that sets up a woman, who, at least in name, "offers herself," in an ambiguous and difficult place between desired "object" and temptress.

Just as a woman has served as the vehicle of Rousseau's narcissism or tenor of Rousseau's love, she now serves de Man's exposure of the truth about excuses. In other words, I wonder whether de Man has not repeated Rousseau's crime of reducing woman to an object—either vehicle or tenor—of masculine desire. In effect de Man strips woman of human face in order to name a mechanical repetition, whose errors are arbitrary. Reduced to bare particularity, that is, to mere accident, woman serves to name—as Hegel would warn—the most deadly and mechanical of abstractions. This mechanical repetition divests all acts of their anthropomorphic character. Ironically, then, "woman" is made to deface masculine desire which has already rendered her devoid of human face.

That is, de Man steals from a woman her voice and then excuses himself by blaming woman—as a power that defigures, the power of chance, blind fate. He renders woman victim and then cause of his crime of violation. In fact, de Man repeats the crime of Rousseau.

Like Rousseau, de Man distances himself from crime through a kind of inversion. Woman is innocent of desire or power of seduction; guilt and desire originally belong to the man. But man is innocent of crimes committed in woman's name. The guilty are innocent and the innocent are guilty. De Man names this inversion "irony."

It is curious, however, that irony works as a trope of endless inversion only if it displays a symmetrical structure. That is, irony detaches a remark from evaluative decision only if its inversions oscillate symmetrically. The logic of undecidability suspends evaluation only if determinations possess equal force and thus cancel each other. The deconstruction of responsibility needs symmetries for its effects of detachment and fictionalization. If irony implicates us in whatever act we would wish to deny, de Man also insists that irony detaches, or distances, us from that act. Recall that de Man defines deconstruction in negative and ironic terms: "No other word states so economically the impossibility to evaluate positively or negatively the inescapable evaluation it implies" (EX x). An ironic remark distances itself from whatever evaluations it might imply. The evaluative act, like the seductive rhetoric of a particular woman, is kept at a distance.

The endless reversibility of de Manian irony presupposes sheer metonymy, or random occurrence; otherwise irony collapses into the indirect evaluation which is in fact implied but which irony would continually work to distance. Nonsense, like the bare particular that opens Hegel's *Phenomenology*, is possible only so long as it is dissociated from even the most indirect and tenuous relations. Similarly, the symmetry of irony, like that of Rousseau's ideal love, would return the author of the ironic remark to a state of innocent detachment. Irony fashions itself as self-conscious innocence.

I am claiming that de Manian irony repeats the structure of a "phallocentric"—finally narcissistic—desire. Woman as object is the victim of woman as artificer, in this case, woman as mindless text-machine. In either case, woman signifies brute accident while desire belongs to the man. If women are thought to have any desires at all, their desires appear only as the symmetrical opposite of the desires of men. De Man's Rousseau calls this moment "ideal love." Not once, even if then to be deconstructed, does de Man take up woman's own desire. That is, de Man's allegory occludes the alterity of woman's speech.

What do we hear if we listen to the almost silent voice of the woman? Marion's few words testify not to the random noise which her name signifies for her male interpreters; instead she addresses a different notion of desire: "You are making me very unhappy but I would hate to change places with you" (EX 279). This woman cannot trade places; that is not her desire. Marion, then, appeals to an asymmetrical notion of desire that would resist irony, or endless inversion. Moreover, it is this asymmetry that is necessary for the act of valuation. Marion and Rousseau cannot trade their guilt or innocence. Marion's desire is not the same as Rousseau's. It is Marion's recognition of differences, and not her alleged innocence, that makes her an ethical individual. Absolute randomness, de Manian irony, results from an elision of woman and woman's desire.

De Man does not deny the asymmetries in desire that introduce effects of evaluation and stabilize irony. Irony does, however, subordinate those inevitable evaluations by a mechanism of distancing. It is this gesture of distancing that obfuscates a deconstructive notion of responsibility.

Between tropes that transpose the unfamiliar face of the other into a familiar form and an irony that would detach itself from its own inevitable evaluations, between dialectic and deconstruction, lies a notion of meaning as the power of association. Our very words offer themselves only by way of an amorphous fabric of unfamiliar and never fully conscious associations. If the bare particular absolutely stripped of any and all associations is a myth, so too is de Manian irony. Nothing occurs without a partial relation to something else, or apart from some fabric of associations. These associations motivate meaning and generate interest and desire. If desire plays an originary role in meaning, it is not the desire to possess, or to make familiar, but a desire that responds to the strangeness of seduction—of that which resists possession but not involvement. This concept of desire is best figured by tropes that render the familiar strange and yet not detached by the distance of irony.

Consequently, the ethical concept of responsibility should extend beyond conscious intention and yet not so far as accidents standing apart from a past of associations. Responsibility should own up to all that persuades or motivates action. Motivations orient action even as they are stitched out of the unexpected accidents that mar experience.

Against de Man's use of "metonymy" to designate the dissociations and disjunctions of experience, *metonymy* can also be used to name a process of association that falls short of any trope of identity or totality. My analysis of de Man's text suggests that associations surrounding the name of Marion accumulate an account that is more than random and yet less than necessary. Both Rousseau and de Man are implicated in more than they could ever know.

What does it signify if behind de Man's deconstruction of responsibility lies a partially concealed narrative that informs his interests and desires? If masculine desire turns out to be narcissism and woman to signify senseless repetition, then deconstruction borrows its elements from the tragic tale of Narcissus and Echo. In this tale, woman figures the empty repetition of words that have their origin elsewhere. She serves as puppet—as Marion would be a marionette—for male desire and male narcissism. Like Rousseau's ribbon, woman serves as empty signifier. Her face reflects the narcissism of her male interpreters. Her movements are their pulls on her strings. Consequently, her power of repetition is sterile; that is, the figure of woman as Echo cannot create but only exhaust meaning.

If the deconstruction of meaning and valuation—if de Manian irony—fashions itself after the tale of Narcissus and Echo, then deconstruction would repeat or invert—as would the face staring back in the mirror—but never alter the values belonging to narcissism. As long as woman is denied her own if broken voice, she is without the power of affirmation, the power to create new values. As the abyss, or *Abgrund*, of inversion, de Manian irony threatens to render evaluation finally reactive. As long as woman signifies the abyss of desire rather than the power of seduction, women are allowed to make no advances.[5]

Notes

1. Paul de Man, "Excuses (Confessions)," in *Allegories of Reading* (New Haven: Yale Univ. Press, 1979), 278–301; hereafter abbreviated "EX."

2. EX 293. Also quoted by Jon Werner, "Deconstructing de Man," in *The Nation*, 9 January 1988, 23.

3. Jacques Derrida, "Like the Sound of the Sea Deep within a Shell: Paul de Man's War," *Critical Inquiry* 14 (Spring 1987–88): 590–652; hereafter abbreviated "MW." Reprinted in Werner Hamacher et al., eds., *Responses: On Paul de Man's Wartime Journalism* (Lincoln: Univ. of Nebraska Press, 1989), 127–64.

4. See Richard Bernstein, "Serious Play: The Ethical-Political Horizon of Jacques Derrida," *Journal of Speculative Philosophy* 1 (1987): 111.

5. De Manian deconstruction employs a rhetoric of "persuasion by proof rather than persuasion by seduction." See Paul de Man, *The Resistance to Theory* (Minneapolis: Univ. of Minnesota Press, 1986), 18.

19

Rorty on Derrida: A Discourse of Simulated Moderation

Roger Bell

The text is remarkable in that the reader (here in exemplary fashion) can never choose his own place in it, nor can the spectator. There is at any rate no tenable place for him opposite the text, outside the text, no spot where he might get away with *not* writing what, in the reading, would seem to him to be *given, past*: no spot, in other words, where he would stand before an already *written* text. Because his job is to put things on stage, *he is on stage himself*, he puts himself on stage. *The tale is thereby addressed to the reader's body, which is put by things on stage, itself.* The moment "therefore" is written, the spectator is less capable than ever of choosing his place. This impossibility—and this potency, too, of the reader writing himself—has from time immemorial been at work in the text in general. What here opens, limits, and situates all readings (including yours and mine) is hereby, *this time at last*, displayed: as such. It is shown through a certain composition of overturned surfaces. And through an exact material *mise en scène*.

Or rather—since this sort of exhibition and the "as such" of phenomena are no longer in the last instance in control here, but are rather being maneuvered as inscribed functions and subordinate mechanisms—what is in question here, this time at last, finds itself not displayed but given play, not staged but engaged, not demonstrated but mounted. Mounted with a

283

confectioner's skill in some implacable machinery, with "consummate prudence and implacable logic."

—Jacques Derrida[1]

The contemporary philosophic scene is often represented as finding renewed vitality in its postmodern condition through a purported opening of "conversation" between the dominant, analytic tradition and those interests that have operated at its margins. Tribute to the importance of such "conversations" (an importance the acknowledgment of which dates to the Pluralist Movement in the Eastern Division of the American Philosophical Association) was finally paid on the West Coast in 1987 at the Pacific Division in San Francisco by the inclusion on the main program of "The Philosophy of Jacques Derrida."[2] This session drew the largest audience of the meeting, due to interest in the exchange between Stanley Cavell and Derrida, an exchange that stood in some emblematic way for the very possibility of "conversation" between the analytic and the continental traditions.[3] This "exchange" with its duties, tariffs, fees so obviously extracted (an admission was charged) served to illustrate the limits and difficulty of any real dialogue, making the session's tribute an "event" of the order that defies philosophic interpretation or meaning.

From the very opening of Cavell's presentation I was suspicious that something was amiss. Cavell began with an extended preface in which he described his reservations regarding participation in this session on the work of Derrida and the successful negotiations with the meeting's organizers by which he now stood before us. His announcement that he was unprepared to present a paper on Derrida's work—or, more precisely, that he had not written anything specifically for the "occasion"—was apparently deemed important by Cavell himself (and only by Cavell—I did not observe anyone asking for their money back), as it constituted the bulk of his introductory remarks. Gaining agreement on this one condition, he described his decision to "read" parts of a paper he had previously delivered in Jerusalem, parts which appeared to share a common interest with Derrida, who coincidentally had also been at the same conference. Only after in fact delivering this reading, his contract fulfilled, did he proceed to comment informally upon the nature of this shared interest between his and Derrida's work and its possible consequences for engendering "conversation" across the analytic and continental traditions.

Similarly, Derrida, for this occasion which was to honor his work (at least the "event" seemed so entitled), agreed at the outset not to deliver a paper but merely to comment upon those papers invited regarding his work. The mutual interest that Derrida and Cavell shared on this platform initially seemed to be the general desire *not* to give a paper. But did this apparent interest follow upon the choice of Derrida to be the key speaker, the occasion being his, or, rather, was it the effect of some testimonial style by which both he and Cavell were inadvertently to dis-play a similarity of approach? Herein lay the challenge to "reading" this exchange: the only text actually read was the one Cavell chose out of coincidence, from the Jerusalem meeting. So what could Derrida have made of this, he being a philosopher known for his parasitic approach? Derrida needed to locate something within Cavell's comments and coincidental text upon which to work his deconstructive strategies. And, yet, Cavell's entire strategy was wonderfully Derridean: the importance given to what would appear as mere coincidence, the indirection by which his work reached Derrida's out of, again, coincidentally shared interests.

Afterwards I could not help speculating, somewhat ironically, that there could have been a deception, that the "exchange" could have been made in collusion, this mix of read text and spoken comment, the two of which being so well blended that this "reader/listener" could not always distinguish what was read from spoken. Was the strength of this illusion due to Cavell's oratory skill or to a hidden, prepared "text" by which his reading and comments were reduced to a single narrative that he enacted? Furthermore, this "text" which was so delivered for Derrida's comments, comprising a proper text—the one delivered in Jerusalem, which meant only coincidentally to cross Derrida's—structurally mimicked his, Derrida's, own characteristic signature style (at least for one familiar with his writing). Could this "text" have been a forgery, written by Derrida himself? Indeed, an audacious idea; yet such a thing was suggested by Derrida himself in Derrida's reply to John Searle on a previous occasion for exchange between France and California.[4] Would it have been beyond Cavell and Derrida to pull such a stunt? Again, Derrida simply agreed not to deliver a paper and Cavell not to write one! Such theater of exchange would fulfill all the requirements of the contract, with interest.

Although such speculation is of itself idle, a response to disappointed expectations, it does serve to indicate certain important questions concerning the political realities of the organizational apparatus responsible for such "meetings," the question of professional memberships, of program committees, of negotiating powers, etc. Reopened is the question of the power of those moderating voices and texts within the current philosophic community by which such exchanges hope to become "conversational": in particular, those of Richard Rorty. Taking this question of "moderation" and its apparent absence or ineffectiveness at the San Francisco meetings as a clue,[5] I want to return to Richard Rorty's text, in particular his "conversation" with Derrida in "Philosophy as a Kind of Writing: An Essay on Derrida,"[6] to locate the key philosophemes of a political discourse which in a way prepared for the difficulties that transpired in the Cavell-Derrida exchange.

For Rorty to purport to moderate what is at issue between differing philosophic traditions or styles—the analytic majority and those groups loosely identified under the banner of Pluralism—requires the ability to delineate clearly the respective differences, to discover some basis of commonality that can engender the hoped-for "conversation." This strategy can be seen at work from the first line of Rorty's "Philosophy as a Kind of Writing." Rorty's essay begins by directing his reader through a series of three oppositions concerning physics, ethics, and philosophy, the poles of opposition defined respectively by the Kantian and Hegelian traditions. With this opening Rorty attempts to locate the discursive space in which to approach the question Derrida's text puts to philosophy regarding writing.

Yet Rorty fails to recognize that such delineation, its drawing of limits through placement within traditions, must be provisional, open to revisions informed by the conversation it engenders. The necessity of such provisionality at the point of setting out would be clear, given even a rudimentary understanding of the strategies of *deconstruction* as they are applied in Derrida's "writing" to uncover the hidden "oppositions" within the tradition.[7] Rorty's opening, in locating Derrida on the Hegelian side of such an opposition, forces its own question on reading with regard to the possibility of slippage between these traditions. This would be the very possibility of that "conversation" which Rorty's text presumes to "moderate." But one does not find tentative qualification to this device of opening by mutual exclusion. Rather, Rorty's text, in the eighth paragraph, affirms: "To understand Derrida, one must see his work as . . . ,"[8] without questioning the sense of *"under-*stand," which tautologically invokes an appeal to traditions in and through origins, the very sense of "origins" that deconstruction seeks to expose in its logocentric, metaphysical assumptions, assumptions that efface the question of writing which Rorty's text claims to "(a)ssay."[9] Can Derrida's work be "understood" in this sense of placement within the bounds of such dichotomy? Or does Derrida's text necessarily obscure such dichotomies, scattering the seemingly coherent light of Rorty's opening?

To answer these questions one has merely to point out the difficulty of locating Derrida's text in a space inclusive of Heidegger on the one hand and exclusive of Husserl's neo-Kantianism on the other. Phenomenology, then, is the space within which Derrida's text "begins" and in a surprising way never completely abandons in his poststructuralist deconstructions.[10] So when Rorty writes that Derrida's "writing about language is an attempt to show why there should be no philosophy of language" (PK 93), reading must take careful note of the attached footnote which includes a reference to the text *Speech and Phenomena*, Derrida's early text on Husserl's phenomenology, which equally claims, somewhat outrageously, that there was never anything called perception. And of course Rorty is correct in pointing out that Derrida's problem with "philosophies of language" hinges upon certain difficulties of Platonism to describe what he takes to be the facts. But Rorty misreads this seeming rejection of language, like perception. Here Derrida is Heideggerian; what we take as being "language," as being "perception," is rather a "metaphysics of presence" which leaves behind the phenomenology of the "things themselves." To "recover" language and perception requires rehabilitating our conceptual apparatus, our "philosophy"; and having "a great deal to tell us about philosophy" entails also the same for both "language" and "perception."

Interestingly, when Rorty does address the question concerning language that he takes Derrida to be posing for philosophy, he employs the same concepts, "language" and "perception," but placed in opposition as "text" and "world." Rorty's formulation of Derrida's question is: "What must philosophers think writing is that they resent so much the suggestion that this is what they do?" (PK 95). Of course, Rorty's version of Derrida's answer is formulated in terms of the problems of "representation" and emphasizes Derrida's view that writing is about texts and, according to Rorty's interpretation of certain lines in *Of Grammatology*, not the world. So Derrida is taken to be replacing the world with the notion of the text, assuming an opposition between text and world. The key quote Rorty employs in defense of this interpretation by opposition of Derrida's sense of writing is the line, "There is nothing outside of the text."[11] As provocative as the citation is on the surface, the context makes its meaning quite clear: Derrida is asking, how does one interpret Rousseau's text, read his writing? Derrida's point is simply that the process of making sense of a text, of "critical reading," must work from within that writing itself: "Beyond and behind what one believes can be circumscribed as Rousseau's text, there has never been anything but writing" (OG 159). The point is that Rousseau was a writer and therefore any trace left of his thought must be located in the *play* of signifiers that form the weave of his text. Appropriately, Rorty notes that there is something "funny" about Derrida's "work," namely that he "does not want to comprehend. . .; he wants to play with [texts]" (PK 96). Of course, this sense of "play," its many senses, is very important to Derrida's deconstructive methods. He attempts precisely to locate such play in the system of signifiers, concepts, and oppositions by which the philosophical text is written, that is, its conceptual "give."

However, by the end of section 2 of the essay, Rorty comes to address the more serious side of Derrida's work, namely, deconstruction, but only while simultaneously charging him with a bad side, what he calls a "nostalgic constructivism" of system building. With this move Rorty seeks to locate a conflicting opposition within Derrida himself, a two-sidedness. But is Rorty here missing that strategy of the double game also so important to deconstruction? But this question must be suspended until our reading of Rorty's text can supply the needed "trigger" by which the text opens itself to criticism.

That something is radically amiss becomes obvious in Rorty's interpretation of the longer citations from Derrida's texts regarding the concepts of the "sign" and "differance."[12] On Rorty's interpretation, Derrida holds that the sign is ineffable, "the one expression of the unconditioned"; however, Derrida puts the concept of the sign itself in question by switching the emphasis from the signified to the *signifier* and its tracing of sense. Derrida's point that the sign is the only thing that escapes the instituting question of philosophy, when interpreted in context, is seen to mean that the conditions of the sign's functioning must be critiqued. It is this analysis that leads Derrida to raise the question of the signifier, its institution of sense which moves by way of the play of differance.[13] So rather than being a primitive, unconditioned concept for Derrida, the sign is quite clearly the major focus of his criticism of structuralism, a criticism that links his analysis of the signifier with the concepts of the "trace" and "differance." Rorty's reading here of Derrida's view of the sign is grossly mistaken and alerts the reader to a careful scrutiny of the final piece of evidence that Rorty cites for his interpretation, a long passage from *Speech and Phenomena.*

The second half of this final citation would at first appear clearly to support Rorty's interpretation of Derrida's sign as an ineffable primitive:

> It is because there is no *name* for this—not even essence or Being—not even the name "differance," which is not a name, which is not a pure nominal unity, and continually breaks up in a chain of different substitutions. . . .
>
> There will be no unique name, not even the name of Being. It must be conceived without *nostalgia*; that is, it must be conceived outside the myth of the purely maternal or paternal language belonging to the lost fatherland of thought. On the contrary we must *affirm* it—in the sense that Nietzsche brings affirmation into play—with a certain laughter and with a certain dance.[14]

But careful reading notices that "name" is in italics, that the concept is placed in question. Also, there is the important ellipsis at the paragraph's end. What has Rorty left out here? Why can it not be named? Turning to the source of the citation in *Speech and Phenomena*, a most blatant *censorship* by Rorty's text is seen. Rorty leaves out of the middle of his citation two important paragraphs which include these lines: "What is unnamable here is not some ineffable being that cannot be approached by a name; like God, for example. What is unnamable is the play that brings about the nominal effects, the relatively unitary or atomic structures we call names, or chains of substitutions for names" (DF 159). Here Derrida is warning the reader against just that interpretation Rorty makes, even using his word "ineffable." Or did Rorty steal the word from Derrida, seduced by the temptation? Rather than arguing for an ineffable concept in these lines, Derrida puts the naming function of the sign in question and gives priority to the play of the signifier, this "play" which Rorty's text continually censors. And precisely here is located that needed "trigger" by which Rorty's text does open, his staging of Derrida through a *censorship/eros* of the text. This is Rorty's play/ploy!

Rorty refers to the eros of the text in the opening passages when describing the inheritance of Socratic dialectic in terms of being "inseminated by this ambivalent eros."[15] However, such a dialectic misses the subtle differance of Derrida's "disseminations" (Derrida's title): a proliferation of always different, always postponed meanings. And this difference finally finds its name in the last section of Rorty's text where *censor/censure* and eros are explicitly joined in his staging of an ethics of sexual normalcy which echoes the formal oppositions of his opening: "In normal physics, normal philosophy, normal moralizing or preaching, one hopes for the normal thrill of just the right piece fitting into just the right slot, with a shuddering resonance which makes verbal commentary superfluous and inappropriate" (PK 106). The mechanism of Rorty's text, its "mounting of bodies," is clearly dis-played in these phallocentric lines (see the citation from Derrida's opening section of "Dissemination," "The Trigger," given above). Should the reader still doubt, consider the following paraphrase of Derrida that Rorty "fits into" his schema of normalcy: "Writing, as Derrida says in commenting on Rousseau, is to this kind of simple 'getting it right' as masturbation is to standard, solid, reassuring sex."[16] But here Rorty's reading misses that education which necessarily "supplements" such a nature, by which one ought to "get it right," with cultured pleasure. Rousseau's text describes the natural catastrophe of culture by which the opposition of normalcy that Rorty attempts to invoke is destroyed. As Derrida writes of Rousseau in the relevant section of *Of Grammatology*: "In other words, between auto-eroticism and hetero-eroticism, there is not a frontier but an economic distribution" (OG 155). Rorty's resistance to *reading* Derrida's text here bespeaks the entrenched phallocentric eros of his text, the trace of its censor/censure that finally finds its name in the following lines: "So the normal man sees the abnormal as not quite up to it—more to be pitied than *censured*. The abnormal sees the normal as someone who *never had the courage to come out*, and so died inside while his body lived on—more to be helped than despised" (PK 108, emphasis added). Exposing these censures shows that Derrida's text does not support the opposition(s) by which Rorty reads him. Derrida's eros of dissemination is not the opposite of insemination, entailing its possibility. Has Rorty's writing on Derrida itself fallen prey to just this uncertainty? Can Rorty really miss the impertinence of pronouncing upon the ab-normality of masturbation, of writing, and of philosophy? Does his censorship spread to the phallocentric body of his own text?

Comparing this written text to an earlier, delivered version, entitled "Derrida on Language, Being, and Abnormal Philosophy," for the 1977 APA Eastern Division symposium on "The Philosophy of Jacques Derrida," clearly reveals the extent of Rorty's willingness to disseminate such self-censorship. In this speech a quite different and more reasonable interpretation of the much-quoted line, "There is nothing outside of the text," is given. Here Rorty recognizes correctly that Derrida's critique of the notion of philosophy of language has to do specifically with foundationalist approaches. He relates his views to Hilary Putnam's critique of foundational enterprises and applauds Derrida's contribution (DL 674–76). Likewise, with respect to the question of the "sign," Rorty acknowledges Derrida's criticism of the concept: "In Derrida's most recent work, this dance takes the form of endless plays with words, plays directed toward making us see words as words rather than as signs, as inscriptions rather than vehicles of communication, as anything rather than bearers of reference and truth" (DL 678). Here Rorty is speaking of the "signifier" to which Derrida's philosophy of language does pay so much attention.

Even in the speech's ending, which is quite similar to that of the essay in question, a clear difference of emphasis can be read. In the essay Rorty emphasizes that "normal philosophy" will always have its "abnormal," "parasitic" counterpart. He describes Derrida as a "decadent dialectician" at "crosstalk" with the progress of philosophy, another example of the contingency of paradigm shifts for all inquiry according to the Kuhnian model: "Everybody needs everybody else" (PK 108). The essay ends with Rorty's reticence with respect to judging anything other than the fact of there inevitably being a "conversation": a conclusion (if you can call it that) that leaves open even the pertinence of the question of writing which entitled his essay. By contrast, the spoken address's ending is substantive and positive. Derrida's concern with writing, Rorty states, is important to questioning the concept of "representation" and its tradition beginning with Plato. In the final sentences of the lecture Rorty says:

> In the end, Derrida's most important work may consist in his Freudian naturalization of metaphilosophy rather than in his reinforcement of Wittgenstein or his *aufhebung* of Heidegger. He is the first professional philosopher to have used Freudian notions to talk about philosophy with Freud's own lightheartedness—the first to use them nonreductionistically and playfully. Seeing Plato and the Western tradition as logocentric because phallocentric may be just what we need to help us avoid the condescending pomposity of the normal question about abnormal writing: "But just what is it trying to *say*?" (DL 681)

The published, written version of this lecture, with its italicizing of the final word "say," uses its ending to emphasize the paradox of linguistic usage which always *"speaks"* of *writing* as if it were speech, concealing the existence of any *text*. This operative logocentricism is undoubtedly intended by Rorty's text, but when spoken, in a delivered speech, the italicizing can easily be lost to an audience as a mere inflection. Is this a sign, then, of the equal loss or absence of Rorty's phallocentric censor of Derrida's text within this spoken address to a "Pluralist" audience of the Eastern APA, the constituency of his "moderation?" How can reading account for this discrepancy between the lecture and the essay? Absent in Rorty's address is that which is to become both the phallocentric censorship of Derrida's text and of Rorty's own in the essay. What Rorty conceals in the logocentric self-presence of his thoughts as delivered to the audience of the APA meeting is simply the phallocentric divisiveness operating within his own text, a discourse of self-censorship by which he attempts to set ideas "right."[17]

What is Rorty trying to "get right"? His censorship/censures/caesurae cannot straighten out the indirection and play of Derrida's text, as if Derrida's meanings could be aligned behind the clear-sighted aims of Rorty's neopragmatism. What an ironic play with language allows Rorty to write using censorship as a "moderating" influence! Such irony indicates the full play of his writing's eros as a body politics empowering a deceptive simulation of an opening of "conversation" across its boundaries. But what are the full terms of this deception?

Turning from Rorty's treatment of Derrida, the real basis of the political issue of pluralism and its challenge to the analytic establishment of the APA can be located in a reading of the rest of Rorty's *Consequences of Pragmatism*. That is, the nexus of issues with regard to the profession that engendered the revolt Rorty claims to moderate can be read preserved within his own text. In the text's final pages, the chapter "Philosophy in America Today," my reading was struck by Rorty's restatement in such graphic, political terms of the inherent antagonism between "analysts" and "Continentalists," an antagonism to which he claims to seek moderation. How is the reader to take such divisive "remarks" given room on Rorty's last page?:

> This split between two sorts of intellectual has become deeper in our own century. It is, indeed, no mere matter of academic politics. It is the split imprecisely sketched by Snow's contrast between the "scientific culture" and the "literary culture." It is the antagonism which begins to become explicit when analytic philosophers mutter about the "irrationalism"

which rages in literature departments and when Continental philosophers become shrill about the lack of "human significance" in the works of the analysts. . . . It comes out when analytic philosophers remark that Carnap emigrated while Heidegger joined the Nazi Party, or that Russell saw through Stalinism and Sartre did not, or that Rawls shares the ordinary civilized hope for the rule of law and Foucault does not. (CP 229)

The omission of the full controversy regarding these political issues within the continental tradition indicates both Rorty's limited knowledge and audience.[18] He writes for an analytic audience, thus the purpose of these so clearly pejorative remarks in closing. His "moderation" seeks its own agenda, that of neopragmatism, within the analytic establishment and remains markedly silent regarding the real political sources of the controversy, the question of education,[19] and the existence of a longstanding continental-American tradition within this country.

To follow out the trace of this absence within Rorty's text, the continued invisibility of an existing philosophic perspective within this country's academic departments that views itself as deriving from a continental tradition, one needs to consider the question of emigré scholars indirectly referenced in the above citation. With this question of immigration one can easily see the manner in which Rorty's "moderation" remains a fiction with respect to the real political basis of the "Pluralist Movement." Here the relevant chapter of *Consequences of Pragmatism* is chapter 4, "Professionalized Philosophy and Transcendentalist Culture." Rorty writes:

> By the end of the Second World War, however, the great days of Deweyan philosophy and social science were over. . . . New heroes were needed, and they were found among that extraordinary body of men, the *emigré scholars*. A young American philosopher learning phenomenology from Gurwitsch or Schuetz, or logical empiricism from Carnap or Reichenbach, was trained to think of philosophy as a rigorous discipline, a matter of cooperation in joint inquiry and the production of agreed-upon results. . . . As logical empiricism *metamorphosed* into analytic philosophy, and succeeded in driving phenomenology out into the *academic shadows*, American philosopher's disinterest in moral and social questions became almost total. . . . Dewey had predicted that philosophy would turn away from the seventeenth-century tension between mathematical physics

and the world of common sense, and would take up new problems arising from the social sciences and the arts. But this prediction was completely off target. . . .

What Dewey had predicted for American philosophy did, however, happen elsewhere: both in Continental philosophy and in American highbrow literary culture. (CP 63–64, emphasis added)

These lines clearly illustrate Rorty's accounting of the American philosophic scene. To the name "Anglo-American" philosophy, denoting the analytic perspective in America, there is no comparable name to denote the existence of a likewise immigrated perspective from the continent, the possibility of its metamorphosis on this soil. Such a philosophical perspective is relegated to the invisibility of the "academic shadows," and yet it was out of just those shadows that the "Pluralist" rebellion derived. And here we can see the significance, especially politically, of Rorty's professed desire to "moderate." Rather than recognize the legitimacy of a "Euro-American" philosophy in its own right, he invites recognition of certain key European figures: Heidegger, Sartre, Derrida, etc., that is, "Continental philosophy," which is allowed existence once again within this country only in "American highbrow literary culture," that is, not within the educational institution. Having lived intimately in both perspectives, the analytic and the continental within this country (and across C. P. Snow's dichotomy of science and art, for that matter), I have always been intrigued by the relative differences of the respective discourses and the ease with which individuals within them ignore the other. But here Rorty's "moderation" is a sleight of hand. Naming the "shadows" entails that he has some sense of their possibility, a possibility to which he attests in his silence. Once again the operative word is "*censure*" with respect to his version of "Philosophy in America Today."[20]

That Rorty's "moderation" functions by way of an effacing censure should be clear by this point. The gesture is there, to open "conversation," but the political disenfranchisement remains. The main gesture is to indicate topics rather than the plurality of voices in the American philosophical scene, with the intention, I think, of directing the philosophic malaise of the postanalytic situation towards his hopes for neopragmatism. His project is one of recovering the indigenous American philosophic perspective (if such a thing is conceivable) with his reading of Dewey. In this sense his project is somewhat similar to Cavell's attempt to identify Emerson and

Thoreau as the properly American philosophic origin. Therefore, Rorty's project puts him in a very weak position to "moderate" the dis-agreement between Cavell and Derrida, weakness with respect to *both* sides of that exchange. On Cavell's side of the exchange, Rorty has an obvious invested interest in repressing the identification of philosophic origins in Emerson and Thoreau in favor of his reading of Dewey. From the side of Derrida, Rorty's reading is marked again by censure of the very eros of exchange and meaning. This, in addition to his silencing of any particular Euro-American perspective within which to comprehend the American response to Derrida, leaves him in an untenable position from which to moderate the difficulty of the Cavell-Derrida exchange.

Rorty's text, then, traces a politics that constantly effaces itself, requiring, in effect, a deconstructive reading to locate the locus of its play. In recognizing this strategy operating within Rorty's text one should not be surprised by his pronouncements regarding the impropriety of a politics within the praxis of philosophical discourse, his "offering" at the Mexico conference.[21] The extent of his politics, the machinations of his simulated "moderations," serves only his North American audience. His philosophical pursuits remain parochial. Cornel West in his "Afterword" to *Post-Analytic Philosophy* puts it best:

> Rorty's neo-pragmatism ingeniously echoes the strident anti-humanist critiques—such as those of Martin Heidegger, Jacques Derrida and Michel Foucault—of a moribund bourgeois humanism. Yet his brand of neo-pragmatism domesticates these critiques in a smooth and witty Attic prose and, more importantly, dilutes them by refusing to push his own project toward cultural and political criticisms of the civilization he (and, in varying degrees, we) cherishes. In this way, Rorty circumscribes his ethnocentric posthumanism within a practical arena of bourgeois humanism. . . .
> Rorty leads philosophy to the complex world of politics and culture, but confines his engagement to transformation in the academy and apologetics for the modern West.[22]

The Mexico audience witnessed the weakness of this apologetics and the inappropriateness of such a postmodernism that does not seek to separate what is of value in its historical, intellectual traditions from an official nationalism, having not yet fully reconciled its postmodern condition. But this question of the relation of philosophy and politics is a complicated one, and Rorty's text serves as a useful example.

Although Rorty's text does not itself "moderate" the diversity of views found even in the academy, it exemplifies a kind of censure that prepares for conversation. Even while playing its double game of an implicit censure within a stated, explicit one, Rorty's text serves a phatic function preparing for the possibility of real communication. This state of affairs is well in evidence regarding the wealth of refutations already circulating. A new discursive space has opened up and voices from the margins of the dominant conversation of the North Atlantic are beginning to be heard. These voices continue to critique the community's ethnocentrism, sexism, and racism, in an attempt to reformulate such cultural identities through, in West's words, "preserving the best and rejecting the worst." Pluralism's value, when truly accorded dialogue, is to better serve to judge the provisional vocabularies by which political institutions are appraised with respect to their hegemonic status. The value and task of philosophy in the postmodern, political condition is to identify those structural moves by which the texts of institutions consolidate their power, limit their readings, define the community. Politics, then, as to its relation to philosophy, begins with a concern for meaning, especially its pragmatics within this post-Enlightenment milieu without foundations. Here Rorty's neopragmatist text provides an opening despite the nature of its censures/caesurae/censorship.

Notes

1. Jacques Derrida, "Dissemination," in *Dissemination*, trans. Barbara Johnson (Chicago: Univ. of Chicago Press, 1981), 290–91. Emphasis in the two phrases containing "on stage" was added.

2. I suppose it is necessary at this juncture to point out that this revolt of the "Pluralists" did not occur here in California in the Pacific Division but only in New York. Does this indicate that all is well with regard to such concerns in the avant-garde state, that we as a professional community are here more progressively amenable to pluralism than are our Eastern colleagues? A complacent yes to this question would be more than self-deceptive; it would be arrogant. My question would be, why has the Pacific Division not followed in the footsteps of the Eastern? And here the answer lies in a matter of arithmetic, the greater number of "marginals" in the East and an accompanying economics. This brings us to the root cause of the political "takeover" of the APA's program committee, a source more

fundamental than the desire merely to participate in the profession's annual rites. This story has to do with accreditation.

3. The suitability of Stanley Cavell's particular conversational style for this meeting is corroborated in a book on Derrida by Stephen Melville entitled *Philosophy beside Itself: On Deconstruction and Modernism* (Minneapolis: Univ. of Minnesota Press, 1986). In comparing Cavell's skepticism to Derrida's deconstruction, Melville holds that "Derrida and Cavell stand together at a major crossing in modern philosophy, a point at which what seemed philosophy's search for its own pure and proper ground apart from any psychology or psychologism is radically complicated by what can appear either as philosophy's invasion of psychology . . . or as philosophy's coming to acknowledge psychology as something inevitably internal to itself" (p. 23). Even more appropriate to our purposes here are Melville's comments in the foreword: "The introduction of Stanley Cavell into this book is so apt, for he is the most accomplished of our philosophical conversationalists. Cavell's tact at hearing what we mean when we speak teaches us that in conversation we do not wish simply that our partner be an echo of ourselves, nor do we even seek a mere exchange of experiences and opinions" (p. xxii). The productivity of such a "conversation" is evident in Cavell's readings of Heidegger, Wittgenstein, Emerson, and Thoreau in *This New Yet Unapproachable America* (Albuquerque: Living Batch Press, 1989).

4. Jacques Derrida, *Limited Inc* (Evanston: Northwestern Univ. Press, 1988), 31.

5. Here I must give the credit to Linda Carson, who posed this important question to my colleague, Joel Rudinow, during a presentation he gave at Sonoma State University entitled "Rorty's Philosophical Imperialism," a question for which dialogue was not yet prepared. This question challenged Rorty's text through a particular problematic that had been raised regarding the Cavell-Derrida exchange at the APA in San Francisco, a problematic of reading across just this difference of traditions to which this political "takeover" in the APA of a few years back in New York attests. The question: "How would Rorty 'moderate' the disagreement between Cavell and Derrida?" The difficulty of this question, placed well in advance of my thinking at the time, was the first real clue that Rorty's "moderating" position is fictitious on any level except that of spectacle, the same level of staging by which the APA "moderated" the session, "The Philosophy of Jacques Derrida," in San Francisco by charging admission.

6. Richard Rorty, "Philosophy as a Kind of Writing: An Essay on Derrida," in *Consequences of Pragmatism (Essays: 1972–1980)* (Minneapolis: Univ. of Minnesota Press, 1982), pp. 90–109; the essay hereafter abbreviated "PK"; the volume, "CP."

7. The importance of oppositions in Derrida's method is quite clearly stated in a section of *Of Grammatology* to which an important part of Rorty's

essay refers (without specifying the reference; although Rorty did so in an earlier delivered version): in the section "...That Dangerous Supplement...," the subsection, "The Exorbitant. Question of Method," in *Of Grammatology*, trans. Gayatri Chakravorty Spivak (Baltimore: Johns Hopkins Univ. Press, 1974), pp. 157–64; the volume hereafter abbreviated "OG."

8. PK 93. The quote continues: "the latest development in this non-Kantian, dialectical tradition—the latest attempt of the dialecticians to shatter the Kantians' ingenious image of themselves as accurately representing how things really are."

9. That Rorty's title itself gives directions by means of the colon—"...: An Essay on Derrida"—further evidences the assumed sense of origins found in "understanding." Rather than reading a text, Rorty presumes to read the man, the sense of understanding an "author," to seek the fullness of "speech" which Derrida's text seeks to deconstruct through "writing." In this sense Rorty's approach can be likened to an "assay," an analysis to determine the presence or absence of particular ingredients, mixing both chemical and trial metaphors. But such a drug test does not fit well the methods of deconstruction nor relay much information concerning the particular effects of that writing which Derrida does argue Plato/Socrates located in the pharmacy.

10. From Derrida's thesis defense, "The Time of a Thesis: Punctuations": "Naturally, all of the problems worked on in the Introduction to *The Origin of Geometry* have continued to organize the work I have subsequently attempted in connection with philosophical, literary and even non-discursive corpora, most notably that of pictorial works." In Alan Montefiore, ed., *Philosophy in France Today* (Cambridge: Cambridge Univ. Press, 1983), 39.

11. OG 158: quoted in PK 96.

12. OG 18–19; quoted in PK 102. And SP 158–59; quoted in PK 103.

13. This can be seen if one compares the relevant quote given by Rorty in section 3 (PK 102; OG 18–19) with the one from section 2 (PK 95; OG 17–18) where the text and the book are paired respectively with the signifier and signified. Also, within the quote from section 3 (PK 102; OG 18–19) is the important line: "And the sign must be the unity of a heterogeneity, since the signified (sense or thing, noeme or reality) is not in itself a signifier, a *trace*."

14. PW 103, quoting Jacques Derrida, "Differance," in *Speech and Phenomena* (Evanston, Ill.: Northwestern Univ. Press, 1973), 129–60, p. 159; hereafter abbreviated "DF".

15. PK 91. Rorty writes "eros" in the Greek.

16. PK 106. It is interesting that Rorty leaves the reader without a reference to Derrida's text here by which to check the paraphrase and the context. Has he lost it? In an earlier, delivered version of this paper he did give it: "...That Dangerous Supplement..." in *Of Grammatology*, 141–64. This earlier paper, "Derrida on Language, Being, and Abnormal Philosophy," interestingly levels a charge against continentalists in general that seems an apt description of Rorty's own essay: "It is as if one did philosophy not by presenting arguments against one's predecessors' views, but by violent and *erotic* struggle with one's images of them." P. 679, emphasis added, in *Journal of Philosophy* 74 (1977): 673–81; hereafter abbreviated "DL".

17. Rorty's "sensitivity" to the phallocentrism of the tradition is even given a footnote at the end of the text of his lecture, a "sensitivity" which is censored in the essay: "The reader who finds all this too far-fetched is asked to ponder the connections between (a) the use of 'hard' and 'soft' to qualify 'subject', 'science', 'nose', 'philosophy', and 'argument'; (b) the fact that women (and unathletic male homosexuals) were traditionally best adapted to soft subjects; (c) Plato's distinction between hard-edged Being and amorphous Becoming; (d) Plato's exhortations to mathematics, muscle-building, and military music; (e) Plato's discussion of writing in the *Phaedrus*" (DL 681).

18. The "Heidegger Affair," precipitated by the publication of Victor Farías's *Heidegger et le nazisme* in France, has served to illustrate this complexity of the continental tradition and to reopen the question of a philosophy's relation to politics. Rorty himself has argued for their separation, most recently in terms of the ironist philosopher in *Contingency, Irony, and Solidarity* (Cambridge: Cambridge Univ. Press, 1989), and in his review of Farías's book entitled "Taking Philosophy Seriously," *New Republic* 198 (1988): 31–35.

19. The revolt occurred in New York as a response to the New York State Education Department's review of its doctoral programs. The rating committees, due to ignorance or political intention, claimed that phenomenologists in particular were not qualified to teach in such areas as metaphysics, epistemology, or ethics. This decision was based on the view that their "area" was phenomenology, a manner of classification that has often been perpetuated by the APA. This event, then, is of no minor political consequence for how the profession views itself and the extent of its allowance for real differences of opinion and perspective. To control curriculum at the graduate level is to control more than simply the profession, but to control what counts as philosophy with regard to its dissemination. How else can one understand the long-held identification in this country of the work of such writers as Derrida and Foucault with Comparative Literature and French departments? Can this really be understood as a simple provincialism?

20. To fill out this "shadow," read "Phenomenology in America (1964–1984)" in a book called *Consequences of Phenomenology* by Don Ihde

(New York: State Univ. of New York Press, 1986), pp. 1–26, which attests to the rich and unique approach to doing philosophy that has resulted from a uniquely American metamorphosis of its European beginnings. Having audited Gurwitsch's last class at the New School in New York City before he died, I can personally attest to the radical difference between the emigré scholar and the work being done at that time in the American tradition at Stony Brook. (Even in the case of Derrida and Ricoeur, for instance, one could argue for an American debt to their thought due to their work here in American universities and the fact that they have a much larger following in this country than in France; at the very least that theirs is a cosmopolitan perspective. Interestingly, Derrida has even suggested that deconstruction is a particularly American theory in its conduciveness to interpreting our heterogeneous culture.)

21. This "event" was brought to my attention by my colleague, Joel Rudinow, in a paper he gave at Sonoma State University entitled "Rorty's Philosophical Imperialism." This paper (plus, of course, Foucault) first motivated my consideration of the political discourse operating within Rorty's text. See Rorty's address at the Eleventh Inter-American Congress of Philosophy, Guadalajara, Mexico, November 10–15, 1985, in *Proceedings and Addresses of APA* 59 no. 5 (June 1986): 747–53.

22. Cornel West, "Afterword," in John Rajchman and Cornel West, eds., *Post-Analytic Philosophy* (New York: Columbia Univ. Press, 1985), pp. 267–68.

20

Elements of a Derridean Social Theory

Bill Martin

At the 1988 Eastern Division meeting of the American Philosphical Association (APA), I, along with several hundred others, witnessed yet another chapter in the continuing saga of the nonengagement between the Habermasians and Derrida. Professor Derrida presented a paper on the politics of friendship, which worked through the philosophical discourse of friendship from Aristotle to the twentieth century.[1] Derrida spoke of "a democracy that is yet to come, and which little resembles what goes by that name today." The analysis Derrida gave of received notions of democracy and community criticized especially the fact that, throughout Western history, friendship relations have been founded on a masculine model. The future democracy depends, in part, on the replacement of this model by one that recognizes the possibility of sisterhood.

The respondent, Professor Thomas McCarthy, mainly raised questions about whether Derrida's analysis is capable of founding any very specific social program. In particular, McCarthy asked for a critique of specific institutions. Despite the fact that I think these are important and worthwhile questions (though I do not know that the Habermasians have been any less evasive concerning these matters than some Derrideans), I found that McCarthy did not really engage Derrida for what he *did* say. And this I have found a typical trait of the Habermasian critique of Derrida. All the same, I think that it is in fact necessary to try to flesh out the elements of a

Derridean social theory, and to show why such a theory is not only useful but indeed necessary. This is the area of my research at present, which I would like to present here in outline form.[2] I cannot claim that this outline will necessarily make the Habermasians or other Marxists happy, but I think it will at least lay the groundwork for more productive engagements in the future.

Although the work of Jacques Derrida has exercised broad influence in literary criticism and, more recently, in philosophy, this influence is only beginning to be felt in a comprehensive way in social theory. In this chapter I will outline a social theory that uses Derrida's work as its methodological basis, and I will demonstrate why a social theory of this type is needed. Though Derrida is not himself a social theorist, his work has profound implications for social theory, in two respects: first, as the basis for the critique of contemporary social theories; second, as the basis, on the other side of this critique, for a social theory uniquely suited to a social situation that I call postmodern (the meaning of this term and its significance in this outline will be explicated in due course). In each case, I take Derrida's philosophy as the key to working through three basic problems (or complexes of problems): first, problems concerning the mediums of social interaction and, in particular, systems of signification (systems in which meaning is generated); second, problems concerning the nature of subjectivity and the relation of subjectivity to human agency and responsibility; and third, problems of social relations, inter-subjectivity, and history. These issues are, of course, central to many diverse social theories; that is why I take them to be the issues with which "yet another" social theory has to concern itself. Everything hinges, however, on the sort of matrix within which these issues are elaborated, and the sort of line leading out of this arrangement to a new theory. With Derrida's work serving as a philosophical ground, a theory can be developed that addresses what I take to be the central questions of contemporary society, both on the practical level of the problems of everyday life and on the broader plane of human relations in a thoroughly interconnected matrix of global social relations.

One thing that I want to emphasize is that this theory can be developed entirely out of elements taken from Derrida's work. I stress this point in connection with two concerns:

First, I think that it may be important to remark on my own basic approach to Derrida's work. My view is that Derrida's work is systematic, rigorous, and argumentative. While this work at the same time undermines systems and teases out the limits of reason (by pursuing reason to its limits, I hasten to add), it is not the wild relativism portrayed in some hasty caricatures.[3]

Second, it is also important that a word or two is said about Marxism. A Derridean social theory must necessarily engage with Marxism at many points. The purpose of my outline, however, is not geared so much toward foreshadowing a full-fledged systematic encounter between Derrida and Marxism. Although such an encounter is necessary and very important (and is in fact developing in the work of Gayatri Spivak, Michael Ryan, Gregory Jay, and others), I think it more worthwhile to explore first the possibilities of getting Derrida's philosophy onto the social-theoretical terrain, where any subsequent encounter with Marxism would more usefully be pursued.[4]

With these concerns in mind, we may turn to the particular matrix in which the aforementioned elements may be arranged. Since I am most interested in delineating a set of elements and their arrangement, page references to particular texts have been for the most part relegated to the footnotes. What follows, then, is a proposal for creating a Derridean social theory.

A specifically Derridean social theory must necessarily take problems of language and signification to be central to understanding, first, subjectivity and, then, social relations in their historical settings. Derrida's approach to language stresses that language functions on the basis of a "system of differences" that, in principle, can unfold indefinitely. This claim, on Derrida's part, is in fact nothing more than the pursuit of the programs of Frege and (especially) Saussure to their logical conclusions. Each claimed that a word only has meaning within a linguistic context. For Saussure, a word means what it means by virtue of its distinguishability from other words—its difference. All that Derrida has added to this understanding is the notion that this process of differentiation is potentially endless. But this is also to claim that there is no "final" context, which claim is a form of antifoundationalism. This antifoundationalism would have very significant practical consequences if it turns out that there is a basic relation among language (and other forms of signification—here I will simply use the term *language* as shorthand for all these forms), subjectivity, and social relations.

The arguments for there being a basic relation between language and subjectivity are many and diverse (it is telling, also, that these arguments are propounded in most of the major schools of philosophy today). The position I take on this question will perhaps seem extreme (to those not working in continental traditions, at any rate), although it has had its proponents (again, a diverse group): subjectivity is an *effect* of language. I am less interested in pursuing this argument at great length (responsibility for which I am relieved by the fact that others are already engaged in this pursuit) than I am in drawing the conclusions that must necessarily follow if the language from which subjectivity emerges is itself not fully a "ground" in the traditional sense. Language may be supporting subjectivity, but what is supporting language?

The further ramifications of this question for social relations are clear: if subjectivity is not moored to a secure ground, then social relations would tend to be, if anything, on even less secure ground. If such conclusions were indeed the limit of a "postmodern" (using this term now in the loose sense promoted by Rorty, who equates anti-foundationalism and postmodernism) understanding of things, then there would be no place for social theory (or even for morality), since there would be little more than a purely existential basis for fundamental notions such as responsibility and agency. More can be argued for, however, on the basis of Derrida's theory of language, than mere indeterminacy.[5] In particular, there are two ramifications of that theory that are of prime importance for a Derridean social theory.

First, taken as a "medium," language's social character ensures that subjectivity will also have a social character. On the basis of an understanding that subjectivity in general is rooted in language, we may assert further that the social character of language grounds the view that intersubjectivity is prior to subjectivity in the order of explanation. Already, then, there is the basis for claiming that subjectivity exists in a social matrix, and that, regardless of whether this matrix is itself "ultimately" grounded (in a foundational sense), the expressions of individual agents have meaning at least insofar as this matrix is concerned. Though the effects of indeterminacy will have to be taken account of, there is the basis for a kind of social theory, though not a theory that claims to be foundational. Derrida's arguments concerning the relation of language to subjectivity, which are especially developed in *Speech and Phenomena*, are compelling.[6] However, it may be safely admitted that if the entire thrust of these arguments was only geared toward showing the necessity for practicing social theory in the pragmatic mode, then there would already be a sufficient basis in quite a few other philosophers for moving ahead with this project. Among these would be the American Pragmatists (especially Mead and Dewey), the later Wittgenstein, and, of course, the more naturalistic side of Marx. But there is another side to Derrida's approach to language that, while not necessarily detracting from the pragmatic mode (in fact, that mode will be very important in developing a postmodern social theory), certainly augments that mode in a way not typical of (indeed, uncomfortable for) social theory in the pragmatic mode.

Second, then, I refer to Derrida's problematic of "the other." Given that this problematic is found in several different forms throughout the European traditions from Hegel to Heidegger and beyond, I think it important to spell out what I find to be Derrida's particular contribution to the notion of the other. Derrida's problematic is closely associated with the fact, mentioned earlier, that there is no "ultimate context." Our participation in the world through particular systems of signification is what makes subjects feel and think that there *is* such a context, but this is a kind of metaphysical illusion. When we understand language as the product of difference, we see that, in both theory and practice, the "ultimate context" is simply a horizon that recedes as we approach it. There is always the infinite "beyond," or other. As Derrida argues in a number of studies, including *Of Grammatology* and the essay, "Differance,"[7] this beyond is an "outside" that is also an "inside." The effect of this always-receding context is twofold and even paradoxical: the other makes language *impossible*, and yet it is the other that "calls" us to language by continually confronting the emerging subject with possibilities. The impossibility of language, as a foundational enterprise, is also, then, its possibility.[8]

The ramifications of this problematic for a Derridean social theory would be the following set of claims, which can be argued for on the basis of the framework now outlined. First, that subjectivity, in addition to having its ground in intersubjectivity, is capable of hearing and responding to the call of the other. This I take to be the basis of responsibility, including social responsibility (here the Levinasian side of Derrida's work should especially be stressed). Second, that responding to this call is not, for Derrida, a quasi-mystical matter—as it seems to be for Heidegger. Rather, and third, it is a question of pursuing systems of signification into their "margins," to their limits, to the point where their systematicity begins to break down.[9] One way to describe this Derridean pursuit is "reading against the grain," a formula that would figure prominently in any discussion of history and social relations undertaken in consideration of the elements outlined here (the connection with Walter Benjamin and a kind of "Jewish Marxism" needs to be stressed). Fourth, the notions of (forms of) subjectivity, social relations, responsibility, and history, as reconceived in a specifically Derridean antifoundational mode, can be distinguished from the notions that go by these names in other social theories.

Fifth, these reconceived notions can be used to read against the grain of received history (by which I mean history that has been both created and reported from the perspective of foundational notions of subjectivity and responsibility), to reveal a different history that will be seen to have a different trajectory (one *without* an "outcome") than the mainstream (as opposed to the margins) of history. Finally, the possibility of reading against the grain will be seen to be the beginning of a new practice of signification that could ground the practice of this "different history."

Wittgenstein argued for a similar possibility in both the earlier and later work (he of course had very different conceptions of what the possibility would mean in his early and later periods), namely, that a new politics would require a new language—and that a new language would require a new attitude toward language. Where this possibility was merely glimpsed by Wittgenstein (it was one of his many undeveloped insights), Derrida's work lays the foundation for the systematic justification and articulation of this possibility. And, of course, it is a possibility that Derrida *practices* in his texts. While the framework just set out is in evidence in a number of Derrida's explicitly "political" writings (for instance, "No Apocalypse, Not Now," "Racism's Last Word," "The Ends of Man," etc.),[10] it has not been fully elaborated in a social theoretical way. That is the task to which I hope this outline will contribute.

Beyond the fleshing out of such an outline, a Derridean social theory must take up a number of specific problems, which I will now set out. We need not claim that there is one and only one way of proceeding once we have a basic framework, but I would claim that these problems are indeed central to understanding and acting responsibly in postmodern society.

The first task in this regard is to contextualize the Derridean framework in terms of an account of the social world that it must confront. This contextualization arises from my conviction that any convincing theory of contemporary social relations must be grounded in an understanding of the nature of *contemporary* society. Despite the obviousness of this claim—which is virtually no more than a truism—it is not clear that most contemporary social theories are formulated in light of it. Ironic as it may seem, this major proviso is in many cases not even met in social commentaries that claim to be "postmodern." It is as though a style of theory that is called "postmodern" can be brought to bear on social questions that are conceived to be essentially atemporal. My intuition, on the contrary, is that it is because society has entered a period, or phase, or *something* (perhaps something "out of phase," something that escapes the Hegelian sense of periodization) that is not simply "modern," but certainly *after* modernity, that a style of theorizing called *postmodern* is appropriate. In attempting to come to grips with this only half-named something, this postmodernity, we should both take Hegel at his word and read against the grain of that word. That is, from Hegel we inherit both the notion of periodization, which has led to the formulation of the idea of postmodernity, and the notion of a formulation of a "completion of history" that has seemingly not occurred. My understanding of postmodernity is that it is the "period" (that is not exactly a "period") in which the conditions for the completion of history (in Hegel's sense) are present, but the end of history is forestalled, perhaps permanently. The sense of this impasse is captured in several of Derrida's essays, including "From Restricted to General Economy: A Hegelianism without Reserve," and in a more atmospheric form in *Glas*.[11] It remains for social theory to demonstrate how this impasse, which contains among its chief characteristics the suspension of received notions of subjectivity, responsibility, and praxis, is concretely the situation of contemporary society.[12] What is needed, then, is a "postmodern cartography." (And a distinction can be drawn between this type of social theory which is postmodern because it aims at such a cartography, and those that claim to be postmodern for other reasons—not that this would in all cases be a hard and fast distinction.)

Within this historical contextualization (which is indeed the context of an historical impasse), the thematics of language, intersubjectivity, and responsibility can be taken up anew, in order to argue that there is a way out of the impasse. As part of that argument, however, Derridean notions of language, subjectivity, and responsibility must confront the more typical notions that are found in "modern" social theories. As a key example here, consider the work of Jürgen Habermas. His own social theory is exemplary in its comprehensiveness. Furthermore, Habermas also takes the problem of language to be central to the development of a contemporary social theory—and he is very attentive to what I earlier called the "pragmatic mode."[13] However, Derrida and Habermas end up in two very different places in pursuit of that mode. The comparison of the two thinkers has been undertaken thus far in piecemeal fashion, in part because Derrida is not a social theorist.[14] What needs showing is that a comprehensive social theory that takes a Derridean approach to language as its methodological basis would be a fit competitor to Habermas's. Note that this remark is made from a position of great respect for Habermas, whom many, including this author, regard as the most important social theorist writing today. The whole question of a postmodern social theory enters in again here, in two respects: first, in that Habermas, despite his pragmatic concerns, is foundational in ways to which a Derridean analysis can be specifically sensitive (here Derrida's analysis of speech act theory, carried out in the essays "Signature Event Context" and "Limited Inc," is very important, as this form of philosophy of language motivates Habermas's own arguments concerning communication);[15] second, in that Habermas is concerned to press forward "the unfinished project of modernity."[16] At the center of that program is, of course, the rationalist paradigm, which Habermas takes over from Rousseau and Kant.[17] Here again, Derrida is especially important, because, unlike some postmodernists, he does not simply throw the rationalist baby out with the bathwater. Derrida is concerned to read both with and against the grain of this Enlightenment heritage: he does not (despite what Habermas seems to think) simply want to turn Reason, History, the Subject, etc., on their heads; he wants to understand how their marginal aspects both problematize and interact with, even to the point of making possible, their "central" aspects.[18]

In this regard we might make a useful detour through the work of Donald Davidson, which provides a bridge away from the philosophy of language found in Habermas, and toward Derrida's approach to philosophy of language.[19] I see several reasons why such an engagement is practical. First, Davidson provides, in a way that is not always so clear (or, at any rate, accessible) in Derrida's work, a sense of what it means for language to have a nonfoundational structure.[20] Like Derrida, Davidson has a "minimal" conception of the sign: that is, both Derrida and Davidson take it that there is nothing essential to the sign other than its repeatability.[21] Second, Habermas has admirably attempted to break out of the analytical/continental antinomy by engaging with analytical philosophy of language. I think that this engagement is important for both philosophical and political (even if of a merely "institutional" kind) reasons. Habermas would have been better served, however, by a truth-conditional theory of meaning, such as Davidson's, than a speech-act theory, which actually has as a consequence (at least in the versions associated with Austin and Searle) the very relativism that Habermas wants very much to avoid.[22] Third, Davidson's theory, which also claims to be a pragmatic theory (and to be antifoundationalist), does not recognize the problematics of otherness that I discussed earlier. So that, and fourth, a critique of this pragmatic alternative to the philosophy of language taken up by Habermas serves as a further basis for showing why the problematic of otherness is essential to understanding language, subjectivity, and responsibility. Finally, this comparison will also demonstrate that there are indeed different forms of antifoundationalism, and why it is a matter of practical importance to distinguish among them. It seems to me that only an antifoundationalism of the sort that Derrida offers can allow us to gain access to the margins of history.

Through this matrix of language, subjectivity, and social relations, the move can be made toward more straightforward "political" questions, beginning with: Supposing that we do have the basis for exploring the margins of history, what will we find in those margins? Not surprisingly, we will find marginal subjects, that is, those who have been written out of history, but who are also deeply inscribed in history, both written and lived. These subjects will be diverse, and the question of bringing their marginal voices to life will also be a question of radical diversity—but also a question of a radical *confluence*. I shall explain with an example: Reading against the grain in Hegel, in what I propose to call a "postmodern cartography," we can take the Jews as an exemplary marginal subject. Hegel needs and takes what Jewish civilization had already created, namely, the very notion of narrative history itself and the concept of "civic altruism," which is found in the Jewish understanding that the relation between the human person and God is only actual insomuch as it is enacted in relationships in the human community.[23] What Hegel leaves behind are the Jews themselves. He also leaves behind the Jewish problematic of otherness, in which the Absolute can never be seen or even named—and indeed, the Absolute is always receding (the incarnation of God is always that which *will* come). This problematic is very much in evidence in Derrida (as in his essays, "Shibboleth," "Des Tours de Babel," and "Violence and Metaphysics: An Essay on the Thought of Emmanuel Levinas").[24] This simultaneous presence and absence of the Jews in Hegel can be taken as a model for reading other margins of history. On the basis of this reading, my further argument would be that these different margins, which include women, people of color, the poor, and other outcasts, are not reducible to one another, even if, in terms of what I take to be the basic understanding created by the Derridean reading strategy, these outcasts conform to a certain model of marginality. The irreducibility of these marginalities has as a consequent the notion that a politics of the margins must depend on the possibility of confluence based in the model of marginality, rather than on a monolithic politics based in reducibility to a single, shared condition of life (as in some readings of Marx's notion of the proletariat). What unites these outcasts is, after all, their difference. The articulation of this radical diversity/radical confluence model will amount, in practical terms, to a philosophy of the new social movements.

Finally, then, we must ask what sorts of political engagements and solutions are made possible by this model. This questioning needs to be pursued on two levels: first, in terms of broad theoretical concerns relating to the question of the relation between responsibility and, on the one hand, capitalism, patriarchy, white supremacy, and industrialism, and, on the other hand, communism, feminism, racial equality, and ecological concerns; second, in terms of more "local" concerns—to put it concretely, the question of what people can *do*, what sorts of practice they can and should engage in, given the model outlined here.

Uppermost among my concerns is the question of whether *community* is possible in postmodern society. This question can only be raised in the skeptical mode. That is, it will not do to assume from the start that community is possible and to proceed from there. A thoroughgoing analysis of postmodern society reveals, I think, that we cannot take it as an assumption that community is possible in contemporary society.

Four possibilities can be raised concerning the question of community. First, that community is no longer possible at all, that all the social conditions that have made community possible in the past are now irreparably shattered. I believe that this is a possibility that has to be very seriously considered—no further possibilities can be considered apart from it. Second, that some sort of community is possible in postmodernity itself. In setting out this possibility we incur the responsibility of showing what sort of postmodern community is possible. Third, that community will only be possible again after the impasse of postmodernity is broken. Here we incur the necessity of showing that the time after postmodernity will in some sense be like the time before (and it will of course be an important question whether this would be a desirable thing). Fourth, and finally, that community will be possible only after the impasse of postmodernity is broken, *and* after the notion and the reality of community is recreated.

The outline I have presented here points toward, I think, the fourth possibility. The new community will be the community of radical diversity/radical confluence. This community will emerge by breaking the impasse of postmodernity and, in an interactive sense, the impasse of postmodernity will be broken by the emergence of this community. I should clarify what I mean by the word "will" in this last sentence. I mean that either this community will emerge and the impasse of postmodernity will be broken, *or* there *will not* be a future for humanity. The outcome of this disjunctive pair—which consists in a possibility and the negation of possibility—is far from certain, but with the outline offered here I hope that we have the basis for some creative theoretical contributions to the furtherance of human possibility.

Notes

1. Jacques Derrida, "The Politics of Friendship," trans. Gabriel Motzkin, *Journal of Philosophy* 85 (1988): 632–44. Thomas McCarthy's response, "On the Margins of Politics," also appears in that volume, pp. 645–48.

2. This research project has in fact been carried through, at least in its initial stage. See Bill Martin, *Matrix and Line: Derrida and the Possibilities of Postmodern Social Theory* (Albany: State Univ. of New York Press, 1992).

3. Fortunately, there are now some comprehensive, systematic studies of Derrida's work that begin to make such caricatures less feasible. Two studies in particular should be mentioned: Rodolphe Gasché, *The Tain of the Mirror: Derrida and the Philosophy of Reflection* (Cambridge, Mass.: Harvard Univ. Press, 1986), and Irene Harvey, *Derrida and the Economy of Differance* (Bloomington: Indiana Univ. Press, 1986). Some have criticized these two books for being "too serious." My feeling is that the "seriousness" of these books is fully justified by some of the "playfulness" of some Derrideans, but even more so on independent grounds: that is, Derrida is a serious philosopher. Of course, for those analytic philosophers and others who do not feel that Derrida must be read in order to be condemned, there is little that even the work of Harvey and Gasché can do. My proposal is simply that, whenever people of this bent say something negative about "Derrida" (i.e., something or someone they think of as Derrida), we should always challenge them to cite their source (and not let them off the hook with some protestation that, "I've *tried* to read Derrida—it's just not possible"). It is time to get serious with these people who are helping to destroy philosophy through promoting a proud illiteracy—there are enough forces outside of the academy promoting this; we don't need our colleagues adding to the anti-intellectual current. (I apologize for the sudden manifesto, but—enough is enough!)

4. I do not consider this proposal, however, to be pitched in a "post-Marxist" direction—this term being presently fashionable among some members of the postmodern set. In particular, I think that there is a basis

in Derrida for a kind of historical materialism (though not a "dialectical materialism"—although the dialectic is not nearly so absent from Derrida's work as some readers seem to think), though one that takes as its first task the "materialization of the signifier." The notion of marginal subjects in history that I will outline has a—not coincidental—resemblance to a certain reading of Marx's notion of the proletariat. Concerning the question of postmodernism, I think that we will need a notion of historical disjuncture that owes something to Marx and indeed to Lenin. The Derridean strategy for reading against the grain might be seen as a form of immanent critique based in the materiality of the signifier. And, of course, both Marx and Derrida are well known as readers of Hegel. So, Marx will hardly be absent from the elements outlined here—but, then, I do not think that Marx is absent from either Derrida or the postmodern situation that a Derridean social theory must address.

5. In the new afterword to the book version of *Limited Inc,* Derrida distinguishes what he means by "undecidability" from what is typically meant by "indeterminacy" in the analytic tradition. The former includes, but goes beyond, the latter. See "Toward an Ethic of Discussion," in Derrida, *Limited Inc,* trans. Samuel Weber and Jeffrey Mehlman (Evanston, Ill.: Northwestern Univ. Press, 1988), 111–60.

6. See especially "Meaning as Soliloquy," in Derrida, *Speech and Phenomena,* trans. David B. Allison (Evanston, Ill.: Northwestern Univ. Press, 1973), 32–47.

7. Jacques Derrida, *Of Grammatology,* trans. Gayatri C. Spivak (Baltimore: Johns Hopkins Univ. Press, 1976); *"Differance,"* in *Margins of Philosophy,* trans. Alan Bass (Chicago: Univ. of Chicago Press, 1982), 1–27.

8. This position on the coextensive possibility and impossibility of language is perhaps not so different from a certain reading of Wittgenstein's *Tractatus.* This kind of reading is evidenced in Russell Nieli, *Wittgenstein: From Mysticism to Ordinary Language* (Albany: State Univ. of New York Press, 1987), though I think the author goes a little overboard on some of the mystical aspects of the problems that Wittgenstein was raising concerning language (though Nieli is undoubtedly fair to what seem to have been Wittgenstein's own mystical leanings). Nieli would have been well served by a better sense of the problematics of language and otherness in Heidegger, Levinas, and Derrida. It is noteworthy that Henry Staten does not deal with the question of the possibility of language in his *Wittgenstein and Derrida* (Lincoln: Univ. of Nebraska Press, 1984).

The other point that may be mentioned at this juncture is that Derrida's problematics of otherness is certainly indebted to Heidegger's, as the reader might expect. The chief difference that I would claim for Derrida's view is its *materialism.* That is, Derrida's problematic arises from pursuing the pragmatic mode of language study to its limit, and by raising questions at that limit. On this pursuit, see John Llewelyn, *Derrida on the Threshold of Sense* (New York: St. Martin's Press, 1986).

9. This line of reasoning is clearly evident in the first presentation that Derrida made in the United States, "Structure, Sign and Play in the Discourse of the Human Sciences," in Derrida, *Writing and Difference*, trans. Alan Bass (Chicago: Univ. of Chicago Press, 1978), 278–93.

10. "No Apocalypse, Not Now (Full Speed Ahead, Seven Missiles, Seven Missives)," trans. Catherine Porter and Philip Lewis, *Diacritics* 14.2 (Summer 1984): 20–31; "Racism's Last Word," trans. Peggy Kamuf, *Critical Inquiry* 12 (Autumn 1985–86): 290–99; "The Ends of Man," in *Margins of Philosophy*, 109–36.

11. Jacques Derrida, *Glas*, trans. John P. Leavey, Jr., and Richard Rand (Lincoln: Univ. of Nebraska Press, 1986); "From Restricted to General Economy: A Hegelianism without Reserve," in *Writing and Difference*, 251–77.

12. These notions of suspension and impasse owe a great deal to the analysis in Fredric Jameson's well-known article, "*Postmodernism*, or The Cultural Logic of Late Capitalism," *New Left Review* 146 (1984): 53–92.

13. See lecture 11, "An Alternative Way Out of the Philosophy of the Subject: Communicative versus Subject-Centered Reason," in Jürgen Habermas, *The Philosophical Discourse of Modernity*, trans. Frederick Lawrence (Cambridge, Mass.: MIT Press, 1987), 294–326.

14. Habermas's noncritique of Derrida is found on pp. 161–210 of *The Philosophical Discourse of Modernity*. To say that these pages do not begin to engage the philosophical project of Derrida would be an understatement (they are a bit of a disappointment, not really up to the calibre of critique of which Habermas is capable). Derrida comments on this nonengagement in *Limited Inc*, pp. 156–58.

15. Jacques Derrida, "Signature Event Context" and "Limited Inc a b c . . .," reprinted in Derrida, *Limited Inc*, 1–23, and 29–110, respectively; Jürgen Habermas, "What Is Universal Pragmatics?" in *Communication and the Evolution of Society*, trans. Thomas McCarthy (Boston: Beacon Press, 1979), 1–68; and *The Theory of Communicative Action*, vol. 1, trans. Thomas McCarthy (Boston: Beacon Press, 1984), chap. 3.

16. See Jürgen Habermas, "Modernity versus Postmodernity," *New German Critique* 22 (Winter 1981): 3–14. Also, see the useful collection edited by Richard Bernstein, *Habermas and Modernity* (Cambridge, Mass.: MIT Press, 1985).

17. On Kantian themes in Habermas's thought, see Rick Roderick, *Habermas and the Foundations of Critical Theory* (New York: St. Martin's

Press, 1986), 17–19 and passim.; and Harry van der Linden, *Kantian Ethics and Socialism* (Indianapolis: Hackett, 1988).

18. A useful project here, as yet not pursued (to my knowledge), would be a reading of Derrida's "The Ends of Man" (cited n. 10) in the context of the discussion of humanism in Sartre ("Existentialism Is a Humanism") and Heidegger ("Letter on Humanism"). A further project that suggests itself here would be a reading that moves historically and politically "forward" from Sartre, through structuralism (especially Althusser), to Derrida. These readings would be useful for establishing Derrida's relationship to (the) Enlightenment in a more contextually secure way. I attempt to make a contribution to this discussion in *Matrix and Line*, chap. 2, sec. 1.

19. See especially Donald Davidson, *Inquiries into Truth and Interpretation* (Oxford: Oxford Univ. Press, 1985); and the essays in part 5, "Language and Reality," in Ernest LePore, ed., *Truth and Interpretation: Perspectives on the Philosophy of Donald Davidson* (Oxford: Basil Blackwell, 1986), 307–429.

20. Here the question is especially the use and modifications that Davidson has made of Tarski's semantic conception of truth. See essays 1–5 in *Inquiries into Truth and Interpretation*. Often the subtleties of Davidson's pragmatic reading of the semantic conception are missed, in part because analytic and continental philosophers sometimes have different foci regarding the metaphysics of language and interpretation. Tarski's conception is an attempted end run around problems of metaphysics. In Davidson's reworking, there is no attempt to avoid metaphysics, only to minimize recourse to metaphysics and to define clearly the scope of metaphysics. Whether this attempt succeeds or not, one important aspect of the attempt is that it struggles against metaphysics "from the inside," in a way that is not so foreign to Derrida's attitude toward metaphysics.

21. See S. Pradhan, "Minimalist Semantics: Davidson and Derrida on Meaning, Use and Convention," *Diacritics* 16:1 (Spring 1986): 65–77. It should be added that the term *repeatability* does not cover the range of possibilities that Derrida signifies with the term *iterability*. On this point, see Gasché, *The Tain of the Mirror*, 212–17.

22. Two points need to be raised here. First, Habermas's conflation of the views of language in the work of Michael Dummett and Donald Davidson indicate that there is a bit of confusion and perhaps carelessness in Habermas's investigation of theories of communication; see Habermas, *Theory of Communicative Action*, 1:276, 316–18. (This is reminiscent of the way in which analytic philosophers often lump diverse continental figures such as Derrida, Habermas, and Foucault all together. Davidson and Dummet are really quite different in their views of language; see Michael Dummett, "What Is a Theory of Meaning?" in Samuel Guttenplan, ed., *Mind and*

Language [Oxford: Oxford Univ. Press, 1975], 97–138, in which Dummet discusses his differences with Davidson.) Second, there is the problem that speech-act theories tend to be both foundationalistic and relativistic: foundational in their positing of a self-present subject who knows and speaks, relativistic in what Dagfinn Follesdal and others have tagged a "Humpty-Dumpty theory of meaning" ("a word means just what I say it means"). Chapter 3 of my *Matrix and Line* is a rather extensive treatment of Habermas's approach to language, as compared to Derrida's and Davidson's.

23. Among the many important references here would be Levinas, Buber, and Fackenheim. See especially Emil Fackenheim, "The Shibboleth of Revelation: From Spinoza beyond Hegel," chapter 3 of *To Mend the World: Foundations of Future Jewish Thought* (New York: Schocken Books, 1982). A pair of articles that articulate the point I am making here are: Richard L. Rubenstein, "Civic Altruism and the Resacralization of the Political Order," and Manfred H. Vogel, "The Social Dimension of the Faith of Judaism: Phenomenological and Historic Aspects," in M. Darrol Bryant and Rita H. Mataragnon, eds., *The Many Faces of Religion and Society* (New York: Paragon House, 1985), 3–17, and 45–57, respectively.

24. Jacques Derrida, "Shibboleth," trans. Joshua Wilner, in Geoffrey H. Hartman and Sanford Budick, eds., *Midrash and Literature* (New Haven: Yale Univ. Press, 1986), 307–47; "Des Tours de Babel," trans. Joseph F. Graham, in Joseph F. Graham, ed., *Difference in Translation* (Ithaca, N.Y.: Cornell Univ. Press, 1985), 165–207; "Violence and Metaphysics: An Essay on the Thought of Emmanuel Levinas," in *Writing and Difference*, 79–153.

21

Faceless Women and Serious Others: Levinas, Misogyny, and Feminism

Craig R. Vasey

I had read Levinas's work, and worked hard at understanding it, long before I heard of Dorothy Dinnerstein or Nancy Chodorow.[1] Today, when I read Levinas, I sometimes feel like I am reading Dinnerstein in French, written by a man, and by a man who does not realize that the philosophy he is putting forth is, and needs to be, feminist. In fact, he has so little sense of this that his text frequently employs traditional patriarchal images and assumptions. In this chapter I will exhibit the misogyny of Levinas's text and suggest that it undermines or counters itself by containing a feminist vision or argument, albeit in ignorance. I believe that Levinas's basic categories (the face, the idea of the infinite, language as the relation to the Other, separation, enjoyment and living from, and proximity) and the use he makes of them in his phenomenology of interiority and exteriority—namely, to show the primarily totalitarian and violent nature of Western philosophy and to articulate an alternative to it—define a theoretical position that is practically indistinguishable from feminism. Yet, as I will also show, he has apparently no inkling of this and actually proceeds to repeat certain claims that are fundamental to the violence of patriarchal philosophy. It is my contention that the anti-totalitarian spirit of his thought is more central and indispensable to it than is the misogyny of his imagery.

317

My title, "Faceless Women and Serious Others," gives a first indication of his allegiance to patriarchal values. In Levinas's work, woman is distinguished as the *"tu"* (not the *"vous"*, which for him indicates the moral relationship marked by distance, separation, and language); and whereas "apparition in the face" is the key to ethics and responsibility, Levinas virtually defines woman in terms of makeup and hair style, as the being with a face manipulated or transformed, already by the hand of God, into an object. There are two kinds of personal otherness in Levinas's thought, and the *serious* Other is the *"vous."* I contend that the reason why women are not serious others in Levinas's work is precisely that they are "unfaced" (de-faced?)—at any rate faceless.

LEVINAS'S CRITIQUE OF WESTERN ONTOLOGY

Totality and Infinity begins with the assertion that when the meaning of individuals is derived from their place within a totality, one is talking about the state of war, which Levinas describes as a positioning of individuals from which there is no escaping, and as establishing an order among things "from which no one can keep his distance."[2] In war, nothing is exterior: "War does not manifest exteriority and the other as other; it destroys the identity of the same" (TI 21).

Levinas holds that Western ontology perceives Being as war, which means that it always treats Being as the totality within which or in terms of which individuals can be what they are, and also that it necessarily excludes the reality of otherness. Furthermore, Western philosophy understands *knowing* to be the privileged mode of access to things, and knowing is totalizing—bringing all together into a totality or system. If we accept that reality is traditionally only discussed in terms of Being, then Levinas says we need another concept, the idea of the infinite to express the reality of that which transcends totality. But Levinas does not make the move of conceiving the infinite as something additional, outside of totality, for this sort of move is a repetition of the totalizing gesture; rather, he finds that the infinite can be described paradoxically as *within* the totality, *within* experience (TI 23). It can be described this way, however, only if it can be thought in a way that is not a matter of representation, only if it can be thought in a way that is not objective.

Like Descartes, Levinas asks about the origin of the idea of the infinite, and he contends that it is in the encounter with the Other.

Specifically: "The idea of the infinite is produced in the *opposition* of conversation, in sociality" (TI 197). "The idea of the infinite, the infinitely more contained in the less, is concretely produced in the form of a relation with the face" (TI 196).[3] I think that the intuition here is fairly obvious: to recognize the genuine otherness of the Other is to encounter him on his own terms (in his face), and not in terms of some third thing (e.g., a clear and distinct idea of him). If in Western philosophy the Other is not immediately encountered, if the Other is encountered always through a representation, through an idea, through a noema, or through a world, then the otherness of the Other is not genuinely encountered. The entire "problem of other minds," as it is called in professional philosophy, presupposes that the real otherness of the Other is not, to a sufficient degree, directly encountered but has to be corroborated by some kind of inspection of evidence and inference. But I think Levinas would agree that one will never "solve" the problem of other minds if one can actually start out from the position that the reality of others is not already revealed from the beginning (and, for Levinas, it is revealed from before the beginning).

Levinas contends that Western philosophy is allergic to the otherness of the Other; if, before it will believe in the reality of the thing encountered, philosophy always requires a kind of evidence that direct encounter does not provide, then philosophy has an allergy to that thing. Western philosophy does *not* seem to be allergic to ideas, sense data, universal forms, representations, and so on, but does seem to have an allergic reaction to anything that does not come packaged in some such capsule. By implication, Western philosophy's attention to ethics has inevitably been a waste of time: for if the concern of ethics is the relation to the Other in his otherness, then it cannot be grounded upon an ontology that keeps the Other inaccessible.

LEVINAS'S BASIC CATEGORIES

Like Martin Heidegger, Levinas does not proceed through argumentation but through proposing a description. Also like Heidegger, Levinas's description is produced from the standpoint of a guiding question of oblivion or forgottenness. However, it is not the forgetting of Being that Levinas seeks to remedy; it is *forgetting the Other*.[4]

Levinas makes the case that the otherness of the Other is forgotten, by generating a description of our being-in-the-world that centers on concepts I will divide up into three sets: (a) the face and the infinite, (b) enjoyment and living from, and (c) separation and language. To say that the otherness of the Other is forgotten is to imply that it was, in some sense, known at some time; by summarizing certain features of the sense of these basic categories of his thought, we can indicate, at least in a rudimentary way, what this means.

The Face and the Infinite

The idea of the infinite is the idea of what cannot be brought within the totality, but also of something of a completely different order from any possible "outside." In Levinas's vision of things, faces are particularly important because a face only is *as* a face if it presents itself as one, and this is done through expressing. There is something enigmatic in the thing that presents itself as a face: it commands one's attention just because one is not able to get what it is into one's grasp or under one's control. In the face, a being presents itself and eludes being taken, because what it presents signifies it or gives meaning to it.

> The way in which the other presents himself, exceeding *the idea of the other in me*, we here name face. . . . The face of the Other at each moment destroys and overflows the plastic image it leaves me. . . . It *expresses* itself. . . . To approach the Other in conversation is to welcome his expression. . . . It is therefore to *receive* from the Other beyond the capacity of the I, which means exactly: to have the idea of the infinite. But this also means: to be taught. The relation with the Other, or Conversation, is a non-allergic relation, an ethical relation. (TI 50–51)

Enjoyment and Living From

It is clear that not everything we encounter in the world has a face. The relation to a face is a relation across a certain distance and is accomplished in language. We will return to this in a moment. What is the relation to those faceless things in the world, what Heidegger calls the ready-to-hand? Levinas does not appropriate the Heideggerian account but introduces the notion of *enjoyment* into his account of being-in-the-world. It has frequently been remarked that Heidegger does not give explicit consideration to the body in his account of Dasein; Levinas does, however, and for him being a body is enjoyment.

> The body is a permanent contestation of the prerogative attributed to consciousness of "giving meaning" to each thing; it lives as this contestation. The world I live in is not simply the counterpart or the contemporary of thought and its constitutive freedom, but a conditioning and an antecedence. The world I constitute nourishes me and bathes me. (TI 129)

For Levinas, enjoyment is an intentionality, but one that is quite different from, and more fundamental than, the *consciousness of* or representational intentionality emphasized by Husserl. Whereas *consciousness of* is an objectifying intentionality (consciousness of this or that determinant thing), enjoyment is an immersion in what Levinas calls the elemental: "Things come to representation from a background from which they emerge and to which they return in the enjoyment we can have of them" (TI 130). The element is the milieu within which one always is and which one can in a sense "overcome," by creating a separation from it within it, by getting a foothold, by carving out one's own space, a dwelling, through labor and possession (TI 142).

When Levinas uses the phrase "living from," it is to indicate the dependence of the sensitive, bodily being upon a world that is already there, the relationship to which is not mediated or across a distance (e.g., of representation). Furthermore, he affirms the fundamental pleasure or agreeableness of being a body in a world, with felt needs that can be addressed, and for which things are not only tools for accomplishing purposes but also textures, warmth, coolness, variety, etc.

In degree of dependence, the one aspect building upon the other, Levinas claims that enjoyment of being is basic, that through it occurs the opening up of interiority, the withdrawal from immersion in the element, the gathering-unto-oneself that culminates in separation, and that is itself the necessary condition of representation or objectifying consciousness. Enjoyment, which is the happiness of being alive, is thus identified by Levinas as the basis of selfhood:

> In enjoyment throbs egoist being. Enjoyment separates by engaging in the contents from which it lives. Separation comes

to pass as the positive work of this engagement. . . . To be separated is to be at home with oneself. But to be at home with oneself. . . is to live from . . . , to enjoy the elemental. (TI 147)

Another remark about the face is in order. Whereas the face of the Other is the compelling presence that is able to place in question my projects, neither the element nor things we use and possess have faces. This is a feature of the "I-it" relationship, as Levinas sees the latter, wherein I can seize upon a thing and put it to use to serve my interests. If Levinas emphasizes the face in his desire to believe that those who want to take ethics seriously are not dupes, it is because he claims that the beginning of moral consciousness is the recognition of the Other in the face, the experience of being confronted by Another, the experience of someone facing up to me.

Separation and Language

As we have seen, Levinas calls the relation to the face "conversation": it is addressing and being addressed, it is being called to and called upon, it is being held accountable to respond. There is accountability where I can be called to account, where I recognize the otherness of Another, where a thing presents itself as a face and makes me face up to it. The featurelessness of the element and the availability of objects for my use, are in clear contrast to the face. Neither respect nor disrespect is a possible attitude toward what has no face. If the latter relationship is an "I-it," the former is an "I-you." It is essential to note that for Levinas it is not an "I-thou."

Language is an essential aspect of the relation with the face for Levinas, for he says "speech proceeds from absolute difference" (TI 194), and "the essence of language is the relation with the Other" (TI 207). This assertion is based, I believe, on Levinas's view that what is special about a thing that announces or presents itself as a face, is that it signifies its own presence, attends itself, but also always fails to be identical to its presentation. In an early passage on "discourse," he writes:

Manifestation καθ' αυτό consists in the being telling itself to us independently of every position we would have taken in its regard, *expressing itself.* Here . . . the being is not placed in the light of another but presents itself in the manifestation that should only announce it; it is present as directing this very manifestation—present before the manifestation, which only manifests it. . . . The face is a living presence; it is expression. The life of expression consists in undoing the form in which the existent, exposed as a theme, is thereby dissimulated. The face speaks. The manifestation of the face is already discourse. He who manifests himself comes, according to Plato's expression, to his own assistance. He at each instant undoes the form he presents. (TI 65–66)

We come now to separation. Separation is the condition for the "manifesting" of this quote; only a being that can withdraw from the orderedness of a totality, that can collect itself and gather-unto-itself, can manifest itself and undo the form in which this manifestation occurs. "Separation" refers to this condition, the basic feature of self-ness: an "I" is a separated being, a being that is at home with itself, a being that can "come home to itself" or "gather itself unto itself." The expression Levinas uses is *"le recueillement,"* which is rendered in translation as "recollection." Separation arises on the fact of enjoyment, says Levinas, but the interiority of recollection is not a being-distanced *from* the world, it is "a solitude in a world already human" (TI 155). Thus recollection refers us to an otherness that is neither the otherness of the element and possessions, nor the otherness of the face, but an otherness that Levinas characterizes as gentle, as intimate, as discreet.

We thus have three levels of otherness to keep straight, and this is codified in the linguistic conventions "I-you," "I-thou," and "I-it":

The I-Thou in which Buber sees the category of interhuman relationship is the relation not with the interlocutor but with feminine alterity. This alterity is situated on another plane than language and nowise represents a truncated, stammering, still elementary language. On the contrary, the discretion of this presence includes all the possibilities of the transcendent relationship with the Other. It is comprehensible and exercises its function of interiorization only on the ground of the full human personality, which, however, in the woman, can be reserved so as to open up the dimension of interiority. And this is a new and irreducible possibility, a delightful lapse in being, and the source of gentleness in itself. (TI 155)

I will explore this point in the next section through other texts than this one, but for now I want to make the observation that if the relation with feminine alterity is not through language, then this relation is not the relation with a face. This inference follows as well from the consideration that the relation with the face is not the welcome but the critique of the self, its being placed in question. At this rate, if the other of intimacy is feminine, the Other of discourse and the face can only be masculine. The masculine Other is, in *Totality and Infinity*, what I am calling the *serious* Other.[5]

THE PLACE OF THE FEMININE IN LEVINAS'S PHILOSOPHY

Anyone who has read *The Second Sex* is likely to recall the footnote in the introduction where Levinas is taken to task for providing one of the basic themes of de Beauvoir's analysis, woman as the Other. She quotes his *Le temps et l'autre*:

> Is there not a case in which otherness, alterity, unquestionably marks the nature of a being, as its essence, an instance of otherness not consisting purely and simply in the opposition of two species of the same genus? I think that the feminine represents the contrary in its absolute sense. . . . Otherness reaches its full flowering in the feminine, a term of the same rank as consciousness but of opposite meaning.[6]

De Beauvoir comments that this can only have been written from a man's point of view, and that it is an assertion of masculine privilege.

It is unlikely that Levinas was persuaded by this critique, for twenty-five years later he published *Totalité et infini*, in which he develops this point about feminine alterity in several passages; and in another three years he published the Talmudic lesson, "Et Dieu créa la femme,"[7] which, although containing an argument that man and woman are equally human, nonetheless seems to endorse the traditional sociopolitical implications of the woman-as-other thesis.

In spite of similarities between the above quote from *Le temps et l'autre* and affirmations of feminine difference in some of contemporary French feminism, the use of the image of the feminine in *Totality and Infinity* to denote a discreet presence, a nonconfronting presence, a silent language (and "the inhabitant that inhabits [the home] before every inhabitant, the welcoming one par excellence, welcome in itself" [TI 157]), seems fairly straightforwardly an expression of good old-fashioned masculine privilege and arrogance. This appearance is strengthened by passages in the Talmudic lesson published in 1977. A primary lesson Levinas seeks to get across here is that sexual difference is in the service of the humanity of humans, that men and women have different tasks to see to in the joint adventure of human existence:

> The last chapter of Proverbs comes to mind, where woman is glorified; she makes possible the life of men, she is the house of men; but the husband has a life outside the house, he sits in the city council, he has a public life, he is in the service of the universal, he is not limited to interiority, to intimacy, to the home, without which, however, he could accomplish nothing. (DC 135)

Such words provide fairly strong evidence that *chez* Levinas the innovative concept of feminine otherness has little to do with any challenge to the sociopolitical traditions of patriarchy. The title of my paper derives from another passage in "Et Dieu créa la femme," however. This section of the text is entitled "L'apparence":

> There is, in the feminine, face and appearance, and God was the first hairdresser. He created the first illusions, the first make-up. To build a feminine being is also to give appearance its due. "Her hair needed attention." There is, in the feminine face, and in the relations between the sexes, this call for the lie [*au mensonge*] or for an arrangement beyond the savage directness of the face to face, for the relation between humans encountering each other in the responsibility of the one for the other. (DC 143)

Taken together with the treatment of "feminine alterity" in *Totality and Infinity* as the "*Je-Tu*" relation, this passage provides reason for saying that for Levinas, woman is faceless, because she is un-faced. She is unfaced even though she has a face, because this face is not meant to speak but to welcome, not to call others to account but to be responsible *for* them and to serve their projects. In her, the face becomes appearance only, not manifestation and self-signifying expression. The seriousness of discourse and accountability, of a public life, does not suit such a being. Such a being does not undo its manifestation of itself in its face but merges with this manifestation, and for just this reason is ultimately faceless. On the subject of the feminine face as object, *Totality and Infinity* says, "Equivocation constitutes the epiphany of the feminine" (TI 264). Levinas even indicates that this is part of the disrespect and objectification shown women, for

> disrespect presupposes the face. Elements and things remain outside of respect and disrespect. It is necessary that the face have been apperceived for nudity to be able to acquire the non-signifyingness of the lustful. The feminine face joins this clarity and this shadow. . . . In this inversion of the face in femininity, in this disfigurement that refers to the face, non-signifyingness abides in the signifyingness of the face. (TI 262–63)
>
> The face, all straightforwardness and frankness, in its feminine epiphany dissimulates allusions, innuendos. It laughs under the cloak of its own expression, without leading to any specific meaning, hinting in the empty air, signaling the less than nothing. (TI 264)

THE ACCOUNT OF SUBJECTIVITY IN THE LATER WORK

In *Autrement qu'être ou au-delà de l'essence* there is no talk of feminine alterity and no direct implication that the relation to the Other in the face is masculine.[8] But one is justified in suspecting that if this is so, it is perhaps because Levinas is now exploring the relation to "prefacial otherness" (if I may be permitted!), that is, the theme of "proximity." Proximity designates being-related, being-linked to the other, being-obligated to the other before being able to relate oneself, or before being in a position to forge a bond oneself, or before being able to obligate oneself. And "proximity" means, in the later work, a nonseparatedness, nonautonomy, nonidentity that Levinas claims is a condition for being-a-self. In this work, the self is conceived as "the other-in-me" and thus as "the seed of madness" (*le grain de folie*, AQE 86). To be a self is to be already submitted to another, to be by virtue of another, and to be for another; Levinas eventually evokes the maternal body to convey his meaning: "*le psychisme comme corps maternel*" (AQE 85)—the self as maternal body. In a sense this just develops a line of thought from *Totality and Infinity*, that the face of the Other is the origin of exteriority and significance, and hence that the separation and identity of the self begin with the situation of "living from" the maternal Other and encountering the possibility of significance in her face. But it is more strongly suggested now that the Other is the ground of the self, which must begin in nonseparatedness.

THE FEMINIST MEANING OF THIS PHILOSOPHY OF THE OTHER: IF THE SELF IS THE OTHER, THE SELF IS THE (M)OTHER

Although he himself never says this, it is clear from the logic of the accounts in *Totality and Infinity* that for Levinas *woman* is the always already forgotten Other, the taken-for-granted, hence always-overlooked Other; without her, there is no being-at-home, no dwelling, no enjoyment of the elements, no separation, no consciousness of, no encounter with the serious face of the Other (who is, by implication, essentially masculine). But this always already overlooked Other is what makes the selfhood of the self possible and is indeed part of selfhood according to the later work: the self is the Other-in-me. There is no me that is not always already "*othered.*"

A consequence of this, for Levinas, is that the freedom of the self is *not* fundamental—against such thinkers as Jean-Paul Sartre. Rather, the self is always already subjected and bound to the Others, already in debt, already obligated. Community in the relation to the Other has genuine priority over individuality in Levinas's conception of the self.

In English we can pun on this very conveniently; we can say, there is no me that is not always already *mothered.* And when you see how natural this pun is in English, it is all the more remarkable to find that Levinas leaves mothers out of his discussion entirely! As a stepfather, I can be gratified by his account of filiality, especially in *Ethics and Infinity,*[9] where he insists that biological ties are not essential, but I find it disturbing that he speaks always and only of *paternity,* and of the *father* finding *him*self in the son.

Indeed, Levinas's view that the self is uncompromisingly responsible for the Other (he approvingly quotes Dostoyevsky: "We are all responsible for all for all men before all, and I more than all the others"),[10] applies better to the kind of labor, devotion, commitment, and sacrifice expected of mothers concretely every day than to that which is really expected of fathers. This is clear to feminist writers like Dinnerstein, and it is compatible with Levinas's failing to take the feminine other, the feminine face, seriously.

More than acknowledging that the self is (m)othered, however, his later work wants to be clear on two points: that being-othered is not something simply past, and that, indeed, the crucial sense of *"l'autre-en-moi"* is not conveyed until we think the self as a (m)othering body, not only a (m)othered body. That is, selfhood consists in inescapable responsibility to and for the Other, a responsibility Levinas would have us recognize as being assigned to us by the fact that we can be addressed, by *the fact* that we can be appealed to and called upon. And *this* seems to be due only to the presence in the self, as one of the features that *make* a self, of the signifying face, the exteriority, of the mother.

The denial of the feminine in Levinas's early and best-known work is classic. In his own discourse, he seeks to instruct us that the condition of selfhood is the Other, that Western ontology seems animated by an absolute allergy to otherness, that in reality the Other has primacy, that this is being constantly covered up and obscured in Western philosophy, and that consequently there is no real affirmation of plurality or difference, no ethics, even in Western moral philosophy. In the course of this argument, his description of Same-Other relations employs gender categories based on traditional sex roles, but absolutizes these roles and repeats the marginalization of women from the serious world of public life and the moral sphere of accountability, which are thereby masculinized. By not assuming a feminist stance, by not associating his critique with the critique of patriarchal culture and philosophy, his exposition of the forgetting of the Other loses much of its credibility. We must, he told us, learn to see the primacy of the Other, learn to affirm the irreducibility of difference. But the Other whose otherness turns out to be the most difficult to recognize and affirm is, *even in his thought*, feminine! This is why I said at the beginning that reading Levinas reminds me of reading Dinnerstein, Chodorow, and object relations feminist theorists; but *they* explore the dynamics of the tendency to deny the primary indebtedness to the mother, and look toward an organization of life, and a theory of life, that will be reoriented away from the violence of this denial. Levinas only exemplifies this tendency.

Levinas does not make the obvious political observation; although he takes the Other seriously, affirming the infinite responsibility to the face, he describes woman as indefinable and unrecognizable. His willingness to have a place for faceless, unrecognizable Others indicates that his early philosophy is no remedy to our allergic condition and is at best only a moment in the diagnosis. In his later work, he seems to give the emphasis to this "prefacial" relationship and to shift his interest away from the relation with the confrontational face of the serious Other, to trying to understand the prefacial presence of the Other in the self. At least in doing this he makes a more legitimate use of feminine imagery—the maternal body and responsibility for someone whom you do not yet know. But here he still does not seem to see that such a philosophy of the Other is not only a departure from Western philosophy, but even more so from patriarchal philosophy, or that among the greatest flaws of Western philosophy, as of Western culture generally, must be counted patriarchy and its essentially violent nature.

Notes

1. Nancy Chodorow, *The Reproduction of Mothering: Psychoanalysis and the Sociology of Gender* (Berkeley: Univ. of California Press, 1978); Dorothy Dinnerstein, *The Mermaid and the Minotaur: Sexual Arrangements and the Human Malaise* (New York: Harper & Row, 1976).

2. Emmanuel Levinas, *Totality and Infinity: An Essay on Exteriority*, trans. A. Lingis (Pittsburgh: Duquesne Univ. Press, 1969), 21: hereafter "TI." Translation of *Totalité et infini: essai sur l'extériorité* (The Hague: Martinus Nijhoff, 1961).

3. English translations of Levinas nearly always use *infinity* rather than *the infinite*. My own preference for the latter stems from Levinas's obvious interest in Descartes's concept of the infinite (TI 210–12), and the fact that Levinas's word in French is *l'infini* rather than *l'infinité*, the same choice Descartes makes (*infinitum* rather than *infinitas*). Translations of such passages have been modified.

4. The expression "forgetting the Other" does not occur in Levinas's writings; I suggested it as a way of capturing a basic point of his thought in my unpublished *thèse du troisième cycle*, "L'oubli de l'autre: le solipsisme épistémologique et la fondation dialogique de la morale" (Université de Paris-Nanterre, 1982).

5. For other descriptions of the category of otherness that is taken seriously, that confronts and commands, that manifests itself through language, and appears from a height, see TI 101, 155, 171, 200, 213.

6. Emmanuel Levinas, *Le temps et l'autre* (Paris: Presses Universitaires de France, 1979); quoted in Simone de Beauvoir, *The Second Sex*, trans. H. M. Parshley (New York: Vintage Books, 1952, 1974), xix.

7. Emmanuel Levinas, "Et Dieu créa la femme," in *Du sacré au saint: cinq nouvelles lectures talmudiques* (Paris: Editions de Minuit, 1977), 122–48; hereafter "DC."

8. Emmanuel Levinas, *Autrement qu'être ou au-delà de l'essence* (The Hague: Martinus Nijhoff, 1974), henceforth "AQE." English translation, *Otherwise than Being; Or, Beyond Essence*, trans. A. Lingis (The Hague: Martinus Nijhoff, 1981).

9. Emmanuel Levinas, *Ethics and Infinity: Conversations with Philippe Nemo*, trans. R. Cohen (Pittsburgh: Duquesne Univ. Press, 1985), 71.

10. Levinas, *Ethics and Infinity*, 101.

Contributors

Babette E. Babich is assistant professor of philosophy at Fordham University, Lincoln Center. Her research and publications focus primarily on Nietzsche and Heidegger and other topics in continental philosophy. She is currently completing a manuscript, "Science in the Light of Art: Toward a Nietzschean Philosophy of Science."

Roger Bell is lecturer in philosophy at Sonoma State University. His publications include "Building It Postmodern, in LA? Frank Gehry and Company," in *After the Future: Postmodern Times and Places* (1990). He is currently working on a manuscript, "Philosophy and Architecture: The Cases of Wittgenstein and Derrida," and organizing a collection of essays on the general relation of philosophy and politics.

Peg Birmingham is the Edward J. Mortola Scholar in Philosophy at Pace University—New York City. She is completing a manuscript on Heidegger's practical philosophy, "The Inviolability of the Possible: Heidegger on Agency and Responsibility."

John D. Caputo is professor of philosophy at Villanova University. He is the author of *Radical Hermeneutics: Hermeneutics, Deconstruction, and the Hermeneutic Project* (1987); *Heidegger and Aquinas: An Essay on Overcoming Metaphysics* (1982); and *The Mystical Element in Heidegger's Thought* (1978). He is currently preparing a study in ethics entitled "Sacred Anarchy" with the support of a National Endowment for the Humanities Fellowship.

Tina Chanter is assistant professor of philosophy at Louisiana State University. In 1990–91 she was a fellow at the University of Virginia Commonwealth Center for Literary and Cultural Change. Her publications include articles on Heidegger, Derrida, Levinas, and Kristeva. Her book, *The Ethics of Eros: Levinas, Irigaray, and the Problem of the Feminine*, is forthcoming from Routledge.

Rebecca Comay teaches philosophy and literary studies at the University of Toronto. She is the author of a book on Hegel and Heidegger,

On the Line: Reflections on the Bad Infinite, forthcoming from State University of New York Press. She is currently at work on a book manuscript on Heidegger and Benjamin, "Pausing for Breath."

Arleen B. Dallery is associate professor of philosophy at La Salle University in Philadelphia, Pennsylvania. She served as executive co-director of the Society for Phenomenology and Existential Philosophy from 1986 to 1990. Her most recent publications include two articles on French feminist theory: "Sexual Embodiment: Beauvoir and French Feminism" and "The Politics of Writing (the) Body: *Ecriture feminine*."

François Dastur is maître de conferences in philosophy at the University of Paris I (Panthéon-Sorbonne). She teaches general philosophy and history of philosophy (German philosophy) and is attached to the Phenomenological Seminar, a research unit of the Centre National de la Recherche Scientifique. She has published several articles in French and English on Husserl, Heidegger, and Merleau-Ponty and is the author of *Heidegger et la question du temps* (1990).

Joseph C. Flay is professor of philosophy at Pennsylvania State University. In addition to *Hegel's Quest for Certainty* (1984), he has published articles on Hegel and on Hegel's relationship to contemporary philosophy. He is presently writing a book on Hegel's *Logic* and is engaged in extended investigation into the nature of space and time.

Véronique M. Fóti is assistant professor of philosophy at Pennsylvania State University. She has published many articles and chapters in books on Heidegger, Hölderlin and Celan, Derrida, and Merleau-Ponty, as well as topics in continental rationalism and Greek philosophy. She is the author of *Heidegger and the Poets: Poiēsis/Sophia/Technē* (forthcoming from Humanities Press) and is currently editing a book on Merleau-Ponty.

Klaus Held holds a chair in philosophy at the Bergische Universität of Wuppertal, Germany, and is president of the Deutschen Gesellschaft für phänomenologische Forschung. Among his publications are editions of Husserl's and Heidegger's works, as well as many articles and books on phenomenology, ancient philosophy, and political philosophy, including *Lebendige Gegenwart* (1966), *Heraklit, Parmenides und der Anfang von Philosophie und Wissenschaft* (1980), *Stato, interessi e mondi vitali* (1980), and *Treffpunkt Platon* (1990).

Samuel IJsseling is professor of philosophy at the Institute of Philosophy of the Catholic University of Louvain, Belgium, where he lectures on the history of modern and contemporary philosophy and on continental philosophy of language. Since 1974 he has been director of the Husserl Archives in Louvain and for several years has served as vice president of the Deutsche Gesellschaft für phänomenologische Forschung. He has published many articles and several books, including *Rhetoric and Philosophy in Conflict* (1976).

David Farrell Krell is professor of philosophy and chair at DePaul University in Chicago. He is the author of *Daimon Life: Heidegger and 'Lebensphilosophie'* (forthcoming from Indiana University Press); *Of Memory, Reminiscence, and Writing: On the Verge* (1990); *Intimations of Mortality: Time, Truth, and Finitude in Heidegger's Thinking of Being* (1986); and *Postponements: Woman, Sensuality, and Death in Nietzsche* (1986). He is editor and translator of a wide range of books and articles by Martin Heidegger, including *Basic Writings, Nietzsche,* and *Early Greek Thinking.*

Bill Martin is assistant professor of philosophy at DePaul University in Chicago. He received his Ph.D. from the University of Kansas. He has published articles on social theory, contemporary European philosophy, analytic philosophy, and contemporary Jewish philosophy. He is the author of *Matrix and Line: Derrida and the Possibilities of Postmodern Social Theory* (1992).

Ladelle McWhorter is associate professor of philosophy at Northeast Missouri State University in Kirksville, Missouri. She is the editor of *Heidegger and the Earth: Essays in Environmental Philosophy* (1990) and has written articles on Foucault, including essays in *The Question of the Other* (1989) and *Crises in Continental Philosophy* (1990).

Mario Moussa is assistant professor of philosophy at Worcester Polytechnic Institute. He received his Ph.D. from the University of Chicago's Committee on Social Thought and is the author (with Susan Bordo) of "Rehabilitating the 'I'," in *Questioning Foundations*, forthcoming from Routledge.

Robert Mugerauer is associate professor of community and regional planning in the School of Architecture at the University of Texas at Austin. He has published articles on literary theory and criticism; the theory of geography, landscape, and the built environment; and the interpretation of architecture and planning. In addition, he has edited (with David Seamon) *Dwelling, Place, and Environment* (1985) and is author of *Heidegger's Language and Thinking* (1988).

William J. Richardson is professor of philosophy at Boston College and a practicing psychoanalyst. He is author of *Heidegger: Through Phenomenology to Thought* (1974) and several articles on Heidegger. He is also co-author (with John P. Muller) of *Lacan and Language: A Reader's Guide to the* Ecrits (1982) and *The Purloined Poe: Lacan, Derrida, and Psychoanalytic Reading* (1988).

P. Holley Roberts is a graduate student in philosophy at Vanderbilt University in Nashville, Tennessee, where she is completing her dissertation on Gadmer's hermeneutics. She served as assistant editor for the journals *Soundings* and *Quarterly Review* and co-edited *Crises in Continental Philosophy* (1990).

Charles E. Scott is professor of philosophy at Vanderbilt University in Nashville, Tennessee, where he is also director of the Robert Penn Warren Center for the Humanities. He served as executive co-director of the Society for Phenomenology and Existential Philosophy from 1986 to 1989. He is the author of *The Language of Difference* (1987) and *The* Question *of Ethics* (1990).

Anthony J. Steinbock is completing doctoral studies at the State University of New York at Stony Brook; his dissertation examines the role of *Heimwelt* and *Fremdwelt* in Husserl's theory of intersubjectivity. He also received fellowships to study in Bochum, Germany, and in Paris. Several of his translations of articles by contemporary German philosophers have been published.

John van Buren is assistant professor of philosophy at Fordham University in New York. He is the author of *The Young Heidegger* (forthcoming from Indiana University Press), translator of Martin Heidegger, *Ontologie (Hermeneutik der Faktizität)* (forthcoming from Indiana University Press); and co-editor, with Theodore Kisiel, of *The Early Heidegger: New Texts, New Perspectives* (forthcoming from State University of New York Press).

Craig R. Vasey is assistant professor of philosophy at Mary Washington College in Fredericksburg, Virginia, where he is co-director of the Race and Gender Curriculum Project. He received his Ph.D. from Brown University, and the Doctorat du troisième cycle from the Université de Paris—Nanterre.

Cynthia Willett is assistant professor at the University of Kansas in Lawrence. Her publications include "The Shadow of Hegel's *Logic*," in *Essays on Hegel's Logic* (1990); "Hollywood Comedy and Aristotelian Ethics: Reconciling Differences," in *Sexual Politics and Popular Culture* (1990); and "Hegel, Antigone, and the Possibility of an Ecstatic Dialectic," in *Philosophy and Literature* (1990).

Edith Wyschogrod is professor of philosophy at Queens College of the City University of New York. She is the author of *Saints and Postmodernism: Revisioning Moral Philosophy* (1990); *Spirit in Ashes: Hegel, Heidegger, and Man-Made Mass Death* (1985); and *Emmanuel Levinas: The Problem of Ethical Metaphysics* (1974), and the co-editor of *Lacan and Theological Discourse* (1989).

Index